Praise for Cloud Native Data Center Networking

Cloud Native Data Center Networking is a must-read book for anyone deploying and automating a modern spine-and-leaf, agile data center fabric. The book's focus on automation and simplification is the future of networking.

—*Donald Sharp, FRRouting Maintainer*

Great read for any network engineer who wants to apply cloud native concepts to today's enterprise networks, but isn't sure where to start. The book has something for all levels of expertise, from high level architecture discussions to hands-on implementation examples you can follow.

—*Anthony Miloslavsky, Network Engineer*

Dinesh Dutt is the greatest evangelist for data center networks and network device disaggregation. The clarity of his thinking and his capability to explain hard concepts with simple words never stops to amaze me.

—*Silvano Gai, former University Professor and Fellow*

Cloud Native Data Center Networking
Architecture, Protocols, and Tools

Dinesh G. Dutt

Beijing • Boston • Farnham • Sebastopol • Tokyo

Cloud Native Data Center Networking
by Dinesh G. Dutt

Published by O'Reilly Media, Inc., 1005 Gravenstein Highway North, Sebastopol, CA 95472.

O'Reilly books may be purchased for educational, business, or sales promotional use. Online editions are also available for most titles (*http://oreilly.com*). For more information, contact our corporate/institutional sales department: 800-998-9938 or corporate@oreilly.com.

Development Editor: Andy Oram	**Indexer:** WordCo Indexing Services, Inc.
Acquisitions Editor: John Devins	**Interior Designer:** David Futato
Production Editor: Katherine Tozer	**Cover Designer:** Karen Montgomery
Copyeditor: Octal Publishing, LLC	**Illustrator:** Rebecca Demarest
Proofreader: Sonia Saruba	

November 2019:   First Edition

Revision History for the First Edition
2019-11-19:   First Release
2020-01-03:   Second Release

See *http://oreilly.com/catalog/errata.csp?isbn=9781492045601* for release details.

978-1-492-04560-1

[LSI]

This book is dedicated to all who make networking—the network designers and architects who plan the systems, the engineers, and the operators who bring them into being. And especially to the open source networking community: may the fire never stop.

Table of Contents

Preface

Clouds come floating into my life, no longer to carry rain or usher storm, but to add color to my sunset sky.
    —Rabindranath Tagore, *Stray Birds*

Cloud native data center networking. That's quite a mouthful to chew if you're a reader. Or to bite off if you're the writer. Let's unpack the easy pieces first.

This is a book about building a robust, scalable network infrastructure for data centers. So if you're a network architect or network operator looking to understand, build, or validate your thinking about data centers, this book is for you. If you're a data center operator responsible for not just the network, but also compute and storage, and you're looking to get up to speed on the current thinking in network design of data centers, this book is for you. And if you're a network developer looking to find information that's scattered or is oral knowledge only, this book is for you.

More precisely, this book is about the design of a specific kind of data center network, the cloud native kind. If you search online for "cloud native," you'll find that it's typically associated with a specific kind of application design—microservices—and on a specific operating system—Linux—and that it relies on a lot of open source code. But those are means. The ends are about building robust, agile, scalable applications that allow the business to keep pace in a fast-moving world. When applied to networks, it means building a network that matches the applications and business needs in a way that is robust, flexible, scalable, and efficient to operate.

I picked the term "cloud native" to focus on the same ends in creating a network. You might not be building a network that scales to the the size of Amazon or Google, but I assume that you want to build a network that has these characteristics: affordable, high capacity, easy to manage, agile, and reliable. That's a lot of adjectives, but I hope to touch upon all of these areas before we're done.

And this book is not just for people deploying microservices-based applications. As hip as that is along with Kubernetes, building a reliable and predictable network is something everybody aspires to, whether you're doing containers or virtual machines or using bare-metal servers.

I do not pursue or want to push any vendor's agenda, whether or not I worked for them in the past. If you see examples or text that reflects a vendor, it is only because of my familiarity with the vendor or tool rather than an endorsement. Biases always creep in, and I'm willing to be called out so that I can correct them. That said, I'll readily admit up front that I'm an advocate of open source tools, because I believe we can build better systems that way.

Audience

As stated earlier, I write mostly for network architects and network operators, but also application developers writing networked applications. I assume that you know what TCP/IP is and what sockets are; I presume not much more. This book attempts to straddle theory, the application of theory to the data center, and practice. As such, the focus is not just on presenting technical information as a text book might, but always within the context of its application in designing a data center. The book does not cover aspects of the data center that have nothing to do with networking such as physical location selection, power and cooling choices, physical layout, and so on.

How This Book Is Organized

The book is broken into three sections:

Architecture
    The first two chapters cover questions of architecture. The story begins with what led to the need for a new architecture and the description of the new network architecture.

Technology
    The next nine chapters cover various pieces of technology and how together they add flesh and blood to the skeleton that is provided by the architecture. We consider the choices, the protocols, and the design that uses the architecture to create a living network.

Practice
    The remaining chapters cover the practice of using the technologies described on the architecture. They largely cover the configuration and validation of networks, including applying the ethos of "less but better" to how network configurations are done.

Another focus of the chapters is my hope to unite the disparate fields of compute and networking, to bring the two teams together, in the hopes of making data center engineers and architects "renaissance men and women" whose knowledge is broad and deep because they can discern the wheat from the chaff. With the advent of network disaggregation, Linux as an operating system (OS) with powerful networking capabilities, applications that are more distributed than ever, and high-quality open source routing suites, the artificial separation between the network and the compute need no longer apply. You can engineer newer solutions that fit more elegantly together and function efficiently.

As expansive as this book might feel, there is much that I have not covered. Security, Intermediate System to Intermediate System (IS-IS), new routing protocols (do we need them?), more advanced topics such as data center interconnect, network analysis, and much more. I apologize for leaving them out. I ran out of time, pages, and energy. And I feared of testing your patience with a larger tome.

Software Used in This Book

In keeping with one of the key principles behind cloud native, examples, configuration snippets, and such are derived from respected and widely used open source software. This also helps keep the book vendor neutral. There are four primary pieces of open source software that I use:

- Linux kernel, as the network OS; version 4.18 or later.
- FRR, for routing; version 7.1 mostly.
- Ansible, for automation; version 2.8.
- Vagrant, for simulating many of the network topologies on my laptop and showing running code, v 2.2.5. I also use the libvirt extension of Vagrant because it makes spinning up large networks fast.

The software that I put on GitHub has been run on my laptop, which uses Intel's i7-8550U processor with 16 GB RAM and 16 GB swap. This includes simulating the Clos topology with Vagrant, running Ansible, and so on. I've found that this allows me to work normally as I run some of the software. Things do slow down if I have a lot of browser tabs open.

In case of any discrepancy between the code in the book and the GitHub repository, the working code wins.

For routers, I use Cumulus Linux as the distribution; for servers, Ubuntu release 16.04. I also provide configuration in places for Arista's Extensible Operating System (EOS), primarily because Arista provided a Vagrant box (but not after version 4.20.0F, sadly) so that I can build networks using EOS and Vagrant.

Please don't hesitate to provide honest feedback.

The samples are available on GitHub (*https://github.com/ddutt/cloud-native-data-center-networking*). The code is licensed under GPLv2.

Conventions Used in This Book

The following typographical conventions are used in this book:

Italic
> Indicates new terms, URLs, email addresses, filenames, and file extensions.

`Constant width`
> Used for program listings, as well as within paragraphs to refer to program elements such as variable or function names, databases, data types, environment variables, statements, and keywords.

`Constant width bold`
> Shows commands or other text that should be typed literally by the user.

`Constant width italic`
> Shows text that should be replaced with user-supplied values or by values determined by context.

 This element signifies a general note.

 This element indicates a warning or caution.

Using Code Examples

Supplemental material (code examples, exercises, etc.) is available for download at *https://github.com/ddutt/cloud-native-data-center-networking*.

This book is here to help you get your job done. In general, if example code is offered with this book, you may use it in your programs and documentation. You do not need to contact us for permission unless you're reproducing a significant portion of the code. For example, writing a program that uses several chunks of code from this book does not require permission. Selling or distributing examples from O'Reilly books does require permission. Answering a question by citing this book and quoting example code does not require permission. Incorporating a significant amount of example code from this book into your product's documentation does require permission.

We appreciate, but do not require, attribution. Attribution usually includes the title, author, publisher, and ISBN. For example: "*Cloud Native Data Center Networking* by Dinesh G. Dutt (O'Reilly). Copyright 2020 Dinesh G. Dutt, 978-1-492-04560-1."

If you feel your use of code examples falls outside fair use or the permission given above, feel free to contact us at *permissions@oreilly.com*.

O'Reilly Online Learning

 For more than 40 years, *O'Reilly Media* has provided technology and business training, knowledge, and insight to help companies succeed.

Our unique network of experts and innovators share their knowledge and expertise through books, articles, conferences, and our online learning platform. O'Reilly's online learning platform gives you on-demand access to live training courses, in-depth learning paths, interactive coding environments, and a vast collection of text and video from O'Reilly and 200+ other publishers. For more information, please visit *http://oreilly.com*.

How to Contact Us

Please address comments and questions concerning this book to the publisher:

O'Reilly Media, Inc.
1005 Gravenstein Highway North
Sebastopol, CA 95472
800-998-9938 (in the United States or Canada)
707-829-0515 (international or local)
707-829-0104 (fax)

We have a web page for this book, where we list errata, examples, and any additional information. You can access this page at *https://oreil.ly/cloud-native-data-center-networking*.

Email *bookquestions@oreilly.com* to comment or ask technical questions about this book.

For more information about our books, courses, conferences, and news, see our website at *http://www.oreilly.com*.

Find us on Facebook: *http://facebook.com/oreilly*

Follow us on Twitter: *http://twitter.com/oreillymedia*

Watch us on YouTube: *http://www.youtube.com/oreillymedia*

Acknowledgments

Writing this book was hard. Harder than I imagined. Just like running a marathon is not like running a longer 10K, writing a 450-page book is not like writing a longer 80-page book. My previous two experiences in writing books of 80 to 90 pages was a far cry from this one. It was made pleasurable thanks to the numerous interactions and feedback I received in writing this book.

Andy Oram. The editor of this book, my partner in the crime of writing the previous two books, this book would be but a pale shadow without your editing. There are unexpected pleasures in any undertaking. Andy has been that in the writing of this book. You were always there, weekends and nights included, when I needed some help, a nudge to find the right words to say, or discard. I never stopped being surprised when you'd respond almost immediately to emails sent at midnight! And that you let me include a poem you wrote about networks, I'm honored and grateful.

The folks who reviewed this book. Anthony Miloslavsky, the book is much better for your extensive and thoughtful feedback across the entire book. Donald Sharp, I appreciate the feedback across many of the chapters, but the multicast chapter would simply not have been possible without you. Sean Cavanaugh, the automation chapter is so much better because of your comments and pointers. Curt Brune, thank you for reviewing the ONIE pieces and providing valuable feedback. And to Silvano Gai, my dear friend, and the only person I've ever tried to emulate professionally, thank you for the detailed discussions on several chapters and your review of many of the early chapters. Your knowledge and humanity are a rare combination. Grazie di tutto, mio caro amico.

To Roopa Prabhu, David Ahern, Vivek Venkataraman, Daniel Walton, Wilson Kok, Purna Bendale, Rama Darbha, and Eric Pulvino. Thank you all for the many questions I bothered you with during the course of this book and for the several years of partnership, laughter, tears, and all the in-betweens during our time together at Cumulus. Pete Lumbis, thank you for being a sounding board, for laughing at my bad lines, and encouraging me to continue anyway. Christian Franke and Don Slice, thank you for helping answer questions on IS-IS and OSPF. To Shrijeet, who'll kill me if I don't mention him after all the years. And I'll find something to thank him for, there's much to choose from.

I'm very grateful to Bart Dworak at Microsoft, who, thanks to Sean Cavanaugh's suggestion, spent time talking at length about his experiences with network automation, which helped shape the content of that chapter. Barak Gafni provided feedback on my previous "EVPN in the Data Center" book which helped correct and clarify some points in the EVPN and network virtualization chapters. To Lincoln Dale, thank you for answering my questions about Arista. This book might not have come to life if it had not been for Narayan Desai inviting me to give a network tutorial at SRECon 2016. The positive feedback from that talk led to O'Reilly asking me to write this book. Thanks Narayan.

To Cisco and Cumulus, where I learned so much about networking, the packets and the people kind, and where I had the chance to work with some of the brightest minds. Two people to whom I am especially grateful are Tom Edsall at Cisco and JR Rivers at Cumulus.

To the open source community for all the amazing work you do. Emacs, my editor for more than 25 years and the one I used to write this entire book, as well. The Linux community, my primary desktop now since version 0.99, which I got by spending an entire day downloading the Slackware floppies, oh so long ago. Ubuntu for making the Linux experience so smooth. HashiCorp for Vagrant and the Ansible team for Ansible.

To my parents for their encouragement and support in my writing, as in everything else, throughout my life. To Shanthala for helping me lighten up and for lighting up my days. And Maya, for being patient as I poured my time into this book. I do look forward to the day when I can include your cartoons in a book I can write. Yes, I see the eyeroll already.

## CHAPTER 1

The Motivations for a New Network Architecture

Once upon a time, there was what there was, and if nothing had happened there would be nothing to tell.

—Charles de Lint

If applications had never changed, there'd be some other story to tell than the one you hold in your hands. A distributed application is in a dance with the network, with the application leading. The story of the modern data center network begins when the network was caught flat-footed when the application began the dance to a different tune. Understanding this transition helps in more ways than just learning why a change is necessary. I often encounter customers who want to build a modern network but cling to old ways of thinking. Application developers coming in from the enterprise side also tend to think in ways that are anathema to the modern data center.

This chapter will help you answer questions such as:

- What are the characteristics of the new applications?
- What is an access-aggregation-core network?
- In what ways did access-aggregation-core networks fail these applications?

The Application-Network Shuffle

Figure 1-1 shows how applications have evolved from single monoliths to the highly distributed microservices model. With each successive evolution, the requirements from the networks have also evolved.

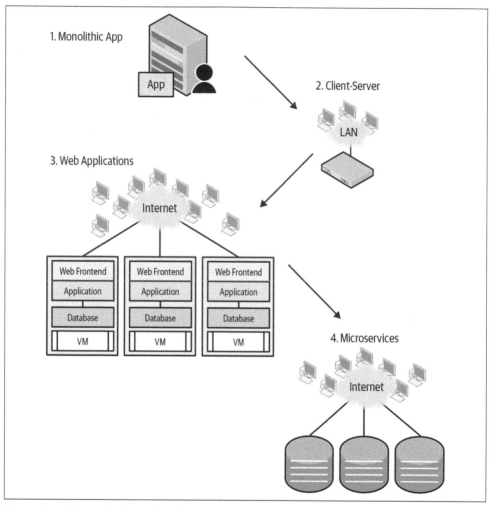

Figure 1-1. The evolution of application architecture

In the era of single monolithic applications, usually running on a mainframe, the network demands were minimal. The interconnects were proprietary, as were the protocols (think of SNA or DECnet). Keeping in line with the nascent stage of networking and distributed applications, the bandwidth requirements from the network were negligible by today's standards.

The next generation of applications arose with the spread of workstations and PCs. This wave was characterized by the rise of the *client-server architecture*. The networks began to become more sophisticated, as characterized by the rise of the *local area network* (LAN). Network demand increased, although it was still paltry by today's standards. As time went by, the data exchanged by applications went from only text and pictures to include audio and video. As befits a growing technology, interconnects and protocols abounded and were mostly proprietary. Ethernet, Token Ring, and Fiber Distributed Data Interface (FDDI) were the most popular interconnects. Interconnect speeds topped out at 100 Mbps. The likes of Novell's IPX and Banyan Systems' VINES competed with IP for supremacy of the upper-layer network protocols. Enterprises were wary of the freely available and openly developed TCP/IP stack. Many bet on the commercial counterparts. Applications were walled within the enterprise without any chance of access from the outside because most of the upper-layer protocols were not designed for use at scale or across enterprises. Today, all of these commercial upper-layer protocols have been reduced to footnotes in the history of networking. Ethernet and TCP/IP won. Open standards and open source scored their first victory over proprietary counterparts.

Next came the ubiquity of the internet and the crowning of the TCP/IP stack. Applications broke free of the walled garden of enterprises and began to be designed for access across the world. With the ability for clients to connect from anywhere, the scale that the application servers needed to handle went up significantly. In most enterprises, a single instance of a server couldn't handle all the load from all the clients. Also, single-instance servers became a single point of failure. Running multiple instances of the server fronted by a load balancer thus became popular. Servers themselves were broken up into multiple units: typically the web front end, the application, and the database or storage.

Ethernet became the de facto interconnect within the enterprise. Along with TCP/IP, Ethernet formed the terra firma of enterprise networks and their applications. I still remember the day in mid or maybe later 1998 when my management announced the end of the line for Token Ring and FDDI development on the Catalyst 5000 and 6500 family of switches. Ethernet's success in the enterprise also started eroding the popularity of the other interconnects, such as Synchronous Optical Network (SONET), in the service provider networks. By the end of this wave, Gigabit Ethernet was the most popular interconnect in enterprise networks.

As compute power continued to increase, it became impossible for most applications to take advantage of the full processing power of the CPU. This surfeit of compute power turned into a glut when improvements in processor fabrication allowed for more than one CPU core on a processor chip.

Server virtualization was invented to maximize efficient use of CPUs. Server virtualization addressed two independent needs. First, running multiple servers without requiring the use of multiple physical compute nodes made the model cost effective. Second, instead of rewriting applications to become multithreaded and parallel to take advantage of the multiple cores, server virtualization allowed enterprises to reuse their applications by running many of them in isolated units called *virtual machines* (VMs).

The predominant operating system (OS) for application development in the enterprise was Windows. Unix-based operating systems such as Solaris were less popular as application platforms. This was partly because of the cost of the workstations that ran these Unix or Unix-like operating systems. The fragmented market of these operating systems also contributed to the lack of applications. There was no single big leader in the Unix-style segment of operating systems. They all looked the same at a high level, but differed in myriad details, making it difficult for application developers. Linux was stabilizing and rising in popularity, but had not yet bridged the chasm between early adopters and mainstream development.

The success of the internet, especially the web, meant that the online information trickle became a firehose. Finding relevant information became critical. Search engines began to fight for dominance. Google, a much later entrant than other search engines, eventually overtook all of the others. It entered the lexicon as a verb, a synonym for web-based search, much like Xerox was used (and continues to be in some parts of the world) as a synonym for photocopy. At the time of this writing, Google was handling 3.5 billion searches per day, averaging 40,000 per second. To handle this scale, the servers became even more disaggregated, and new techniques, especially cluster-based application architectures such as MapReduce, became prominent. This involved a historic shift from the dominance of communication between clients and servers to the dominance of server-to-server traffic.

Linux became the predominant OS on which this new breed of applications was developed. The philosophy of Unix application development (embodied in Linux now) was to design programs that did one thing and one thing only, did it well, and could work in tandem with other similar programs to provide all kinds of services. So the servers were broken down even more, a movement now popularized as "microservices." This led to the rise of containers, which were lighter weight than VMs. If everything ran on Linux, booting a machine seemed a high price to pay just to run a small part of a larger service.

The rise of Linux and the economics of large scale led to the rise of the cloud, a service that to businesses reduced the headaches of running an IT organization. It eliminated the need to know what to buy, how much to buy, and how to scale, upgrade, and troubleshoot the enterprise network and compute infrastructure. And it did this at what for many is a fraction of the cost of building and managing their own infrastructure. The story of the cloud is more nuanced than this, but more on that later.

The scale of customers supported in a cloud infrastructure far exceeded the technologies deployed in the enterprise. Containers and cloud networking also enabled a lot more communication between the servers, as it was in the case of the new breed of applications like web search. All of these new applications also demanded a higher bandwidth out of the network, and 10 Gigabit Ethernet became the common interconnect. Interconnect speeds have kept increasing, with newly announced switches supporting 400 Gigabit Ethernet support.

The scale, the difference in style of application communication, and the rise of an ever more distributed application all heaped new demands on the network to handle these new requirements. Let us turn next to the network side of the dance, look at what existed at that time and see why it could no longer keep step to the new beat.

The Network Design from the Turn of the Century

Figure 1-2 shows the network design that held sway at the end of the last century. This was the network that the modern data center applications tried to dance with. This network design is called *access-aggregation-core*, often shortened to access-agg-core or just access-agg.

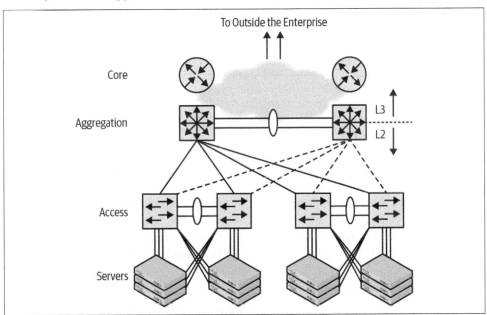

Figure 1-2. Access-aggregation-core network architecture

The endpoints or compute nodes are attached to access switches, which are the lowest layer of Figure 1-2. The aggregation switches, also called *distribution switches*, in turn connect up to the core network, thus connecting the access network to the rest of the world. Explicit links between the aggregation switches and the core switches are not shown because they vary across networks, and are mostly irrelevant to the discussion that follows.

The reason for two aggregation switches, of course, was to avoid having the network isolated when one of the aggregation switches failed. A couple of switches was considered adequate for both throughput and redundancy at the time, but ultimately two proved inadequate.

Traffic between the access and aggregation switches is forwarded via bridging. North of the aggregation boxes, packets are forwarded using routing. So, aggregation boxes were Janus boxes, with the south-facing side providing bridging and the north-facing side providing routing. This is indicated in Figure 1-2 by the presence of both L2 and L3, referring to Layer 2 networking (bridging) and Layer 3 networking (routing).

Directionality in Network Diagrams

Network engineers draw the network diagram with the network equipment on top and the compute nodes at the bottom. Cardinal directions such as "north" and "south" have specific meanings in such a diagram. Northbound traffic moves from the compute nodes into the network and leaves the enterprise network toward the internet; southbound traffic goes from the internet back to local compute nodes. In other words, this is classical client-server communication. East-west traffic flows between servers in the same network. This traffic was small in the client-server era but is the dominant traffic pattern of modern data center applications, which are highly clustered, distributed applications.

The Charms of Bridging

The access-agg-core network is heavily dependent on bridging, even though it came into being at a time when the internet was already fast becoming a "thing." If IP routing was what powered the internet, why did networking within an enterprise turn to bridging and not routing? There were three primary reasons: the rise of silicon-switched packet forwarding, the rise of proprietary network software stacks within the enterprise, and the promise of zero configuration of bridging.

Hardware packet switching

On both the service-provider side—connecting enterprises to the internet—and in the rise of client-server applications, vendors specializing in the building of networking gear began to appear. Networking equipment moved from high-performance workstations with multiple Network Interface Cards (NICs) to specialized hardware that supported only packet forwarding. Packet forwarding underwent a revolution when specialized Application-Specific Integrated Circuit (ASIC) processors were developed to forward packets. The advent of packet-switching silicon allowed significantly more interfaces to be connected to a single box and could forward packets at a much lower latency than was possible before. This hardware switching technology, however, initially supported only bridging.

Routers, Bridges, and Switches—Overlapping Terms

Is a router a switch? Or is a switch a synonym for bridging? This question has stayed for a long time on network engineer's minds. One customer, early in my Cumulus days, held the idea that switch meant only bridging, that disaggregated switches were therefore capable only of bridging, and thus that Cumulus Linux could only do bridging. Over the course of a single afternoon, he went from a skeptic to deploying a fairly large network running Cumulus Linux, as I eliminated this source of confusion and suggested a pure routing-based design for their network. However, the waters were muddied enough that VMware called the bridging module it built into its hypervisor software a "software switch," and it largely did only bridging.

I believe this distinction arose because hardware-based packet forwarding was first called a *hardware switch*, later shortened to just *switch*. But hardware packet forwarding supported only bridging for a long time because the IP routing lookup was too complex to design in hardware. So switching meant packet forwarding in hardware, and hardware packet forwarding meant bridging only.

However, after packet-switching silicon began supporting routing, as well, there was no need to restrict switches to bridging. Some use the terms "L2 switch" for switches that offer only bridging, whereas an "L3 switch" can also do routing. Many vendors still use this distinction to drive different pricing and licensing for bridging versus routing ports.

In this book, I use switch to mean a router or a bridge, and explicitly call out its function when appropriate.

I also stick with common industry terminology by using *packet* at both the bridging (link) and routing layers (no one says frame switching). In the standard Open Systems Interconnection (OSI) model, the link layer exchanges frames instead of packets.

Proprietary enterprise network stacks

In the client-server era of networking, IP was just another network protocol. The internet was not what we know now. There were many other competing network stacks within enterprises. Examples of such networks were Novell's IPX and Banyan VINES. Interestingly, all these stacks differed only above the bridging layer. Bridging was the sole given. It worked with all the protocols that ran at the time in different enterprise networks. So the access-agg-core network design allowed network engineers to build a common network for all of these disparate network protocols instead of building a different network for each specific type of network protocol.

The promise of zero configuration

Routing was difficult to configure—and in some vendor stacks, it still is. IP routing involved a lot of explicit configuration. The two ends of an interface must be configured to be in the same subnet for routing to even begin to work. After that, routing protocols had to be configured with the peers with which they needed to exchange information. Furthermore, they had to be told what information was acceptable to exchange. Human error is either the first or second leading cause for network failures (after hardware failures) according to multiple sources (*https://oreil.ly/RitXm*). Routing was also slower and more CPU-intensive than bridging (though this has not been true for well more than two decades now).

Other protocols, such as AppleTalk, promoted themselves on being easy to configure.

When high-performance workstations were replaced by specialized networking equipment, the user model also underwent a shift. The specialized network devices were designed as an appliance rather than as a platform. What this meant was that the user interface (UI) was highly tailored to issuing routing-related commands instead of a general-purpose command-line shell. Moreover, UI was tailored for manual configuration rather than being automatable the way Unix servers were.

People longed to eliminate or reduce networking configuration. Self-learning bridges provided the answer that was most palatable to enterprises at the time, in part because this allowed them to put off the decision to bet on an upper-layer protocol, and in part because they promised simplification. Self-learning transparent bridges promised the nirvana of *zero configuration*.

How Self-Learning Transparent Bridging Works

This sidebar summarizes how self-learning works in case you haven't studied it or you need a refresher. Lots of books cover bridging in more detail.

A bridge contains multiple interfaces and forwards packets from one interface to the others. Each interface is identified by the MAC address (also called the Ethernet address) built in by the manufacturer. A bridge builds the lookup table automatically without any user configuration by snooping on the packets as it switches them.

Every packet in a packet-switching network carries two MAC addresses: the source and the destination. The bridge also looks up the destination MAC address to see whether it knows which interface the system lives on. If it does not know, it sends the packet out to all of the interfaces except the interface from which it received the packet. This way, if the destination MAC address exists in the network, the packet will eventually be delivered to it.

Sending a packet out to all of the interfaces when the MAC address is not in the lookup table is called *flooding*. It includes a *self-forwarding check* that prevents the bridge from sending the packet out the interface from which it came.

Packets with a destination MAC address that is not present in a bridge's MAC table are called *unknown unicast* packets. Broadcast and unknown multicast packets are also flooded, because such packets must be delivered to every end station.

After the node with that MAC address originates a packet, the bridge learns what interface it lives behind. This is called *learning*. The next time around, the bridge just forwards the packet out that interface. Thus, it builds a forwarding table of the network over time. Hence the name *self-learning bridge*. It is also called a *transparent bridge* because packets are not explicitly addressed to the bridge to reach the destination. This is unlike routing in which routed packets have a destination MAC addressed to a router's interface.

Building Scalable Bridging Networks

Bridging promised the nirvana of a single network design for all upper-layer protocols coupled with faster packet switching and minimal configuration. The reality is that bridging comes with several limitations as a consequence of both the learning model and the Spanning Tree Protocol.

Broadcast storms and the impact of Spanning Tree Protocol

You might wonder whether self-learning bridges could result in forwarding packets forever. If a packet is injected to a destination that is not in the network or one that never speaks, the bridges will never learn where this destination is. So, even in a simple triangle topology, even with self-forwarding check, the packet will go around the triangle forever. Unlike the IP header, the MAC header does not contain a time-to-live (TTL) field to prevent a packet from looping forever. Even a single broadcast packet in a small network with a loop can end up using all of the available bandwidth. Such a catastrophe is called a *broadcast storm*. Inject enough packets with destinations that don't exist, and you can melt the network.

To avoid this problem, a control protocol called *Spanning Tree Protocol* (STP) was invented by Radia Perlman. It converts any network topology into a loop-free tree, thereby breaking the loop. Breaking the loop, of course, prevents the broadcast storm.

STP presents a problem in the case of access-agg networks. The root of the spanning tree in such a network is typically one of the aggregation switches. As is apparent from Figure 1-2, a loop is created by the triangle of the two aggregation switches and an access switch. STP breaks the loop by blocking the link connecting the access switch to the nonroot aggregation switch. Unfortunately, this effectively halves the possible network bandwidth because an access switch can use only one of the links to an aggregation switch. If the active aggregation switch dies or the link between an access switch and the active aggregation switch fails, STP will automatically unblock the link to the other aggregation switch. In other words, an access switch's uplinks to the two aggregation switches behave as an active-standby model. We see the solution to this limitation in "Increasing bandwidth through per-VLAN spanning tree" on page 11.

Over time, vendors developed their own proprietary knobs to STP to make it faster and more scalable, trying to fix the problems of slow convergence experienced with standard STP.

The burden of flooding

Another undesirable problem in bridging networks is the flooding (see the earlier sidebar for a definition) that occurs due to unknown unicast packets. End hosts receive all of these unknown unicast packets along with broadcast and unknown multicast packets. The MAC forwarding table entries have a timer of five minutes. If the owner of a MAC address has not communicated for five minutes, the entry for that MAC address is deleted from the MAC forwarding table. This causes the next packet destined to that MAC address to flood. The *Address Resolution Protocol* (ARP), the IPv4 protocol that is used to determine the MAC address for a given IP address, typically uses broadcast for its queries. So in a network of, say, 100 hosts, every host receives at least an additional 100 queries (one for each of the 99 other hosts and one for the default gateway).

ARP is quite efficient today, so there is no noticeable impact from handling a few hundred more packets per second. But that wasn't always the case.

And most applications were not as thoughtful as ARP. They were quite profligate in their use of broadcast and multicast packets, causing a bridged network to be extremely noisy. One common offender was NetBIOS, the Microsoft protocol that ran on top of bridging and was used for many things.

The invention of the virtual local area network (VLAN) addresses this problem of excessive flooding. A single physical network is divided logically into smaller networks, each composed of nodes that communicate mostly with one another. Every packet is associated with a specific VLAN, and flooding is limited to switch ports that belong to the same VLAN as the packet being flooded. This allows a group within an enterprise to share the physical network with other groups without affecting other similar groups sharing the same physical network. In IP, a broadcast is contained within a subnet. Thus, a VLAN is associated with an IP subnet.

What Is a Subnet?

IP addresses can be grouped such that one consecutive group of addresses is indicated by the initial bits they share—the mask—and the length of this mask. For example, in IPv4, 1.1.1.0/24 represents a subnet that groups 256 addresses ranging from 1.1.1.0 to 1.1.1.255.

Increasing bandwidth through per-VLAN spanning tree

Remember that access switches were connected to two aggregation switches and that STP prevented loops while halving the possible network bandwidth.

To allow both links to be active, Cisco introduced *per-VLAN spanning tree* (PVST); that is, it built a separate spanning tree for every VLAN. By putting the even VLANs on one of the aggregation switches and the odd VLANs on the other, for example, the protocol allowed the use of both links: one link by the even group of VLANs, and the other link by the odd group. Effectively, the spanning tree topology for a given VLAN for an access switch looked as shown in Figure 1-3.

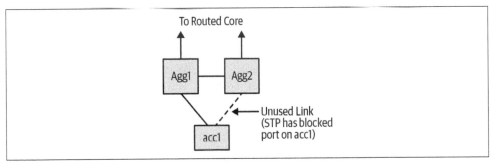

Figure 1-3. Active STP topology for a VLAN in an access-agg-core network

Redundancy at the IP level

One more problem needed to be solved, this time with the IP layer. Because the aggregation switches represented the routing boundary, they were the first-hop router for all the hosts connected under them via the access switches. When assigning an IP address to a host, the first-hop router's IP address is also programmed on the host. This allowed the hosts to communicate with devices outside their subnet via this first-hop router.

After a host is notified of the default gateway's IP address, changing it is problematic. If one of the aggregation switches dies, the other aggregation switch needs to continue to service the default gateway IP address associated with the failed aggregation switch. Otherwise, hosts would be unable to communicate outside their subnet in the event of an aggregation switch failure. This undermines the entire goal of the second, redundant aggregation switch. So a solution had to be invented such that both routers support a common IP address but have only one of them be active at a time as the owner of that IP address.

Because of the topology shown in Figure 1-3, every broadcast packet (think ARP) will be delivered to both aggregation switches. In addition to having only one of them respond at a given time, the response also had to ensure the MAC address stayed the same.

This led to the invention of yet another kind of protocol, called the First Hop Routing Protocol (FHRP). The first such FHRP was Cisco's Hot Standby Routing Protocol (HSRP). The standard FHRP protocol in use today is called Virtual Router Redundancy Protocol (VRRP). FHRP allowed the two routers to keep track of each other's liveness and ensure that only one of them responded to an ARP for the gateway IP address at any time.

Mitigating failure: In-Service Software Upgrade

Because there were only two aggregation switches, a single failure—or taking down a switch for any reason, such as an upgrade—resulted in halving the available bandwidth. Network operators wanted to avoid finding themselves in this situation. So, network vendors introduced dual control-plane cards on an aggregation switch. This was done so that if one control-plane card went down, the other card could take over without rendering the entire box unusable. The two control planes ran in active-passive mode: in other words, only one of them was active at a time. However, in the initial days, there was no synchronization of state between the two control-plane cards. This translated to an extended downtime during a control-plane card failure because the other control-plane card had to rebuild the forwarding state again.

In time, Cisco and other vendors developed a feature called *In-Service Software Upgrade* (ISSU). This allowed the control-plane cards to synchronize state with each other through proprietary protocols. The idea was to let a control plane go down (due to maintenance or a bug, for instance) by switching over automatically to the standby control plane without incurring either a cold start of the system or a prolonged period of rebuilding state.

This feature was extremely complex and caused more problems than it resolved, so few large-scale data center operators use it.

All of the design choices discussed so far led to the network architecture shown in Figure 1-2.

Now, let's turn to why this architecture, which was meant to be scalable and flexible, ended up flat-footed in the dance with the new breed of applications that arose in the data center.

The Trouble with the Access-Aggregation-Core Network Design

Around 2000, when the access-agg-core network architecture became prominent, the elements seemed reasonable: a network architecture that supported multiple upper-layer protocols, and was fast, cheap, simpler to administer, and well suited to the north-south traffic pattern of client-server application architecture. Even though this architecture was not as robust as operators would've liked—even with added protocols and faster processors, life went on. As an example of the fragility of this architecture, the nightmare that is a broadcast storm is familiar to anybody who has administered bridged networks. Even with STP enabled.

Then the applications changed. The new breed of applications had far more server-to-server communication than in the client-server architecture—traffic followed a more east-west pattern than north-south. Further, these new applications wanted to scale far beyond what had been imagined by the designers of access-agg-core. Increased scale meant considering failure, complexity, and agility very differently than before. The scale and different traffic pattern meant that networks had a different set of requirements than the one they were working with.

The access-agg-core network failed to meet these requirements. Let's examine its failures.

Unscalability

Despite being designed to scale, the access-agg-core network hit scalability limits far too soon. The failures were at multiple levels:

Flooding
> No matter how you slice it, the "flood and learn" model of self-learning bridges doesn't scale. MAC addresses are not hierarchical. Thus, the MAC forwarding table is a simple 60-bit lookup of the VLAN and destination MAC address of the packet. Learning one million MAC addresses via flood and learn, and periodically relearning them due to timeouts, is considered unfeasible by just about every network architect. The network-wide flooding is too much for end stations to bear. In the age of virtual endpoints, the hypervisor or the host OS sees every single one of these virtual networks. Therefore, it is forced to handle a periodic flood of a million packets.

VLAN limitations
> Traditionally, a VLAN ID is 12 bits long, leading to a maximum of 4,096 separate VLANs in a network. At the scale of the cloud, 4,096 VLANs is paltry. Some operators tried adding 12 more bits to create a flat 24-bit VLAN space, but 24-bit VLAN IDs are a nightmare. Why? Remember that we had an instance of the STP

running per VLAN? Running 16 million instances of STP was simply out of the question. And yes, Multi-Instance STP (MSTP) was invented to address this, but it wasn't enough.

Burden of ARP

Remember that aggregation boxes needed to respond to ARPs? Now imagine two boxes having to respond to a very large number of ARPs. When Windows Vista was introduced, it lowered the default ARP refresh timer from a minute or two to 15 seconds to comply with the RFC 4861 ("Neighbor Discovery for IP version 6") standard. The resulting ARP refreshes were so frequent that they brought a big, widely deployed aggregation switch to its knees. In one interesting episode of this problem that I ran into, the choking up of the CPU due to excessive ARPs led to the failure of other control protocols, causing the entire network to melt at an important customer site. The advent of virtual endpoints in the form of VMs and containers caused this problem to become exponentially worse as the number of endpoints that the aggregation switches had to deal with increased, even without increasing the number of physical hosts connected under these boxes.

Limitations of switches and STP

A common way to deal with the increased need for the east-west bandwidth is to use more aggregation switches. However, STP prevents the use of more than two aggregation switches. Any more than that results in an unpredictable, unusable topology in the event of topology changes due to link and/or node failures. The limitation of using only two aggregation switches severely restricts the bandwidth provided by this network design. This limited bandwidth means that the network suffers from congestion, further affecting the performance of applications.

Complexity

As shown in the study of the evolution of access-agg-core networks, bridged networks require a lot of protocols. These include STP and its variants, FHRP, link failure detection, and vendor-specific protocols such as the VLAN Trunking Protocol (VTP). All of these protocols significantly increase the complexity of the bridging solution. What this complexity means in practice is that when a network fails, multiple different moving parts must be examined to identify the cause of the failure.

VLANs require every node along the path to be VLAN aware. If a configuration failure leads a transit device to not recognize a VLAN, the network becomes partitioned which results in complex, difficult-to-pin down problems.

ISSU was a fix to a problem caused by the design of access-agg-core networks. But it drags in a lot of complexity. Although ISSU has matured and some implementations do a reasonable job, it nevertheless slows down both bug fixes and the development of new features due to the increased complexity. Even the software testing becomes more complex as a result of ISSU.

As a final nail in this coffin, reality has shown us that nothing is too big to fail. When something that is not expected to fail does indeed fail, we don't have a system in place to deal with it. ISSU is similar in a sense to nonstop Unix kernels, and how many of those are in existence today in the data center?

Unless the access-agg-core network is carefully designed, congestion can quite easily occur in such networks. To illustrate, look again at Figure 1-3. Both the Agg1 and Agg2 switches announce reachability to the subnets connected to acc1. This subnet might be spread across multiple access switches, not limited to just acc1. If the link between Agg1 and acc1 fails, when Agg1 receives a packet from the core of the network destined to a node behind acc1, it needs to send the packet to Agg2 via the link between Agg1 and Agg2, and have Agg2 deliver the packet to acc1. This means the bandwidth of the link between Agg1 and Agg2 needs to be carefully designed; otherwise, sending more traffic than planned due to link failures can cause unexpected application performance issues.

Even under normal circumstances, half the traffic will end up on the switch that has a blocked link to the access switch, causing it to use the peer link to reach the access switch via the other aggregation switch. This complicates network design, capacity planning, and failure handling.

Failure Domain

Given the large scales involved in the web-scale data centers, failure is not a possibility but a certainty. Therefore, a proportional response to failures is critically important.

The data center pioneers came up with the term *blast radius* as a measure of how widespread the damage is from a single failure. The more closely contained the failure is to the point of the failure, the more fine-grained is the failure domain and the smaller is the blast radius.

The access-agg-core model is prone to very coarse-grained failures; in other words, failures with large blast radiuses. For example, the failure of a single link halves the available bandwidth. Losing half the bandwidth due to a single link failure is quite excessive, especially at large scales for which at any given time, some portion of the network will have suffered a failure. The failure of a single aggregate switch brings the entire network to its knees because the traffic bandwidth of the entire network is cut in half. Worse still, a single aggregate switch now will need to handle the control plane of both switches, which can cause it to fail, as well. In other words, cascading failures resulting in a complete network failure is a real possibility in this design.

Another example of cascading failures is due to the ever-present threat of broadcast storms when the control plane becomes overwhelmed. Instead of merely diverting traffic from a single node, broadcast storms can bring the entire network down either because that node is overwhelmed or because of a bug in it.

Unpredictability

A routine failure can cause STP to fail dramatically. If a peer STP is unable to send hello packets in time for whatever reason (because it is dealing with an ARP storm, for example), the other peers assume that there is no STP running at the remote end and start forwarding packets out the link to the overwhelmed switch. This promptly causes a loop and a broadcast storm kicks in, completely destroying the network. This can happen under many conditions. I remember a case back in the early days when the switching silicon had a bug that caused packets to leak out blocked switch ports, inadvertently forming a loop and thus creating a broadcast storm.

STP also has a root election procedure that can be thrown off and result in the wrong device elected as the root. This happened, for example, at a rather large customer site, during my Cisco days, when a new device was added to the network. The customer had so many network failures as a result of this model that it demanded that switch ports be shipped in a disabled state until they were configured. With the ports administratively disabled by default, STP on a newly added switch didn't accidentally join a network and elect itself the root.

The presence of many moving parts, often proprietary, also causes networks to become unpredictable and difficult to troubleshoot.

Inflexibility

In Figure 1-4, VLANs terminate at the aggregation switch, at the boundary of bridging and routing. It is not possible to have the same VLAN be present across two different pairs of aggregate switches. In other words, the access-agg-core design is not flexible enough to allow a network engineer to assign any available free port to a VLAN based on customer need. This means that network designers must carefully plan the growth of a virtual network in terms of the number of ports it needs.

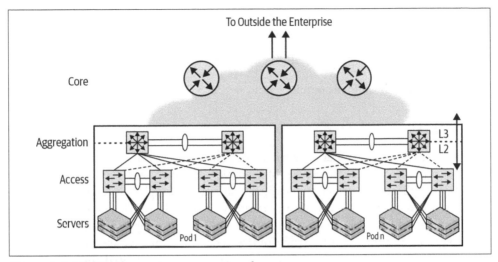

Figure 1-4. Multipod access-agg-core network

Lack of Agility

In the cloud, tenants come and go at a very rapid pace. It is therefore crucially important to provision virtual networks quickly. As we've discussed, VLAN requires every node in the network to be configured with the VLAN information for proper functioning. But adding a VLAN also adds load on the control plane. This is because with PVST, the number of STP hello packets to be sent out is equal to the number of ports times the number of VLANs. As discussed earlier, a single overwhelmed control plane can easily take the entire network down. So adding and removing VLANs is a manual, laborious process that usually takes days.

Also as discussed earlier, adding a new node requires careful planning. Adding a new node causes a change to the number of STP packets the node needs to generate, potentially pushing it over the edge of its scaling limit. So even provisioning a new node can be a lengthy affair involving many people to sign off, each crossing their fingers and hoping all goes well.

The Stories Not Told

Bridging and its adherents didn't give up without a fight. Many solutions were suggested to fix the problems of bridging. I was even deeply involved in the design of some of these solutions. The only thing that remains for me personally from these exercises is the privilege of working closely with Radia Perlman on the design of the Transparent Interconnection of Lots of Links (TRILL) protocol. I won't attempt to list all the proposed solutions and their failures. Only one of these solutions is used in a limited capacity in the modern enterprise data center. It is called *Multichassis Link Aggregation* (MLAG) and is used to handle dual-attached servers.

The flexibility promised by bridging to run multiple upper-layer protocols is no longer useful. IP has won. There are no other network-layer protocols to support. A different kind of flexibility is required now.

Summary

In this chapter, we looked at how the evolution of application architecture led to a change in the network architecture. Monolithic apps were relatively (in comparison to today's applications) simple applications that ran on complex, specialized hardware and worked on networks with skinny interconnects and proprietary protocols. The next generation of applications were complex client-server applications that ran on relatively simple compute infrastructure that relied on complex networking support. The current class of applications are complex large-scale distributed applications that demand a different network architecture. We examine the architecture that has replaced the access-agg model in the next chapter.

## CHAPTER 2

Clos: Network Topology for a New World

Redwoods have an enormous surface area that extends upward into space because they have a propensity to do something called reiteration. A redwood is a fractal. And as they put out limbs, the limbs burst into small trees, copies of the redwood.

—Richard Preston

Form is destiny—in networking even more than in life. The structure of the network lays the foundation for everything that follows. Plant a tree and its roots control the flow. Build a torus-like access road and you get a rich, well-knit neighborhood. Design your network as a Clos, and you get this book.

The structure of the new world is the Clos topology (named after one of its inventors, Charles Clos). The cloud native data center infrastructure pioneers wanted to build something that could scale massively. The Clos topology is like a redwood tree, using a somewhat fractal model to scale out. Networking in a Clos topology is pretty much what this book is about. So understanding the Clos topology and its properties is a key requirement for any network engineer or architect.

This chapter is designed to address questions such as:

- What is Clos topology and how is it different from access-agg-core topology?
- What are the characteristics of Clos topology?
- What are the consequences of the Clos topology for data center networking?
- How do you scale a Clos topology?
- What problems turn up in a Clos topology?

We discuss how the Clos topology connects to outside networks in Chapter 9.

Introducing the Clos Topology

Figure 2-1 shows the most common illustration of a basic Clos topology. It shows two layers of switches, one called the *spine* and the other called the *leaf*. Hence, the layout is also commonly called a *leaf-spine* topology.

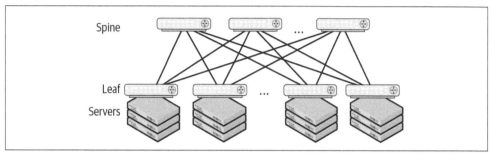

Figure 2-1. Illustration of a common Clos topology

Every leaf is connected to every spine node. The spines connect the leaves to one another, and the leaves connect the servers to the network. It is common practice to put the servers and the leaf switch in a single hardware rack, with the switch at the top of the rack. So the leaf is often called a *top of rack* (ToR) switch. In this book, I use the terms ToR and leaf interchangeably when referring to the tier to which servers connect.

I've used the same shade for both spine and leaf switches to show that both the spine and the leaf can be the same type of device. Although not mandated by the Clos topology, the use of homogeneous equipment is a key benefit of this architecture. We discuss why later in the chapter.

This topology produces a high-capacity network, because there are more than two paths between any two servers. Adding more spines increases the available bandwidth between leaves. Adding more links between a leaf and a spine is not recommended to achieve this goal. We explain more on why this is so in a bit.

The spines serve a single purpose: to connect the different leaves. Compute endpoints are never attached to spines. The spines do not provide any other service, either. Thus, the spines are different from the aggregation switches of the access-agg-core architecture described in Chapter 1, although they structurally occupy the same position. In other words, in a Clos topology, all functionality is pushed to the edges of the network, the leaves and the servers themselves, rather than being provided by the center, represented by the spines.

Clos grows in a very consistent way thanks to having what's called a *scale-out* architecture. You increase the amount of work supported by the network by adding more leaves and servers. The spines are then used only to scale the available bandwidth between the edges. In contrast, in the access-agg-core architecture, the scaling of services was provided by beefing up the aggregation box's CPUs. Such an architecture is called a *scale-in* architecture.

In Clos, all functionality except interconnection is pushed out to the edges, so the control-plane load on a spine increases only marginally as more leaves are added to it. For example, the spines are not responsible for responding to the Address Resolution Protocol (ARP) requests of the end stations, like an aggregate switch would. As a consequence, we'll soon see how easy it is to determine the maximum number of servers that can be connected in such a network.

Drawing Clos Topology

If you look up *Clos* in Wikipedia or in the original paper by Charles Clos, the picture of the Clos topology looks different from the one I drew as a leaf-spine topology. The picture looks more like the one shown in Figure 2-2.

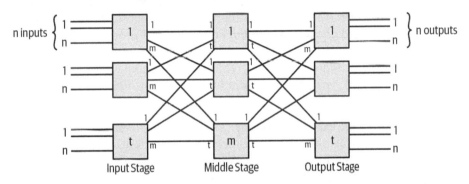

Figure 2-2. Classic three-stage Clos topology

The topology is described as having three stages: input, middle, and output. The input stage has *n* inputs and *m* connections to the middle stage, whereas the output stage has the *n* outputs and *m* connections to the middle stage. Each input stage switch is connected once to every middle stage switch. Each middle stage switch is connected to each output stage switch once. There are *t* input stage switches and *t* output stage switches, so the middle stage has *t* inputs and *t* outputs.

Although this looks very different from Figure 2-1, it actually maps neatly to it. If you imagine the output stage switch folded back so that it lies on the same side of the middle stage switch as the input stage switch, you can easily see that the middle stage switches are spine switches, and the input and output stage switches are just the leaves. If you make the *n=m=t*, you get the leaf-spine topology I drew earlier, which is what network practitioners use today.

A Deeper Dive into the Clos Topology

Let's now take a deeper look at the Clos topology to better understand its properties.

Use of Homogeneous Equipment

Using this topology, Charles Clos made it economical to build very large telephony networks with relatively small switches. In a similar fashion, we can use the Clos topology to build very large packet-switched networks using simple fixed-form-factor switches—a game changer. The new topology and the economics that go along with it modernize everything from how we think about failure to how we buy switches, how we do inventory management, and how we manage the network.

Routing as the Fundamental Interconnect Model

A fundamental limitation of the access-agg-core network is its ability to support only two aggregation switches. Readers might be wondering how the Clos topology can then support more than two spines. The short answer is that the Spanning Tree Protocol (STP) is not used as the switch interconnect control protocol. Does this mean bridging is not supported in Clos topologies? Bridging is mainly supported only at the edges, meaning within a single rack. To achieve bridging across racks, we use a more modern network virtualization solution such as the Virtual eXtensible Local Area Network (VXLAN), which we cover in Chapter 6.

Before the industry settled on IP routing within the data center, various solutions were proposed to support bridging as the interconnect without STP. Solutions such as TRILL and Shortest Path Bridging (SPB) came up. Cisco's proprietary FabricPath was deployed in some networks. However, these solutions were immature even though they were based on ideas straight out of networking 101. Further, bridging had outlived its usefulness as the main connectivity method because IP networks were about the only upper-layer protocol in use. Just about every packet-switching silicon supported IP routing at the same cost, latency, and bandwidth as bridging, thus removing the pragmatic concerns around routing's traditional slowness.

So how does routing allow for more than two spine switches? By supporting something called Equal-Cost Multipath (ECMP) routing. This allows a packet to be forwarded along any of the available equal-cost paths. For example, in Figure 2-1, a leaf can reach any other leaf using any spine, and the cost to reach any leaf is the same.

At the most basic level, therefore, the Clos topology was accompanied by switching (pun intended) to routing rather than bridging as the primary packet forwarding model.

Flows and Congestion

When there is more than one next hop to a destination, a router can either randomly select one to forward the packet, or ensure that all packets belonging to a flow use the same next hop. A flow is roughly defined as a group of packets that belong together. Most commonly, a Transmission Control Protocol (TCP) or User Datagram Protocol (UDP) flow is defined as the five-tuple of source IP address, destination IP addresses, the Layer 4 (L4) protocol (TCP/UDP), the L4 source port, and the L4 destination port. Packets of other protocols have other definitions of flow.

A primary reason to identify a flow is to ensure the proper functioning of the protocol associated with that flow. If a node forwards packets of the same flow along different paths, these packets can arrive at the destination in a different order from the one in which they were transmitted by the source. This out-of-order delivery can severely affect the performance of the protocol and, consequently, of the applications using the protocol. However, it is also critical to ensure maximum utilization of all the available network bandwidth; that is, all the network paths to a destination. Every network node makes decisions that balance these two constraints.

To ensure that all packets associated with a flow take the same next hop, routers (hardware or software) use *flow hashing*. This means that for every packet, the router creates a hash of the packet headers, coupled with some other information such as incoming port. Some fixed number of bits of the hash are used as a modulo on the number of available hops to select for the next hop. This method of determining the next hop for a flow allows routers to ensure that all packets associated with a flow take the same path without requiring them to maintain per-flow state.

An important factor to understand is that flow hashing leads to equal distribution of flows across the links, but not equal distribution of packets, because different flows have different numbers of packets. This means that although the flows are distributed evenly, the total bandwidth is not. This causes congestion on the links, with some flows using more than their fair share of packets. Flows with a relatively large number of packets are called *elephant flows*, whereas flows with relatively few packets are called *mice flows*. Networks exhibit the classic heavy-tailed distribution, in which a few flows make up the majority of bandwidth used. The problem of many elephant flows ending up on the same link causing congestion and affecting the mice flows on that link is the so called *elephant–mice problem*.

Even without the elephant–mice problem, with certain traffic patterns, flow hashing can result in some links being preferred over other links. This unbalanced uplink utilization is called *traffic polarization*. Most packet-switching silicon provide the ability to change certain parameters of the hash to see whether the polarization can be either mitigated or eliminated.

Oversubscription in a Clos Topology

In packet-switched networks, *oversubscription* of a switch is defined as the ratio of downlink to uplink bandwidth. In leaves, downlinks are the server-facing links, and uplinks are the spine-facing links. So an oversubscription ratio of 1:1 means that the total downlink bandwidth is equal to the total uplink bandwidth. If the bandwidth from the servers is twice as much as the bandwidth going toward the spines, we say that the oversubscription ratio is 2:1. Unless there's an additional tier, as we discuss in "Scaling the Clos Topology" on page 29, the spines do not have an oversubscription definition in the simple, two-tier Clos topology of Figure 2-1.

Assuming equal speed links for uplink and downlink, a 1:1 ovsersubscription ratio means that every downlink has a corresponding uplink. But not all data centers preserve a 1:1 oversubscription at the leaf. Many use a 2:1 or 4:1 oversubscription ratio. But most data centers ensure that higher tiers (discussed in "Scaling the Clos Topology" on page 29) in the Clos network have a 1:1 oversubscription ratio. So in a three-tier or four-tier Clos network, an oversubscription ratio that is not 1:1 might be found at the leaf level, but only at that level. Of course, as you build out the data center, operators might choose to start with higher oversubscription (2:1 or so) and bring it to 1:1 only as the bandwidth demand soars.

A 1:1 oversubscribed network is also called a *nonblocking* network (technically, it is really *noncontending*), because traffic from one downlink to an uplink will not contend with traffic from other downlinks. However, even with an oversubscription ratio of 1:1, the Clos topology is technically only *rearrangably nonblocking*. Depending on the traffic pattern, flow hashing can result in packets from different downlinks using the same uplink (as described in "Flows and Congestion" on page 23). If you could rearrange the flows from different downlinks that end up on the same uplink to use other uplinks, you could make the network nonblocking again. Hence the name rearrangably nonblocking.

Assuming we're using n-port switches for both leaf and spine, and assuming a 1:1 oversubscription, the maximum number of servers that can be connected in the Clos topology shown in Figure 2-1 is $n^2/2$. To understand this better, let's use four-port switches. In Figure 2-3, if all the switches are four-port switches, it is easy to see how only eight servers can be connected to such a Clos network. The leaves L1-L4 have two ports facing the server and one port to each spine. That allows each leaf to connect to two servers. The same four-port switch as a spine can hook up to four leaves. Thus four leaves multiplied by two server ports per leaf is eight servers. Using the formula provided, $4 \times 4/2 = 8$ servers.

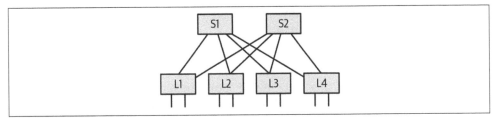

Figure 2-3. Illustrating Clos math with four-port switches

If you use more realistic numbers, such as 64-port switches, the total number of servers that can be connected is $64^2/2 = 2{,}048$ servers. If you double the number of ports on the switch and buy 128-port switches, the total number of servers quadruples to $128^2/2 = 8{,}192$ servers. This assumes that all n-ports are of the same bandwidth.

The total number of switches needed in a fully built-out two-tier Clos topology with n port switches is $n + n/2$. For a 64-port switch, therefore, the total port count is $64 + 64/2 = 96$ switches. To understand this, consider that each spine switch can support n leaf switches. Every leaf switch can connect half its ports to the spines and the other half to the servers. A spine can connect all n ports to leaves. So an n-port switch will have n leaves connecting to $n/2$ spines, yielding the formula just shown.

Although 2,048 servers is large enough for most small- to middle-sized enterprises, how does this design get us to the much-touted tens of thousands or hundreds of thousands of servers? We address that in "Scaling the Clos Topology" on page 29.

Interconnect Link Speeds

The most common implementation of the Clos model I've seen is to have servers at one speed and the *inter-switch link* (ISL) at a higher speed. For example, a 1GbE (Gigabit per second Ethernet) server link is used with a 10GbE ISL; a 10GbE server link is used with a 40GbE ISL. As of this writing, a 25GbE server link coupled with a 100GbE ISL is becoming the trend.

The main reason for using higher-speed uplinks is that you can use fewer spine switches to support the same oversubscription ratio. For example, with 40 servers connected at 10GbE, the use of 40GbE uplinks requires only 10 spines, whereas using 10GbE uplinks would require 40 spines. This four-fold reduction in the number of spines is important for most data center operators because it significantly reduces the cost of cabling. It also reduces the number of switches that they need to manage. A third reason is that a larger capacity uplink ISL reduces the chances of a few long-lived high-bandwidth flows overloading a link. All of these factors are desirable to most data center operators today.

A few data center operators use the same, relatively low, link speed for uplinks and downlinks. This is done for three reasons.

The first and primary reason is to allow the building of much larger networks, even with smaller port count switches. For example, 32-port 40GbE switches were the state of the art around 2013. Using only 40GbE ports means that the total number of servers possible in a two-tier network would be $32^2/2 = 512$. If instead you split up each 40GbE port into 4 ports of 10GbE, you can get a maximum of 108 ports of 10GbE (the switch implementation prevents getting the entire 128 ports of 10GbE). With 108 ports of 10GbE, you can build a much larger network: $108^2/2 = 5,832$.

The second reason is much better load balancing. Using more switches at the lower speed means, based on the example in the previous paragraph, using 54 spine switches instead of just 16 (half of the 32 40GbE ports). With 54 potential next hops to choose from instead of 16, the risk of the elephant–mice problem is greatly reduced.

Finally, the loss of a link or spine node means a much finer failure domain (see "Failure Domain" on page 15). This is because, sticking with our previous example, the loss of a link would mean a reduction of only 1/54th of the bandwidth.

So far, only a few very large data center operators have used the equal speed uplink architecture.

Practical Constraints

The numbers calculated theoretically in the earlier section do not totally correspond with reality. The reasons have nothing to do with the Clos topology; rather, it's to do with the technological limitations associated with cooling, rack-sizing standards, server packaging, and switching silicon technology. Let's consider some of these.

Rack space limitations limit servers to 40 per rack in the larger data centers. But cooling and power availability dictate that most racks house maybe less than 40 servers per rack. Most sites are designed for around 10 KVA (Kilo-Volt-Amperes) power. If you want to stay with air cooling, 45 KVA is the the limit of possible power today. Depending on location, the power limitations hold many enterprises back to 20 servers per rack. The addition of Graphical Processing Units (GPUs) can also add to the power consumption of a server, further reducing the number of servers you can fit in a rack. I've run into enterprises using microserver technology to fit 96 servers into a single rack. But the common numbers I've seen are 20 or 40 servers per rack.

So as shown in Figure 2-4, with 40 servers per rack, on a 64 10GbE–port switch, we have 24 free ports. If we use only 20 of these for an uplink bandwidth of 200GbE, we get an oversubscription ratio of 400:200 or 2:1.

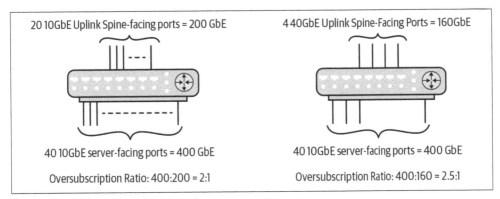

Figure 2-4. Illustrating the oversubscription ratio

With this math, you can hook up $64 \times 40 = 2{,}560$ servers in a two-tier Clos. This is higher than the theoretical number of 2,048 servers (64×32). Most operators combine the 24 ports of 10GbE into 6 ports of 40GbE (assuming the switching silicon supports it) but use only 4 for a 4-spine network. As shown in Figure 2-4, this leads to an oversubscription of 400:160 or 2.5:1 (40 ports of 10G is 400, and 4 ports of 40G is 160). This is quite acceptable for these small data centers.

What about oversubscription in data centers with enough power for only 20 servers per rack? It's a little more complicated.

Switching silicon commonly available today is 32 or 64 ports of 100GbE and 32 ports of 40GbE. As mentioned earlier, enterprises decide on one of the 10GbE/40GbE or 25GbE/100GbE speed combinations and stick to them. I haven't seen other occurrences such as 10GbE/100GbE, although 1GbE/10GbE was quite common in earlier times. Switching silicon design and cabling technologies also prevent a simple way to hook up 10GbE with 100GbE. Because servers in most enterprises are not capable of 40GbE or 100GbE worth of traffic, a bunch of 40GbE or 100GbE ports are split into 10GbE or 25GbE ports, and those are used to connect to servers. If you assume 25GbE server-facing links, and not more than 40 servers per rack, you need 10 100GbE server-facing ports ($10 \times 100 = 25 \times 40$). For a 1:1 oversubscription, you need 10 100GbE uplink, spine-facing ports. Putting the downlink and uplink requirements together, a use of just 20 switch ports lets you hook up the servers with spines with full 1:1 oversubscription. This leaves too many unused ports on a switch. Therefore, organizations with smaller server footprints choose to dual-attach servers, to end up with 40 server-facing ports.

The ones that use more servers per rack, such as 96 servers per rack, end up with 96×25, or 24 ports, of 100GbE with 8 ports of 100GbE left over for uplinks. That leads to an oversubscription ratio of 3:1, or if they use only 4 ports of 100GbE, an oversubscription ratio of 6:1.

In short, although data center operators want a larger port count switch for building larger networks, they also want a smaller port count switch for each leaf. To meet these needs, silicon switch vendors usually provide two (if not more) variations of switching silicon, one for the spines and one for the leaf. Broadcom's Trident and Tomahawk families are an example of this division.

Fine-Grained Failure Domain

With more than two spines, the loss of a single link or a spine node is not catastrophic. Large web-scale providers and some others use as many as 16 or 32 spines. Four spines is the smallest I have encountered. So with 16 spines, the loss of a single spine node or link results in only a 1/16th reduction of total bandwidth. Even with four spines, the loss is one-quarter as opposed to half.

Furthermore, the loss of a single link affects only traffic to and from the leaf that lost the link to the spine. The rest of the network continues to use full bandwidth. Link failures are far more common than node failures, so this failure domain is as fine grained as it gets. The same failure domain analysis also kicks in when a node is upgraded.

Consider a topology with spines S1 through Sn and leaves L1 through Lm. When the link fails between, say, leaf L1 and spine S1, all other leaves stop using S1 to reach L1. It is possible for traffic landing on S1 to reach L1 by bouncing the traffic off another leaf and spine. For example, S1 can send the packet to L1 via L2 and S2. But traffic bouncing back and forth between leaves and spines would result in congesting the links from those leaves. This in turn would cause collateral damage to traffic that is not even flowing to or from the affected leaf. But unlike STP, routing protocols restrict the impact of a failed link to just the nodes attached to that link, and nothing else.

In contrast to losing a spine or a link to a spine, the loss of a leaf affects all the servers connected to it. In large data centers, this is not too troublesome because they have hundreds and thousands of racks, so work on the lost servers can simply be abandoned and rescheduled on other servers. Smaller data centers place two leaf switches in each rack and connect the servers in each rack to both leaves. We discuss this further in "Host Attach Models" on page 36.

Systemic control-plane failures can affect the entire network. Smaller data centers don't have much protection from such failures except to reduce the chances of such failures by using robust and mature control protocols and keeping the network simple. Larger data centers break up the network into sections and ensure that no single point of failure exists across these sections. But note that there are no systemic failures of the style found in access-agg networks due to the use of routing, not bridging, for packet switching.

Scaling the Clos Topology

So far, we've seen how a two-tier Clos topology can support 8,192 servers. How does this design get us to the much-touted tens of thousands or hundreds of thousands of servers? For that, we show how elegantly the Clos topology scales to build much larger networks.

The important thing to remember is that as we add additional tiers, we assume a 1:1 oversubscription ratio between each set of layers except at the lowest tier.

There are a couple of ways to build a three-tier Clos network. Illustrating them is most easy using four-port switches. Therefore, Figure 2-5 shows a two-tier Clos constructed out of four-port switches, followed by two variations of a three-tier Clos also using four-port switches.

In a two-tier Clos topology, the spines use all four ports to connect to leaves, whereas the leaves use two ports to connect to the servers and two ports to connect to the two spines. This leads to a total of eight servers, as predicted by the formula we mentioned earlier, $4 \times 4/2 = 8$.

One way to build a three-tier Clos topology is to take the two-tier Clos topology of Figure 2-5(a) but instead of attaching servers directly to the leaves, create another tier by attaching another row of switches. This leads to the topology shown in Figure 2-5(b). Because we can support eight servers with a two-tier topology, we can support eight new rows of switches, which now become the leaf switches. These are also four-port switches, which means they have two server-facing ports and two uplinks. Thus, we get 16 servers with a 3-tier Clos using 4-port switches. The model in Figure 2-5(b) is a three-tier model popularized by Facebook. I call this the *virtual chassis model* because some vendors build a single large chassis-based switch that houses the two layers represented by the dashed box (see "A Different Kind of Chassis for Clos" on page 36 for more details).

Another way to build a three-tier Clos topology is to take two ports from the spine switches in the two-tier Clos topology and use them to connect to another layer of switches (the top layer in the figure), as shown in Figure 2-5(c). This model is used by Microsoft, Amazon, and many other mid- to very-large-sized data center operators. This model is commonly called the *pod* or *cluster* model. Each group of four switches that were originally part of the two-tier Clos topology now form a unit often called a *pod* or a *cluster*. Figure 2-5(c) shows that we can have four pods using only four-port switches. The new layer of switches that connects the pods is called by different names: some refer to this tier as *super-spine* switches or *inter-pod spine* switches, whereas others just relabel the three tiers in which the spine becomes the top-most tier, and what we called spine-leaf in the two-tier Clos topology becomes leaf-ToR in the three-tier Clos topology. In this book, we follow the leaf, spine, super-spine terminology.

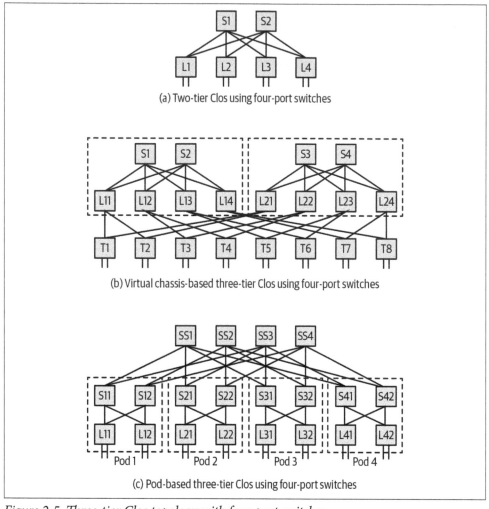

(a) Two-tier Clos using four-port switches

(b) Virtual chassis-based three-tier Clos using four-port switches

(c) Pod-based three-tier Clos using four-port switches

Figure 2-5. Three-tier Clos topology with four-port switches

This topology adheres to maintaining an oversubscription of 1:1. As expected with a four-port switch, we get an ECMP of two at every level of the topology up to the leaf layer.

These pictures are meant simply to illustrate the way in which three-tier topologies are built. You might conclude that with only four-port switches, we need more switches than servers. But this is not true in the real world. Just like the formula for a two-tier Clos, the number of servers that can be supported by a three-tier Clos network built up of n-port switches is $n^3/4$. For a 64-port switch, the total number of servers that can be supported is $64^3/4 = 65,536$. Remember, in a 2-tier Clos, the number of servers that could be supported was 2,048. This is a significant bump up. With

128-port switches, we can support $128^3/4 = 524{,}288$ servers. This equation holds true for both ways of building three-tier Clos networks.

The total number of switches needed in a fully built-out three-tier Clos topology is given by the formula $n + (n^2)$. With 64-port switches, we get $64 + (64^2) = 4{,}160$ switches. To understand this, let's use the pod model, knowing that the total from this model will also be the same for the virtual chassis model. Each pod has as many spines as half the number of ports, $n/2$, and each spine supports as many leaves as half the number of ports, which is also $n/2$. So each pod has $(n/2 + n/2) = n$ switches. Each spine connects up to half the number of its ports into a super-spine switch, and we know that there are as many super-spine switches as ports, which is n. So each of the n super-spine switches hook into a network of n spine switches, producing a total number of switches given by the formula $n + (n \times n) = n + n^2$ switches.

Comparing the Two Three-Tier Models

Where there is a choice, there is a question of which is better. This section contrasts the benefits of the virtual chassis model and pod model based on two criteria: workloads on the network, and ease of growth.

Application Matchup

The two models differ in how even the flow of traffic is, which in turn has implications for division of labor on your network.

Referring back to Figure 2-5, in the virtual chassis model (b), the path from any one of the leaves (labeled T× in the figure) to any other leaf is much more uniform than in the pod model (c). The pod model has an average of three hops from any server in a pod to another server in the same pod, but five hops to another server in a different pod. So there are two distinctly different latencies, one within the pod and one across pods. In the virtual chassis model, every server is on average five hops away from every other server, so the latency is much more uniform across the entire network.

Therefore, the models serve different workload needs. Data centers that tend to run a single application, such as Facebook, tend to use the virtual chassis model. On the other hand, data center operators that operate a cloud and that need to localize customer instances tend to use the pod model. The pod model also allows the operators to run different applications in each pod, varying the size of the pod as necessary. However, it is not uncommon for sites with a single application to use the pod model.

Data Center Build Out

As much as possible, data center operators do not want to recable the network. After it's cabled, they're willing to add new nodes or links and replace failed units, but they prefer not to recable an existing link from its current position to another one. With that perspective in mind, let us see how we can incrementally build out each of the two topologies as required. By "incrementally build out," I mean how you can start with only as many switches as you need initially and build out to the full planned capacity. Needless to say, when fully built out, both the pod and the virtual chassis architecture use the same total number of switches for a given capacity.

In the virtual chassis model, you start with the minimum number of super-spine and spine switches inside a virtual chassis to build out the network. This number must be multiplied by the number of virtual chassis necessary to preserve the desired oversubscription. In addition, you'll need enough leaf switches to handle the minimum server count. In the pod model, you can start with fewer super-spine switches if most of the traffic is confined to the pod. Unfortunately, this is not possible in the virtual chassis model.

Assuming 32-port 100GbE switches—a common model as of this writing—you can build a pod topology for a 200-server cluster using five leaf switches (assuming 40 servers per rack) and five spine switches, assuming an oversubscription ratio of 2:1 (two server-facing ports for every uplink port) for a total of 10 switches. In the virtual chassis model, you'll need five virtual chassis, each with one spine and five super-spine switches for a total of $(5 + 1) \times 6 + 5$ switches = 41 switches.

For this reason, most data center operators that I've seen tend to use the pod model to build out data centers. The virtual chassis model is often used when the data center operator has a very clear expansion plan and knows that the upfront investment will not be wasted.

Implications of the Clos Topology

In this section, we consider some of the implications of the Clos topology. These observations are important because they affect the day-to-day life of a network operator. Often, we don't integrate the impacts of a new environment or design choice into all aspects of our thinking. These second-order derivatives of the Clos network help a network operator to reconsider the day-to-day management of networks differently from how they did previously.

Rethinking Failures and Troubleshooting

Because Clos topology allows for building large networks with relatively smaller switches, network operators can decide to replace large chassis-based multirack switches with multiple switching silicon with a simple, fixed-form-factor (usually a rack) switch powered by a single switching silicon. A key benefit of these fixed-form-factor switches is that they fail in simple ways. In contrast, a large chassis can fail in complex ways because there are so many "moving parts." Simple failures allow simpler troubleshooting and, better still, more affordable sparing, allowing operators to swap-out failing switches with good ones instead of troubleshooting a failure in a live network. Thus, resilience becomes an emergent property of the parts working together rather than a feature of each box.

Cabling

Fixed-form-factor switches create the need to manage a lot of cables. The larger network operators all have some homegrown cable verification technology. An open source project called Prescriptive Topology Manager (PTM), which I coauthored, handles cable verification. This idea has been copied and used as vendor-specific solutions. One large customer I knew said PTM saved them from several headaches because they had as much as 30% cabling failures, and PTM helped the company catch a problem during cabling as opposed to encountering it as the hidden source of application performance problems. In Chapter 18, we look at how we can build a cabling check using an Ansible playbook. This provides most of the benefits of PTM for those whose platforms don't support PTM.

Simplified Inventory Management

Building a large network with only fixed-form-factor switches also simplifies inventory management. Because any network switch is like any other, or there are at most a couple of variations, it is easy to stock spare devices and replace a failed one with a working one. This makes the network switch or router inventory model similar to the server inventory model. This simplified inventory was a prominent reason for switching to the standard Intel/Linux model for servers.

Network Automation

With so many fixed-form-factor switches, it is no longer possible to manually configure the network. Network automation becomes a must-have as opposed to a nice-to-have architecture. We discuss network automation in greater detail in Chapter 10.

Some Best Practices for a Clos Network

In this section, we cover some best practices in a Clos topology. The two mentioned here specifically address mistakes that I've seen made by engineers who still hold on to the access-agg-core way of thinking.

Use of Multiple Links Between Switches

The most common way to increase available bandwidth in the access-agg-core network is to add additional links between the access switch and the aggregation switch and convert these multiple links into a port channel (aka bond or link aggregation). So wouldn't it be a good idea to add more links between the leaf and spine, or between the spine and super-spine, in a similar way instead of adding an additional spine?

The answer is no, in most cases. The reason is how routing protocols typically behave in such a topology when links fail. To understand this, let's use a stripped-down topology of a Clos network, redrawn in Figure 2-6.

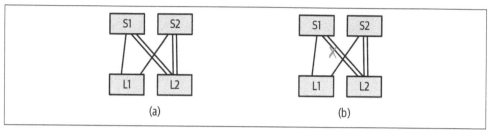

Figure 2-6. Illustrating the problem of using multiple links

Figure 2-6(a) shows multiple links between switch L2 and the spines S1 and S2. It doesn't matter whether these links are bonds or just individual routed links. From the perspective of L1, it sees two equal-cost paths to L2, via both S1 and S2. So far, so good.

Now consider a failure of one link between L2 and S1, as shown in Figure 2-6(b). From the perspective of L1, it still sees two equal-cost paths to L1. This results in it sending equal amounts of traffic through both S1 and S2 destined to L2. This is bad because S1 has only half the bandwidth of S2. As a result, random flows suffer increased packet drops or increased latency. When this manifests as degraded application performance, the problem can be difficult to track down.

If the two links are treated as a bond, the behavior is different with different routing protocols. In Border Gateway Protocol (BGP), we can use a feature called *link bandwidth extended community* to send proportional traffic to S1 and S2, but the way to make this work in the presence of multiple links and link failures is not commonly supported. Using Open Shortest Path First (OSPF) or Intermediate System to Intermediate System (IS-IS), the link failure would result in a drop in cost of the link, and L1 would simply stop using S1 as a path to L2. So OSPF and IS-IS cannot handle this, either.

Therefore, do not consider using multiple links for increased bandwidth. Instead, add additional spine (or leaf) nodes and keep the link count uniform between nodes.

Use of Spines as Only a Connector

The pure Clos model uses spines only as connectors for leaf nodes. But sometimes spines play another role as well, such as exit points to the external world, as shown in Figure 9-1. In such a scenario, some operators might decide to connect only some of the spines to the external connecting router. This is bad because it results in those spines receiving more than their share of traffic. For instance, a spine used for both internal and external communication will be asked to handle more traffic than the model assumes. This additional traffic can cause hotspots on those spines. Furthermore, these special-case spines change the failure characteristics of the network. For example, if only two out of four spines are used for connectivity to the external world, the loss of a link to one of these two spines halves the bandwidth available for external communication.

So ensure that if you use the spines for anything other than as connectors, no spine is treated specially. In that way, you preserve the fine-grained failure domain and reduce the risk of hotspots. This is a simpler mental model of the spines and makes it easier to understand what's going on with the network. Despite what vendors say, simple is not a pejorative word. It is a strength, not a weakness.

Use of Chassis as a Spine Switch

Some network operators are afraid to deal with three-tier Clos networks. So they think that for the spine if they can use a chassis switch with far more ports than the leaf, they can build a larger network using just a two-tier network. For example, with a 256-port chassis spine switch and a 64-port leaf switch, you can build 256×32 — 8,192 servers instead of the 2,048 switches available with just 64-port switches. More important, the network engineer might be concerned with the cost and effort of cabling in a three-tier network, compared to sticking with just the two-tier network.

Although this proposition can sound attractive, there are many considerations that argue against it. Smaller networks can get by with just a two-tier network. But as networks grow larger, there is a trade-off to be made between cost and complete network failure. A two-tier network has less protection from a systemic failure than a three-tier network.

Furthermore, as described in the previous chapter, when a chassis switch fails, it fails in complex ways, complicating the task of troubleshooting. With a fixed-form-factor switch, you can replace the problematic switch, restoring the health of the network, and troubleshoot the problematic switch outside the live network.

Another reason to reconsider the use of the chassis switch approach is that it makes a simple inventory management more complex, as discussed in "Simplified Inventory Management" on page 33. Finally, larger 128-port single-switch ASIC fixed-form-factor switches are already available, allowing you to build a larger network without resorting to the chassis switches.

I know of customers who chose the chassis switch approach and regretted this choice due to the reasons described. As LinkedIn, Dropbox, and many others have documented publicly, they all have moved away from chassis-based solutions to only fixed-form-factor switches.

A Different Kind of Chassis for Clos

A chassis is a modular piece of hardware that houses linecards along with one or more central management linecards. The linecards have the switching ports. All the linecards are connected via a proprietary backplane or cross-connect. A common moniker for this internal cross-connect is the *crossbar*. The aggregation box in the access-agg-core model is almost always this kind of chassis.

With the advent of Clos, a different kind of chassis has evolved. This is exemplified by designs such as Facebook's Backpack. The *raison d'etre* for these designs is to reduce the cabling cost of building a large data center. To do this, you build a chassis using a Clos topology as the crossbar across all the linecards of a chassis. For example, you can take the virtual chassis model of Figure 2-5(b) and build a single hardware box that houses the two-tier Clos topology in the box labeled *virtual chassis* as the cross-connect. The externally visible ports are the outputs of all the leaves in the picture. The crossbar runs a standard routing protocol just like the external Clos topology.

The entire chassis solves only the cabling problem. Unlike a traditional chassis, this chassis has no central linecard or cards that manage the entire chassis. Each linecard is managed as a separate router. The internal Clos cross-connect can optionally be exposed to the external world, depending on the implementation.

This is not a very popular model, but a few prominent companies have adopted this model in their data center.

Host Attach Models

In the modern data center, hosts with one or two NICs are most common. Servers either connect to the network via a single attach point to a single leaf or are dual-attached, as shown in Figure 2-7, with one link each to two different leaves. The dual-attached NICs are popular in the enterprise data center, but are not used in large data centers. The primary reason for dual attachment is that the operator cannot afford losing even a single rack of servers if a leaf goes down, either due to a planned maintenance or failure. This is usually the case with smaller data centers.

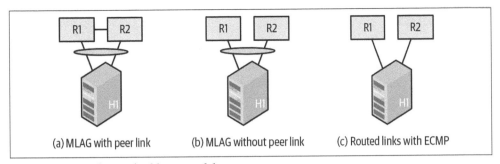

| (a) MLAG with peer link | (b) MLAG without peer link | (c) Routed links with ECMP |

Figure 2-7. Dual-attached host models

When hosts are dual-attached, some operators choose to use them only in active-standby mode; that is, only one link is active at a time. In this case, the operator is interested only in ensuring that a link failure doesn't cut off a server from the network. But most operators prefer to use both links. In this case, there are three possible models, as shown in Figure 2-7. The most common model I've seen is using the two links on the host as a bond (aka port-channel or link aggregation). This is shown in Figure 2-7(a). From the server side, it looks like a standard IEEE 802.3ad bond. On the switch side, the most common method is to use a vendor-proprietary protocol commonly called MLAG. Different vendors have their specific name for this proprietary protocol. Cisco calls it vPC, whereas Cumulus calls like CLAG, and Arista calls it MLAG. This protocol offers the magic to make the host think it is connected to a single switch with a bond (or port channel).

When MLAG is used in conjunction with a network virtualization technology such as Ethernet VPN (EVPN), the link between the two leaves connecting the host might not be present, as shown in Figure 2-7(b).

A third model is to use routing from the host to use both links in forwarding traffic. This is shown in Figure 2-7(c).

In the older enterprise networks, one other model called *MAC pinning* was common with the use of dual NICs with a hypervisor. In this model, the two NICs were used such that the hypervisor deliberately chose load-balanced packets across the two links based solely on the source MAC address of the packet.

Summary

In this chapter, we delved deep into many aspects of the Clos topology, which is the fundamental building block of the modern data center. In the next chapter, we consider a primary implication of Clos topology: the rise of network disaggregation.

References

Clos, Charles. "A study of non-blocking switching networks." *Bell System Technical Journal*, Vol 32, Issue 2, March 1953. (*https://oreil.ly/0oniD*)

## CHAPTER 3

Network Disaggregation

Breaking up is like knocking over a Coke machine. You can't do it in one push. You gotta rock it back and forth a few times, and then it goes over.

—Jerry Seinfeld

Jerry might as well have been speaking about *network disaggregation*. After all, disaggregation is a breakup. Hardware and software are no longer satisfied to be living under the same roof. They each want to follow their dream, find their true north. This chapter follows the hardware half of this breakup. The next chapter follows the software half.

Network disaggregation is one of the key fallouts from the new architecture introduced in Chapter 2. At the end of this chapter, you should be able to answer questions such as these:

- What is network disaggregation?
- Why is it important?
- What are the key enabling technologies for network disaggregation?
- Who are the key players in the hardware market for network disaggregation?
- How do operations with a disaggregated switch differ from a traditional one?

What Is Network Disaggregation?

The term "network disaggregation" has its roots in the movement that preceded it by a decade or more, server disaggregation." With server disaggregation, the compute node was broken up into a series of components—CPU, the hardware housing the system, OS, applications and so on—and each component could be purchased separately, typically from different vendors. In the broadest of terms, disaggregation involves breaking up the hardware from the software that make up a device such that each can be purchased separately. Typically, each was manufactured by a different company. In a similar fashion, network disaggregation (or more accurately "switch disaggregation" or "network switch disaggregation") is the breakup of the router/bridge into its hardware and software (which includes the network OS) components, allowing each to be purchased separately.

The primary reasons for disaggregation are to reduce the cost of the entire system and to allow each piece to develop and innovate independently of the other pieces. Application architects who have been examining the motivations behind microservices will see a parallel pattern here.

Figure 3-1 illustrates the main components of a network switch, specifically that of a fixed-form-factor switch. There are obviously many more components involved, such as RAM, disk, and so on. But in network disaggregation, these are the main components of interest.

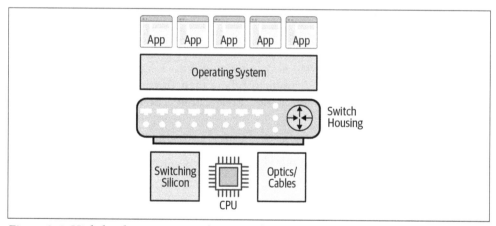

Figure 3-1. High-level components of a network switch

As mentioned earlier, in broad terms, a network switch can be broken up into hardware and software. The hardware can be broken further down into packet-switching silicon, the CPU, the box itself holding everything together, optics, and cables. The software can be broken down into the OS and applications. Applications include routing suite, monitoring and configuration agents, and other pieces that make up the control plane of the switch.

Even as of this writing, a network switch is most often bought from a single vendor; for example, Cisco. Typically, the switch is entirely proprietary and tightly integrated, with the vendor making (or contracting out the manufacturing of) all the pieces shown in Figure 3-1: packet-switching silicon, the box housing the CPU, the optics and cables that connect to it, and in rare occasions even the software. Vendors like

Cisco still design their own packet-switching chips while also building products based on off-the-shelf switching chips.

This is not very different from how servers were once manufactured and sold. Sun Microsystems made its own CPU (Sparc), its own workstation (along with monitors, keyboards, mice, and other peripherals, including cables to hook them all up), and its own OS (SunOS and then Solaris). Applications ranged from the ones that Sun itself made to third-party applications such as word processors and presentations. The same model was repeated by SGI, HP, IBM, and many others. Although some standardized layers arose such as POSIX, some chunk of software had to be specific to each vendor.

Personal computers (PCs) used a different model (and name) from the workstations. The CPU was made by one company, Intel (and then a few more over time); the hardware—including cables, monitors, keyboards, and the box itself that housed all of this—was made by a different company, usually IBM (although, eventually many more competed for this market); and the OS was made by an entirely different company, most dominantly, Microsoft (and others in time). Applications were made by Microsoft itself and eventually many others. Interestingly, the entire PC was initially sold by a single company, IBM, and it was only in time that others started shipping IBM or "IBM-compatible" PCs with Microsoft's OS, and then later Linux.

History has shown which model won out in the end. The question that the very large data center operators began asking in the networking industry was, "Why shouldn't the network be disaggregated?"

A General Perspective on Disaggregation

As Mark Twain said, "History doesn't repeat itself, but it often rhymes." Disaggregation is one of those rhymes that occur at various times in history, across different areas. This is especially true since the dawn of the industrial revolution, with its focus on the specialization of labor to innovate faster and the economy of large numbers to bring down costs. Initially, a field is immature. As a consequence, there are many approaches to solving a common set of problems. Companies form around these approaches and battle it out in the marketplace. Because there is no clear winner, there is little incentive for a third party to come up to serve a common need across the different companies. Over time, as a few winners begin emerging, it starts to become easier and more advantageous for third parties to emerge and solve a specific piece of the problem far more efficiently and cheaply than a single monolithic vendor can. Sometimes, this differentiation is built into the model itself, as in the case of PCs. Sometimes, the differentiation arises naturally due to various other factors. These factors, specifically the gradual dominance of Ethernet and IP, were in play when Broadcom and Mellanox diversified from building NICs to Ethernet switches.

Why Is Network Disaggregation Important?

If you're a network engineer or architect, I predict network disaggregation is in your future. Already, just about every company, be it Cisco or Juniper, has a product based on merchant packet-switching silicon. Arista's entire philosophy is built around not developing its own packet-switching silicon, but using the merchant silicon. Most vendors use Linux as the base OS. How much of Linux's networking functionality they use and how much of Linux they expose is the only key difference between the companies with respect to the OS. Although this is not publicly well known or available to most people, Cisco and Arista sell just their boxes to some of the largest data center operators and let those operators run their OS. It is a matter of time before network disaggregation in its complete state will be how people consume networking equipment. Therefore, it is important to understand it, learn how to work with it, and separate the myths from the reality so that you can choose wisely.

Disaggregation is a business model, not a technical issue, though there are technical decisions that are affected by this. As such, it is important more for business reasons than technical ones. Let's examine some reasons why network disaggregation is important.

Controlling Costs

Controlling the costs of building network infrastructure is probably the biggest reason that the large data center operators pursue network disaggregation. The product designs of vendors such as Cisco, Juniper, and Arista limited their customers' choices. Consider the case of optics and cables. Every incumbent allowed only the optics and cables they sold to work with their switches. Buying cables from elsewhere was not supported. As a consequence, vendors charged 10 to 20 times more for the cables than they would otherwise cost. This was a huge money spinner for the vendors. Since the advent of network disaggregation, every incumbent has slowly but reluctantly relaxed this practice.

But capital expense is only a small part of the cost. The operating expense—in other words, the cost of managing the network—is far more expensive. The administration of these boxes was mostly manual and thus not amenable to scaling. The network vendors were loath to solve this problem fast enough for the data center operators. Network vendors have slowly come around to making routers more manageable in time, but the price of network operations as provided by traditional vendors remains more difficult and complex compared to the compute nodes.

Avoiding Vendor Lock-In

The next primary reason for network disaggregation arose from a strong desire on the part of network operators to avoid vendor lock-in and to allow them to move specific pieces or the entire software to other, more adept vendors.

Some naysayers decried network disaggregation, saying vendor lock-in can occur in software, and that's a valid point. After all, we're all stuck with PowerPoint and Word. But, if the vendor is the open source community, the outcome can be different. Using Linux as the network operating system (NOS), for example, offers much less risk of vendor lock-in than using any proprietary OS. Using well-defined features and usage constructs also decreases the potential to get into vendor lock-in.

In other words, vendor lock-in is always a danger. It is a reflection of our unwillingness to change as easily as we'd like to. All you can do, as David Foster Wallace said, is make sure the demons that push vendor lock-in are as little in the driver's seat as possible. A disaggregated platform has the tendency to push against vendor lock-in more than an integrated switch.

Standardization of Features

A part of avoiding vendor lock-in is to ensure that the operator can focus on only standard features. With vendor-specific ASICs, it's easy to become trapped into proprietary solutions such as Qfabric, FabricPath, and Overlay Transport Visualization (OTV).

Having well-known packet-switching silicon also helps network operators evaluate the competitive strengths of different NOS vendors along measures such as resource usage, routing convergence, and speed. We can determine these things more evenly than when each vendor is working off a proprietary ASIC.

I'll conclude with a third benefit that isn't widely discussed but is based on my own observations. I notice that merchant silicon vendors deliver more regular upgrades than integrated silicon, making it easier for operators to plan upgrades. OS and original design manufacturer (more on this in a moment) vendors who provide a good quality and cadence that matches the arrival of new silicon have a better shot at winning customers.

What Made Network Disaggregation Possible Now?

Network disaggregation arose because of three primary factors. The first reason is the realization by the pioneers of the modern data center that traditional network vendors were slowing down their business. This was especially true when it came to operating networks. The second reason was the adoption of the Clos topology instead of access-agg topology. This eliminated the need for complex proprietary features required for bridging and reduced the feature set to a standardized minimum. That made it easy for these pioneering companies to take on the task of building a NOS themselves. The third factor was the rise of independent packet-switching silicon vendors. These vendors sell the packet-switching silicon to other companies producing switches, instead of integrating the chips into switches that they themselves produce. The switching silicon chips made by these companies are often called *merchant silicon*. These chips have grown to be extremely sophisticated, and today they are among the first to support new features.

Thus, these pioneering companies asked Chinese and Taiwanese manufacturers to build a network switch for them, initially based on Broadcom's Trident chipset, but later with chips from other merchant silicon vendors.

 A network switch without a NOS is also called a *bare-metal switch*, using the term "bare metal" differently from the concept behind bare-metal servers.

The rise of a fixed-form-factor chassis also made it easier for the development of new NOS players. Cumulus Networks and Big Switch Networks took different approaches to the NOS problem (which we discuss in Chapter 4). Since then, they have been joined by many other companies looking to capitalize in the new area of a disaggregated network OS.

Difference in Network Operations with Disaggregation

There are two primary differences in operations involving a disaggregated switch. Both are day-zero problems, meaning that the network engineer faces them right at the outset of the journey into network disaggregation. The first difference is the procurement of the hardware and software, and the second is the sequence of operations to be performed after these pieces arrive.

But first, a quick brush with terminology. Manufacturers of just the hardware—that is, the switching box itself, without any software on it—are called *original design manufacturers* (ODMs). Unlike a traditional switch, for which the vendor such as Cisco or Juniper tells the manufacturer the specifications by which to build the device and owns the design, the ODM of a disaggregated switch designs the box.

Purchase and Support

A traditional switch purchase involves contacting a single company such as Cisco or Arista to order the switch. Cables are also typically sold by this company. For a disaggregated switch, the customer must place an order for the hardware with one company, acquire the NOS from another company, the cables from a third company, and so on.

The common problem I've found with mid-sized to large enterprises in acquiring bare-metal switches is their own internal acquisition model. It did not help that many of the ODMs had never sold directly to such enterprises. They had manufactured and sold tens of thousands of units to a few large web-scale companies, but they did not know how to sell tens and hundreds of units to a large number of different enterprises. On the software side, enterprises had built requirements for years based on the advice of the vendors and consultants trained in the old access-agg model, where the length of the feature list was a proxy for the quality of the product. Therefore, a scrawny startup had to spend time to add features that customers didn't need to take business away from a vendor the customer didn't like.

To be fair, many, if not all, of the early adopters discovered ways to work around these issues or directly dealt with them by changing the existing rules to get the new players in. But as network disaggregation started going more mainstream, these real problems prevented many enterprises from committing to this model.

Customers also worried that they no longer had a single vendor responsible for a misbehaving network. This has not been true pretty much from the time the first NOS vendor stepped up. For example, Dell offers the support for the systems in which its hardware appears, and Cumulus offers support when the ODM is Quanta or Edgecore. So the network engineer has a single throat to choke in case of a problem with the disaggregated switch, just as in the case of a traditional switch.

First Boot

A vertically integrated switch is shipped with a preinstalled NOS, which cannot be changed. A bare-metal switch has no inherent NOS. Customers can install any supported NOS on it. If the switch is received without a NOS, the network engineer must know how to install a NOS on it. This is not unlike a sysadmin installing an OS on a server. However, network engineers are not familiar with this paradigm. So receiving a switch that doesn't boot to a recognizable NOS prompt leaves them unsure of the next step. We discuss what is to be done in such a case next.

Some switch manufacturers (such as Mellanox) address this issue by shipping the box with the NOS already installed. Some NOS vendors sell switches with a preinstalled NOS (an example of this is Cumulus Express by Cumulus Networks). But these companies are merely easing a customer's workload. The switch they sell can be replaced with another NOS by the customer.

Open Network Installer Environment

The PC had a reference design, produced by IBM, that every PC manufacturer had to adhere to. This meant that PCs manufactured by various companies all met a specification that the OS (Windows, Linux, etc.) could rely on and take as a basis for software. Unfortunately, the switch ODMs had no such reference design, so the switch manufactured by each ODM was different in myriad tiny ways. Pioneering NOS companies such as Cumulus Networks recognized this problem and had started work on it. But Cumulus itself was just a tiny startup without the power to influence the ODMs.

Facebook then started an initiative, Open Compute Project (OCP), with Intel, Rackspace, Goldman Sachs, and Andy Bechtolsheim, to provide a new design for equipment to build efficient data centers. According to OCP's website (*https://oreil.ly/ gkdKw*), the new design "...was 38% more energy efficient to build and 24% less expensive to run than the company's previous facilities—and has led to even greater innovation." OCP also undertook to standardize the design of bare-metal network switches. The first and chief need was for a firmware that would allow a bare-metal switch to install and provision a NOS in a scalable, automated way. Cumulus had already designed such a piece of software, called Open Network Installer Environment (ONIE). OCP adopted this and declared that any bare-metal switch needs to support ONIE to be OCP-compliant. As a result, every ODM that wanted to play in the disaggregated market supports ONIE.

Why not PXE?

ONIE serves a single purpose: to allow a NOS to be installed on a bare-metal switch. On the compute side, Pre-boot eXecution Environment(PXE) accomplished this task of installing an OS on a server. However, PXE worked only on servers with the x86 CPU. Servers running other chipsets such as ARM or PowerPC had to use a different bootloader called u-boot. Bare-metal switches were shipped with both PowerPC and x86 chipsets. ONIE wanted to be the single installer independent of the chipset.

ONIE needed to also support some additional enhancements over PXE and u-boot. For example, IPv6 support was required from day one. Another requirement was to provide an environment that a NOS installer could use to provide additional simplifications, such as determining the NOS image based on the model and CPU of the switch.

Instead of relying on a specific firmware image, ONIE designers chose to simply use Linux itself as the bootloader. This makes ONIE vastly more powerful as it ties itself to the feature set available in a standard Linux kernel.

How Does ONIE Work?

ONIE uses a Linux kernel (the latest versions use kernel version 4.9.95) with a Busy-box (*https://oreil.ly/5GknD*) environment to provide the desired functionality. Busybox is described by its developers as the Swiss Army knife of embedded Linux that "combines tiny versions of many common UNIX utilities into a single small executable." This allows the user to run various shell scripts to configure and automate the install and boot process. Busybox was designed to provide a familiar but stripped-down replacement for the usual Unix and Linux command-line utilities, suitable for limited environments such as embedded systems.

The NOS installer can also use many standard Linux tools and the shell (albeit with some options stripped out) to script the install. Because Busybox is essentially Linux, it supports pretty much any common protocol such as HTTP and the older Trivial File Transfer Protocol (TFTP), as well as various Ethernet drivers and even wireless (although not by default). The same applies to its locally attached storage. As long as Linux supports a protocol or device, ONIE can use it to install the NOS.

One important point to note is that ONIE uses only the management Ethernet port(s) for network access. It does not use the switching silicon ports for network access. The switching silicon comes with its own sophisticated driver, and attempting to use this inside ONIE was considered too heavyweight and unnecessary. All network switches ship with one or more management Ethernet ports, which are serviced by the standard Ethernet drivers in the Linux kernel.

Finally, ONIE kicks in only when a NOS isn't installed or the NOS configures it to run again. Otherwise, on reboot, the switch boots with the installed NOS.

The selection of where to load the NOS from follows the following order:

1. Local USB flash drive
2. URL from the DHCP server
3. URL obtained via DNS Service Discovery
4. Probing over any IPv4 or IPv6 link local neighbors
5. Probing over HTTP
6. Probing over TFTP

In the case of probing, ONIE uses ping and ping6 to the subnet local address (255.255.255.255 in case of IPv4 and ff02::1 in case of IPv6) to get a list of locally attached IP addresses to ping. ONIE then uses a series of default filename specifications to probe for an installer image. If it finds a NOS installer image using any of these techniques, it attempts to download and install the image obtained. If this installation fails, ONIE moves on to try the next method in the chain. This continues in a loop forever until a NOS is installed.

Before installing the NOS, ONIE sets up a bunch of environment variables for the NOS installer to use if required. Examples of these environment variables include the switch hostname (obtained via Dynamic Host Configuration Protocol [DHCP], for example), the switch's serial number, and the vendor ID. The NOS installation script can use the values from these preconfigured variables to take specific actions.

ONIE can also be updated using the same process, except that the OS image pointed to will be ONIE's new image instead of a NOS.

ONIE has a dedicated website (*http://onie.org*) with a lot of well-documented examples.

The Players in Network Disaggregation: Hardware

In this section, we look at the major players on the hardware side of network disaggregation. The primary objective of this section is to highlight the vast number of players involved in this space, as well as to provide network engineers with some names so they can continue the investigation. We cover the players in the software part of network disaggregation in the next chapter.

Packet-Switching Silicon

Without the rise of companies specializing in good-quality merchant silicon with enough features to make them usable in data centers, network disaggregation might never have taken off. Today, switch vendors often rely on these products to support important new features. For example, VXLAN support was commercially available for the first time on merchant silicon, not on the packet-switching silicon produced by the traditional network vendors.

Broadcom is the pioneer and the clear leader in the merchant silicon market. They make the Trident family of chips, which are primarily used as leaf (also called top of rack [ToR]) switches. It also makes the Tomahawk family, which are used in spines, and the Jericho chipset for internet-facing or so-called *enterprise edge* routers.

Mellanox is the next player that has been around for a very long time. Its Spectrum family of chips is its flagship product for use in both ToR and spine switches.

Barefoot is one of the newer players in the switching-silicon market. The company's claim to fame is its programmable packet-switching silicon. Both Cisco and Arista have switching products based on Barefoot's silicon.

Innovium, Marvell, and a few others also manufacture merchant silicon. A chip with 64 ports of 100GbE is commonly available today from multiple merchant-silicon vendors. The holy grail among all of these manufacturers is to achieve the ability to fit 128 100GbE ports on a single switching silicon. Including 128 ports of 100GbE on a single switching chip makes it possible to build very large networks. With the introduction of Innovium's Teralynx 7 and Broadcom's Tomahawk 3, you can now get either 128 ports of 100GbE or 32 ports of 400GbE. Of course, the goal posts keep getting moved.

ODMs

Edgecore, Quanta, Agema, and Celestica are the most popular switch manufacturing ODMs. They almost exclusively support the Broadcom family of switches. Dell is the other major ODM switch manufacturer; it also sells more traditional switches that bundle its own NOS, which cannot be replaced by the customer.

White Boxes and Brite Boxes

Bare-metal switches are also called *white-box switches*, because they lack a well-known brand label. As more incumbents began getting on the disaggregation bandwagon, they started advertising their hardware as capable of running NOSes other than their own, but they still branded the switch with their well-known brand. Such boxes were called *branded white boxes* or *brite boxes*. Dell is a good example of a brite-box vendor. They have their own OS while also allowing third-party NOSes such as Cumulus and Big Switch to run on top of its hardware. For many enterprises, brite boxes are far more attractive because they have one less new factor to deal with, and a single trusted player, the box manufacturer.

CPU Complex

During the early days, ODMs shipped with PowerPC-based CPUs. As in the server market, Intel x86 chips now rule the roost on high-end boxes. But unlike the desktop versions, the switch versions are typically less powerful and use less power as a consequence. On the lower-end boxes, like those used for network management only, ARM-core chips are the de facto standard.

Both of these CPUs are easy to run Linux on.

The Standards Bodies

The OCP (*https://oreil.ly/5QDmg*), introduced in "Open Network Installer Environment" on page 46, is the main organization responsible for network disaggregation. Any vendor that wants to advertise a disaggregated switch needs to make it adhere to the specifications put out by OCP. For example, ONIE is a mandatory requirement for the OCP stamp of approval. On the software side, the Linux Foundation (*https://oreil.ly/qwstw*) is the primary organization behind anything Linux. It also supports the open source routing suite, FRR (*https://frrouting.org*). Open Network Foundation (ONF) (*https://oreil.ly/HngbK*) is another organization whose charter is to play in the open networking space. The organization primarily focuses on a different model for a NOS, OpenFlow, which we discuss in the next chapter.

 The Internet Engineering Task Force (IETF), the key standards body that rules over the TCP/IP suite of protocols and the internet, is not involved in any way in network disaggregation. Network disaggregation is not a technical problem and hence is outside its jurisdiction. The Institute of Electrical Engineers (IEEE) continues to be the standards body for standardizing Ethernet and for the development of new Ethernet speeds. With the current dominance of routing, there is no role in the modern data center for the bridging parts of IEEE, specifically the 802.3 division of the standard.

Common Myths About Network Disaggregation

Incumbents are always terrified of disaggregation. It usually means lower revenues, lower profit margins, and far less possibilities for vendor lock-in. To counter the rise of disaggregation, network vendors have spread a bunch of myths as part of a FUD (Fear, Uncertainty, Doubt) campaign. The idea was to sow fear that network engineers stood to lose something essential when companies moved to white-box switches. Let's unpack each of their claims here:

It is a very DIY endeavor
Do it yourself (DIY). This was the most common meme I heard repeated during my time at Cumulus. It was as if the network engineers had to solder the switching ASIC and the CPU onto the board, turn the screws to close the box, and write routing protocols and other critical code to make the white box work. It was certainly true that network engineers accustomed to walled-garden command lines were unnerved by the wide open access of the Linux shell, and using Linux was not easy. But an unfamiliar user interface, the Linux shell, does not constitute a DIY.

It's only for the very big data center operators
This was one of the first myths that I encountered. Intertwined deeply in this myth were the other memes we discuss in this section, such as the boxes were difficult to manage or required a lot of assembling. Even as they tried to dissuade small- and medium-sized customers with the idea that the costs of disaggregating were too high, the incumbents were offering unusually deep discounts to the largest data center operators in an effort to keep them from pursuing the bare-metal switch model. They also made network automation seem too inconsequential for anyone but the largest data center operators and attempted to provide even more integrated solutions that exacerbated vendor lock-in.

Without a "single throat to choke," support is a mess

Users not accustomed to dealing with hardware and software separately found this urban legend easy to accept. The truth is that even the earliest white-box NOS pioneers provided a single-throat-to-choke model, regardless of whether they made the hardware.

The feature set is limited

Having managed vendor lock-in by selling a complex feature set as a boon rather than a bane, traditional networking vendors pointed to a "meagre" feature set as a problem with white box switches. At the same time, these very same vendors charged extra to even enable routing on their products. Compared to the large complex feature set required by bridging, the simple feature set of routing was not a curse, but a blessing. Furthermore, disaggregation allowed operators to try different operating systems. For example, operators can try operating systems from vendors who support a much more complex feature set, and one with good support for data center networking, and decide which one they prefer. In the process, they don't need to buy new hardware to try out new software.

Disaggregated switches are of poor quality

In the early days of Cumulus networks, JR Rivers, one of its founders, would go to customer meetings with a network switch that had its top removed and its insides exposed. He did that to show that the Cumulus ODM box was the same box as the brand name product that the customer was currently using. The quality difference in the manufacture of the ODM boxes is another myth propagated by the incumbents. Given the wide range of ODM manufacturers available, it's possible that some of the switches could have been worse than others, but in general, the quality of these switches was the same as the equivalent products from the incumbents because the same companies manufactured both boxes.

Not a Panacea

On the flip side, the followers of many early adopters felt that buying white-box switches would automatically make their networks better. But a box is rarely a substitute for good practice. Just running Linux as the NOS will not automatically fix anything unless the user changes their way of thinking and the practice of building and managing networking.

Some Best Practices for Engaging with Network Disaggregation

During my years dealing with customers attempting to deploy white-box or brite-box switches, I have noticed a few patterns that in my opinion hinder their engagement

---

with network disaggregation. The basic idea in writing this section is to provide some guidance from my experience for a more successful engagement. "Successful" does not necessarily mean buying into network disaggregation, but at least being able to arrive at a stage at which decisions can be made on a more informed basis:

Decide how to handle spares
> If a box fails, would you prefer to have a spare in your inventory that you can just replace, or to return the box to the switch manufacturer and have them ship you a new one ASAP? Remember that unlike older chassis boxes or integrated switches, bare-metal switches are much less expensive and so make it easier for you to host spares. If you prefer to have the switch manufacturer quickly ship you a spare, pick one with a turnaround time acceptable to you.

Pick cables and optics that have been tested by the NOS vendor
> Although you can theoretically pick up any cable and optics, experience has taught me that not all are made equal, neither in quality nor in the availability of information needed to add support for it. Ask the NOS vendor for their list of tested cables and optics, at least for the initial engagement phase.

Rethink your network design
> Do not work by the old model of looking at feature lists to determine which NOS is better. The more minimalist or essentialist your network design, the better the network will be. If you're thinking this means that you need to compromise on the quality of your network, you're falling into the old school of network design. We discuss this and other concepts of network redesign in Chapter 12.

Summary

In this chapter, we introduced network disaggregation, a key new development in the world of networking. The repercussions of this choice will echo far into the future. We examined the pieces that make up a network switch along with the changes in operations for a network engineer deploying bare-metal switches. We also examined some of the myths surrounding network disaggregation and a few tips in making an initial foray into network disaggregation successful. Some consider white-box switches a fad that had its moment in the sun. I think we're still rocking it back and forth. The breakup will go mainstream soon. In the next chapter, we look at the NOS in more detail.

References

- NOS list maintained by OCP (*https://oreil.ly/NXxCU*).

## CHAPTER 4

Network Operating System Choices

All models are wrong, but some are useful.
—George E.P. Box

All operating systems suck, but Linux just sucks less.
—Linus Torvalds

The breakup at the heart of cloud native data center networking was engineered by the network operators dissatisfied with the degree of control the vendors were willing to cede. Whenever a breakup occurs, the possibilities seem limitless, and there's a natural tendency to explore new ideas and ways of being that didn't seem possible before. But after a while, we realize that some of the old ways of being were actually fine. Just because we did not like watching yet another episode of *The X Files* with pizza every Friday evening did not mean that pizza was the problem. We don't need to throw out the things that work with the things that do not.

Thus, it was that the evolution of the modern big data and cloud native applications gave rise to a whole new set of ideas about how to do networking. Some were born out of the necessity of the time, some were truly fundamental requirements, and some are still testing their mettle in the new world. In this chapter, we follow the possibilities and models explored by the software half (the better half?) of network disaggregation.

The chapter aims to help you answer questions such as the following:

- What are the primary requirements of a cloud native NOS?
- What are OpenFlow and software-defined networking? Where do they make sense and where do they not?
- What are the possible choices for a NOS in a disaggregated box?

- How do the models compare with the requirements of cloud native NOS?

Requirements of a Network Device

In the spirit of Hobbes, the state of NOS around 2010 could be summarized as: proprietary, manual, and embedded. The NOS was designed around the idea that network devices were appliances and so the NOS had to function much like an embedded OS, including manual operation. What this meant was that the NOS stood in the way of everything that the cloud native data center operators wanted. James Hamilton, a key architect of Amazon Web Services (AWS), wrote a well-read blog post titled "Datacenter Networks Are in my Way" (*https://oreil.ly/bYEmD*) discussing these issues.

Operators buying equipment on a vast scale were extremely conscious of costs—the cost of both the equipment and the cost of operating it at scale. To control the cost of running the network, the operators wanted to change the operations model. Thus, a primary factor distinguishing a cloud native networking infrastructure from earlier models is the focus on efficient operations. In other words, reduce the burden of managing network devices. The other distinguishing characteristic is the focus on agility: speed of innovation, the speed of maintenance and upgrades, and the speed with which new services and devices can be rolled out. From these two needs arose the following requirements of any network device in the cloud native era:

Programmability of the device
> For efficient operations that can scale, automation is a key requirement. Automation is accomplished by making both device configuration and device monitoring programmable.

Ability to run third-party applications
> This includes running configuration and monitoring agents that don't rely on antiquated models provided by switch vendors. It also includes writing and running operator-defined scripts in modern programming languages such as Python. Some prefer to run these third-party apps as containerized apps, primarily to isolate and contain a badly behaving third-party app.

Ability to replace vendor-supplied components with their equivalents
> An example of this requirement is to replace the vendor-supplied routing suite with an open source version. This is a less common requirement for most network operators, but it is essential for many larger-scale operators to try out new ideas that might solve problems specific to their networks. This is also something that researchers in the academia would like. For a very long time, academia has had very little to contribute to the three lowest layers of the networking stack, including routing protocol innovations. The network was something you innova-

ted *around* rather than *with*. The goal of this requirement was to crack open the lower layers to let parties other than the vendors make relevant contributions in networking. As an example of the innovation that can result, imagine the design, testing, and deployment of new path optimization algorithms or routing protocols.

Ability for the operator to fix bugs in the code
This allows the operators to adapt to their environment and needs as quickly as they want, not just as quickly as the vendor can.

In other words, the network device must behave more like a server platform than the embedded box or specialized appliance that it had been for a long time.

The Rise of Software-Defined Networking and OpenFlow

The first salvo in the search for a better operating model came from academia, which was battling a different problem. The networking research community faced a seemingly insurmountable problem: how to perform useful research with a vertically integrated switch made up of proprietary switching silicon and a NOS that was not designed to be a platform? Neither the network vendors nor the network operators would allow any arbitrary code to be run on the switch. So the academics came up with an answer that they hoped would overcome these problems. Their answer, expressed in the influential OpenFlow (*https://oreil.ly/nkAvT*) paper, was based on the following ideas:

- Use the flow tables available on most packet-switching silicon to determine packet processing. This would allow researchers to dictate novel packet-forwarding behavior.

- Allow the slicing of the flow table to allow operators to run production and research data on the same box. This would allow researchers to test out novel ideas on real networks without messing up the production traffic.

- Define a new protocol to allow software running remotely to program these flow tables and exchange other pieces of information. This would allow researchers to remotely program the flow tables, eliminating the need to run software on the switch itself, thereby sidestepping the nonplatform model of the then-current switch network operating systems.

Flow tables (usually called Access Control List tables in most switch literature) are lookup tables that use at least the following fields in their lookup key: source and destination IP addresses, the Layer 4 (L4) protocol type (Transmission Control Protocol [TCP], User Datagram Protocol [UDP], etc.), and the L4 source and destination ports (TCP/UDP ports). The result of the lookup could be one of the following actions:

- Forward the packet to a different destination than provided by IP routing or bridging
- Drop the packet
- Perform additional actions such as counting, Network Address Translation (NAT), and so on.

The node remotely programming the flow tables is called the *controller*. The controller runs software to determine how to program the flow tables, and it programs *OpenFlow nodes*. For example, the controller could run a traditional routing protocol and set up the flow tables to use only the destination IP address from the packet, causing the individual OpenFlow node to function like a traditional router. But because the routing protocol is not a distributed application—an application running on multiple nodes with each node independently deciding the contents of the local routing table—the researchers could create new path forwarding algorithms without any support from the switch vendor. Moreover, the researchers could also try out completely new packet-forwarding behavior very different from traditional IP routing.

This separation of data plane (the packet-forwarding behavior) and control plane (the software determining the population of the tables governing packet forwarding) would allow researchers to make changes to the control plane from the comfort of a server OS. The NOS would merely manage resources local to the device. Based on the protocol commands sent by the control-plane program, the NOS on the local device would update the flow tables.

This network model, having a central control plane and a distributed data plane, became known as *software-defined networking* (SDN). The idea was to make the flow tables into a universal, software abstraction of the forwarding behavior built into switching silicon hardware. This was a new approach to breaking open the vendor-specific world of networking.

More Details About SDN and OpenFlow

Figure 4-1 shows the two central components of a switch with SDN. Figure 4-1(a) shows how OpenFlow manages a network run by devices with flow tables governing packet forwarding, as shown in Figure 4-1(b).

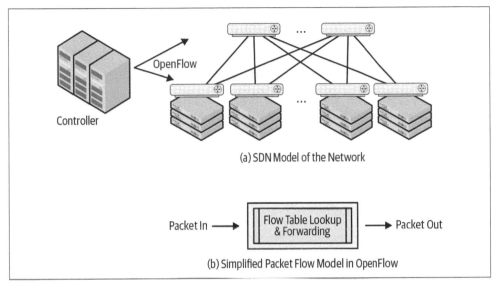

(a) SDN Model of the Network

(b) Simplified Packet Flow Model in OpenFlow

Figure 4-1. OpenFlow and SDN

Figure 4-1(a) shows that configuration and monitoring can be done at a central place. The network operator has a god's view of the entire network. The hope was that this model would also relieve network operators of trying to translate their network-wide desired behavior into individual box-specific configuration.

Figure 4-1(b) shows that the switching silicon can be quite simple with OpenFlow. The original flow tables consisted of only a handful of fields. To allow for interesting ideas, OpenFlow advocates wanted to make the flow table lookup key very generic: just include all of the fields of the packet header up to a specific size—say the first 40 or 80 bytes. An example of this approach that was often cited was the automatic support for new packet headers, like new tunnel headers. We discuss tunnels in more detail in Chapter 6, but for the purpose of this discussion, assume that the tunnel header is a new packet header inserted before an existing packet header such as the IP header. Because the lookup involved all of the bytes in the packet up to a certain length, the table lookup could obviously handle the presence of these tunnel headers, or other new packet headers, if programmed to recognize them.

The flow tables on traditional switching silicon were quite small compared to the routing or bridging tables. It was quite expensive to build silicon with very large flow tables. So the OpenFlow paper also suggested to not prepopulate the flow tables, but to use them like a cache. If there was no match for a packet in the flow table, send the packet to the controller. The central controller would consult its software tables to determine the appropriate behavior for the packet and also program the flow table so that subsequent packets for this flow would not be sent to the central controller.

FoRCES

What few people know about SDN is that the separation of the control and data planes was an idea pursued in the very body that standardizes distributed routing protocols, the IETF. There was a working group within the IETF called Forwarding and Control Element Separation (FoRCES). A key component of the Linux networking stack, the Netlink API (*https://oreil.ly/nLe5-*), is one of the outputs of the FoRCES working group. I remember some initial chatter around FoRCES. A former colleague of mine was even working on this at Intel. But the idea never got any traction, either with vendors or the operators.

The Trouble with OpenFlow

OpenFlow ran into trouble almost immediately out of the gate. The simple flow table lookup model didn't really work even with simple routing because it didn't handle ECMP (introduced in "Routing as the Fundamental Interconnect Model" on page 22). On the control-plane side, sending the first packet of every new flow to a central control plane didn't scale. These were both fundamental problems. In the networking world, the idea of sending the first packet of a flow to the control plane had already been explored in several commercial products and deemed a failure. This was because they didn't scale, and the caches thrashed far more frequently than the developers originally anticipated.

The problems didn't end there. Packet switching involves a lot more complexity than a simple flow table lookup. Multiple tables are looked up, and sometimes the same table looked up multiple times to determine packet-switching behavior. How would you control the ability to decrement a TTL, or not, to perform checksums on the IP header, handle network virtualization, and so on? Flow table invalidation was another problem. When should the controller decide to remove a flow? The answer was not always straightforward.

To handle all of this and the fact that a simple flow table isn't sufficient, OpenFlow 1.0 was updated to version 1.1, which was so complex that no packet-switching silicon vendor knew how to support it. From that arose version 1.2, which was a little more pragmatic. The designers also revised the control plane to prepopulate the lookup tables and didn't require sending the first packet to a controller. But most network operators had begun to lose interest at this point. As a data point, around 2013, when I started talking to customers as an employee of Cumulus Networks, OpenFlow and SDN were all I was asked about. A year and a half or two years later, it rarely came up. I also didn't see it come up with operators I spoke to who were not Cumulus customers. It is rarely deployed to program data center routers, except for one very large operator: Google.

OpenFlow didn't succeed as much as its hype had indicated for at least the following reasons:

- OpenFlow conflated multiple problems into one. The programmability that users desired was for constructs such as configuration and statistics. OpenFlow presented an entirely different abstraction and required reinventing too much to solve this problem.

- The silicon implementation of flow tables couldn't scale inexpensively compared to routing and bridging tables.

- Data center operators didn't care about research questions such as whether to forward all packets with a TTL of 62 or 12 differently from other packets, or how to perform a lookup based on 32 bits of an IPv4 address combined with the lower 12 bits of a MAC address.

- OpenFlow's abstraction models were either too limiting or too loose. And like other attempts to model behavior, such as Simple Network Management Protocol (SNMP), these attempts ended up with more vendor lock-in instead of less. Two different SDN controllers would program the OpenFlow tables very differently. Consequently, after you chose a vendor for one controller, you really couldn't easily switch vendors.

- Finally, people realized that OpenFlow presented a very different mindset from the classic networking model of routing and bridging, and therefore a lower maturity level. The internet, the largest network in the world, already ran fairly well (though not without its share of problems). People did not see the benefit of throwing out what worked well (distributed routing protocols) along with the thing that did not (the inability to programmatically access the switch).

My Insight into OpenFlow's Limitations

Openflow had just come out and was garnering a lot of attention. I along with some others was invited to visit a large network operator to explain our position on Openflow, because this customer was very interested in OpenFlow's potential. These were still OpenFlow 1.0 days. So it was easy to beat down OpenFlow. We told the senior executives and engineers at this meeting that we would address their concerns with a better OpenFlow than OpenFlow. Everybody was very happy, talks of trials happened, problem solved. At that point, I posed a question, "Imagine you have what we're promising you in your labs today. How would you use it? What would be your first goal in testing it?" One of the senior people in the meeting said, "Oh Dinesh, it's quite simple. I'll use it to configure VLANs and retrieve statistics from the interfaces." I recall a distinct feeling of falling off my chair. I asked him to explain a little more because I felt clearly mistaken about what he was saying. It was at that meeting I realized the pain of the network operators due to the lack of programmability and the paucity of SNMP. Metaphorically, the customer lacked a can opener but was asking for a jackhammer.

When I began to hear similar echoes from other customers and operators, my feeling that OpenFlow was the wrong tool became firmer.

OVS

Open Virtual Switch (OVS) (*http://www.openvswitch.org*) is a well-regarded open source implementation of the OpenFlow switch on Linux. *ovs-vswitchd* is the user space application that implements the OpenFlow switch, which includes the Open-Flow flow tables and actions. It does not use the lookup tables or packet forwarding logic of the Linux kernel. So *ovs-vswitchd* reimplements a lot of standard code such as Address Resolution Protocol (ARP), IP, and Multiprotocol Label Switching (MPLS). The flow tables in *ovs-vswitchd* are typically programmed by an OpenFlow controller. As of this writing, OVS was at version 2.11.90 and supports OpenFlow protocol version 1.5. The website provides more details on all this. Use of OVS is the most widespread use of OpenFlow I've encountered.

OVS comes with a component called OVSDB server or just OVSDB, which is used to configure and query OVS itself. The OpenFlow controller can query the OVS state via OVSDB using the schema exported by OVSDB server for such queries. The OVSDB specification has been published as RFC 7047 (*https://oreil.ly/BNuoF*) by the IETF. Figure 4-2 shows the relation between the OpenFlow controller, OVSDB, and OVS.

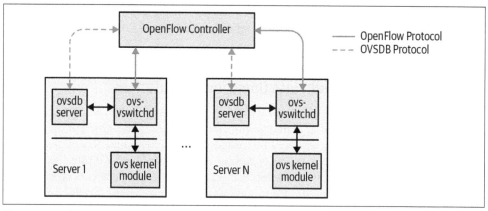

Figure 4-2. OVS components and OpenFlow controller

OVSDB is also used by hypervisor and OpenStack vendors to configure OVS with information about the VMs or endpoints they control on hardware switches. For example, this latter approach is used to integrate SDN-like solutions that configure OVS on hypervisors with bare-metal servers that communicate with the VMs hosted by the hypervisors. In such a model, the switch NOS vendor supplies an OVSDB implementation that translates the configuration specified by OVSDB into its NOS equivalent and into the switching silicon state. VMware's NSX is a prominent user of OVSDB. Switches from various prominent vendors, old and new, support such a version of OVSDB to get their switch certified for use with NSX.

You can configure OVS to use Intel's Data Path Development Kit (DPDK) to perform high-speed packet processing in user space.

The Effect of SDN and OpenFlow on Network Disaggregation

OpenFlow and the drums of SDN continue to beat. They are by no means moribund. In some domains such as wide area networks (WANs), the introduction of software-defined WAN (SD-WAN) has been quite successful because it did present a model that was simpler than the ones it replaced. Also, as a global traffic optimization model on the WAN, it was simpler and easier to use and deploy than the complicated RSVP-TE model. Others have come up with a BGP-based SDN. Here, BGP is used instead of OpenFlow as the mechanism to communicate path information for changing the path of certain flows, not every flow. Another use case is as the network virtualization overlay controller such as VMware's NSX product.

But within the data center, as a method to replace distributed routing protocols with a centralized control plane and a switch with OpenFlow-defined lookup tables, my observations indicate that it has not been successful. Outside of a handful of operators, I have rarely encountered this model for building data center network infrastructure.

The authors of OpenFlow weren't trying to solve the problems of the cloud native data center or of disaggregated networking. Their promise to provide something like a programmable network device intrigued many people and drew them down the path of OpenFlow.

But SDN muddied the waters of network disaggregation quite a bit. First, it made a lot of network operators think that all their skills acquired over many years via certifications and practice—skills in distributed routing protocols and bridging—were going to be obsolete. Next, traditional switch vendors used this idea of programming to say that network operators had to learn coding and become developers to operate SDN-based networks. This made many of them averse to even considering network disaggregation. And I know of other operators who spent a lot of time trying to run proof-of-concept (PoC) experiments to verify the viability of OpenFlow and SDN in building a data center network, before giving up and running back into the warm embrace of traditional network vendors. Furthermore, many of the vendors who sprang up around the use of SDN to control data center network infrastructure supported only bridging, which, as we discussed, doesn't scale.

NOS Design Models

If OpenFlow and SDN didn't really take off as predicted, what is the answer to the NOS in a disaggregated world? Strangely, the OpenFlow paper alluded to a different approach, but rejected it as impractical. From the paper:

> One approach—that we do not take—is to persuade commercial "name-brand" equipment vendors to provide an open, programmable, virtualized platform on their switches and routers so that researchers can deploy new protocols.

Alas, the cliché of the road not taken—again. Let us examine the various NOS models in vogue. We begin by looking at the parts that are common before examining the parts that are different.

Here are the two common elements in all modern network operating systems:

Linux
> This is the base OS for just about every NOS. By base OS, I mean the part that does process and memory management and nonnetworking device I/O, primarily storage.

Intel x86/ARM processors
> A NOS needs a CPU to run on. Intel and ARM are the most common CPU architecture for switches. ARM is the most common processor family used on lower-end switches: those that have 1GbE Ethernet ports or lower. The 10GbE and higher speed switches using Intel are typically dual-core processors with two to eight gigabytes of memory.

These two elements can be found in both the new disaggregated network operating systems and the traditional data center switch vendors. The most well-known holdout from this combination is Juniper, whose Junos OS uses FreeBSD rather than Linux as its base OS. However, the next generation of Junos, called Junos OS Evolved (*https://oreil.ly/_Sy_W*), runs on Linux instead of FreeBSD.

An OS acts as the moderator between resources and the applications that want to use those resources. For example, CPU is a resource, and access to it by different applications is controlled by process scheduling within the OS.

Every OS has a user space and a kernel space, distinguished primarily by protected memory access. Software in kernel space, except for device drivers, has complete access to all hardware and software resources. In the user space, each process has access only to its own private memory space; anything else requires a request to the kernel. This separation is enforced by the CPU itself via protection rings (*https://oreil.ly/MujUb*) or domains provided by the CPU. An OS also provides a standard

Application Programming Interface (API) to allow applications to request, use, and release resources.

In any switch, disaggregated or otherwise, the CPU complex is connected to the packet-switching silicon, the management Ethernet port, storage, and so on, as shown in Figure 4-3.

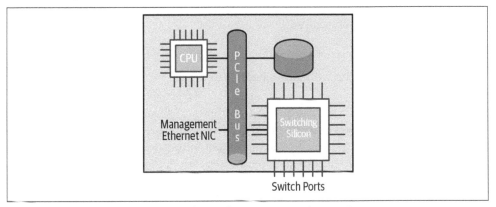

Figure 4-3. CPU and packet-switching silicon in a switch complex

The packet-switching silicon is connected to the CPU via a peripheral input/output bus, usually Peripheral Component Interconnect express (PCI). The interconnect bandwidth between the packet-switching silicon and the CPU complex is only a fraction of the switching silicon capacity. For example, a common switching silicon available circa 2018 has 32 ports of 100GbE, which adds up to 3.2 Terabits per second. However, the interconnect bandwidth varies between 400 Mbps and at most 100 Gbps, though it rarely reaches the upper bound.

The main tasks of a NOS are to run control and management protocols, maintain additional state such as counters, and set up the packet-switching silicon to forward packets. Except when OpenFlow is used, the NOS on a switch is not in the packet-forwarding path. A small amount of traffic is destined to the switch itself, and those are handled by the NOS. Packets destined to the switch are usually control-plane packets, such as those sent by a routing protocol or bridging protocol. The other kind of packet that the NOS sees consists of erroneous packets, for which it must generate error message packets.

Thus, the NOS on the switch sees a minuscule percentage of the total bandwidth supported by the packet-switching silicon. For example, the NOS might process at most 150,000 packets per second, whereas the switching silicon will be processing more than 5 billion packets per second. The NOS uses policers to rate-limit traffic hitting it and prioritizes control protocol traffic over the others. This ensures that the NOS is never overwhelmed by packets sent to it.

All of the parts discussed so far are the same across all the network operating systems designed from the turn of the century. The reliance on embedded or real-time operating systems such as QNX and VxWorks is so past century, though a couple of vendors (see this NOS list (*https://oreil.ly/aOKJA*) maintained by the Open Compute Project [OCP]) still seem to rely on them.

Modern network operating systems however, differ in the following areas, each of which is examined in upcoming sections:

- Location of the switch network state
- Implementation of the switching silicon driver
- Programming model

Each of these pieces affects the extent of control a network engineer or architect is able to exercise. The first two considerations are interconnected, but I have broken them up to highlight the effect of each on the network operator. Furthermore, a solution chosen for one of these considerations doesn't necessarily dictate the answer to the others. We'll conclude the comparison by seeing how each of the choices address the requirements presented in "Requirements of a Network Device" on page 54.

Location of Switch Network State

Switch network state represents everything associated with packet forwarding on the switch, from the lookup tables to Access Control Lists (ACLs) to counters. This piece is important to understand because it defines to a large extent how third-party applications function in the NOS.

There are three primary models for this.

Vendor-specific user space model

The most common model at the time of this writing stores the network state only in NOS-vendor specific software in the user space. In other words, the ultimate source of truth in the NOS in such a model is the vendor-specific software. In this model, the vendor-supplied control protocol stack writes directly to this vendor-specific data store. Cisco's NX-OS and DPDK-based network operating systems implement this model.

Hybrid model

The second model, which is the hybrid model, is a variation of the first model. The ultimate source of truth in these cases is the same as the first model, the vendor-specific user-space vendor stack. However, the NOS also synchronizes parts of this state with the equivalent parts in the kernel. For example, in this model, the NOS synchronizes the routing table with the kernel routing table. Only a subset of the total state is synchronized. For example, I know of a NOS that synchronizes everything except bridging state. Another NOS synchronizes only the interfaces and the IP routing state, including the ARP/ND state. The rest are not synchronized in the kernel. In most cases, vendors also synchronize changes in the other direction: any changes made to the kernel in those structures are also reflected in the vendor's proprietary stack.

So is there a rationale behind which states are synchronized, why those and not the others? I have heard different reasons from different NOS vendors. Some NOS vendors treat the switching silicon as the only packet forwarder in the system. When the CPU sends a packet to the switching silicon, it expects that chip to behave very much as if the packet came in on a switching silicon port, and to forward the packet in hardware; the same is assumed in the reverse direction. So the only state that is synchronized is whatever is necessary to preserve this illusion. In this way, the only packet-forwarding model used is the switching silicon's model. In other cases, the vendor's user-space blob is synchronized with the kernel state only to the extent that it allows certain large network operators that use only routing functions to write their own applications on top of such a NOS. This is done primarily to retain (or acquire) the business of such large-scale network operators.

In either case, the vendor-provided applications, such as control protocol suites, update state directly in the vendor-specific user space part rather than in the kernel.

Arista's Extensible Operating System (EOS), Microsoft's SONiC, IP Infusion's OcNOS, Dell's OpenSwitch, and many others follow this hybrid model, albeit with each differing in what parts are synchronized with the kernel.

Complete kernel model

The third model, one that is relatively new, is to use the Linux kernel's data structures as the network state's ultimate source of truth. The kernel today supports just about every critical construct relevant to the data center network infrastructure, such as IPv4, IPv6, network virtualization, and logical switches. Because packet forwarding is happening in the switching silicon, this model requires synchronizing counters and other state from the silicon with the equivalent state in the kernel. I'm assuming that in this model, the NOS vendor does not use any nonstandard Linux API calls to perform any of the required functions. Cumulus Linux is the primary NOS vendor behind this model.

At some level, you can argue that most vendors follow the hybrid model, even one like Cumulus, because not everything from the switching silicon is always available in the Linux kernel. However, the discussion here is about the general philosophy of the model rather than the state of an implementation at a particular point of time. The Linux kernel is sophisticated, mature, and evolving continuously through the work of a vibrant community.

Let's now consider what models permit when you want to run a third-party application on the switch itself. The vendor-specific user space-only model requires modifications to the application to use the NOS vendor's API. Even simple, everyday applications such as *ping* and Secure Shell (SSH) need to be modified to work on such a NOS. The kernel model will work with any application written to work with the standard Linux API. For example, researchers wanting to test out a new routing protocol can exploit this model. Furthermore, because the Linux API almost guarantees that changes will not break existing user-space applications (though they might need to be recompiled), the code will be practically guaranteed to work on future versions of the kernel, too. In the hybrid model, if the third-party application relies only on whatever is synchronized with the kernel (such as IP routing), it can use the standard Linux API. Otherwise, it must use the vendor-specific API.

Programming the Switching Silicon

After the local network state is in the NOS, how is this state pushed into the switching silicon? Because the switching silicon is a device like an Ethernet NIC or disk, a device driver is obviously involved. The driver can be implemented as a traditional device driver—that is, in the Linux kernel—or it can be implemented in user space.

As of this writing, the most common model puts the driver in user space. One of the primary reasons for this is that most switching silicon vendors provide the driver in user space only. The other reason is that until recently, the Linux kernel did not have an abstraction or model for packet-switching silicon. The kernel provides many device abstractions such as block device, character device, net device, and so on. There was no such equivalent for packet-switching silicon. Another reason for the prevalence of the user-space model is that many consider it simpler to write a driver in user space than in the kernel.

How does the user-space driver get the information to program the switching silicon? When the network state is in the user space, the user-space blob communicates with the driver to program the relevant information into the silicon. When the ultimate source of truth is in the kernel, the user-space driver opens a Netlink socket and gets notifications about successful changes made to the networking state in the kernel. It then uses this information to program the switching silicon. Figure 4-4 shows these two models.

The small, light block just above the silicon switch represents a very low-level driver that's responsible for interrupt management of the switching silicon, setting up DMA, and so on.

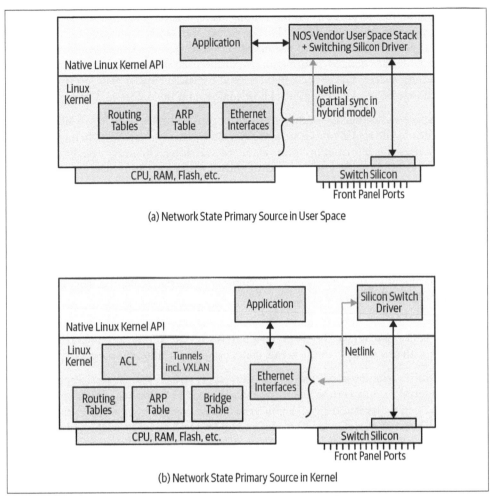

Figure 4-4. *How a user-space switching-silicon driver gets information*

Netlink

The magic of synchronizing the network state in the kernel with the user space or using the information to program the switching silicon is possible because of a feature in the Linux kernel called *Netlink*. Netlink is both an API to program the state of various networking structures in the kernel and a publish–subscribe bus. Netlink is provided as a socket family in the Linux kernel, AF_NETLINK. A user-space process can create an AF_NETLINK socket and use the socket methods of send and recv to program the networking structures in the kernel. More than one process can open an AF_NETLINK socket and program the kernel.

For example, to add an entry to the routing table, a user-space process such as the routing protocol opens an AF_NETLINK socket and sends a message formatted as per the rt_netlink kernel API. If the update is successful, the kernel sends a Netlink message with the changed information to all the user-space processes that have an open Netlink socket. The process that issued the change request also receives a copy of this change besides receiving an acknowledgment on the successful change.

A user-space switching silicon driver can also open Netlink socket. Thus, all successful updates to the routing table are also received by this user-space switching-silicon driver. It uses this information to program the switching silicon to reflect the kernel state. For example, a user who wants to shut down a switching-port interface can issue the Linux command `ip link set down swp1`. The program "ip"—which belongs to the iproute2 family of commands—opens a Netlink socket and sends an appropriately formatted message to shut down the interface. The kernel then shuts down the reflected interface in the Linux kernel. The kernel also sends a notification of this link shutdown to all user-space processes that have an open Netlink socket. Thus, the user-space silicon-switching driver receives notification of the link down. It can consequently send the appropriate commands to the switching silicon to shut down the actual port on the chip.

Similarly, in the hybrid NOS model, the vendor stack can also synchronize its internal routing tables (and any other tables it supports) with the kernel, and update its internal state with any changes in the kernel tables caused by a different process.

The Netlink socket provides various message types to allow a user-space process to signal interest in only certain events from the kernel. For example, a user-space process can open a socket and signal an interest only in changes to interface state. In such a case, the kernel does not send successful changes of other types, such as in the routing table, to this socket. *ifplugd*, a popular user-space Linux tool that monitors interface state, works in this fashion.

Just about every facet of the network state in the Linux kernel is programmable and notifiable via Netlink. Netlink is also extensible. It supports user-definable message types for use, say, between a user-space component and a brand new kernel component. Whenever a user-space process doesn't drain the notification packets from the Netlink socket fast enough, causing packets to be dropped in the kernel, the process gets an error message on the next I/O operation. The process must then reopen the socket and resynchronize the state with the kernel. To avoid such scenarios, it is recommended that the buffer size for Netlink sockets be set to a large size.

You cannot open a Netlink socket on a remote host. However, nothing prevents a user from writing a simple application that acts as a proxy between remote clients and a local Netlink socket. For example, one can imagine a central controller programming individual devices using Netlink, much like OpenFlow. As mentioned earlier ("FoRCES" on page 58), Netlink arose from the work in FoRCES around separating control and data planes.

Switch Abstraction Interface

Because the silicon switch driver is in the user space, most NOS vendors have defined their own Hardware Abstraction Layer (HAL) and a silicon-specific part that uses the silicon vendor's driver. This has enabled them to support multiple types of switching silicon by mapping logical operations into silicon-specific code. The HAL definition is specific to each NOS vendor.

Microsoft and Dell defined a generic, NOS-agnostic HAL for packet-switching silicon and called it Switch Abstraction Interface (SAI). They defined as much as they needed from a switching silicon to power Microsoft's Azure data centers and donated the work to the OCP. OCP adopted this as a subproject under the networking umbrella. Microsoft requires that any switching silicon support SAI for it to be considered in Microsoft Azure. Therefore, many merchant silicon vendors announced support for SAI; that is, they provided a mapping specific to their switching silicon for the abstractions supported by SAI. As originally defined, SAI supported basic routing and bridging and little else. Development of SAI has continued since then and is an open source project available on GitHub (*https://oreil.ly/WmmhP*).

SAI makes no assumptions about the rest of the issues we defined at the beginning of this section. In other words, SAI does not address the issues associated with supporting third-party applications on a NOS. SAI neither assumes that the packet forwarding behavior is the switching silicon's nor does it assume that the Linux kernel is the ultimate source of truth.

Switchdev

To counter the lack of a kernel abstraction for packet-switching silicon, Cumulus Networks and Mellanox, along with some other kernel developers, started a new device abstraction model in the Linux kernel. This is called *switchdev*.

Switchdev works as follows:

- The switchdev driver for a switching silicon communicates with the switching silicon and determines the number of switching ports for which the silicon is configured. The switchdev driver then instantiates as many Netdev devices as there are configured silicon ports. These netdev devices then take care of offloading the actual packet I/O to the switching silicon. netdev is the Linux model for Ethernet interfaces and is used by NICs today. By using the same kernel abstraction, and adding hooks to allow offloading of forwarding table state, ACL state, interface state, and so on, all the existing Linux network commands such as ethtool, iproute2 commands, and others automatically work with ports from packet-switching silicon.

- Every packet forwarding data structure in the kernel provides well-defined back-end hooks that are used to invoke the switching silicon driver to offload the state from the kernel to the switching silicon. Switching silicon drivers can register functions to be called via these hooks. For example, when a route is added, this hook function calls a Mellanox switchdev driver which then determines whether this route needs to be offloaded to the switching silicon. Routes that do not involve the switching silicon are typically not offloaded.

So when the kernel stores all the local network state, programming the switching silicon is more efficient using switchdev.

Switchdev first made an appearance in kernel release 3.19. Mellanox has provided full Switchdev support for Mellanox's Spectrum chipset.

API

When the kernel holds the local network state in standard structures, the standard Linux kernel API is the programming API. It is not vendor specific and is governed by the Linux kernel community. When the user space holds the local network state, the NOS vendor's API is the only way to reliably access all network state. This is why operators demand vendor-agnostic APIs. Despite the Linux kernel API already being vendor agnostic, the kernel model is considered as just another vendor model by operators. Thus, some operators demand that the vendor-agnostic API be provided even on native Linux.

These so-called vendor-agnostic APIs are a continued throwback to the position of network devices largely as appliances rather than platforms. So the operators continue the pursuit of a uniform data model for the network devices via the vendor-agnostic APIs. No sooner have the operators defined an API, a new feature added by the vendor causes a vendor-specific extension to the API. This happened a lot; for example, with the Management Information Base (MIB) data structures consulted by SNMP. It happened with OpenFlow. It's happening with NETCONF. I am reminded of the Peanuts cartoon's football gag (*https://oreil.ly/0tkqW*) in which Lucy keeps egging Charlie Brown to kick the ball, only to pull it out from under him at the last minute. I fear operators are treated similarly when their vendor-agnostic models are promptly polluted by vendor-specific extensions.

The Reasons Behind the Different Answers

The different models of where network state is stored and the differences in switch silicon programming have two primary causes, in my opinion:

- The time period when they were first conceived and developed, and the network features of the Linux kernel during that period
- The business model and its relation to licensing

Timing is relevant because of the evolution of the Linux kernel. As of this writing, Linux kernel version 5.0 has been released. Vendors framed their design on the state of the Linux kernel at the time the vendor decided to adopt the Linux kernel. As such, they miss out as evolving versions of Linux provide more features, better stability, and higher performance. The timing of the model and its relation to the kernel is as follows:

1. The first model was developed around 2005. The Linux kernel version was roughly 2.4.29. Cisco's NX-OS had its roots in the OS that was built for its MDS Fibre Channel Switch family. NX-OS first started using the Linux kernel around 2002, when Linux 2.2 was the most stable version. Furthermore, NX-OS froze its version of the Linux kernel in the 2.6 series because it did not really need much from the kernel.

2. Arista, which was the primary network vendor pushing for the hybrid model, started operations around 2004. Although I do not know the origins of its Linux kernel model, it largely stayed with Linux kernel version 2.6 (Fedora Release 12, from what I gather) for a long time. The latest versions of its OS as of this writing runs Linux kernel version 4.9.

3. Cumulus Networks, which heralded the beginning of the third NOS model, uses the Debian distribution as its base distribution model. This means that whatever kernel version is running in the Debian distribution it picked, is largely the kernel version it has. As of this writing, it is based on version 4.1, with significant backports of the useful features from the newer Linux kernels. In other words, although the kernel version is supposed to be 4.1, it contains fixes and advanced features picked from the newer Linux kernels. By staying with the base 4.1 kernel, software from the base Debian distribution work as is.

Licensing considerations were another critical reason why the different NOS models developed and persisted. The Linux kernel is under the GNU General Public License (GPL) version 2. So if a NOS vendor patches the kernel, such as by improving the kernel's TCP/IP stack, it must release it back to the community if the vendor intends to make a publicly usable version of its kernel. In 2002, when the Linux kernel was still relatively nascent, NOS vendor engineers felt that they did not want to help competitors with the improvements of the kernel networking stack. So they switched to designing and developing a user-space networking stack. Kernel modules can be proprietary blobs, although the Linux community heavily discourages their use. This idea continued with later NOS vendors, which developed new features (consider VRF, VXLAN, and MPLS) in the user space in their own private blob.

Finally, working in an open source community involves a different dynamic from the ones for-profit enterprises are used to. First, finding good, talented, and knowledgeable kernel developers is difficult. Next, unless organizations are sold on the benefits of developing open source software, they are loathe to develop something in the open that they fear potentially enables competitors and reduces their own value proposition. NOS vendors such as Cumulus Networks built their businesses on developing all network-layer features exclusively in the Linux kernel, and so working closely with the kernel community was part of their DNA.

User Interface

Network operators are used to a command line that is specific to a networking device. The command-line interface (CLI) that networking devices provide is not a programmable shell, unlike Linux. It is often a modal CLI—for instance, most commands are valid only within a specific context of the CLI. For example, `neighbor 1.1.1.1 remote-as 65000` is only valid within the context of configuring BGP. You enter this context by typing several prior commands such as "configure" and "router bgp 64001." Linux commands are nonmodal and programmable. They're meant to be scripted. Network operators are used to typing "?" rather than pressing TAB to get the command completions, not typing "--" or "-" to specify options to a command, and so on. What this means is that when dropped into a Bash shell, most network operators are too paralyzed to do anything. They type "?" and nothing happens. They press Tab and most likely nothing happens. A network operator not used to the Bash shell or, more important, used to the traditional network device CLI will be at a loss on how to proceed.

There's a popular saying: "Unix is user-friendly. It just is very selective about who its friends are." Just because the Linux kernel makes for a powerful and sophisticated network OS, doesn't automatically mean that Bash can be the only CLI to interact with networking on a Linux platform. Linux grew up as a host OS and as such does not automatically make things easy from a user interface perspective for those who want to use it as a router or a bridge. Furthermore, each routing suite has its own CLI. FRR, the routing suite we use in this book, follows a CLI model more familiar to Cisco. BIRD, another popular open source routing suite, uses Juniper's Junos OS-like syntax. goBGP uses a CLI more familiar to people used to Linux and other modern Go-based applications.

Therefore, there is no single, unified, and open source way to interface with networking commands under Linux. There are open source packages put out by Cumulus such as *ifupdown2* that work with Debian-based systems such as Ubuntu, but they don't work with Red Hat–based systems. FRR seems like the closest thing to a unified, homogeneous CLI. It has an active, vibrant community, and people are adding new features to it all the time. If you're configuring a pure routing network, FRR can be your single unified networking CLI. If you're doing network virtualization, you have to use native Linux commands or *ifupdown2* to configure VXLAN and bond (portchannel) interfaces, though there are efforts underway to add this support to FRR. Pure bridging support such as MSTP will most likely remain outside the purview of

FRR. The FRR community is also working on a management layer that can support REST API, NETCONF, and so on.

To summarize, using the Linux kernel as the native network OS doesn't mean that Bash shell with the existing command set defined by iproute2 is the only choice. FRR seems the best alternative, though interface configuration is limited to routed interface configuration as of this writing.

Comparing the NOS Models with Cloud Native NOS Requirements

Let's compare the three models of NOS with regard to the requirements posed by the cloud native NOS. Table 4-1 specifies the requirement as it applies to running on the switch itself.

Table 4-1. Comparing the NOS models

Requirement	User-space model	Hybrid model	Kernel model	Kernel model with switchdev
Can be programmable	Proprietary API	Proprietary API	Mostly open source	Open source
Can add new monitoring agent	NOS-supported only	Mostly NOS-supported only	Mostly yes	Mostly yes
Can run off-the-shelf distributed app	NOS-supported only	Mostly NOS-supported only	Yes	Yes
Can replace routing protocol suite	No	No	Yes	Yes
Can patch software by operator	No	No	On open source components	On open source components
Support new switching silicon	NOS vendor support	NOS vendor support	NOS vendor support	Switching silicon support

Illustrating the Models with an Example

Let us dive a bit deeper into exploring how the hybrid and kernel space models work when a third-party application is involved. We can ignore the pure user-space model here, because every networking application must be provided by the vendor and runs in user space without kernel involvement. In the following sections, I describe applications on Arista's EOS, even though EOS is not a disaggregated NOS, though other disaggregated network operating systems behave in a somewhat similar fashion. I use EOS primarily because it is one I'm familiar with, though not as much as I am with Cumulus.

Ping

Let's see what happens when the *ping* application is used to see whether an IP address is reachable. Let's assume that we're trying to *ping* 10.1.1.2, which is reachable via switch port 2. In both models, we assume the kernel's routing table contains this information.

First, in both the kernel and the hybrid models, the switching silicon ports are represented in the Linux kernel as regular Ethernet ports, except they're named differently. Cumulus names these ports swp1, swp2, and so on, whereas Arista names them Ethernet1, Ethernet2, and so on.

In either model, some implementations might choose to implement a proprietary kernel driver that hooks behind the netdevs that represent the switching silicon ports. Other implementations might choose to use the kernel's Tun/Tap driver (described later in "Tun/Tap Devices" on page 77) to boomerang the packets back to the NOS vendor's user-space component, which handles the forwarding. In the case of Cumulus, the proprietary driver is provided by the switching silicon vendor whose silicon is in use on the switch. In the case of Arista, the proprietary driver is provided by Arista itself.

The switching silicon vendor defines an internal packet header for packet communication between the CPU complex and the switching silicon. This internal header specifies such things as which port the packet is received from or needs to be sent out of, any additional packet processing that is required of the switching silicon, and so on. This internal header is used only between the switching silicon and the CPU complex and never makes it out of the switch.

In regard to the kernel driver responsible for sending the packet to the switching silicon, when a *ping* command is issued, the following sequence of actions occurs:

1. The application, *ping*, opens a socket to send a packet to 10.1.1.2. This is just as it would on a server running Linux.

2. The kernel's routing tables point to swp2 as the next hop. The switching silicon's tx/rx driver delivers the packet to the switching silicon, for delivery to the next-hop router.

3. When the *ping* reply arrives, the switching silicon delivers the packet to the kernel. The switching silicon's tx/rx driver receives the packet, and the kernel processes the packet as if it came in on a NIC.

4. The kernel determines the socket to deliver the packet to, and the *ping* application receives it.

Figure 4-5 presents this packet flow. As shown, the user-space switching-silicon driver is not involved in this processing.

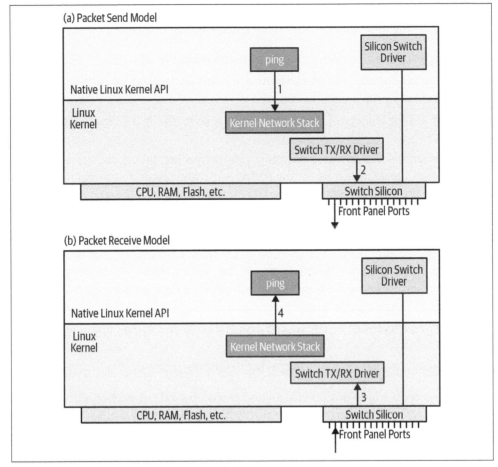

Figure 4-5. *Native kernel packet tx/rx flow*

Even though the same sequence of commands occurs on an Arista switch, too, the Arista switch requests the switching silicon to treat this packet as if it came in on one of its ports and to forward it appropriately. This request is indicated via the internal packet header mentioned earlier. In other words, the switching silicon redoes the packet forwarding behavior even though the kernel had already done the right thing. This allows Arista to claim that all packets, locally originated or otherwise, are forwarded the same way, via the switching silicon. In other words, the packet forwarding behavior is that of the silicon, not the Linux kernel.

There are other commercial network operating systems that use virtual network devices called Tun/Tap to create switch ports inside the kernel that map to the switching silicon ports. The primary behavior of a Tun/Tap device is to boomerang the packet back from the kernel into the user space. In such a case, the NOS vendor implements packet forwarding in its user-space stack when running as a VM. The sequence of steps for the *ping* now works as shown in Figure 4-6:

1. The application *ping* opens a socket to send a packet to 10.1.1.2.

2. The kernel does the packet forwarding for this packet and sends it out port et2, as specified by the kernel routing table.

3. et2 is a Tun/Tap device, so the packet is sent to the NOS vendor's user-space stack.

4. The user-space stack performs any vendor-specific processing necessary and then uses the actual driver for the packet-switching silicon to transmit the packet out the appropriate front-panel port.

5. When the *ping* reply is received, the switching silicon delivers the packet to the user-space stack.

6. After processing the packet, the user-space stack writes the packet to the appropriate Tun/Tap device. For example, if the reply is received via the switching-silicon port 3, the packet is written to et3, the Tun/Tap port corresponding to that port.

7. The kernel receives this packet and processes it as if it came in on a regular network device such as a NIC.

8. Ultimately, the kernel hands the packet to the *ping* process.

This completes the loop of packet send and receive by a third-party application such as *ping*. Some NOS vendors who implement the hybrid model also use the Tun/Tap model when running on a real switch.

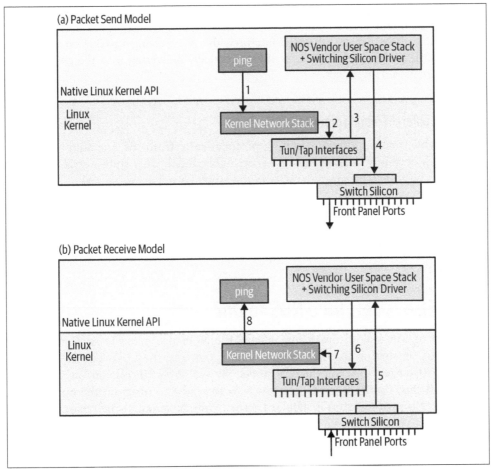

Figure 4-6. Tun/tap packet tx/rx flow

Tun/Tap Devices

The Linux kernel supports two virtual network devices called the Tun driver (for tun-nel) and the Tap driver. The Tun driver supports routing, whereas the Tap driver sup-ports bridging. Together they support user-space network stacks. In the original design, Tun devices were used to implement features such as encryption/decryption software for Virtual Private Network (VPN) use in user space. They were also used to add support for IP tunneling protocols such as Generic Routing Encapsulation (GRE).

Tun/Tap drivers create a network device called /dev/tapN (where N is a number that increases as tap devices are added). The user-space stack binds to this device. If the network lookup tables, such as routing and bridging tables, have entries that point to the Tap device, the kernel forwards the matching packet to this interface, and the packets are then received by the user-space stack. When the user-space stack sends a packet to the Tap device, the kernel interprets this as receiving a packet on a regular network device and processes it as such, eventually delivering it to the application that is the packet's recipient.

Running a different routing protocol

If you want to run a different routing protocol suite from the one supplied by the vendor, it's certainly possible in the kernel-only model. This suite needs to run on Linux and be able to program the state in the Linux kernel using Netlink.

In the hybrid mode, if the routing protocol suite needs to program state that is not synchronized with the kernel, it needs to be modified to use the NOS vendor's API. Even if this third-party routing suite wants to program the kernel, it must adopt the peculiarities of the NOS vendor's implementation of switching silicon interfaces in the kernel.

What Else Is Left for a NOS to Do?

Besides programming the switching silicon, the NOS also needs to read and control the various sensors on the box, such as power, fan, and the LEDs on the interfaces. The NOS also must discover the box model, the switching silicon version, and so on. Besides all this, the NOS needs to know how to read and program the optics of the interfaces. None of this stuff is standard across white boxes and brite boxes. So a NOS vendor must write their own drivers and other patches to handle all of this. The NOS of course has lots of other things to provide such as a user interface, possibly a programmatic API, and so on.

Summary

The primary purpose of this chapter was to educate you on cloud native NOS choices. The reason this education is important is that these choices impose some fundamental consequences on the future of networking and the benefits they yield. The model chosen has effects on what operators can do: what applications they can run on the box, what information they can retrieve, and perhaps what network protocol features are supported.

The philosopher and second president of India, Sarvepalli Radhakrishnan, is quoted to have said, "All men are desirous of peace, but not all men are desirous of the things that lead to peace." In a similar fashion, not every choice leads to the flourishing of a NOS that is true to the cloud native spirit. So being thoughtful about the choices is very important, especially for network designers and architects. Network engineers, too, can cultivate their skillsets for each of the choices. The information in this chapter should help you determine which choices are easy today but possibly gone tomorrow, and which choices truly empower your organization. In the next chapter, we move up the software stack to examine routing protocols and how to select one that's appropriate for your needs.

References

- Hamilton, James. "Datacenter Networks are in my Way" (*https://oreil.ly/D_Zpr*).
- McKeown, Nick, et al. "Linux kernel documentation of switchdev" (*https://oreil.ly/ltVy9*).
- "OpenFlow: Enabling Innovation in Campus Networks" (*https://oreil.ly/nkAvT*).
- NOS list, Open Compute Project (*https://oreil.ly/aOKJA*).

## CHAPTER 5

Routing Protocol Choices

A name indicates what we seek. An address indicates where it is. A route indicates how we get there.
   —John F. Schoch

Unicast routing is a fundamental enabling technology for the cloud native data center. And though unicast routing is as old as the internet, its application in the data center has led to some head scratching. Some of the head scratching led to enhancements and change to routing protocols in adapting them to data centers. But some of the reexaminations of old practices resulted in erroneous pronouncements. These errors are either based on an excessively strict application of theory to the Clos topology (saying, for instance, that link-state protocols are too chatty) or on popular misconceptions (for instance, that BGP is too slow).

Another barrier to proper routing within the data center is that, for many network operators raised on building bridged networks, routing seems an arcane art. So this chapter is an attempt to clear the cobwebs in the path to a better understanding routing and routing protocols, specifically with their application to Clos topology. With the rise of technologies such as Kubernetes, even nonnetwork engineers have to take a look at routing; Kube-router and Calico require an understanding of routing and routing protocols.

This chapter should help you answer questions such as the following:

- How does routing work?
- What are the types of routing protocols?
- What is the fit of routing protocols to Clos topologies?
- What are unnumbered interfaces and why do they matter?

- How can I determine the routing protocol that best fits my needs?

People comfortable about their knowledge of routing and routing tables can skip the following section. In the rest of this chapter, I use "routing" as shorthand for "unicast routing." Multicast routing appears in a separate chapter. This chapter also avoids delving into specifics of BGP or OSPF routing protocols. We have separate chapters to address those specifics.

Routing Overview

In the simplest of terms, *routing* is the process of using a packet's destination IP address to forward the packet from its source to its destination.[1] A device that forwards a packet using routing is called a *router*.

IP routing requires each router to make packet forwarding decisions independently of the other routers. Thus, an IP router is interested only in finding the next hop on the way to a packet's final destination. You can say that IP routing is a little myopic this way. But this myopia is a strength because it allows IP to route easily around failures. A popular quote attributed to John Gilmore, one of the founders of the Electronic Frontier Foundation, is: "The Net interprets censorship as damage and routes around it." When he says "The Net," he's really talking about IP routing. Unless the router is on the same subnet (more on this in a bit) as the destination of a packet, the next hop will be another router, which repeats the routing process, until the destination is reached.

A router finds the next hop for a packet by looking up the packet's destination IP address in a lookup table called the *routing table*. The router then forwards the packet out the network interface returned by this lookup.

To expand this description a little more, routing consists of the following steps:

1. Look up the destination IP address of the packet in the routing table to get a list of next-hop entries.
2. Select one next hop from this list.
3. Determine the MAC address of this next hop.
4. Update the packet and frame headers, a task that includes rewriting the destination MAC address and TTL in the IP header.
5. Forward the packet out the network interface specified by the selected next hop.

---

1 Because IP is the only network layer in practice, we use IP in place of the more generic term "network layer."

IPv6

IPv4 and IPv6 coexist today, with IPv4 remaining more popular. These versions handle routing in similar ways. So we use IPv4 for the examples in this chapter with the understanding that similar issues apply to IPv6.

How Routing Table Lookups Work

Briefly, a routing table contains entries whose key is the IP *address prefix* and whose result is a list of *next hops*.

A routing table does not contain an entry for every possible IP address that is reachable in the network. Instead, addresses are grouped into *subnets*, where a subnet is a group of addresses that share the same number of leftmost bits. The number of shared bits is denoted by a *mask length* (an alternate but older model is to denote the shared bits with a *network mask*). An IP *address prefix* is defined as the start of the shared bits along with the mask length. For example, the address prefix 1.1.1.0/24 (each number before a . is 8 bits, and thus with three numbers we have 24 bits) includes every IP address from 1.1.1.0 to 1.1.1.255 because the upper 24 bits, 1.1.1, are shared across all those addresses.

Figure 5-1 illustrates these concepts. In the figure, each first line expands the address or address prefix on the left into the associated four octets of 8 bits, for a total of 32 bits. The first line expands 1.1.1.0/24, showing that each of the first three octets contains 1 in binary, whereas the last octet is shown full of asterisks (*), meaning that the bit can be either 0 or 1. Thus, the addresses 1.1.1.1 and 1.1.1.16 will be matched by the prefix 1.1.1.0/24. But the address 1.1.2.1 will not be matched by this prefix, because the upper 24 bits of 1.1.2.1 differ from the upper 24 bits of the prefix entry.

Figure 5-1. Illustrating IP address prefix and match

Why is this interesting? An address prefix allows us to aggregate a bunch of addresses into a single entry. Consider a router with two links that can reach a block of about two hundred addresses. It might be able to reach the first set of these addresses, starting from 1.1.1.1, via link 1, whereas it reaches the second set of these addresses, starting from 1.1.1.129, via link 2. The routing table on this router needs only two entries —one for 1.1.1.0/25, and the other for 1.1.1.128/25—instead of two hundred routing table entries.

In a different scenario, let's assume that only two addresses in the address block, say 1.1.1.31 and 1.1.1.67, live on link 1, whereas the rest live on link 2. I now need three routing table entries, one each associating 1.1.1.31/32 and 1.1.1.67/32 with link 1, and one entry for 1.1.1.0/24 that associates the rest of the addresses with link 2. This is still a significant savings over listing every one of the two hundred addresses.

Thus, given a lookup table containing these three address prefixes, a routing table lookup for 1.1.1.31 needs to return link 1, and a routing table lookup for 1.1.1.2 needs to return link 2. This is done by selecting an entry with the longest prefix length from a given set of matching prefixes. For 1.1.1.31, the entry with the longest matching prefix is 1.1.1.31/32, whereas for the address 1.1.1.2, the entry with the longest matching prefix is 1.1.1.0/24. Therefore, this match algorithm is called the *longest prefix match* (LPM).

This ability to represent multiple IP addresses with a single entry in the routing table enables IP networks to scale. Because an IPv4 address is 32 bits, there can be almost four billion IPv4 addresses. Building a routing table that big would be impossibly expensive and inefficient. An IPv6 address is 128 bits, which represents a mind-boggling total address space of 340,282,366,920,938,463,463,374,607,431,768,211,456.

A routing table entry has a list of one or more next hops. Each next hop in the list contains the outgoing interface, and optionally the next-hop router's IP address. When the next hop is another router, the next-hop entry contains the IP address of the next-hop router. When a packet reaches a router that has an interface with either the destination address itself or with an IP address in the same subnet as the destination address, routing is successfully terminated. In this case, the router looks up the IP neighbor table (also called the ARP/ND table), using the destination address and the outgoing interface to determine the MAC address of the destination node. Finally, it forwards the packet to that node. This last step of delivering the packet to a node with a given destination MAC address can involve traversing a bridged network.

If there is no entry in the ARP/ND table, the network stack uses the Address Resolution Protocol (ARP) for IPv4 addresses, or the Neighbor Discovery Protocol (NDP) for IPv6 addresses, to determine the MAC address associated with the IP address.

Besides a successful termination, routing also terminates in case of the following two failures:

- There is no available route to pursue.
- The packet cannot be forwarded due to an error.

In such cases, the packet is dropped and an error message is often returned to the source of the packet. These error messages are what is called the *Internet Control Message Protocol* (ICMP).

How Routes Are Chosen

Consider the simple network shown in Figure 5-2.

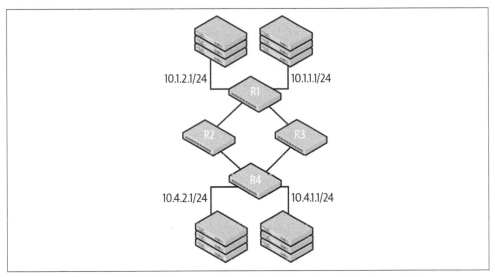

Figure 5-2. A sample network

In the figure, the routers are shown with a single link to the rack of servers. In reality, there are separate physical links from R1 and R4 to each server in a rack. The single link is a logical link that represents the subnet that all the servers are a part of. R1 has an address of 10.1.1.1/24 on the 10.1.1.0/24 subnet, an address of 10.1.2.1/24 on the 10.1.2.0/24 subnet, and so on.

We say that the networks 10.1.1.0/24 and 10.1.2.0/24 are attached to router R1, and the networks 10.4.1.0/24 and 10.4.2.0/24 are attached to router R4. Individual servers on the 1.1.1.0/24 network get addresses such as 10.1.1.2/24, 10.1.1.3/24, and so on. The same applies to the servers connected to the 10.4.2.0/24 network, where the servers get the addresses 10.4.2.2/24, 10.4.2.3/24, and so on. So, when server 10.1.1.2 sends a packet to 10.4.2.20, the routing path is from R1 to R4.

If a prefix has multiple next hops, the routing lookup selects one. Typically, the router selects the same next hop for all packets belonging to a flow, to avoid reordering packets within a flow. As defined in "Flows and Congestion" on page 23, a flow is a set of packets sharing the same five traits: source IP address, destination IP address, Layer 4 (L4) protocol, source port, and destination port.

Every routing table entry can also have additional attributes. The attributes associated with each entry include information such as which entity created this entry.

Types of Routing Table Entries

A routing table contains three kinds of entries:

Connected routes

These are routes associated with the addresses associated with a device's interfaces. The network stack (the Linux kernel or the vendor stack) adds these entries automatically when the address assignment occurs. For example, when you add an IP address 10.1.1.1/24 to an interface in the Linux kernel, the kernel adds the route to 10.1.1.0/24 (the subnet) to the routing table automatically. Thus, when a packet is addressed to the peer on the other side of the link, the kernel knows how to forward the packet correctly. Connected routes enable communicating with directly connected peers without requiring a routing protocol.

Static routes

Static routes are routes added manually, by an administrator. For example, in very small networks, the network administrator might configure the default route pointing out the interface connected to the service provider's network because there is no routing protocol configured between the service provider and the enterprise. Static routes are always obeyed and take precedence over routes that are populated via a routing protocol. A static route is marked as unusable when it has no operational next-hop interface (i.e., the link is down).

Dynamic routes

These are routes that are populated by a routing protocol after it computes the shortest path to various destinations that it learns by communicating with its peers. These typically form the bulk of the entries in a routing table. On servers, the Dynamic Host Configuration Protocol (DHCP) automatically adds a default route pointing to the gateway that it learns via communication with a DHCP server. This is an example of a dynamic routing entry being added by something other than a routing protocol.

The discussion in this chapter is all about routes populated via a routing protocol. But before we get there, let's consider how a routing stack resolves conflicts between these three kinds of entries.

RIB and FIB

Can a router run multiple protocols? What happens if a router receives information from a remote router about a prefix that is also a connected route? Or if a network operator accidentally adds a static route that overrides a connected route?

These questions are some of the many conflicts that arise because multiple entities (routing protocols, the network stack, the operator) provide the same or conflicting information. To resolve such questions, routing implementations split the routing table into two parts. The first is associated with the control-plane software and is called the Routing Information Base (RIB). The other is used in the data path during packet forwarding and is called the Forwarding Information Base (FIB). In this book, when we say "routing table," we mean the FIB.

The RIB contains all the different pieces of information learned via all the different ways (connected, static, and routing protocols). A software component called the *RIB manager* selects the prefixes to be sent to the FIB from all these different methods. Every routing protocol is assigned a unique number called the *distance*.[2] In case multiple protocols provide the same prefix, the RIB manager picks the prefix from the protocol with the lowest distance. Connected routes have the lowest distance. Static routes have a lower distance than that of routes obtained via a routing protocol. The RIB manager then pushes the winning entry into the FIB used during packet forwarding. The difference between RIB and FIB is illustrated in Figure 5-3.

---

2 To the purists, yes, BGP uses two distances, a detail we won't bother with until we get to it in Chapter 15.

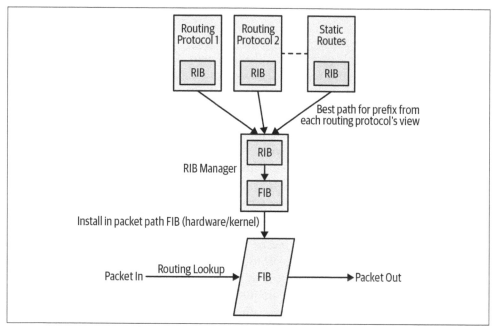

Figure 5-3. RIB versus FIB

Linux Routing Table Display

If you're coming from an environment that uses a traditional vendor stack, you're used to the display of the routing table that looks like this (taken from an Arista box):

```
eos#show ip ro

VRF: default
Codes: C - connected, S - static, K - kernel,
       O - OSPF, IA - OSPF inter area, E1 - OSPF external type 1,
       E2 - OSPF external type 2, N1 - OSPF NSSA external type 1,
       N2 - OSPF NSSA external type2, B I - iBGP, B E - eBGP,
       R - RIP, I L1 - IS-IS level 1, I L2 - IS-IS level 2,
       O3 - OSPFv3, A B - BGP Aggregate, A O - OSPF Summary,
       NG - Nexthop Group Static Route, V - VXLAN Control Service,
       DH - Dhcp client installed default route

Gateway of last resort:
 S       0.0.0.0/0 [1/0] via 192.168.121.1, Management1

 C       10.10.0.0/24 is directly connected, Vlan10
 O       10.20.0.0/24 [110/20] via 10.127.0.0, Ethernet1
                                via 10.127.0.2, Ethernet2
 C       10.127.0.0/31 is directly connected, Ethernet1
 C       10.127.0.2/31 is directly connected, Ethernet2
 C       10.254.0.1/32 is directly connected, Loopback0
```

```
O        10.254.0.2/32 [110/10] via 10.127.0.0, Ethernet1
                               via 10.127.0.2, Ethernet2
C        192.168.121.0/24 is directly connected, Management1

eos#
```

The output of the Linux kernel on the peer router to this router (taken from a router running Cumulus) looks like this:

```
vagrant@vx:~$ ip route show
default via 192.168.121.1 dev eth0
10.10.0.0/24  proto ospf  metric 20
        nexthop via 10.127.0.1  dev swp1 weight 1
        nexthop via 10.127.0.3  dev swp2 weight 1
10.20.0.0/24 dev vlan20  proto kernel  scope link  src 10.20.0.1
10.127.0.0/31 dev swp1  proto kernel  scope link  src 10.127.0.0
10.127.0.2/31 dev swp2  proto kernel  scope link  src 10.127.0.2
10.254.0.1  proto ospf  metric 20
        nexthop via 10.127.0.1  dev swp1 weight 1
        nexthop via 10.127.0.3  dev swp2 weight 1
192.168.121.0/24 dev eth0  proto kernel  scope link  src 192.168.121.44
vagrant@vx:~$
```

The output of `ip route show` in Linux is the output of the kernel FIB, not the RIB. As a consequence, information maintained by the RIB, such as distance, is not shown in the output. A couple of unfamiliar terms, which denote Linux implementation-specific controls, are worth describing:

metric
:   A number used internally by the Linux kernel when there are multiple routes with the same distance. The kernel always chooses entries with the lower metric. This can be used, for example, to implement something advanced like ip fast reroute, where the backup routes are prepopulated with a higher metric, and so is used only when the main route entry becomes invalid.

weight
:   Used when there are multiple next hops, to identify the proportion of traffic distribution across the next hops. For example, consider a route with two next hops, one with a weight of 2 and the other with a weight of 1. The kernel sends two-thirds of the packet flows over the next hop with a weight of 2 and one-third of them over the next hop with a weight of 1. Typically, all next hops have the same weight, and flows are equally distributed across all the next hops.

To see the distance in the RIB, operators have to examine the routing table from the perspective of a routing protocol stack, such as Free Range Routing (FRR). The display in that case looks more like a traditional vendor stack's display:

```
vx# show ip route
Codes: K - kernel route, C - connected, S - static, R - RIP,
       O - OSPF, I - IS-IS, B - BGP, E - EIGRP, N - NHRP,
       T - Table, v - VNC, V - VNC-Direct, A - Babel, D - SHARP,
```

```
            F - PBR,
            > - selected route, * - FIB route

  K>* 0.0.0.0/0 [0/0] via 192.168.121.1, eth0, 00:37:56
  O>* 10.10.0.0/24 [110/110] via 10.127.0.1, swp1, 00:36:20
    *                          via 10.127.0.3, swp2, 00:36:20
  O   10.20.0.0/24 [110/10] is directly connected, vlan20, 00:36:38
  C>* 10.20.0.0/24 is directly connected, vlan20, 00:36:38
  O   10.127.0.0/31 [110/100] is directly connected, swp1, 00:37:55
  C>* 10.127.0.0/31 is directly connected, swp1, 00:37:56
  O   10.127.0.2/31 [110/100] is directly connected, swp2, 00:37:54
  C>* 10.127.0.2/31 is directly connected, swp2, 00:37:56
  O>* 10.254.0.1/32 [110/110] via 10.127.0.1, swp1, 00:37:47
    *                          via 10.127.0.3, swp2, 00:37:47
  O   10.254.0.2/32 [110/0] is directly connected, lo, 00:37:55
  C>* 10.254.0.2/32 is directly connected, lo, 00:37:56
  C>* 192.168.121.0/24 is directly connected, eth0, 00:37:56
  vx#
```

The action of the RIB is clearly visible in this output. The route to 10.127.0.0/31 is announced in two separate lines: one starting with O to show that OSPF announces it, and one starting with C to show that it is directly connected. The connected route wins over the OSPF announced route, as seen by the asterisk (*) before the directly connected route. OSPF has a distance of 110, by default.

Routing Protocols Overview

A routing protocol communicates route reachability information to its peers to allow the automatic building of a consistent forwarding topology across all the routers in the network. There are many ways to define a routing protocol. All convey the same basic essence.

A routing protocol performs the following main tasks:

1. Tracks local state (links, addresses, and such)
2. Exchanges information about reachability to destinations
3. Computes shortest paths to the destinations that routers learn about from communicating with their peers
4. Programs the routing table with the next hops for these destinations

There are many ways to accomplish these tasks. For instance, one protocol might centralize the path computation (task 3), whereas another lets each router do the path computation autonomously. The former model leads down the path of OpenFlow and a centralized control plane. The latter is how the internet works and is the classic IP routing model. We focus on the classic IP distributed routing protocol model. However, even this classic model comes with many approaches to solving the puzzle of routing a packet. We consider the two primary approaches and their differences in the next few sections.

Distance Vector Protocols Versus Link-State Protocols

There are two primary approaches to designing a routing protocol in the classic mold: *distance vector* protocols and *link-state* protocols. The Routing Information Protocol (RIP), Enhanced Interior Gateway Routing Protocol (EIGRP), and BGP are examples of distance vector protocols. The only practical choice for a distance vector protocol in the data center is BGP. OSPF and IS-IS are examples of link-state protocols. Let's see the most basic differences between the approaches.

The primary difference between these two types of routing protocols is how they choose to convey route information. A distance vector protocol carries the distance to each destination network. A link-state protocol, on the other hand, carries information about the connectivity of a router to its neighbors. Let's tease apart the meaning in these words a little more.

Consider Figure 5-2 again. The end goal of either approach is for all routers R1 through R4 to know how to reach the destination networks 10.1.1.0/24, 10.1.2.0/24, 10.4.1.0/24, and 10.4.2.0/24. Let's focus only on the propagation of routes from R1 toward R4. This focuses the discussion on the distribution of the 10.1.1.0/24 and 10.1.2.0/24 networks. By ignoring the 10.4.x.x network propagation, we simplify the discussion.

In either approach, the routers are first configured to indicate who they can communicate with. R1 is told that it can talk to R2 and R3, R2 is told it can talk to R1 and R4, and so on. Routers need first to establish that they can talk to each other before they can exchange route advertisements. The routers also must be configured to indicate what information they can originate.

Distance Vector Dissected

A distance vector protocol advertises R1's routes through the simplified sequence shown in Figure 5-4.

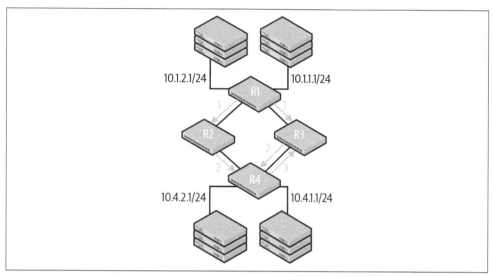

Figure 5-4. Sample distance vector routing protocol packet exchange from R1 to R4

❶ R1 advertises to R2 and R3 that it can reach the two networks with a distance of 1. It does this because it has been configured to know that its routing peers are R2 and R3. It has also been configured to glean the subnet information about these two networks from the logical routed interfaces. If a router is not explicitly configured to advertise a locally attached subnet or address, the router will not advertise it.

❷ R2 receives this information. It has no other information about how to reach those two networks. So, it accepts R1's advertisement as the best path to reach the two networks. Now, from R2's perspective, the way to reach either of the networks is via link P1 leading to R1. R2 now advertises this information to the other router it is configured to communicate with, R4. But in its advertisement, it increments the value of the distance to 2. In other words, each hop increments the distance by a cost before advertising the information to the other routers. R3, meanwhile, does the same thing as R2.

❸ Let's assume that R4 receives R2's advertisement before R3's. Because R4 has not learned any other way to reach the two networks, it computes that R2 is the best path to reach the two networks. The only routers R4 has been configured to talk to are R2 and R3. Because R4 learned the distance to the two networks via R2, the only router left to announce it to is R3. And so R4 announces to R3 that it can reach the two networks with a distance of 3. R3 receives R4's advertisement. However, it already has computed that it knows the two networks R4 is talking about, and that they are reachable with a distance of 1. Because a distance of 3 is higher, it does not change the information that the best way to reach the two networks is via R1. Thus, it has nothing new to advertise to its only other connected router, R1. Remember that R3 already advertised that it can reach the two networks with a cost of 2 to R4, after it received R1's advertisement.

When R4 receives R3's advertisement sent in step 2, it computes that the two networks are again reachable with a cost of 2, the same as via R2. R4 now updates its information to say that it can reach the two networks via R2 and R3. Because the distance to the subnets 10.1.1.0/24 and 10.1.2.0/24 didn't change on receipt of R3's advertisement, R4 has nothing further to advertise to R2.

At the end of this packet exchange, all routers know how to reach the two networks efficiently, and we're done. One minor detail is that R4 and R1 each need to choose a "best route" to reach each other. For instance, even though both R2 and R3 are equidistant from R1, R4 must select one as the best path, and the other as a equal-cost path to the best path (this part varies among distance-vector protocols, but is done this way in BGP).

Link-State Dissected

Link-state protocol packet exchange is more complicated than the one shown for distance vector.

1. As shown in Figure 5-5(a), all routers initially exchange their own link-state information with their peers. This is different from how distance vector protocols behave. After establishing the peering session, if there are no routes to advertise, a router running a distance vector protocol sends no further traffic to its peers. In contrast, with a link-state protocol, after session establishment, each router advertises its link-state information to its peers. Even those routers with only links to other routers, such as R2 and R3, exchange this link information with their peers. R2, for example, advertises to R1 that it has two links, one to R1 and the other to R4. R1 and R4, of course, advertise their reachability to their locally attached subnets as well, except that they advertise them via locally attached links to those subnets (there are other ways such as via redistribute, but we'll ignore them for now). We use colors (or shades in grayscale) to identify the Link-State Advertisements (LSAs) of the various routers as being different.

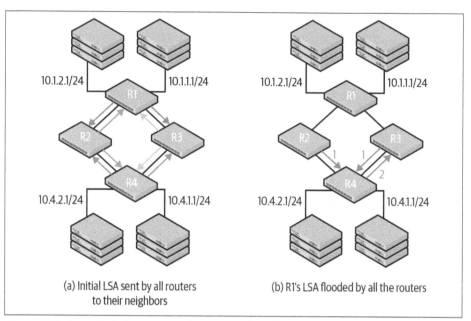

10.1.2.1/24   R1   10.1.1.1/24   10.1.2.1/24   R1   10.1.1.1/24

R2   R3   R2   R3

R4   R4

10.4.2.1/24   10.4.1.1/24   10.4.2.1/24   10.4.1.1/24

(a) Initial LSA sent by all routers   (b) R1's LSA flooded by all the routers
to their neighbors

Figure 5-5. Sample link-state routing protocol packet exchange

2. Unlike in a distance vector protocol, when a router receives an LSA from a peer router, it floods the packet to all its other peers without modifying it, if either it has no knowledge of the LSA or the information received in this LSA is newer than the one it currently has. The flooding rules can be complicated depending on the specific link-state protocol, but the basic behavior of flooding without modifying is the same across all of them. The only change to the LSA is that each router increments the age of the LSA field before flooding. Flooding, of course, doesn't send the packet out the port it came in. This flooding of R1's LSA by the other routers is shown in Figure 5-5(b). The numbers indicate the order in which the packets are sent. R4 floods R2's LSA to R3, assuming it received R2's LSA before it received R3's. R4 ignores R1's LSA received from R3 because it is identical to R1's LSA received from R2. Similarly, R3 discards R4's sending of R1's LSA as it is identical to the one received from R1 itself.

3. When this process is complete, all four routers contain identical copies of every other router's LSA.

4. After a router receives an LSA, independently of its propagating that LSA, it triggers a path recomputation. This path computation involves figuring out the shortest path to every other router. Let's assume that, as in the distance vector example, R4 receives the information via R2 before it receives the information via R3. R4 figures out first that it can reach R1 via R2. Because R1 has announced that it is connected to the two subnets, R4 also computes that the shortest path to

those subnets is via this path it computed to R1. When it receives R3's LSA, it updates this information to state that it can reach R1 and its connected subnets via both R2 and R3.

Summarizing Distance Vector Versus Link-State Route Exchange

Thus, we can summarize the difference between distance vector and link-state protocols as follows. In distance vector protocols, a router tells its neighbors only its reachability cost to every destination subnet, not of how it learned this information. In link-state protocols, a router tells its neighbors only about whom it is connected to; every router works out the reachability to a destination subnet from this link-state information. It's commonly said that in a distance vector protocol, a router gossips about everybody in the network with its neighbors, whereas in a link-state protocol every router in the network gossips about its neighbors with everybody else.

Of course, the resulting routes chosen by each router are the same at the end of the process that each protocol undertakes.

Comparing Distance Vector and Link-State Protocols

We now explore some key characteristics of both distance vector and link-state protocols. We examine a few more of the differences in the following section with the context of their application in a Clos topology. The book *Interconnections* by Radia Perlman (Addison-Wesley), listed in the references section of this chapter, provides additional comparative information.

Scaling in Link-State and Distance Vector Protocols

In distance vector protocols, every node carries only the information about the distance of prefixes from its neighbors. This is because in distance vector protocols, every router tells its neighbor only about its view of the world. The information is consolidated as it passes from one router to the next.

In link-state protocols, every router carries information about the neighborhood of all routers in the network. This can become quite big as networks expand. Furthermore, keeping every router up to date about the neighborhood changes of every other router increases the number of messages exchanged by the routing protocol. To limit the amount of chatter and the memory consumed by large networks, link-state protocols break the network into a hierarchy. IS-IS calls uses the intuitive term *level* for each part of the hierarchy, whereas OSPF calls it an *area*. Within a given level or area, all routers know about one another's neighborhood in all the glory required by link-state. But a router in one area does not know the detailed link-state information about another area if it does not have an interface in that area. In such cases, the router only knows what an *area border* router advertises. In other words, across areas or levels, link-state protocols become just like distance vector protocols. But unlike distance vector protocols, the prefixes carried across areas are always tagged separately from those in the same area.

OSPF supports only two levels of hierarchy: *backbone area* and *nonbackbone area*. IS-IS supports multiple levels, but there wasn't a description of how to make that support work until recently. Tony Li, one of the authors of the BGP and a highly regarded network architect and engineer in the internet, recently introduced a draft (*https:// oreil.ly/teXbg*) to specify this behavior.

How many routers would be too many for a single level? Given the horsepower of modern data center routers, numbers in the hundreds are not considered worrisome. I know of deployments where at least 384 nodes in a single level aren't considered a problem. Although I don't know of any larger deployments personally, I've heard of FRR's IS-IS implementation successfully tested with a 1,000 nodes in a single level, with routers running a modern Intel CPU.

Multipathing in Distance Vector and Link-State Protocols

Consider the topology in Figure 5-6, in which R1 through R7 are routers. From R7's perspective, there are two paths to reach 1.1.1.0/24, via R5 and via R6. R6, however, has two paths to 1.1.1.0/24, one via R3 and the other via R4, whereas R5 has a single path, via R2. A distance vector routing protocol considers only the distance through each connected router, not the number of possible paths. R6 can multipath, but that is a decision local to R6. So R7 assumes that it has two equal-cost paths to reach 1.1.1.0/24: one via R6 and the other via R5. It sends half the traffic to 1.1.1.0/24 via R6 and the other half via R5. This is a gross oversubscription of the path via R5, and an undersubscription of the path via R6. As for R6, even though it treats both R3 and R4 as equal cost, it still marks only one of them as its *best path* for 1.1.1.0/24.

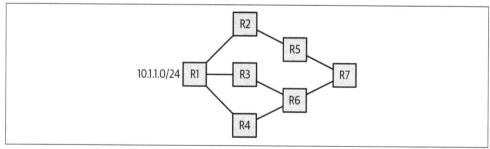

Figure 5-6. Sample topology showing the effect of multipath

With a link-state routing protocol, instead, R7 has the information to know that the path through R6 is more attractive than the path through R5. However, the *shortest path first* (SPF) algorithm does not take this into account. R7 treats both paths as being equal cost and sends the same amount of traffic to both R5 and R6 instead of one-third to R5 and two-thirds to R6. So the information about the link states for R5 and R6 didn't alter computations at R7. The end result is the same for both link state or distance vector.

No News Is Good News

Consider another scenario in which the link between R1 and R4 goes down in Figure 5-6. From R7's perspective, this failure has no effect on its reachability to 1.1.1.0/24. When a distance vector protocol is in use, R6 might not even bother to update R7 about this link failure (unless R6 marked the path through R4 as best path). In a link-state protocol, R6 notifies R7, and the update is propagated to all routers. In fact, R4 also notifies every router about this link change. R7 recomputes its path to 1.1.1.0/24 and finds no difference from its existing state (it is still reachable via R5 and R6).

So, whereas the distance vector protocol required no recalculation, the link-state protocol in this case forced R7 to spend some time recomputing paths when there was no need to. When link-state protocols were new, this was considered a big problem due to the low-powered CPUs that routers used. To mitigate this issue, the *incremental shortest path first* algorithm was invented. This algorithm is now used in just about every implementation that I'm aware of.

Propagation Delay in Link-State and Distance Vector Protocols

The break in the link between R1 and R4 in Figure 5-6 also causes changes to the forwarding states of the other routers. For example, R3 no longer has multipathing to R4 (previously it could reach R4 via R1 and R6, but now only via R6). R1 must find its path to R3 (via R4), R2 now has multipathing to R4 (R1-R3-R6-R4 and R5 R7 R6-R4), and so on. How efficiently do all these changes occur between the two models, in terms of time required to arrive at the final state, number of messages exchanged, and so on? The time taken to arrive at the final and correct state is called *convergence*. There is node-specific convergence and a network-wide convergence.

In link-state, because the original router's link-state information is forwarded without any modification, information propagates to all the nodes rapidly. All of the routers can run their path computation in parallel because they all have the updated information. In distance vector, a router cannot forward any updates without computing the distance first, because what a router advertises is its distance to a prefix. So, theoretically, link-state protocols should converge faster than a distance vector protocol. Distance vector protocols might also have other mechanisms, such as running a holddown timer to avoid the "count to infinity" problem. All of this gives rise to the reputation of distance vector protocols for slow convergence compared to their link-state siblings. This isn't true of BGP, especially in the data center. We cover this a little later in this chapter.

Furthermore, this rapid propagation of LSAs takes place only within the same level. Across levels, the consolidation of LSAs by the area border routers slows things down.

Multiprotocol Support

Networks need to recognize multiple Layer 3 (L3) protocols, notably IPv4, IPv6, and MPLS. IPv6 is the heir apparent of IPv4, and has been waiting in the wings forever (well, actually for 20 years, which in internet time seems forever) to take over the mantle from IPv4 as the key protocol. MPLS is another routing solution that uses 20-bit labels to guide a packet through the network.

Networks also handle Layer 2 (L2) or MAC addresses. On top of all this, a single network can be carved into multiple virtual networks (something we study in Chapter 6), and a routing protocol needs to know how to carry the addresses of these virtual networks without getting them mixed up. Each of these variants in the information carried is commonly known as a *network address family*.

Routing protocols that can transport routing information for multiple address families are called *multiprotocol* routing protocols. Thus, both BGP and IS-IS are multiprotocol routing suites. OSPF had to undergo an evolution to an incompatible upgrade called OSPFv3 just to support IPv6. OSPFv3 is trying to be a multiprotocol routing suite, but it supports only IPv4 and IPv6 at this point, and not all implementations support advertising IPv4 prefixes with OSPFv3. IS-IS is more versatile because it not only advertises IPv4 and IPv6, but also advertises MPLS labels. BGP supports all of these and more, including MAC addresses, flow information, and multicast addresses.

In short, both link-state and distance vector protocols can be multiprotocol routing protocols, but BGP leads in its range of supported address families.

Unnumbered Interfaces

In routing parlance, a numbered interface is one with its own unique IP address. Consequently, an *unnumbered* interface is one without its own unique IP address. An unnumbered interface borrows the IP address from another operational interface.

Borrowing an IP address, of course, leads to a dependency that could become a problem. If an interface goes down, it deletes any associated IP addresses. For example, a link failure causes the interface to become unoperational, it gives up its IP address. So unnumbered interfaces commonly borrow the loopback interface's IP address (the globally valid one, not the one from the host-only 127.x.x.x subnet), because that interface is always present.

In networks, numbered interfaces provide a mechanism to better troubleshoot connectivity issues. In *traceroute*, if each interface has a unique IP address, this shows up in the *traceroute* output. This allows a network operator to know which link the *traceroute* is traversing, during troubleshooting, for example. This use with *traceroute*, coupled with scrappy support in vendor implementations, made unnumbered interfaces a motherless child in networking.

Clos networks change this decision significantly. In Clos topologies, the best practice is to allow just a single link between two nodes in adjacent tiers. This makes it easy to identify the link traversed between two adjacent nodes. Assigning a separate IP address per interface is redundant. Further, best practice within the data center recommends not advertising interface addresses in order to reduce the attack vector for malware and reduce the FIB size. Numbered interfaces also complicate automation of router configuration. For these reasons, in the data center, unnumbered interfaces are a big win.

OSPF and IS-IS have supported unnumbered interfaces from the start. Few vendors support it, especially for OSPF over Ethernet, but it exists. FRR (*https://frrouting.org*), the popular open source routing suite, supports unnumbered interfaces for OSPF and IS-IS.

BGP runs on top of the Transmission Control Protocol (TCP), whereas link-state protocols use a link-local multicast address to send their messages. This means the link-state protocols do not need to know the address of their peer, only what interface to send packets out of and receive packets from. BGP, on the other hand, by using TCP, requires the network stack to determine what interface to communicate on. This it does by having the network stack route the BGP packet to its peer like any other packet.

Traditionally, BGP uses a connected route or requires another routing protocol (such as OSPF or IS-IS) to set up the routing to reach the remote peer. Strange as it may sound, this makes sense in the use case for which BGP was originally derived: in-service provider networks. But in the data center, when BGP is used, it is the only protocol in use—no other protocol such as OSPF or IS-IS is used with it. Therefore, BGP requires a connected route, which means every interface needs to use a specific IP address from a subnet that the remote peer is on, as well. For example, if you use 10.1.1.0/31 as the IP address of an interface, BGP can now establish communication with a peer whose IP address is 10.1.1.1/31 because the network stack sets up the 10.1.1.0/31 as a connected route. (The 10.1.1.0/31 prefix includes both 10.1.1.0 and 10.1.1.1 addresses.) In other words, BGP requires a different IP address per interface, which is exactly the opposite of unnumbered interfaces.

Along with the routing team at Cumulus, I came up with a way to make BGP work without requiring the assignment of an interface address. We call this *unnumbered BGP* and it has been available in FRR for several years now. Unnumbered BGP is how

I've seen every data center operator using FRR deploy BGP. We cover unnumbered BGP in "BGP Unnumbered: Eliminating Pesky Interface IP Addresses" on page 316.

In short, the use of unnumbered interfaces is possible today with both distance vector and link-state protocols. However, not all data center vendor routing stacks support unnumbered interfaces with either distance vector or link-state protocols.

Routing Configuration Complexity

How does the configuration of a link-state protocol compare to its distance vector rival? A simpler, easier-to-understand configuration helps in building an error-free network. Human configuration errors are among the primary leading causes of network errors. It is therefore useful to consider whether one style of protocol offers significant benefit over another.

BGP is famous for being complex to configure, with more knobs than the population of some of the tiny island nations. Does this therefore favor link-state protocols?

To help answer this question, let's examine the basic pieces of a routing protocol configuration. Every routing protocol requires the configuration to answer the following mandatory questions:

- Who am I?
- Whom do I talk to?
- What do I tell them?

Routing protocols have a bunch of other things to configure such as logging, timers, protocol-specific knobs, and so on. I don't discuss them because they're not relevant to the conversation here. I cover them in sufficient detail in Chapter 13 and Chapter 15.

Who am I?

Every router configuration contains an identity field, usually called a *router ID*. This allows other routers to know who originated the information under consideration. This can be useful in troubleshooting, too. The router ID is usually a 32-bit integer typically written out as an IPv4 address in BGP and OSPF (v2 and v3). The common practice is to have a router ID that is typically the IP address of the loopback interface. IS-IS uses a system ID that has the rather long format, XX.XXXX.XXXX.XXXX.XXXX.XX, to identify the speaker.

If no router ID is configured, most implementations pick the first interface with a valid IP address and use that IP address as the router ID. This can lead to unexpected behavior, so it is better to assign the router ID explicitly. This is the same for both link-state and distance vector protocols.

Whom do I talk to?

This is the next critical piece of information to configure. In link-state protocols, this is as simple as the name of the interface to which the neighbor is connected. Although many network operators fail to use this model, it is highly recommended because it simplifies automating the configuration tremendously. Most vendors support this model.

In addition, you need to configure the level of the link in the IS-IS hierarchy (or the area of the link in OSPF).

In BGP, the choice is much more complex. Not only do you need to configure the IP address of the peer, you also must configure a key BGP concept concerning the neighbor, called the Autonomous System Number (ASN). (We discuss a little more about ASNs in Chapter 15.) If either the IP address or the ASN is configured incorrectly, the peering session will not come up and no routes can be exchanged with that peer.

In FRR, you can configure the interface over which you want BGP to peer with the neighbor. You can also eliminate specifying the exact peer ASN. This makes BGP configuration as simple as OSPFs.

Routing stacks from Cisco and others attempt to simplify configuration by assigning all routers at a given level in the Clos tier the same ASN, including the routers at the lowest rung of the Clos topology. They use one of the infinite knobs available to allow the leaves to see one another's prefixes. This is needlessly complex. Plus, when all of the leaves have the same ASN, you lose the ability to easily identify the origin of a route or the path associated with the route. This affects effective troubleshooting in many situations. So, I don't recommend using ASNs like this. This is a hack to make automation easy. Ask the vendor to support unnumbered BGP instead.

What do I tell them?

The next question is what to advertise to the routing peers after the communication is established. In link-state protocols, configuring the interface over which the router will communicate automatically advertises that interface's IP address. For other interfaces such as loopback, you can add a clause to advertise the address on that interface without attempting to peer.

In distance vector protocols, network statements specify which prefixes to advertise.

For supporting multiple network address families, each address family must be "activated" to start the advertisement.

In both kinds of protocols, the prefix must be in the local routing table before the protocols advertise the information. Another common practice in both protocols is to use the "redistribute" model of advertising. This involves picking the addresses assigned via another method—connected or static, for instance—and advertising them.

So here, both link-state and distance vector protocols have roughly comparable complexity when it comes to the essential pieces.

Routing Protocols in Clos Networks

Many decisions about routing protocols were conceived in the days when links were skinny and networks sparsely connected. Let's now examine the behavior of link-state and distance vector protocols where it matters to this book: in the richly connected data center network. (See Chapter 2 for discussion of data center network topologies.)

Figure 5-7 shows a three-tier Clos topology with the L* routers representing leaf routers, S* routers representing spine routers, and SS* routers representing super-spine routers. There are two pods, Pod 1 and Pod 2, using the architecture described by Figure 2-5(c) in Chapter 2.

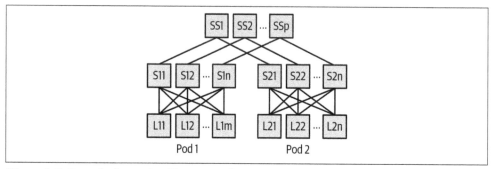

Figure 5-7. Sample three-tier Clos network

Using the normal link-state deployment model, in each pod, the leaf and spine router links belong to the level 1 (area 1). The spine and super-spine router links belong to level 2 (or backbone) area.

Link-State Versus Distance Vector When Links or Nodes Fail

In this section, we examine what happens in each of the distance vector and link-state protocols when a link or node fails in a Clos topology.

BGP's behavior in a Clos network

BGP's behavior here revolves around the assignment of an ASN to each node. The ASN is one of the central concepts in BGP. Every BGP speaker (a router running BGP protocol) must have an ASN.

Remember that prefixes in BGP are carried with the complete path of that prefix's advertisement. The path that is encoded in the prefix is the list of ASNs. This list is called the ASPATH.

Assuming that the ASN of a router in Figure 5-6 is its numbered suffix, R1's ASN is 1, R6's ASN is 6, and so on. The advertisement for prefix 10.1.1.0/24 from R6 to R7 carries the ASPATH of 6-3-1.

Using the BGP deployment model described in Chapter 15:

- Each leaf gets its own ASN.
- All spines within a single pod get the same ASN.
- Spines in each pod get a different ASN from the spines in other pods.
- All super-spines get the same ASN.

This allocation model avoids BGP's path-hunting problem, and results in a simple *top-down routing*. Top-down routing means packets cannot bounce between levels of a Clos tier. Figure 5-8 illustrates what we mean by top-down routing. The figure shows packet flows that are not permitted as a consequence of top-down routing. As an example, traffic from SS2 cannot reach SS0 as indicated by the crossed out link.

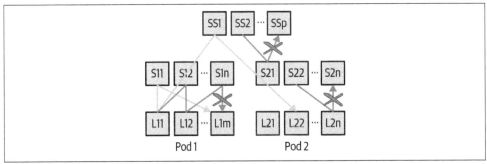

Figure 5-8. Possible and impossible packet forwarding with BGP in Clos

This means that leaves can talk to one another, spines in a pod cannot talk to one another, and the super-spines cannot talk to one another.

Now let's consider what happens when there are changes in the network.

For example, in Figure 5-7, if a link between a leaf and spine goes down, such as between L11 and S11, S11 sends an update withdrawing reachability to L11 and its locally attached prefixes to the other leaves connected to it. Those leaves remove L11 as reachable for S11 and its prefixes. To illustrate this, in Figure 5-7, L11 updates the other connected spines about its lost connectivity to S11. Those spines drop this update, because they share the same ASN. S11 also sends an update about its lost connectivity to L11 and its prefixes to the super-spines it's connected to. They update their routing tables to indicate that they cannot reach L11 and its prefixes via S11. That's it. No other route updates propagate anywhere else. Updates can't get simpler than this.

L11 withdraws reachability to the loopback IP address of S11 because reachability to the other leaves is still possible via the other leaves. But because the spines could never talk to each other because of how ASNs were configured, L11's update to the other spines is dropped by them.

 In the data center, the best practice is to set the BGP's *advertisement interval* timer to 0 so that updates are immediately dispatched. The default value for advertisement interval in service provider space is 30s, so the administrator must explicitly change the interval to 0.

Link-state protocol's behavior in a Clos network

With IS-IS or OSPF, each pod is in its own level or area, level 1 or the nonbackbone area. The leaves are the area border routers. The leaves and spines form the level 2 (or backbone) routers.

Let's consider what happens when the link between S11 and L11 goes down:

1. S11 sends a new LSA with the link between S11 and L11 removed. This propagates throughout the pod, hitting the leaves and then the other spines. A single node can receive multiple copies of the same packet because of the way LSA flooding works in a link-state protocol.

2. Similarly, L11 sends its updated LSA with the link between L11 and S11 removed. This LSA is flooded like S11's LSA.

3. Every node in the network recomputes its SPF based on these new LSAs.

4. The leaves realize that they can no longer use S11 as a way to reach L11 and thus remove it from the next hops as a way to reach L11 and its prefixes.

5. All of the leaves also compute the area summary routes to announce to the other backbone area routers. S11, which saw the change, sends the new updates to its neighbors in the backbone area, the super-spines. This update propagates through the backbone area until all routers in the backbone area have received it. This includes leaves in other pods. We're assuming that the spines are not summarizing in this case (see the "Route Summarization in Clos Networks" on page 105 for details on summarization).

6. Every backbone area router recomputes its routes. The spine routers remove S11 from their next-hop list to reach L11 and its prefixes. The leaves in the other

pods find no changes after the computation and thus have no local routing updates.

One possible benefit of link state's additional computation and message exchange is that any in-flight packets to L11 can find their way to T11 eventually. However, it is very likely that these packets can loop or arrive out of order. Loops can happen while the forwarding topology converges to the final state. This is true of all routing protocols, which is why a TTL is present in the IP header. Before a router forwards a packet, it decrements the TTL, and when the TTL is going to be decremented to 0, the packet is dropped.

TCP does not work well if it encounters too many out-of-order packets. It assumes packet loss and throttles its congestion window, thereby reducing performance. Therefore, the tiny benefit of link-state protocols can be undermined by TCP's reaction to misordered packets.

Route Summarization in Clos Networks

Routing scales. This is why it is used in building very large networks, be it the internet or the largest data centers in existence today. Routing scales because of its ability to summarize IP addresses. Route summarization is the ability to advertise a single prefix that covers reachability to several networks. As described earlier in this chapter, the prefix 10.1.1.0/24 summarizes the routes for the 256 addresses from 10.1.1.0 to 10.1.1.255. Similarly, 10.1.0.0/16 summarizes the routes to 64,000 addresses. These are significant savings. How does route summarization work in Clos networks?

A Clos network summarizes routes only on the leaves. We cannot summarize at the spines, because the link failure between a spine and a leaf will either render that route unreachable or cause additional congestion in the network. Consider that in Figure 5-8, the spines announced a summary route of 10.1.0.0/16 which covered all the prefixes announced across all leaves. If S11 loses connection to L11, because it is announcing a summarized route, it can still attract traffic to L11's prefix; for example, from the other pods or from the external world. But S11 has either no way to deliver the packet to L11 (the case with BGP) or it leads to bouncing the packet off other spines and leaves (in the case of OSPF or IS-IS).

If you don't allow a subnet to stray beyond a single rack, the leaf needs to just announce subnet prefixes. In the early years of the current data center networks described in this book, merchant-switching silicon had no more than 16K entries in the routing table. So, if you just announced subnet prefixes, the switching silicon had enough routing table entries to hold the information pertaining to the entire data center (and yes, data centers were also smaller by today's standards). These days, merchant-switching silicon supports up to 256K of routing table entries. So supporting up to 256K endpoint addresses (rather than subnet prefixes) throughout the data center is a possibility, one that is exploited by network virtualization solutions such as EVPN. Nevertheless, it's good network design to restrict a subnet to a single rack if you can. In Chapter 6, we consider summarization in large networks with network virtualization.

Security and Safeguards

Peering in routing protocols involves configuring both peers. This is a sufficiently high bar to avoid malware drive-by attacks. Routing protocols also support security measures to prevent unauthorized peering, and to protect packet integrity. Within the data center, security for routing protocols isn't usually a concern. But with the advent of routing protocols on the hosts via Kube-router and Calico, it's important to protect the security and integrity of the routing state from accidental or malicious errors introduced by the end host.

The minimum additional configuration to secure your routing protocol is to assign a password that needs to be exchanged for the peering to continue. BGP, OSPF, and IS-IS all support assigning passwords and password exchange. All these routing protocols provide password authenticated peering.

BGP runs on top of TCP and so, in theory, can support additional security mechanisms. Examples of such mechanisms are Transport Layer Security (TLS) and TCP Authentication Option. Unfortunately, no implementation supports BGP with these options. BGP can also be used with IPsec, although that is uncommon.

OSPF runs on top of IP and so can support encryption of the protocol exchange itself using IPsec in addition to passwords. IS-IS runs on top of Ethernet and so has no other security option besides passwords.

Calico and Kube-router use BGP, so good security for BGP is important. I know of some Cumulus customers that have deployed FRR with OSPF on the hosts, but this is a rarity.

It is also important to ensure that the routing protocol has safeguards in place to prevent human errors or malware from advertising prefixes that cause a network failure. For example, you should configure the protocol to ensure that only certain prefixes are accepted from neighbors, and that only certain prefixes are announced to a neighbor (just the default route, for example).

Route filtering is the most common way to ensure such safeguards. Route filtering is supported either via *route-maps* or a filtering language in most routing suites. FRR supports route-maps. BGP has the most extensive support for configuring route-maps, both inbound and outbound, for specific neighbors and for everyone. OSPF and IS-IS provide inbound route filtering via a *distribute-list* command.

In summary, BGP has the most extensive support for security and safeguards. This is all the more appropriate because application infrastructure software tools are beginning to use BGP on the hosts on which they run.

Bidirectional Forwarding Detection

Bidirectional Forwarding Detection (BFD) is a standard protocol that detects faults in the path between two routers. Such faults include failures in cables, interfaces, and possibly the forwarding pipeline itself. The protocol is sufficiently granular to detect faults in time scales of less than a second. Though BFD is typically configured in conjunction with a routing protocol (as shown in Chapter 13 and Chapter 15), it is a separate protocol and works independent of any specific routing protocol or media.

Detecting faults quickly is important in high-speed networks. Some faults can be difficult to notice immediately, such as when a cable fails in one direction but continues to work in the other direction. All routing protocols run timers to detect faults, but if the routing protocol has to detect all failures on its own, the administrator has to run the keepalive or hello timers at high frequencies, say less than a second. But this places an undue burden on the routing process. Also, if there are multiple routing protocols, such as an internal protocol like OSPF alongside an exterior protocol such as BGP, having each of them run fast timers to catch the same condition seems redundant and excessive. BFD was invented to address these conditions. With the use of BFD, the routing protocols can run with more relaxed timers. When BFD detects a failure, it notifies the routing protocol to take the appropriate action such as tearing down the routing session associated with that link.

When routers are connected via a shared medium, as they used to be in the access-agg model, BFD plays an even more important role because it catches problems that cannot be caught easily in a point-to-point links, such as link failures. But in the data center, all inter-router links are point to point. And so, you might wonder, isn't BFD redundant because cable breaks are caught instantly? However, BFD is used to catch problems that don't result in a complete failure, such as unidirectional cables or faulty silicon. The only fault that BFD doesn't catch is where a routing protocol process itself has hung and is unresponsive. Only the routing protocol timers can catch this error. But it should be rare in robust routing stacks.

BFD is defined in RFC 5880 (*https://oreil.ly/DyyOe*) and RFC 5881 (*https://oreil.ly/pOhSl*). There are many different BFD modes. The most common implementation uses the two independent unidirectional sessions called Asynchronous mode. FRR supports BFD. One final note: BFD works only between routers; it does not support links between bridges.

Requirements of a Routing Protocol in the Data Center

A routing protocol in the data center needs to satisfy a number of basic requirements. Beyond that, there are advanced requirements applicable to a large set of networks. Finally, we can consider requirements that one might call futuristic or less crisp. This classification is based on my experience dealing with hundreds of customers—during my time at Cisco and Cumulus—along with discussions I've had with other industry experts.

Basic Requirements

Given the dominance of the Clos topology in the data center, the basic requirements of a routing protocol are as follows:

- Distribute network prefixes for the networks of choice for the data center. In just about every case, this involves at least IPv4 prefixes. In some cases, IPv6 prefixes might be required.
- Support for fast convergence of routing state across the network.
- Support for draining traffic from a node to be taken down for maintenance or end of life. Examples of such support include the overload bit in IS-IS, the max-metric option in OSPF, and the various choices in BGP to drain traffic.
- Support for network configuration that is friendly to automation.

Advanced Requirements

The next requirements address requirements that stem from more advanced deployments such as those involving network virtualization or routing on the host:

- Multiprotocol support. This is increasingly required in enterprises looking to run legacy applications that require a bridged network or have other multitenancy requirements. Network virtualization support is the main requirement here.
- Support for large-scale networks; that is, from a few routers to tens of thousands routers.
- Support for running on servers. With the advent of Calico and Kube-router, routing protocols might also run on servers, not just on routers. So a routing protocol that works on hosts as well as on routers is important. Servers usually run open source versions of routing protocols, notably FRR, BIRD (*https://oreil.ly/yxwVa*), or goBGP (*https://oreil.ly/wsm3J*).
- As few protocols as necessary. This point becomes particularly important when requiring multiprotocol support. The main reason I emphasize this point is that fewer protocols implies fewer things that can go wrong, and fewer places you

need to look to troubleshoot an issue. Using a single eBGP session is better than using OSPF + PIM + iBGP (more on this in the next chapter).

- Support for a large number of prefixes. This starts to become important when servers can advertise individual container addresses or when EVPN is used.
- Support for filtering inbound and outbound advertisements.
- Support for securing communications (establishment at least).

Rare or Futuristic Requirements

This last list contains requirements stemming from uses that an extremely limited set of advanced deployments have been considering:

- Support for MPLS and Segment Routing. This is largely found at some of the most advanced network operators.
- The ability to obtain the physical connectivity of the entire network from a single node (or just a handful of nodes). Some network operators desire this connectivity information in order to run global path optimization algorithms at a central location and push down routes for individual flows that need additional optimization to the individual nodes.
- Scaling advertisement of prefixes to millions of routes.

Choosing the Routing Protocol for Your Network

Several factors determine the proper choice of protocol for your network. Many are technical, but there are nontechnical factors, too. In my experience, most customers I've dealt with, and networks I've heard of from friends and other sources, use BGP as the routing protocol within the data center. OSPFv2 comes a close second, and that's it. I have not heard of other routing protocols used within the data center. Sometimes, the protocol used is tied into a more complex product, as in the case of Cisco's ACI (Application-Centric Infrastructure) product where IS-IS is used as the base protocol along with BGP. Customers cannot necessarily control this choice.

Here are some questions to help you decide which routing protocol is best for your network. The one criterion I follow is to use as few protocols as possible.

- Do you need to support only IPv4? (The world's your oyster.)
- Do you need to support EVPN? (Done. Answer is BGP.)
- Do you need to support IPv6?
- Do you need the router to peer with a host? (Done. Answer is BGP.)

- Does your vendor support unnumbered interfaces? (Use them.)
- Do you have in-house expertise in a specific protocol?
- Does your vendor support EVPN with eBGP only? (Choose it.)

Summary

The goal of this chapter was to demystify routing and routing protocols. Details of specific protocols are left to later chapters, but with the help of the questions in the previous section, you hopefully have the ability to make an informed decision, rather than give in to a particular vendor's choice.

In the spirit of the "zen of python," let me suggest a "zen of routing protocols":

```
Beautiful is better than ugly.
Simple is better than complex.
Complex is OK, complicated is not so good.
So just because you can, doesn't mean you must.
One is better than many.
Unnumbered is better than numbered.
Readability counts.
Although practicality beats purity, strive to automate.
A knob is sometimes better unused.
A good-enough network lasts longer than a perfect one.
```

May this guide you in your answers to seek a good enough routing protocol for your network.

References

- Perlman, Radia. 1999. *Interconnections*: Bridges, Routers, Switches, and Internetworking Protocols. New York: Addison-Wesley Professional.
- Keshav, Srinivasan. 1997. *An Engineering Approach to Computer Networking*: ATM Networks, the Internet, and the Telephone Network. New York: Addison-Wesley Professional.

## CHAPTER 6

Network Virtualization

It's what we come for, to gawk at all those layers, exposed.
—Wendy Barker

Cloud computing is possible only because of the technologies that enable resource virtualization. If you're going to have multiple virtual endpoints share a physical network, but different virtual endpoints belong to different customers, the communication between these virtual endpoints also need to be isolated from one another. In other words, network is a resource, too, and *network virtualization* is the technology that enables the sharing of a common physical network infrastructure. In the data center, the use of network virtualization is not limited to cloud computing. This chapter therefore aims to acquaint the network engineer or architect with this fundamental technology.

This chapter helps a network engineer or architect answer the following questions:

- What is network virtualization?
- What are the uses of network virtualization?
- What are the different choices in network virtualization?
- What are the control-plane choices for network virtualization?
- How does bridging and routing work with VXLAN?

What Is Network Virtualization?

Network virtualization enables a network operator to carve a single physical network into multiple isolated, virtual networks. The concept is similar to server virtualization. In server virtualization, the compute element consisting of a CPU, memory, and I/O interfaces is carved into multiple virtual compute elements. Each virtual compute element believes it is the only instance running on the machine and is unaware of the other virtual compute elements. The VM sees an abstraction of the CPU, memory, and I/O interfaces that are actually being shared and switched around among multiple VMs. The server virtualization software, called a *hypervisor*, provides a generic abstraction of a compute element and isolates each virtual instance from the others.

In packet networks, each virtual network assumes it owns the following resources:

- Interface or link
- Forwarding tables
- Other tables such as for enforcing policies (access control, for example) and performing other packet manipulation (Network Address Translation [NAT], for example)
- Packet buffers and link queues

At a higher level of abstraction, each virtual network assumes it *is* the entire network. To allow this illusion, each virtual network is isolated from other virtual networks. To enable the illusion of owning the entire address space, the packet forwarding table is partitioned across the multiple virtual networks. To ensure isolation of traffic between virtual networks, either a complete interface is allocated to a virtual network, or a single interface is logically carved out for each virtual network sharing that link.

To enable efficient sharing, the partitioning of the resource is dynamic and fine-grained. Each resource is tagged with the virtual network it belongs to. For example, to enable sharing a physical interface across multiple virtual networks, the packet header carries a *virtual network identifier*. Packet header lookups in forwarding and flow tables are then qualified with this virtual network ID of a packet. Just as there can be more virtual networks than physical interfaces, a relatively few packet buffers and link queues can serve a much larger set of virtual networks due to the scarcity of these resources in comparison to the number of virtual networks that are present. This is especially true on switches, more than for network interface cards on end hosts. So packet buffers and queues typically have no minimum guaranteed buffers or queues per virtual network.

Virtual networks have been implemented so many times, in so many different ways, as we'll see later. Each technology has its own name and its own jargon. The name of the field identifying the virtual network is different in each of these technologies. VLAN uses VLAN ID, VRF uses a name typically, VPNs have a VPN ID, VNID stands for VXLAN Network ID, and so on. There isn't a single term to encompass all of these into one abstract ID such as virtual network identifier. I use VNID to mean this term, but its official expansion is the one associated with VXLAN. And as a testimony to this absence, often there is no uniform ID used end to end to identify the virtual network associated with a packet.

We examine network virtualization in more detail after we understand the uses of network virtualization in the data center. We will map the different kinds of network virtualization to these use cases later in the chapter.

Uses of Network Virtualization in the Data Center

There are three primary use cases for network virtualization in the modern data center:

- Forcing traffic through certain services
- Providing Layer 2 (L2) connectivity over a Layer 3 (L3) network
- Multitenancy
- Separating switch management traffic from data traffic

Let us examine each a little bit more.

Forcing Traffic to Take a Certain Path

The first use case is to use network virtualization to force traffic through certain nodes that provide a specific service. A simple example is a firewall between traffic external to the data center and the internal network. For example, servers can communicate with one another internally to return the results of an external query. Therefore, it is important to ensure the security of the data center by ensuring that these externally facing servers alone can communicate with the external world, and that an attack on these servers does not compromise the the internal network. (I assume the firewall itself is not compromised.) This is a common use case of network virtualization inside the data center.

Figure 6-1 shows a typical design for this use case. Figure 6-1(a) shows the physical connection between an external network and a single internal network. Figure 6-1(b) shows how the separation is accomplished by creating separate virtual networks for the external network and the internal network. Traffic between the internal and external virtual networks must pass through the firewall because the firewall is the only node with legs in both the internal and external network. Figure 6-1(b) might look like a traditional firewall setup, but here the two edge routers are really the same router. Its routing table is split into two, so that one side (the internal network) cannot talk to the other side (the external network) directly.

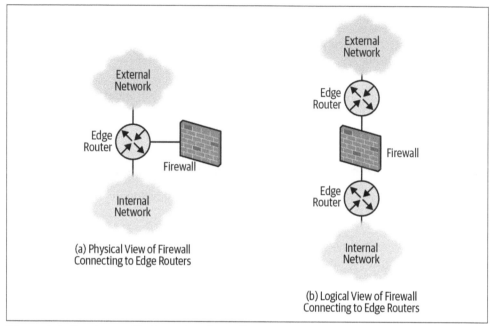

Figure 6-1. Forcing traffic through a firewall

If there are multiple internal networks, each with different policies for communicating with the outside world, creating multiple virtual networks is a practical solution for this use case.

This use case for network virtualization is also valuable when compliance requirements force certain classes of traffic to be explicitly authorized in order for communication to occur. By forcing such traffic into separate virtual networks and using firewalls alone to allow the flow of traffic across the virtual networks, the network engineer can demonstrate compliance (via logs, for example).

Applications That Require L2 Adjacency

Many applications, predominantly in the enterprise space, still rely on L2 connectivity. For example, VMware demands that L2 connectivity be maintained to support VMotion. Even though it has been demonstrated that VMotion can work without requiring L2 connectivity, it is either not supported by VMware or the VMware administrators are reluctant to let go of a tried and tested method. Another example is the use of L2 multicast (or broadcast) to detect new cluster members and to maintain cluster membership.

Whatever the reason, this requirement to maintain L2 connectivity requires that it work over an L3 network because the modern data center with the Clos topology is inherently L3. Network virtualization is used to provide this functionality.

Cloud

The final case for network virtualization is in clouds. Clouds are inherently multitenant, with a cloud service provider supporting multiple customers on a common, shared infrastructure, be it compute or networking. Network virtualization is a fundamental technology for this use case.

Separating Switch Management Network from Data Traffic

The most ubiquitous use of network virtualization in the data center is its use to keep the switch management traffic separate from the data traffic. Every switch has a separate, out-of-band Ethernet port that is used only to have management servers communicate with the switch. For example, switch management tasks such as image download, access via SSH, configuration via network automation, monitoring via SNMP, and other solutions are all commonly performed over this separate out-of-band management network. This Ethernet management port is not connected to the packet-switching silicon and doesn't need the switching-silicon driver to be present to configure the switch. This is the most common way I've encountered in how operators manage switches (routers or bridges, just to be clear). Data traffic that is, the traffic for which this network exists—does not use this management network. We discussed the notion of a default route in Chapter 5. Data traffic requires a different default route compared to the one for this management network. The only way for a switch to have two separate default routes is via the use of Virtual Routing and Forwarding (more on this in a moment). *Management VRF* is a well-known concept among network operators.

Network Virtualization Models

Network virtualization solutions can be classified along two major dimensions: by the service abstraction they provide (L2 or L3), and whether they are inline or overlay based. There are other ways to classify network virtualization solutions, such as by the type of encapsulation used, but I consider those as details rather than a high-level classification model. Another way to dissect network virtualization is by the nature of the control plane. However, I consider that an orthogonal discussion, which we examine separately. Another virtualization abstraction is that of network namespaces used in containers, which we examine in Chapter 7.

Service Abstraction: L2 or L3

Although networking is traditionally divided into seven layers, from the perspective of network virtualization, the only ones that matter are L2 and L3. Above these two layers, the functionality is more a service virtualization than network virtualization. Both L2 and L3 network virtual networks are popular, in and out of the data center.

L2 virtual networks

As an L2 service abstraction, a virtual L2 network makes no assumptions about the network layer on which the packet is routed. It assumes that the packet forwarding uses the L2 (or MAC) forwarding table and that addresses are unique across the entire L2 layer. But a virtual L2 network does not make IP addresses unique across virtual L2 networks, the way it does for a MAC address. The granddaddy of virtual networks is the *virtual local area network* (VLAN) which provided an L2 service abstraction.

In traditional bridging (including with VLANs), STP constructs a single tree across the bridged network to forward all packets, including unicast and multidestination packets (unknown unicast, multicast, and broadcast). Thus, unicast and multidestination frames follow the same path. With VLANs, often a separate tree is created per VLAN.

Not all virtual L2 network technologies support this model, especially those that do not use STP. The model of a single path for unicast and multidestination frames is not supported, for instance, by EVPN with VXLAN, standard TRILL, or Cisco's Fabric-Path. Many network operators were initially wary of this difference in behavior in EVPN and TRILL networks. But after they realized that applications did not suffer as a consequence of this change, network operators stopped worrying about this difference in forwarding behavior between virtual and physical bridged networks.

L3 virtual networks

As an L3 service abstraction, a virtual L3 network provides unique L3 addresses. Just as in a physical networks, a virtual L3 network is often—if not always—an IP network. Every virtual L3 network gets its own copy of the routing table. Each virtual network's routing table is populated similar to a physical network's routing table: either administratively or dynamically by a protocol or by the network stack. If the routing table is populated by a routing protocol, there are either separate instances of the routing protocol—one per virtual L3 network—or there is a single instance of the routing protocol that can distinguish between the addresses of the different virtual L3 networks. Both models are quite popular and common.

The most common virtual L3 networking technology is the VPN. VPNs rely on a fundamental abstraction required to support virtual L3 networks called *Virtual Routing and Forwarding* (VRF). The primary task of VRF is to provide a separate routing table for each virtual L3 network. This is often done by adding a VRFID field to the routing table lookup. In the simplest implementation of VRF, the VRFID is derived from the packet's incoming interface. The packet itself doesn't provide any information from which the VRFID can be derived. However, a VPN carries a VPN ID in the packet.

VPNs have since evolved to support virtual L2 networks, as well. So a VPN supporting a virtual L3 network is often called an L3VPN to distinguish it from an L2VPN.

Inline Versus Overlay Virtual Networks

The other primary classification axis for virtual networks is whether the virtual network is implemented as an inline network or an overlay network. In the inline model, every hop between the source and destination is aware of the virtual network the packet belongs to and uses this information to do lookups in the forwarding table. In the overlay network model, only the edges of the network keep track of the virtual networks; the core of the network is unaware of virtual networks. VLAN and VRF are examples of the inline model of virtual networks, whereas MPLS, VXLAN, and other IP-based VPNs are examples of the overlay model. I've encountered customer deployments where 32 to 64 VRFs were used.

The primary benefits of the inline model are transparency and reduced packet header overhead. However, requiring every node along the path be aware of virtual networks makes the model very unscalable and inefficient. It scales poorly because, as we get to the core of the network, the core devices must keep track of every single virtual network to forward packets properly. It is inefficient because any change to the virtual network affects every node in the network. The more moving parts there are, the more possibility there is of introducing an error and causing unexpected problems. Anybody who has deployed VLANs is well aware of these two problems. The same holds for VRFs, as well.

Therefore, overlay virtual networks are more popular and preferred in the data center, especially when hundreds or thousands of virtual networks are required. For this reason, we focus on overlay based virtual networks for the rest of this chapter.

Network Tunnels: The Fundamental Overlay Construct

I've often said, when the going gets tough, the network engineer gets another tunnel going. In one case after the next, when faced with a seemingly insurmountable problem, network tunnels have been devised to come to the rescue. Network tunneling is a mature technology, and so they're used in constructing overlay virtual networks, too.

A network tunnel is a simple enough construct: add an additional set of packet headers to hide the original packet header. These additional packet headers, called the *tunnel header*, contain a new source and destination address and are inserted above the original packet's header. The network between the tunnel endpoints is now blissfully unaware of everything below the tunnel header. Another way to think of a network tunnel is as a virtual link with the new tunnel header providing the required abstraction. In fact, a tunnel is created as a pseudo-network interface on all networking stacks that I'm aware of.

Let's use Figure 6-2 to understand packet forwarding in network tunnels. R1, R2, and R3 are routers, and their routing table state is shown in the boxes above them. Each arrow illustrates the port the router needs to send the packet out to reach the destination associated with that entry. As shown by its routing table, R2 knows only how to forward packets destined to R1 or R3. So, as shown in Figure 6-2(a), when a packet from A to B reaches R2, R2 drops the packet. In Figure 6-2(b), R1 adds a new header to the packet, with a destination of R3 and a source of R1. R2 knows how to forward this packet. On reaching R3, R3 removes the outer header and sends the packet to B because it knows how to reach B. Between R1 and R3, the packet is considered to be in a network tunnel. A common example of network tunnels is the use of VPNs.

The behavior of R1, R2, and R3 resembles the behavior of a virtual network overlay. A and B are in a private network that is unknown to the core router R2. This is why overlay virtual networks are usually implemented by a network tunnel.

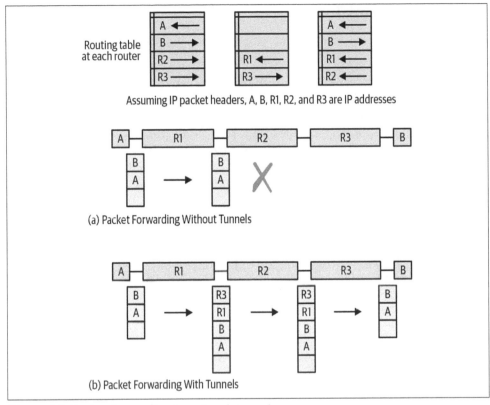

Figure 6-2. Packet forwarding in network tunnels

In an overlay virtual network, a tunnel endpoint (R1 and R3 in Figure 6-2) is termed a *network virtualization edge* (NVE). The ingress NVE, which marks the start of the virtual network overlay (R1 in our example), adds the tunnel header. The egress NVE, which marks the end of the virtual network overlay (R3 in our example), strips off the tunnel header. The network connecting the NVEs is called the *underlay*.

The tunnel header also carries the virtual network ID of the packet. The remote tunnel endpoint can thus direct the packet to the correct virtual network.

Network tunnels can be either point-to-point or point-to-multipoint. In a point-to-point tunnel, there is exactly a single endpoint at each end of the tunnel. In a point-to-multipoint tunnel, there are multiple egress tunnel endpoints for a single ingress endpoint. It is possible for some traffic to be sent to a single destination even in a point-to-multipoint tunnel, making it appear to be point-to-point. L3 tunnels are typically point-to-point tunnels, whereas L2 tunnels can be either.

Benefits of Network Tunnels

Network tunnels are extremely popular for the following reasons:

Scalability

As discussed earlier, network tunnels support greater scalability, especially in the data plane. Consider the Clos topology. Except for the lowest layer, none of the other layers in the Clos topology need to know anything about virtual networks. Furthermore, each switch at the lowest layer needs to know only the virtual networks that are connected to it. In public clouds, which can have millions of virtual networks, this is the only solution. The largest public cloud operators go further by pushing the tunneling layer all the way to the endpoints themselves, achieving even greater scalability.

Avoidance of a complete equipment upgrade

By restricting only those devices that need to know about virtual networks to support network tunnels, the network operator does not need to forcibly upgrade existing equipment to support virtual networks. Needless to say, this is a significant benefit.

Simplified administration

This same model also simplifies administration of virtual networks by requiring configuration only of those nodes that need to know of a virtual network. The fewer the moving parts, the simpler, less error prone, and therefore more reliable a network becomes.

Flexibility

One last benefit of network tunnels is that we can use them for other purposes besides building virtual networks. This flexibility is also manifest in the knowledge that different levels of the Clos topology (the host or the lowest layer of Clos) have about virtual networks. One design illustrating this flexibility is to have only certain dedicated pods support virtual networks, if the entire network doesn't require it. This solution can then grow out of a single pod into more pods as desired instead of upgrading the entire equipment because you might need it some day.

You might have noticed that all of the advantages stem from a single design choice: restricting knowledge only to the edges of the network and leaving the rest of the network free from this knowledge. This also supports the *immutable infrastructure* model of building networks. After you build and configure the network, no further changes are required, freeing the network in the future from errors that might introduced by configuration changes or new features.

The Drawbacks of Network Tunnels

No solution is without its drawbacks, and so it goes for network tunnels. In the discussion that follows, if a specific drawback can be overcome, we discuss the solution, as well.

Packet load balancing

Tunneled (or encapsulated) packets pose a critical problem when used with existing networking gear. That problem lies in how packet forwarding works in the presence of multiple paths to a destination. A node has the choice of either randomly selecting a node to which to forward the packet, or ensuring that all packets belonging to a flow take the same path.

As defined in "Flows and Congestion" on page 23, a flow is roughly defined as a group of packets that belong together. Most commonly, a TCP or UDP flow is defined as the five-tuple of source IP address, destination IP addresses, the Layer 4 (L4) protocol (TCP/UDP), the L4 source port, and the L4 destination port. Packets of other protocols have other definitions of flow.

A primary reason to identify a flow is to ensure the proper functioning of the protocol associated with that flow. If a node forwards packets of the same flow along different paths, these packets can arrive at the destination in a different order from the order in which they were transmitted by the source. This out-of-order delivery can severely affect the performance of the protocol. However, it is also critical to ensure maximum utilization of all the available network bandwidth; that is, all the network paths to a destination. Every network node makes decisions that balance the two types of optimization.

When a packet is tunneled, the transit or underlay nodes see only the tunnel header. They use this tunnel header to determine what packets belong to a flow. An L3 tunnel header typically uses a different L4 protocol type to identify the tunnel type (for example, IP GRE) uses IP protocol type 47). For traffic between the same ingress and egress NVE, the source and destination addresses are always the same. However, a tunnel usually carries packets belonging to multiple flows. But this flow information is embedded within the tunnel header. Because existing networking gear cannot look past a tunnel header, all packets between the same tunnel ingress and egress endpoints take the same path. Thus, tunneled packets cannot take full advantage of multipathing between the endpoints. This leads to a dramatic reduction in the utilized network bandwidth. Early networks had little multipathing, and so this limitation had no practical impact. But multipathing is quite common in modern networks, especially data center networks. So this problem needed a solution.

A clever fix for this problem was to use UDP as the tunnel. Routers (and bridges) have load balanced UDP packets for a long time. Like TCP, they send all packets associated with a UDP flow along the same path. When used as a tunnel header, the destination UDP port identifies the tunnel type. The source port is not used. So the tunnel ingress sets the source port to be the hash of the five-tuple of the underlying payload header. Ensuring that the source port for all packets belonging to a TCP or UDP flow is set to the same value enables older networking gear to make maximal use of the available bandwidth for tunneled packets without reordering packets of the underlying payload. The Locator Identity Separation Protocol (LISP) was the first protocol to adopt this trick. VXLAN copied the idea.

NIC behavior

On compute nodes, a NIC provides several important functions to enhance performance. One such function is offloading TCP segmentation; another is checksum computation for packets at the IP, TCP, and UDP layers. Performing these functions in the NIC hardware frees the CPU from having to perform these compute-intensive tasks. Thus, end stations can transmit and receive at substantially higher bandwidth without burning costly and valuable CPU cycles.

The addition of packet encapsulations or tunnels foils this. Because the NIC does not know how to parse past these new packet headers to locate the underlying TCP/UDP/IP payload or to provide additional offloads for the tunnel's UDP/IP header, the network performance takes a significant hit when these technologies are employed at the endpoint itself. Although some of the newer NICs understand the VXLAN header, this problem has been a primary reason VXLAN from the host has not taken off. So people have turned to the network to do the VXLAN encapsulation and decapsulation. This in turn contributed to the rise of EVPN.

For an application engineer, this specifically has an impact on whether to pick solutions such as Flannel or Weave (discussed in Chapter 7) with Kubernetes, Mesos, or even OpenStack.

Maximum transmission unit

In an L3 network, every link is associated with a maximum packet size, called the maximum transmission unit (MTU). Every time a packet header is added, the maximum allowed payload in a packet is reduced by the size of this additional header. The main reason this is important is that modern networks typically do not fragment IP packets, and if end stations are not configured with the proper reduced MTU, the introduction of virtual networks into a network path can lead to difficult-to-diagnose connectivity problems.

Lack of visibility

Network tunnels obscure the ecosystem they plow through. Classic debugging tools such as *traceroute* will fail to reveal the actual path through the network, presenting instead the entire network path represented by the tunnel as a single hop. This makes troubleshooting painful in networks using tunnels.

Network Virtualization Solutions for the Data Center

There are lots of overlay and inline virtual network solutions, but only a small subset are deployed in the data center.

VLAN

VLAN is deployed almost universally at the edge of the network; that is, in the first-hop router. Even some of the largest networks use this model. But because VLAN is limited to a single hop, this is less interesting as a virtual network solution. However, it is often used to simplify deployment, as shown in the following section.

VRF

This is a simple construct to provide isolated routing tables on a node. Mapping isolated routing tables across multiple nodes to provide end-to-end traffic isolation is a problem left to other constructs.

VRF is an inline solution. Every node along the path from the source to destination is aware of virtual networks. This requires each node to be responsible for independently associating a packet to its virtual network. Nodes do this by deriving the virtual network from the packet's incoming interface.

A single physical interface is typically carved into multiple logical interfaces by using the VLAN tag. The VLAN in this case is not an L2 construct, but merely a tag to separate the virtual networks. Because VLANs are terminated at each L3 hop, each router along the way can use a different VLAN to represent the same VRF. However, to simplify deployment, improve network observability, and create a more robust, predictable network, the same VLAN usually identifies a VRF across the entire shared infrastructure.

VXLAN

VXLAN is a stateless, L2 tunnel that allows you to build a single L2 virtual network over an L3 network infrastructure. This is the predominant overlay virtual network solution that I have encountered in the data center. It is relatively new (less than a decade old at the time of this writing). In the data center, VXLAN is coupled with VRF to provide a full bridging and routing overlay solution.

VXLAN uses UDP over IP as the encapsulation technology to allow existing network equipment to load balance packets over multiple paths, a common requirement in data center networks. VXLAN is primarily deployed in data centers. In VXLAN, the tunnel edges are called VXLAN Tunnel Endpoints (VTEPs).

The VXLAN header looks like Figure 6-3.

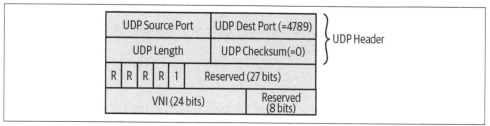

Figure 6-3. VXLAN header format

As mentioned in the section on load balancing, the UDP source port is computed at the ingress VTEP using the inner payload's packet header. This allows a VXLAN packet to be correctly load balanced by all the transit nodes. The rest of the network forwards packets based on the outer IP header.

VXLAN is a point-to-multipoint tunnel. Multicast or broadcast packets can be sent from a single VTEP to multiple VTEPs in the network.

The Inside Story of VXLAN

Educated readers can see several oddities in the VXLAN header. Why did we need yet another tunneling protocol? Why are 24 bits devoted to the Virtual Network Instance (VNI)? Why are there so many reserved bits? The entire VXLAN header could have been just four bytes, so why is it eight? Why have a bit that is always 1? The main reason for all this is historical, and I am mostly responsible.

Circa 2010, AWS had taken off in a big way, especially its Elastic Compute Service (ECS). VMware, the reigning king of virtualizing compute, approached Cisco, the reigning king of networking, for help with network virtualization. VMware wanted to enable its enterprise customers to build their own internal AWS-like infrastructures (called private clouds). They wanted an L2 virtual network, like VLANs, but based on an overlay model with the ability to support millions of virtual networks. They also wanted it to be IP-based due to IP's ubiquity and its superior scalability compared to L2-based technologies. The use of MPLS was a nonstarter, because MPLS was considered too complex and not supported within an enterprise.

As one of the key architects in the data center business unit at Cisco, I was tasked to come up with such a network tunnel. I first looked at IP-GRE, but quickly rejected it because we wanted a protocol that was easy for firewalls to pass through. Configuring a UDP port for passage through a firewall was easy, whereas an L4 protocol like GRE was not. Moreover, GRE was a generic encapsulation, with no specific way to identify the use of GRE for purposes other than network virtualization. This meant that the header fields could be used differently by other uses, preventing underlying hardware from doing something specific for network virtualization. I was tired of supporting more and more tunneling protocols in the switching silicon, each just a little different.

I already needed to support the OTV, a proprietary precursor to EVPN, and LISP protocols. I wanted VXLAN to look like OTV and for both to resemble LISP because LISP was already being discussed in the standards bodies. But there were already existing OTV and LISP deployments, so whatever header I constructed had to be backward compatible.

So I allocated 24 bits for the VNI, because many L2 virtual networks already supported 24-bit VNIs and I didn't want to build stateful gateways just to map VNI between different tunneling protocols. The reserved bits and the always-1 bit are there because those bits mean something else in case of LISP and OTV. In other words, the rest of the header format is a consequence of trying to preserve backward compatibility. The result is the VXLAN header you see.

Other Network Virtualization Solutions

Network Virtualization over GRE (NVGRE) was used by Microsoft instead of VXLAN, but I don't know whether it still uses it. Some other early pioneers used the original IP-GRE tunnel. VMware is pushing for a new network tunnel called Geneve to provide an enhanced and extensible feature set over a single network tunnel type, but I haven't encountered much real-world deployment of Geneve yet.

NVGRE (*https://oreil.ly/X3Q7P*) is already an informational standard published by the IETF. A similar approach is currently in progress for Geneve (*https://oreil.ly/ SAobK*). Geneve is also supported in the Linux kernel, both in the native kernel stack and as part of OVS.

The other granddaddy of network tunnels, MPLS, has also been considered for use in the data center by some large and sophisticated network operators, but I'm not aware of an actual deployment using one.

Practical Limits on the Number of Virtual Networks

As we discussed earlier, inline and overlay models support different numbers of virtual networks. In this section, we examine the numbers.

The primary factors that affect the actual deployed numbers depend on the following:

- Size of the virtual network ID in the packet header
- Limits enforced by hardware
- Scalability of the control plane and software

- Deployment model

The maximum number of virtual networks is the lowest number that results from all these factors. The factors are listed in the order in which that factor absolutely limits the upper bound. For example, if the packet header supports only four thousand virtual networks, there is little that can be done to increase that by any of the other factors, except maybe using more complex deployment strategies. Similarly, if the packet-switching silicon supports only 512 virtual networks, the ability for the packet header to support 16 million virtual networks might be irrelevant.

Size of Virtual Network ID in Packet Header

The size of the virtual network ID in the packet header is a key limiting factor for the number of virtual networks that can be supported on a single common physical infrastructure. This number applies equally to inline and overlay networks. Common limits follow:

- VLAN has 12 bits in its header to carry the virtual network. This means that it can support at most four thousand virtual networks in a contiguous physical network.
- MPLS supports 20 bits, which takes its limit to one million virtual networks, although MPLS could theoretically support even more by just adding another MPLS label.
- VXLAN and GRE support 24 bits, and so can run 16 million simultaneous virtual networks.

Hardware Limitations

The next factor that limits the number of virtual networks supported in a network is the limit enforced by hardware. For example, even though VXLAN supports 16 million virtual networks, most packet-switching silicon supports only 16K to 64K virtual networks on a single device. The hardware limit depends not just on what the packet forwarding table supports, but also on other tables such as ACL tables. But, if all virtual networks do not need to be known across all devices—for example, they're restricted to a single pod—you can support a significantly larger number of virtual networks across the data center than what a single device can support.

Scalability of Control Plane and Software

The control plane for network virtualization (discussed in "Control Protocols for Network Virtualization" on page 128) provides the next practical limit on the number of virtual networks; here's why:

- A single instance of the control protocol carrying information about all the virtual networks is more scalable than when a separate instance of the control protocol is involved for each virtual network. For example, if a different process is invoked for each control-plane instance, supporting 16 million processes (the potential outcome because VXLAN has a VNID of 24 bits) is clearly impractical.
- If a control protocol encodes the virtual network with a specific ID size, that is the limit that can be supported, regardless of the other considerations we've discussed.

In overlay networks, the core switches are unaware of the virtual networks in the packet-forwarding plane. But in the control plane, the control protocol can still be holding state information about all of the virtual networks because the core switches might be relaying the information from one leaf to the other leaves. This places an additional burden on the control protocol, though this is typically not the primary limiting factor.

Besides these limits, there might be other software scaling issues such as the implementation of the control protocol, the synchronization of the software state to the hardware, and so on. Asking for vendor-tested or supported limits is important here.

Deployment Model

If the network deployment pushes all knowledge of virtual networks to the endpoints, and even the first-hop router is ignorant of virtual networking, scalability in the control plane is the only limit governing the number of virtual networks supported. Of course, the upper bound is still the size of the virtual network ID in the tunnel header.

Automation also changes how many virtual networks can be deployed. I know of a customer who couldn't deploy an overlay model, but managed to run more than 128 inline virtual networks with the help of network automation.

If you use iBGP, you can also push limits upward by locating the iBGP route reflector in the network, on servers, instead of on the core routers.

Another critical factor that has nothing to do with software or hardware limits is the imperative for a fine-grained failure domain. Successful public cloud operators like to limit the failure domain as much as possible and make it possible to identify which virtual networks are affected when a given failure occurs. So they might not actually deploy as many virtual networks as possible.

Here are the typical ranges I have seen for inline solutions in the modern data center:

VRF
    From 2 to 64 virtual networks, occasionally 128.

VLAN

These can attain four thousand virtual networks, but because VLANs are restricted to a single hop at the edge of the network, this limit is less interesting.

VXLAN

Because their use with EVPN is only now gaining prominence, I have not encountered numbers greater than four thousand. This is also because most of the deployments of EVPN with VXLAN run legacy enterprise applications on a Clos topology.

The more successful public cloud operators start the virtual network on the host itself and run a proprietary distribution model for the information. So their scaling numbers are vastly different—and not publicly disclosed.

Control Protocols for Network Virtualization

This section examines the control plane for packet forwarding in network virtualization. The primary goal is to leave you with an understanding of the two available models and help you determine which is the better answer for your network.

Relationship of Virtual and Physical Control Plane

Control planes for inline network virtualization typically involve running multiple instances of the standard control plane for a physical network. VLANs, for example, use multiple instances of STP. In the traditional and most popular model, PVST ran a separate instance of STP per VLAN. Due to scaling limits, the standards bodies evolved a variation called MSTP that has gained traction, albeit slowly.

In a somewhat different model, VRF commonly uses multiple instances of the routing protocol, one per VRF. But a single routing protocol process usually supports all these instances.

In the overlay model, a control-plane protocol for virtual networks needs to exchange at least the following pieces of information:

- A mapping of the inner payload's destination address to the tunnel header's destination address
- A list of virtual networks supported at each overlay endpoint

Additional pieces of information might be exchanged—such as the type of tunnel used—depending on the control protocol and features used.

The Centralized Control Model

The primary question that arises in picking a control protocol is how virtual networking is incorporated, especially in the modern data center. Is a virtual network overlay an application that runs over the physical network infrastructure, or is it an inherent part of the networking rubric itself?

I wrote an article arguing that virtual networking in the modern data center is actually an application. I opined, like some others, that overlay virtual networks represented the real use of SDNs (whose history I described in "The Rise of Software-Defined Networking and OpenFlow" on page 55). VMware's NSX, Nuage Networks, and Midokura, among others, embodied this model. Because the virtual endpoints are known only to the compute endpoints, it makes logical sense to have the creator of the virtual endpoint also distribute the mapping information and start the network overlay at the compute endpoint.

VXLAN evolved largely as a response to this model and was adopted by the most successful public cloud operators. Linux's OVS (discussed in "OVS" on page 60) was an example of this model. It included a global database called OVSDB that stored the mapping information, along with some other information. This database was queried to retrieve the relevant information by each overlay endpoint. To allow for bare-metal servers, which did not have any virtual endpoints to communicate with servers that used virtual endpoints, the first-hop router was designated to provide the tunneling function. Routers from various vendors supported OVSDB so that a central controller could set up network tunnels between bare-metal servers and virtual endpoints. This solution was also written as an IETF standard document (RFC 7047 (*https://oreil.ly/GSXcH*)).

However, the centralized model didn't succeed quite as well as was expected.

The Protocol-Based Control Model

Disappointments with VXLAN led to the second model, which uses the control protocols running on the network devices themselves to distribute this mapping information. EVPN is an example of such a solution. EVPN has become quite popular and is increasingly seen as the most acceptable model for deploying overlay virtual networks. This is popularly called the controller-less VXLAN solution.

With the advent of open source routing solutions, such as FRR that support EVPN, I have started to see customers deploying EVPN on the compute endpoints to implement a controller-style solution with the overlay starting on the compute endpoints themselves, but using EVPN instead of OVSDB or other similar protocols.

We discuss EVPN in more detail in Chapter 17.

Vendor Support for Network Virtualization

This section surveys the support for virtual networks in both the open networking ecosystem and traditional networks. We also briefly examine the work in various standards bodies associated with these technologies.

Merchant Silicon

The era of custom switching ASICs built by networking companies seems to be nearing its end. Everyone is increasingly relying on merchant-silicon vendors, as described in Chapter 3, for switching chips. As if to highlight this very switch (pun intended), just about every traditional networking vendor first supported VXLAN on merchant-switching silicon. Broadcom introduced support for it with its Trident2 platform, adding VXLAN routing support in Trident2+ and in the upcoming Trident3 platforms. Mellanox first added support for VXLAN bridging and routing in its Spectrum chipset. Other merchant-silicon vendors such as Barefoot Networks, Marvell's Prestera, and Innovium Networks also support VXLAN, including bridging and routing. All these chips also support VRF. Some switching silicon, especially the newer ones at the time of this writing—such as Mellanox's Spectrum and Broadcom's Trident3—support using IPv6 as the VXLAN tunnel header, whereas the older ones mostly do not. VXLAN, however, happily encapsulates and transmits inner IPv6 payloads.

Software

The Linux kernel itself has natively supported VXLAN for a long time. VRF support in the Linux kernel was added by Cumulus Networks in 2015. This is now broadly available across multiple Linux distributions (for example, Ubuntu had basic IPv4 VRF support as early as version 16.04, released in April 2016). For a stable release of the Linux kernel with full VRF support, target the 4.14 release of the kernel.

Cumulus Linux in the open networking world, as well as all traditional networking vendors, have supported VXLAN for several years. Routing across VXLAN networks is newer. Although the Linux kernel has supported routing across VXLAN networks from the start, some additional support that was required for EVPN has been added. Linux kernel version 4.18 has all the support required for EVPN.

Standards

The IETF is the primary body involved with network virtualization technologies, especially those based on IP and MPLS. VXLAN is an informational RFC, RFC 7348 (*https://oreil.ly/azt3Y*). Most of the network virtualization work takes place under the auspices of the NVO3 (Network Virtualization Overlay over L3) working group at the IETF. Progress is slow, however. Except for some agreement on basic terminology, I'm not aware that any work from the NVO3 working group is supported by any major networking vendor or by Linux. However, EVPN related work is occurring in the L2VPN working group. EVPN in conjunction with VXLAN is still in the draft stages of the standards workflow. But the specification itself has been stable for quite some time. Multiple vendors, along with the open source routing suite FRR, support EVPN with most of its major features.

Illustrating VXLAN Bridging and Routing

Nothing works as well as a packet flow walk-through when trying to understand a protocol. VXLAN is no different. In this section, we use a sample network to illustrate how VXLAN forwarding works, for both the bridging and routing scenarios. There are many questions associated in each of these scenarios. In this section, we concern ourselves only with the data plane; that is, packet forwarding in VXLAN. We study how the various tables get populated via a control plane in Chapter 16. We will also ignore implementation details—specifically silicon implementation—and focus only on the functionality and functional tables. Likewise, we'll postpone some of the more advanced concepts of VXLAN, such as ARP suppression, to a later chapter. We also assume that the switches act as VTEPs; in other words, they do VXLAN encapsulation and decapsulation.

Let's begin with a terse overview of basic bridging and routing in the context of VXLAN, ignoring errors from the network to keep things simple:

1. In bridging, packet forwarding works by looking up a packet's destination MAC address in the MAC table. Every packet, whether it is routed or not, is typically looked up in a MAC table if the receiving interface is a bridged interface.

2. If the received interface is not a bridged interface, such as on interswitch links, the destination MAC address must be owned by the receiving interface or else the packet is dropped. If the destination MAC address on the received packet belongs to the router, the packet is flagged for routing. In case of a bridged interface, the MAC address of the local router is flagged for delivery to a logical interface belonging to the router on that bridge. This is commonly called a Switched VLAN Interface (SVI). If the destination MAC address belongs to the switch's routed interface, the packet is flagged for routing. These concepts are illustrated in Figure 6-4.

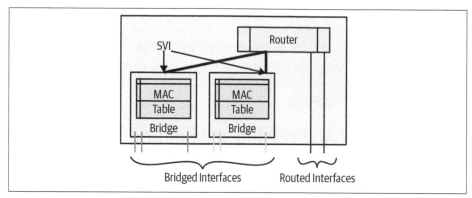

Figure 6-4. SVI and routed interfaces in a switch

3. If the destination MAC address is not addressed to the router, the switch performs a MAC table lookup given the incoming VNI and the destination MAC address. If the outgoing interface is a VXLAN tunnel, the VXLAN tunnel header is added to the packet. After the VXLAN header is added to the packet, the new packet gets routed. In this round of routing, the destination IP address used for the routing lookup is the tunnel header's destination IP address, which is the egress VTEP's IP address.

4. If, however, in the previous step, the packet is flagged for routing, the packet forwarding logic does a lookup in the routing table for the destination IP address in the packet and derives an outgoing interface for the packet. (If there are multiple possible outgoing interfaces, just one is selected.) The output of this lookup also identifies the destination MAC address of the packet, including any additional information such as the VNID associated with this MAC address.

5. If the outgoing interface is a bridge interface, logically this MAC address is then looked up in the MAC table again to derive the outgoing interface to send the packet out of. If the outgoing interface specified by this MAC table lookup is a VXLAN tunnel, packet forwarding works as in step 3. Otherwise, the packet is forwarded out the identified outgoing interface.

6. If the destination IP address is a local VTEP IP address and the packet is identified as a VXLAN packet, the VXLAN header is stripped and the underlying packet is thrown back to the start of the packet forwarding logic, to step 1. This could result in the packet going out VXLAN encapsulated again, albeit usually with a different VNID than the one it came in with.

When packets can be encapsulated post-routing or packets can be routed post-decapsulation, this functionality is often referred to as *Routing In and Out of Tunnels* (RIOT).

We use the topology shown in Figure 6-5 to illustrate VXLAN packet forwarding. The physical network contains two virtual networks: a purple VNI (and purple VLAN) with a subnet of 10.1.0.0/24 represented by the darker line connecting a server to a leaf, and a green VNI (and green VLAN) with a subnet of 10.2.0.0/24 and shown with the lighter line connecting a server to a leaf.

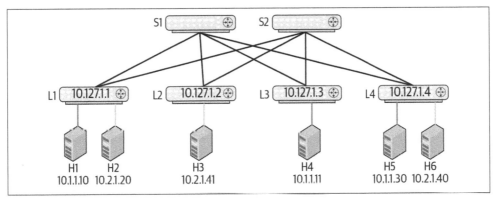

Figure 6-5. Sample topology to explain VXLAN packet flow

The IP addresses shown for leaves L1 through L4 are the VTEP IP addresses of those switches. For example, 10.127.1.3 is the VTEP IP address of L3.

VXLAN Bridging Example: H1 to H5

In this section, we watch a packet travel through a virtual network in the sample topology in Figure 6-5. The endpoints see only their purple virtual network and don't realize that the packet traverses systems that are not part of that network:

1. H1 determines that H5's IP address, 10.1.1.30, is in H1's own subnet. So it determines the MAC address of H5 via ARP. H1 then sends a packet to switch L1 with this MAC address as the destination MAC address and the source MAC address as it's own MAC address. It sends the packet on the purple VLAN.

2. L1 receives this packet and does a lookup in the MAC table with the purple VLAN and the MAC of H5. This is now determined to be the VXLAN tunnel associated with the purple VNID and an egress VTEP of L4, 10.127.1.4.

3. L1 encapsulates the packet with a VXLAN header with the destination VTEP as 10.127.1.4 and the source VTEP as 10.127.1.1.

4. L1 now does a routing lookup on 10.127.1.4 to determine the next hop to reach it. Because there are two possible choices for the next hop, S1 and S2, it uses the hash of the VXLAN header to randomly pick one. Let's assume it picks S2. It then uses the destination MAC address of S2 to send the packet out the interface to S2.

5. S2 receives this packet. Because the destination MAC address belongs to the receiving interface and the interface is a routed interface, S2 does a routing lookup on the destination IP address of the packet, 10.127.1.4. It identifies the packet as coming out of the interface to L4. It then sends the packet to L4 with the destination MAC address set to L4's MAC address and the source MAC address set to itself; in other words, S2.

6. L4 receives this packet. Because the destination MAC address belongs to the receiving interface and the interface is a routed interface, L4 does a routing lookup on the destination IP address of the packet, 10.127.1.4. This matches with its own VTEP IP address, so L4 decapsulates the VXLAN header.

7. The decapsulated packet goes to a MAC table lookup because VXLAN is an L2 overlay tunnel. The destination MAC address on this decapsulated packet is H5's MAC address. The lookup in the MAC table with the purple VNID and this destination MAC returns the result as being out the port to H5. So L4 sends the decapsulated packet to H5.

8. H5 receives this packet. Because the destination MAC address belongs to the receiving interface, H5 accepts the packet and does a routing lookup on the destination IP address, which is 10.1.1.30. This lookup result indicates that the packet is destined to H5 itself, so the host schedules it for local delivery to the process associated with this packet. This terminates the packet delivery.

Figure 6-6 shows the packet headers as the packet progresses from H1 to H5.

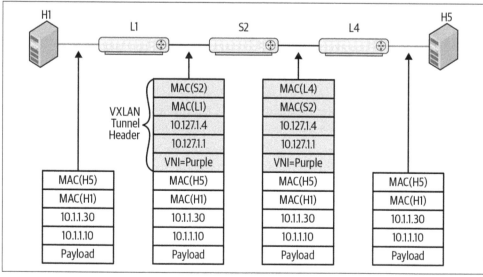

Figure 6-6. Packet headers with VXLAN basic bridging

As shown in the figure, the original packet as crafted by H1 is not modified by any of the VTEPs.

Multidestination frame handling in VXLAN

VXLAN provides two models for handling frames intended for more than one destination. Examples of such frames are broadcast frames, unknown unicast frames, and multicast frames.

In the most common model, the ingress VTEP replicates the frame to every single destination VTEP. This is called *head-end replication* because the ingress VTEP (or the head) replicates a copy of the packet to every destination. To avoid creating duplicate packets and loops, no VTEP receiving such a packet replicates the packet to any other VTEP.

The primary benefit of this approach is that it doesn't require additional control protocols to provide multidestination frame handling and so is quite simple. The disadvantage of this approach is that it doesn't work well if you have to replicate the packet to a very large number of VTEPs or if the number of multidestination frames in the network is small. It is not uncommon for packet-switching silicon to efficiently support replicating to anywhere from 128 to 750 VTEPs. Beyond that, the overhead starts to become noticeable. If the most common multidestination frames are ARP requests, cluster discovery packets, and cluster membership packets, this model works quite well because such traffic consumes very little bandwidth. However, if there is extensive multicast traffic, due to solutions such as IPTV or traditional applications, this solution is not optimal.

The second model creates an routed multicast in the underlay to deliver the packets to multiple destination VTEPs. In such a scenario, the ingress VTEP uses an IP multicast address as the destination IP address, and uses multicast routing to forward the packet (we cover multicast routing in Chapter 8). All nodes in the underlay—VTEPs and transit nodes such as spines—will need to support multicast routing with this option.

As discussed in "Multicast Routing Protocol" on page 165, the most commonly used multicast routing protocol is called PIM-SM. However, the EVPN draft recommends using PIM Source-Specific Multicast (PIM-SSM) because it is more appropriate for this use case. Nonetheless, PIM-SSM is not commonly deployed in enterprise networks. On the other hand, PIM-SM requires additional protocols such as Multicast Source Discovery Protocol (MSDP) for a reliable deployment. We do not have the space to get into explaining leaf03 multicast here. But deploying routed multicast is sufficiently painful that everybody avoids it if possible.

The primary benefit of using multicast is that it can efficiently handle both large numbers of VTEPs and large amounts of multidestination traffic. But the disadvantages far outweigh any advantage. Besides the complexity of enabling PIM and dealing with routed multicast, this model has many other limitations. To ensure that for every virtual network only the associated VTEPs get the packet, each virtual network must be in its own multicast group. But this would result in far too many multicast groups to scale well. So the administrator must now manually map all of the virtual networks into a smaller number of multicast groups. This in turn leads to some VTEPs receiving Broadcast, Unknown unicast, and Multicast (BUM) packets for virtual networks in which they have no interest. Mapping a virtual network to a multicast group also adds significant configuration complexity. An administrator must configure the mapping of virtual network to multicast group on every single VTEP. There is no simple way to ensure that this configuration is consistent and correct across all the VTEPs.

Most, if not all, data center operators, service providers, and cloud service providers disable the use of multicast due to its complexity. But some enterprises think they need this either because they truly have a lot of L2 multicast traffic or because certain vendors push the use of this model in the name of efficiency. So unless your network has a significant quantity of multidestination frames, avoid using routed multicast in the underlay.

VXLAN and Routing: H1 to H6

Let's consider now the scenario in which H1 wants to talk an endpoint in a different subnet, H6. Because H6 is in a different subnet, the packet must be routed. This invokes the functionality we termed RIOT earlier.

As Figure 6-5 shows, the 10.1.1.x and 10.2.1.x subnets are spread across multiple leaves. In such a scenario, the common model is to have every VTEP carrying a subnet be the default gateway for that subnet. So for example, H1, H4, and H5 will all use the same default gateway address, but L1 routes H1's packets, L3 routes H4's packets, and L4 routes H5's packets. This is called the *distributed routing* model.

It is also possible to have only a subset of routers perform the routing for a subnet. For example, for the 10.2.1.x subnet, it is possible to have only leaf L2 be the router. This is called the *centralized routing* model. We discuss the deployment scenarios for the different models in a later chapter. For the example that follows, we assume the distributed routing model.

Here are the steps in the packet flow when H1 sends a packet to H6:

1. Because H1 knows that H6 is in a different subnet based on H1's IP address (10.1.1.10/24 is in a different subnet from 10.2.1.40), it sends a packet with the destination MAC set to the default gateway, which in this case is L1's MAC address.

2. L1 receives this packet. Seeing that it is addressed to the router, L1 proceeds to route the packet. Because the subnet representing H6's IP address is spread

across multiple leaves, the routing (plus ARP) lookup yields the specific egress VTEP associated with H6's IP address. There are two ways the routing lookup can accomplish this. The lookup can yield H6's MAC address directly, or it can yield the router MAC address of the egress VTEP, L4. The former approach is called *asymmetric routing* and the latter is called *symmetric routing*. The control protocol and deployment model dictate which model is picked, and the routing table is populated appropriately. In either model, the VNID in the VXLAN header must be present on both the ingress and the egress VTEP. In the asymmetric model, the VNID used is the VNI that 10.2.1.0/24 belongs to, green in this example. In the symmetric model, a new VNI that represents the VRF shared by the 10.1.1.0/24 and 10.2.1.0/24 subnets is used as the VNID in the packet sent from L1 to L4.

3. Independent of the routing model picked by L1, L4 is always the egress VTEP; the VXLAN header always carries the IP address of L4 as the destination IP address. After the VXLAN header is added, packet forwarding works similar to the bridging case, with the VXLAN-encapsulated packet routed to L4 via S2 (or S1).

4. Upon reaching L4, the VXLAN header is stripped because L4 is the egress VTEP and the destination IP address on the received packet is L4's IP address. Because VXLAN is an L2 tunnel, in either routing model, L4 does a MAC table lookup with the decapsulated packet's destination MAC address and the VNI provided in the VXLAN header. In case of asymmetric routing, because the destination MAC address belongs to H6, the packet is bridged directly to H6. In case of symmetric routing, because the destination MAC address is that of the router, L4 does another routing lookup, this time on the decapsulated packet's destination IP address. The routing lookup results in the packet being forwarded to H6.

Figure 6-7 shows the packet headers for asymmetric routing from H1 to H6. The VXLAN header looks much like the bridging case except that the VNI is different because H6 is in a different subnet than H1. However, the MAC addresses of H1's original packet are rewritten at the ingress VTEP, L1. Alternatively, Figure 6-8 shows the packet headers for symmetric routing from H1 to H6. The destination MAC address post-routing at L1 points to L4's MAC address, not H6's. L4 therefore routes the packet to H6.

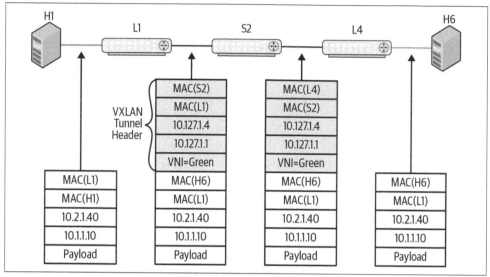

Figure 6-7. VXLAN asymmetric routing packet flow

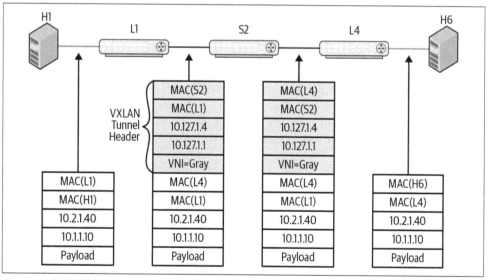

Figure 6-8. VXLAN symmetric routing packet flow

Support for multicast routing in overlay networks

We discussed using multicast in the underlay network as a mechanism to efficiently deliver multidestination overlay network virtualized frames. Additionally, it is also possible that a network migrating from a traditional access-aggregation-core network to the Clos-based network requires multicast routing in the overlay network. Some control protocols such as EVPN have evolved to support this model. However, I have not often encountered this model. In my opinion, adding this level of complexity degrades the reliability and simplicity of Clos-based networks, Given this and because such applications are not commonplace in the data center, I recommend that users seriously consider whether it is better to stay with existing networks if they require multicast overlay.

Summarizing VXLAN Bridging and Routing

As described earlier, VXLAN is an L2 virtual network overlay—a network tunnel. A tunnel typically looks like a single hop to the tunnel endpoints from the perspective of, say, a command such as *traceroute*. Figure 6-9 summarizes this high-level perspective of VXLAN.

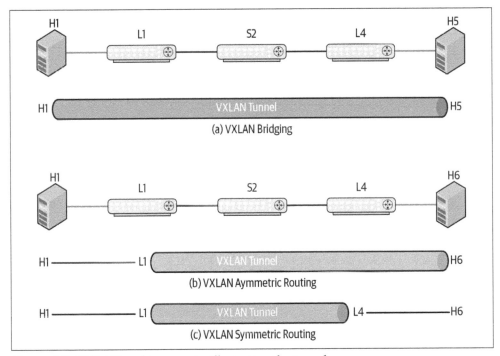

Figure 6-9. VXLAN and traceroute, illustrating the tunnel

In the bridging example, the *traceroute* output from 10.1.1.10 (H1) to 10.1.1.30 (H5) shows only nodes H1 and H6 because the entire packet is considered bridged. The VTEPs themselves are not seen as being part of the path in the case of bridging. So even though the VXLAN tunnel starts at L1 and ends at L4, from the perspective of the end hosts H1 and H6, it looks like they're connected by a wire. This is shown in Figure 6-9(a).

In the case of routing, Figure 6-9(b) shows the world as seen by *traceroute* for asymmetric routing, and Figure 6-9(c) shows the perspective for symmetric routing. So a *traceroute* of asymmetric routing reveals only three hops—H1, L1, and H6—whereas a *traceroute* of symmetric routing reveals four hops—H1, L1, L4, and H6.

In all cases, the VXLAN-encapsulated packet is routed from L1 to L4.

Summary

In this chapter, we studied network virtualization as another fundamental tool used inside the data center. Specifically, we examined three specific virtualization technologies—VLAN, VRF, and VXLAN—and examined their use cases. We noted the pros and cons of network tunnels. In the next chapter, we examine the various networking constructs available on the Linux platform for use with containers, because these form the basis for building efficient communications for microservices.

## CHAPTER 7

Container Networking

Architecture is basically a container of something. I hope they will enjoy not so much the tea-cup, but the tea.
—Yoshio Taniguchi

The evolution of application architectures has led to the current trend of *microservices*. Containers are the teacup delivering the tea that is microservices. If networks exist to serve the applications, it is important to understand what are the networking constructs supported best by containers for an efficient distributed systems design. As a cloud native technology, containers support simpler, more scalable, and sophisticated network options. Thus, the juxtaposition of Kubernetes with open source routing suites allows the reconsideration of how networking is done. Traditional networking features such as routing and tunnels are no longer the sole purview of specialized routers and bridges. An understanding of container networking constructs will therefore help a network engineer or designer use them with traditional routers to build a network that is best suited to the organization's business needs. Because Linux is the de facto leader and host OS in the modern data center, this chapter will focus on the constructs provided by Linux. The goal is not so much to encourage everyone to migrate to Linux and containers as it is to educate and to make you aware of the possibilities. And how some of the pioneers are taking advantage of these possibilities.

How is this chapter on container networking different from the dozens of similar-sounding ones out there? The primary differences I believe are two-fold. First, this is an attempt at addressing networking as a network engineer or architect might consider it, compared to an application engineer. Second, most descriptions I've encountered on this topic deal with a host perspective, assuming that you have no control of the network side of the equation. So they tend to either rule out or gloss over options that might be viable and more robust when the application developer and network engineer can work together. This is one way that the good cloud providers become so efficient as well as a way that I've seen the more innovative data centers out there built. So I hope this chapter has something new to offer to the discussion than the usual assumption that "Application is application, network is network, and never shall the engineers of the twain talk."

Although containers are quite the hip and trending server virtualization technology, virtual machines (VMs) still dominate among deployed technologies. Enterprise data centers are still largely VMware shops. Besides the use of VMs, traditional enterprise applications run much more often on Windows rather than on Linux or over the web. But even these traditional enterprises deploy a decent percentage of Linux VMs, via VMware. From a networking perspective, VMware largely provides only Layer 2 (L2) constructs, is deployed that way, and is a closed piece of software. Linux, on the other hand, has been making significant inroads in its support of networking constructs. As Linux matures and is found in more places, its networking features have also grown. Proprietary operating systems and hypervisors such as VMware and Hyper-V are working to reconstruct the microservices-based application architecture pioneered on Linux.

This chapter helps answer the following questions:

- What container networking constructs are available on Linux?
- What are the constraints and performance characteristics of the various choices?

Introduction to Containers

Containers are defined a couple of different ways, one focused on packaging and the other on the execution environment. As a packaging model, a container bundles the application code together with its dependencies, configuration, and data such that it can run without requiring that these things be provided by the environment in which it runs. As an execution model, a container is an isolation unit that enforces limits on much of a resource—CPU, memory, and so on—that it uses. Thus, a container allows the sharing of resources on a server running a common OS. A single container can run multiple processes.

A container is more heavyweight than a process but less heavyweight than a VM. Like a process and unlike a VM, the container shares the OS with other containers running on the same host. But unlike a process, and akin to a VM, each container has its own private view of the network, including hostname and domain name, processes, users, filesystems, and interprocess communication. New proposals for isolating more features, such as time and syslog, are in progress.

The container execution model is a user space construct built on the dual Linux kernel constructs of *namespaces* and *control groups* or *cgroups*. Cgroups are a Linux kernel feature that enforces limits on the resources consumed by a collection of processes. Namespaces provide the isolation. We begin our discussion of container networking with a discussion of network namespaces.

Container Landscape and Scoping the Discussion

The container landscape is littered with buzzwords and solutions that cater to multiple needs. At a fundamental level, any container network must address the following questions:

- How does a container interface get an IP address?
- How does a container communicate with the external world?
- How does a container communicate with other containers? A container can be running on the same host or on a different node in a multihost scenario.

In this chapter, we discuss mostly the support available from Docker. Docker, although still popular, seems to be making way for containerd, and in Kubernetes circles, its equivalent CRI-containerd. However, these differences do not affect the questions pertinent to us in this book—questions about networking. So we focus the discussion using Docker, but we will not get into Docker-only solutions. Those interested in understanding the different container runtimes can find them on the Kubernetes website (*https://oreil.ly/jFDMm*).

Namespaces

Namespaces are a Linux kernel virtualization construct akin to network and server virtualization. Namespaces virtualize specific resources managed by the kernel, thereby allowing multiple isolated instances of a virtual resource. A process is associated with one such virtual instance of the resource. Multiple processes can belong to a common virtual instance of the resource. From the processes' perspective, they appear to fully own the resource.

Namespaces are fully usable as a virtualization construct since kernel version 3.8. The kernel supports virtualization of the following six resources:

Cgroup
> Virtualizes the view of a process's cgroups as seen via */proc/pid/cgroup* and */proc/pid/mountinfo*, where *pid* is the process ID of the process. One reason for doing this is to prevent containerized applications from discerning that they're running within a container.

Interprocess Communication (IPC)
Virtualizes the various constructs for IPC, such as POSIX message queues, shared memory, semaphores, and so on. This also prevents processes from reaching across their isolation unit to mess with another process's state.

Network
Virtualizes all the networking resources, such as interfaces, sockets, routing table, MAC table, and so on. We discuss network namespaces a little more in the following section.

Mount
Virtualizes the filesystem mount points. This allows each group of isolated processes to think they own the root filesystem, whereas in reality their root is usually just a constrained view of a larger filesystem. chroot, a very old Unix construct, merely constrained the view of the root seen by a single process.

PID
Virtualizes the process ID space. This is also useful as a technique to prevent processes from discovering that they're containerized. Every container has a process with a PID of 1 (the init process) just like on a bare-metal server.

User
Virtualizes the users and the user and group IDs. Every isolated group of processes has a root user that acts as root only within that virtual instance.

UTS
Virtualizes the hostname and domain name such that each isolated unit can set its own hostname and domain name without affecting the others or the parent.

Using namespaces, it is possible to construct a logical router. Many traditional routers have far less-beefy CPUs than servers, so namespaces make it possible to support logical routers more tenably than with VMs. Such a construct allows a network administrator to provide different tenants with their own view and management of a physical infrastructure. Of course, using VMs to provide logical routers means that you can provide each tenant with a different version of the router OS, but I suspect this is less interesting in most cases.

Network Namespaces

The concept of a *network namespace* (aka *netns*) is akin to network virtualization, but a more heavyweight virtualization construct, because it encompasses the entire network stack all the way up to and including the transport layer of the network stack. You can have two separate containers each running a server serving port 80 traffic, for example. The common network virtualization constructs virtualize only a single layer, (L2) or Layer 3 (L3). Multiple such constructs need to be deployed concurrently to provide virtualization of multiple layers.

The Linux kernel creates a loopback interface in the netns when a new netns is created. For example, see the link information in a newly created netns (to make the output fit into the formatting for this book, we trim the columns and text that's irrelevant to this discussion using the ellipsis character (…):

```
$ sudo ip netns add myown
$ sudo nsenter --net=/var/run/netns/myown ip -d link show
1: lo: <LOOPBACK> mtu 65536 qdisc noop state DOWN mode DEFAULT ...
    link/loopback 00:00:00:00:00:00 brd 00:00:00:00:00:00 ...
eui64 numtxqueues 1 numrxqueues 1 gso_max_size 65536 gso_max_segs 65535
```

Network Namespaces Versus Virtual Routing and Forwarding

This sidebar is a bit of a tangent to container networking, but it's here because this is a somewhat important topic. During my time at Cumulus Networks, one critical question on our minds was whether we needed a new Linux kernel construct called VRF or whether we could take advantage of the already existing construct of network namespaces. Some vendors such as 6Wind and Arista had implemented a version of VRF using network namespaces. In the end we decided on adding a new functionality because the isolation provided by network namespaces was too strong. Overcoming it involved going through unnatural contortions that would only confuse network users rather than help them. The goal of adding VRFs was to ensure that most, if not all, applications could support all the common operations of a network engineer without modifying the application. Let's consider a few examples.

The most common deployment model of routers puts the management port in a separate VRF, typically called the *management VRF* (see "Separating Switch Management Network from Data Traffic" on page 115 for details). Because the management port is not shared with the actual data traffic port, assigning the management port to a management network namespace would have worked just as well without the need for a VRF construct. Coming in through the management port would automatically put the user who is using SSH to access the node in the management namespace, as well. So far, so good. Network namespaces seem to do the job fine.

However, network admins are used to running `ping` and `traceroute` commands, looking at routing tables and such, all in the context of the data traffic's VRF, not the management VRF. To do this with network namespaces would require them to consciously jump out of their namespace into the data traffic namespace via, say, the `ip netns exec` command. This is just cumbersome and prone to errors. VRFs allow administrators to accomplish their networking tasks as easily as on traditional routers, without the possibility of errors and without imposing an onerous burden on an already burdened network administrator.

With the implementation of a true VRF construct, network operators can execute *ping* and *traceroute* for specific VRFs via the traditional interface option (the *-I* option to *ping* or the *-i* option to *traceroute*). This is because the VRF implementation in the Linux kernel acts as a virtual interface allowing all commands that bind to an interface to automatically work in the context of a VRF without requiring any changes. Linux supports the notion of a master interface associated with an interface that governed the packet forwarding behavior of an interface. For example, the individual interfaces that make up a bond (or port channel for those more familiar with that name) are slaves to the master interface that is the bond. The VRF uses this same construct to provide the appropriate routing tables and such, as soon as a process binds to the VRF interface.

The next problem that network namespaces face in the context of VRF is the support for what is called *route leaking* between VRFs. A shared resource must often be reachable from multiple VRFs. In such cases, an administrator manually adds routes ("leaks" them, in other words) in one VRF that reaches across into another VRF. It is also common to have a global or internet VRF that encompasses the routing table for reaching entities outside a given VRF if there is no match for a route within that VRF. To leak routes across namespaces involves a contortion using virtual Ethernet interfaces, which make troubleshooting difficult and the general construct more challenging for an administrator to follow.

For these reasons among others, a separate construct specifically targeted to addressing VRFs was added to the Linux kernel. VRFs are usable from kernel version 4.14.

Virtual Ethernet Interfaces

An interface in one netns must use an external connection to send or receive a packet from an interface in a different netns on the same physical system. Linux provides a virtual interface construct called *veth*, for virtual Ethernet, to allow communication outside of a netns. veths are always created in pairs. What goes into one end of a veth automatically comes out the other end. The following snippet shows the creation of veth in pairs:

```
$ sudo ip link add veth1 type veth
$ ip -br link show type veth
veth0@veth1       DOWN            c2:9c:96:5c:fa:bf <BROADCAST,MULTICAST,M-DOWN>
veth1@veth0       DOWN            8a:69:f2:c9:76:e7 <BROADCAST,MULTICAST,M-DOWN>
```

So, to allow communication from inside a netns to the outside, you put one end of the veth into the netns, and the other end into wherever you want the outside communication to go. For example, when you create a container via the docker command, a veth pair is created with one end inside the created container's netns and the other end in the default or host netns. This way you can set up communication between a container and an outside world. Figure 7-1 illustrates such a use of veth in

Linux. NS1 and NS2 are separate net namespaces with a veth interface enabling communication between them.

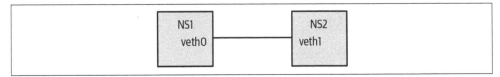

Figure 7-1. veth interfaces in Linux

The most common network interface created inside a container, at least in Docker, is a veth interface, especially when used with the default Docker bridged network. A simple way to check the type of the interface in a container is to execute the ip -d link show command. Some minimal containers such as alpine do not support the -d option to ip link show. In such cases, if you can use the nsenter command, you can do the following (assuming the name of the container you want to inspect is "container1"):

```
$ sudo nsenter -t `docker inspect --format '{{.State.Pid}}'
                container1` -n ip -d link show
1: lo: <LOOPBACK,UP,LOWER_UP> mtu 65536 qdisc noqueue state UNKNOWN ...
default qlen 1
    link/loopback 00:00:00:00:00:00 brd 00:00:00:00:00:00 promiscuity ...
17: eth0@if18: <BROADCAST,MULTICAST,UP,LOWER_UP> mtu 1500 qdisc noqueue ...
    link/ether 02:42:ac:11:00:02 brd ff:ff:ff:ff:ff:ff link-netnsid 0 ...
    veth addrgenmode eui64
$
```

You can see that eth0 is of type veth.[1] This veth interface has an ifindex[2] of 17 and the other veth interface of this pair is at ifindex 18, as shown by @if18 in the interface information. If you examine the output of *ip link show* on the host, you see the following:

```
$ ip -d link show
...
4: docker0: <BROADCAST,MULTICAST,UP,LOWER_UP> mtu 1500 ... state UP ...
    link/ether 02:42:f5:4c:09:f4 brd ff:ff:ff:ff:ff:ff promiscuity 0
    bridge forward_delay 1500 hello_time 200 max_age 2000 ...
32768 vlan_filtering 0 vlan_protocol 802.1Q addrgenmode eui64
18: vethcd16cb7@if17: <BROADCAST,MULTICAST,UP,LOWER_UP> ... master docker0 ...
    link/ether ba:66:d1:d2:70:df brd ff:ff:ff:ff:ff:ff link-netnsid 0 ...
    veth
    bridge_slave state forwarding priority 32 cost 2 hairpin off ...
```

---

1 Docker rewrites the interface name to eth0 to provide the illusion of a bare-metal host environment for the application.

2 ifindex is short for interface index and is a unique ID assigned to every interface in a box.

`vethcd16cb7` is the veth interface with an ifindex of 18, and it is a member of the `docker0` bridge.

Container Networking: Diving In

Container networking has four operating modes:

- No network
- Host network
- Single-host network
- Multihost network

The first mode is used when a container has no desire to communicate with the outside world and so has no network connectivity of any sort. There is no reason to say more about this mode in this chapter.

In the second mode, the container shares the network namespace with the host OS. In other words, the container sees everything that the host sees with no isolation. The benefit of this is that the network performance is almost the same as the host OS network performance, because there are no overheads between the container and the outside world. When run in a privileged mode, the container can modify the host operating system's network state such as routing table, MAC table, interface state, and so on. FRR, the open source routing suite, when running as a container on a server, runs in privileged mode, allowing routing to be provided as a containerized service on a server. This helps, for example, users who deploy all applications as containers and would prefer to not make an exception for just routing. Mesos, the container-based compute cluster–management software, also uses host networking as the default network type. The main disadvantage of this mode is that containers share the network state, thereby making it difficult to have two containers using the same TCP/UDP port number to communicate with the outside world.

Single-host network is the default network provided by Docker. In this mode, containers running on the same host can communicate with one another in addition to communicating with the outside world. We discuss this in more detail in the following sections.

In the final mode, multihost container network allows containers running on different servers to communicate with one another. We discuss this model also in more detail, after discussing the single-host network model.

Single-Host Container Networking

In this section, we examine the two common ways in which containers running on the same host can communicate with one another and with the outside world.

Bridge

When a Docker service is first instantiated, it creates a docker0 device, which is a Linux bridge. Whenever new containers are created via the docker run command without specifying a network option, Docker creates a veth pair of interfaces, assigns one of them to the container's netns, and attaches the other to the docker0 bridge. Additional containers created in a similar fashion have the same behavior. Thus, multiple containers created on the host can communicate with one another because one end of the veth interfaces in each of these containers is connected to the docker0 bridge, as illustrated in Figure 7-2.

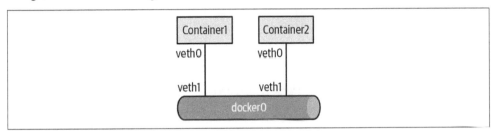

Figure 7-2. docker0 bridge as the default network for containers

Docker uses a default subnet of 172.17.0.0/16 to the docker0 bridge. It assigns the address 172.17.0.1 to the bridge itself. As a container is spun up that has a network interface associated with the docker0 bridge, Docker automatically assigns an unused IP address from the docker0 subnet, 172.17.0.0/16, to the container. Docker also adds a default route in the container's namespace that specifies the next hop as the docker0's IP address, 172.17.0.1. Docker by default also configures any packet from the bridge destined to the outside world to undergo NAT so that multiple containers can share a single host IP address to communicate with entities other than the host.

Figure 7-3 shows the sequence of actions in which container1 wants to communicate with an external web server. Both the host running the Docker container and the web server are on the 192.168.0.0/24 network, Docker is at 192.168.0.23, and the web server is at 192.168.1.2.

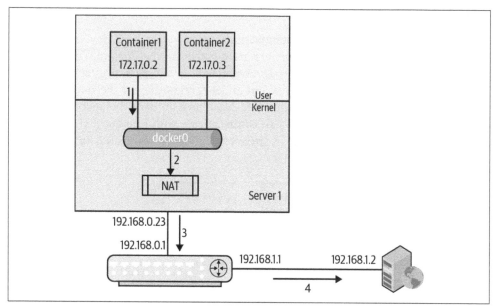

Figure 7-3. External communication via docker0

1. Because the address 192.168.1.2 is outside Container1's subnet of 172.17.0.5/16, it sends the packet to its configured default gateway, which is 172.17.0.1, as part of normal routing.

2. The Linux kernel stack receives this packet, does a route lookup, and decides that the packet is destined to its default gateway, which is 192.168.0.1, an external router.

3. Docker has set up the *iptables* rules so that any communication from docker0 to the outside world undergoes NAT. Therefore the source port and source IP address of the packet are modified before being sent to the external router.

4. The external router routes the packet to the web server.

Example 7-1 shows the output of *iptables*.

Example 7-1. iptables output showing NAT performed on Docker bridge

```
$ sudo iptables -L -t nat
Chain PREROUTING (policy ACCEPT)
target     prot opt source          destination
DOCKER     all  --  anywhere        anywhere        ADDRTYPE match dst-type LOCAL

Chain INPUT (policy ACCEPT)
target     prot opt source          destination
```

```
Chain OUTPUT (policy ACCEPT)
target     prot opt source        destination
DOCKER     all  -- anywhere       !localhost/8  ADDRTYPE match dst-type LOCAL

Chain POSTROUTING (policy ACCEPT)
target     prot opt source        destination
MASQUERADE all  -- 172.17.0.0/16  anywhere    ❶

Chain DOCKER (2 references)
target     prot opt source        destination
RETURN     all  -- anywhere       anywhere
$
```

❶ This line indicates the NAT action post-routing. This line indicates that packets
   with the source address matching the 172.17.0.0/16 subnet and destined to any
   other destination, local or otherwise, must be NAT'd. Masquerade is the iptables
   module that performs NAT, among other things.

If a container wants to communicate with another container associated with the same
bridge, the docker0 bridge bridges the traffic to the appropriate container.

Containers connected to the same network, docker0 for example, can communicate
with one another by default. However, containers connected to other networks on the
same host cannot communicate with one another by default. For example, if we create another bridge called docker1 (via *docker network create docker1*) and create a
Container3 attached to it, Container1 connected to docker0 cannot talk to Con-
tainer3 by default.

Although the bridge mode is commonly used as a single-host mode, you'll see in a
later section how, when combined with a routing daemon on the host OS, we can also
use it for multihost container communication.

Macvlan

As an alternative to using a bridge for single-host container communication, you can
use a Macvlan, an L2 virtual network interface associated with a physical interface.
The kernel driver assigns each Macvlan interface a unique MAC address.[3] The kernel
delivers an incoming packet to the Macvlan interface whose MAC address matches
the packet's destination MAC address, and thereby to the correct container.

Figure 7-4(a) shows the Macvlan network to which the containers are connected, and
the Macvlan network itself is directly attached to a physical interface. The containers
associated with the Macvlan network need to be assigned IP addresses in a subnet

---

3 Docker generates the MAC address with the upper-three bytes set to 02:42:ac, which is an unassigned Organizationally Unique Identifier (OUI).

associated with the upstream interface. In the figure, the upstream router assumes the interface is in the subnet 192.168.0.0/24 with its own interface being assigned the address 192.168.0.1. The host is assigned the address 192.168.0.101/24, and the containers are assigned the addresses 192.168.0.128 and 192.168.0.129.

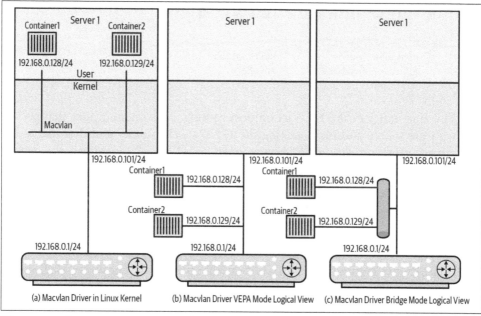

Figure 7-4. Containers using Macvlan as seen by the Linux kernel

This addressing convention raises the first consideration in using Macvlan interfaces. By default, Docker assigns the IP address when a container is spun up. To avoid IP address conflicts with any other noncontainer on the same upstream network, you need to either provide Docker with a range that will not be used by the upstream device's IP address assigner (typically a Dynamic Host Configuration Protocol [DHCP] server) or manually assign the IP address as each container is spun up. Unfortunately, there is no easy, prebuilt method to allow the container interface to request an address assignment using DHCP to the upstream router. You'll need to use a third-party plugin driver or roll your own IP Address Management (IPAM) module to handle such scenarios.

Fortunately, the docker network create command solves part of the problem. Its --ip-range option makes Docker use a smaller range within the subnet to allocate the IP address to the containers. Following is an example command:

```
$ docker network create -d macvlan \
  --subnet=192.168.0.0/24  \
  --ip-range=192.168.0.128/25 \
  --gateway=192.168.0.1  \
```

```
--aux-address="my-router=192.168.0.129" \
-o parent=eth1 macv
```

Although the host and the containers are in the same subnet and run on the same Linux kernel, they cannot ping each other directly. Figure 7-4(b) and (c) show the actual behavior of a Macvlan. To ping the host it is running on, the packet must go up to the upstream device, the router, and then come back. This is called *hairpinning*. As shown in Figure 7-4(b), even containers connected to the same Macvlan device cannot ping one another directly. This is called the *VEPA mode* [4] of the Macvlan driver.

By default, Docker creates a Macvlan network in a different mode called *bridge mode*, shown in Figure 7-4(c). In bridge mode, containers connected to the same Macvlan can talk to each other directly without hairpinning. However, communicating with the host itself still requires hairpinning.

Figure 7-5 compares packet forwarding in a regular bridge versus Macvlan in VEPA mode. The primary benefit of a Macvlan network in VEPA mode over a bridge is better performance. The Macvlan's interface sits directly on the physical interface associated with it. Unlike a bridge, no additional processing is required to deliver a packet from one end of a veth interface to the other end, from there to a bridge, and then to physical interface on its way out. Furthermore, there is no NAT performed in this model. Every container has an externally reachable IP address. However, if containers on the same host need to communicate with one another, putting the Macvlan interface in bridge mode is more efficient because it prevents traffic from being hairpinned to communicate with one another.

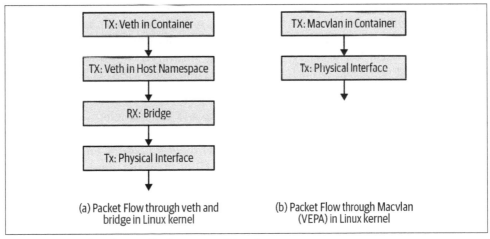

(a) Packet Flow through veth and bridge in Linux kernel

(b) Packet Flow through Macvlan (VEPA) in Linux kernel

Figure 7-5. Packet flow in bridge versus Macvlan

---

4 For Virtual Ethernet Port Aggregator, the IEEE standard that defined this behavior.

There is one caveat when using a Macvlan device. Most NICs accept only 512 or so MAC addresses as their own addresses. Beyond that, the NIC must be put in the poorer-performing promiscuous mode. So ensure that you do not overflow the NICs MAC address filter with too many container MAC addresses.

Multihost Container Networking

So far, we considered container communication constrained to a single host. In this section, we see how multihost container communication works. When considering multihost container communication, you need to address the following questions:

- Are the containers connected at L2 or L3?
- How is address management handled when containers are spread across multiple hosts?
- What are the various implications of the available choices?

Macvlans, discussed earlier, can provide an L2 multihost container networking answer. In this section, we consider two more.

Overlay network

Docker defines a network type called *overlay* for a multihost connectivity. Although the documentation doesn't make it explicit, the overlay network used is VXLAN, which we studied in Chapter 6. This is an L2 network. In other words, the containers spread across the hosts are in the same subnet. In such a scenario, coordinating IP address assignments for the same subnet across hosts is no longer as simple as the local Docker daemon allocating the address on container spinup. Therefore, Docker requires the Swarm functionality when creating an overlay network. Swarm is the Docker control plane that handles IP Address Management (IPAM) across multiple hosts, provides service abstraction, and so on.

There are other overlay solutions, such as Weave and Flannel, that we can use with containers instead of Docker's overlay. Each of these has its own specific agent (Swarm is specific to Docker's overlay) that synchronizes network information such as IP address allocation across multiple nodes. All of them use some form of a distributed key/value store to store the coordination information.[5]

Figure 7-6 shows how everything is hooked up at the data plane; that is, from the perspective of packet forwarding. The containers in the two different servers all belong to the same subnet, 172.17.0.0/24. Server 1 has a VTEP IP address of 192.168.0.23,

---

5 It is rather puzzling to me that none of these solutions has chosen to implement a DHCP relay plugin and use a common DHCP server to coordinate everything rather than using a key/value store.

whereas Server 2's VTEP IP is 192.168.10.41. The routers will have exchanged routing information so that all the routers know how to reach the 192.168.0.0/24 and 192.168.10.0/24 subnets. So a VXLAN-encapsulated packet from Server 1 to Server 2 would be routable across the network shown.

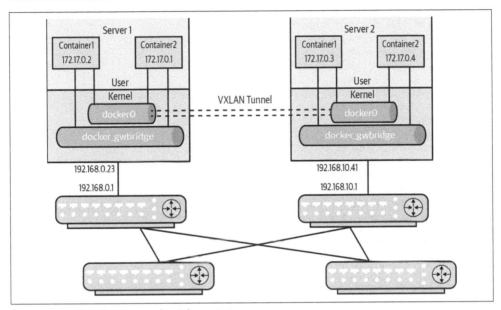

Figure 7-6. Overlay network with containers

From the container's perspective, a veth interface hooked up to a Linux bridge works just as in a single-host bridge network. However, under the covers, the overlay network also creates a VXLAN tunnel between the nodes in the network. The VXLAN tunnel is hooked up to the bridge (typically docker0) to which the veths are connected. Every node that is joined in Swarm (or Flannel or Weave) has a VXLAN tunnel created and attached to the bridge to allow packets to tunnel through the underlay network.

When overlay networking is used, Docker sets up two interfaces inside a container. One is for the communication between containers in the same subnet using the overlay. The other communicates with the outside world. This new interface is also a veth, but it's connected to a different bridge called *docker_gwbridge*. It also gets its own IP subnet. The routing table inside a container is set up to use the appropriate interface for each form of communication. Let's examine this. Consider the following output, which shows a series of commands executed and their resulting outputs. To make the output fit into the formatting for this book, we trim the columns and text that's irrelevant to this discussion using the ellipsis character (…):

```
$ docker network create -d overlay --subnet=172.16.86.0/24 \          ❶
        --gateway=172.16.86.1 --attachable overlay
```

```
kjq9b3psbrvtxdaxnxvp1j52y
$ docker run --rm -itd --network overlay --name test1 alpine        ❷
e02b42e392c05e8d0a34597df7f10687f9afccd597d75f14781c4e787020145c
$ docker attach test1
/ # ip route show                                                    ❸
default via 172.19.0.1 dev eth1
172.16.86.0/24 dev eth0 scope link  src 172.16.86.2
172.19.0.0/16 dev eth1 scope link  src 172.19.0.3
/ # read escape sequence
$ sudo nsenter -t `docker inspect --format '{{.State.Pid}}'          ❹
                   test1` -n ip -d link show
1: lo: <LOOPBACK,UP,LOWER_UP> mtu 65536 qdisc noqueue state ...
default qlen 1000
    link/loopback 00:00:00:00:00:00 brd 00:00:00:00:00:00 ...
numtxqueues 1 numrxqueues 1 gso_max_size 65536 gso_max_segs 65535
111: eth0@if112: <BROADCAST,MULTICAST,UP,LOWER_UP> mtu 1450 qdisc...
    link/ether 02:42:ac:10:56:02 brd ff:ff:ff:ff:ff:ff link-netnsid 0 ...
    veth addrgenmode eui64 numtxqueues 1 numrxqueues 1 ...
113: eth1@if114: <BROADCAST,MULTICAST,UP,LOWER_UP> mtu 1500 ...
    link/ether 02:42:ac:13:00:03 brd ff:ff:ff:ff:ff:ff link-netnsid 1 ...
    veth addrgenmode eui64 numtxqueues 1 numrxqueues 1 ...
$ ip link show veth71a0f27                                           ❺
114: veth71a0f27@if113: <BROADCAST, ... master docker_gwbridge
    link/ether 12:8f:e7:bd:7b:92 brd ff:ff:ff:ff:ff:ff link-netnsid 4
```

❶ We create a new network of the type "overlay."

❷ We create a new container and ask that it use the newly created overlay network.

❸ Inside the container, we view the contents of the IP routing table. We see that the routing table has the default route pointing out 172.19.0.1 and interface eth1.

❹ We exit the container to execute the command from the host because alpine's minimal command set includes a limited version of the iproute2 command set. This output shows that eth1 is a veth whose partner has the ifindex 114 (eth1@if114).

❺ The output of the ip link show veth71a0f27 command shows that this veth is the one with the ifindex 114. It also shows the master interface for this veth is docker_gwbridge; in other words, this interface is a part of the docker_gwbridge bridge.

Packets going through docker_gwbridge undergo NAT by default, just as in the case of docker0 bridge. Although it is possible to change the default IP subnet used by docker_gwbridge, it does not seem possible to change the type to be anything other than a Linux bridge in Docker version 18.09.4.

Direct routing

An alternative to an overlay solution is to use routing, an L3 solution. This solution uses a single-host container network driver, typically the bridge driver, to build multiple host containers that are then connected via routing. NAT for the bridge subnet must be turned off to use this solution. A routing daemon (say ospf or bgp from FRR) running on the individual servers announces either the individual container addresses or the bridge subnet.

Suppressing NAT in Docker

To turn off NAT, create a *daemon.json* file in the */etc/docker* directory containing the following fragment:

```
{
    "ip-masq": false
}
```

Restart docker via `systemctl restart docker` and the masquerade line from the iptables output (described in Example 7-1) will be gone. If this does not happen, you might need to reboot the server.

For the case of advertising only the bridge subnet, when the first container is attached to the bridge, the subnet route is advertised, and when the last container connected to the bridge terminates, the subnet route is withdrawn. This happens automatically using existing routing advertisement logic because the bridge moves its interface state to up when the first container is spun up and attaches to the bridge, and the bridge moves its interface state to down when the last container attached to the bridge terminates.

Drivers such as Calico follow this model. They also provide additional features, such as ensuring that policies are enforced independent of where a container is instantiated.

Kube-router is another solution that we can deploy with Kubernetes to provide a direct routing solution for multihost container connectivity.

Figure 7-7 shows this solution. Notice how this looks very much like the Figure 7-3 architecture, except that there is no NAT in this solution and there is a routing daemon that is advertising the container route. If the routing daemon used is an independent daemon such as FRR, the only route that can be advertised with no additional code is the bridge subnet route. When the routing daemon is part of the driver solution, such as with Kube-router or Calico, individual container addresses can be advertised.

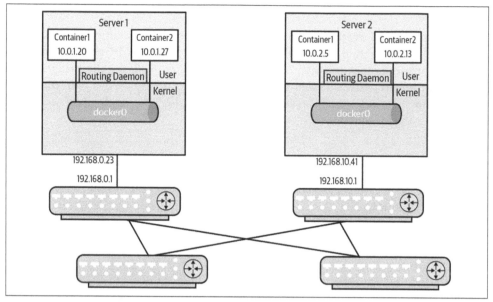

Figure 7-7. Routing for multihost container networking

The one disadvantage of this solution is the inability to assign IP addresses from the same subnet across multiple nodes.

Comparing Different Container Network Solutions

With so many possible choices, what are some things to ponder before deciding on a solution? Based on just performance numbers, my recommendation is to avoid any overlay solution. The performance numbers that I saw in late 2018 indicated that the overlay network driver had terrible performance in comparison to the other drivers. This includes any kind of overlay, including Weave and Flannel, not just Docker's overlay.

Next up, consider Macvlan versus a Linux bridge with respect to the packet flow in the Linux kernel, as shown in Figure 7-5.

As discussed earlier, there is additional processing involved in the veth/bridge case that is not present in the Macvlan case. In addition, these packets are NAT'd unless you explicitly disable it. When a bridge is used in conjunction with a routing daemon to do multihost networking, NAT is not used.

Macvlan devices have no routing table lookup, and in VEPA mode, there's no MAC table lookup, learning, or any of the overheads imposed by the Linux bridge. However, Macvlan increases the complexity of DHCP address assignment, due to the presence of multiple IPAM masters (DHCP server for the hosts and the DHCP IPAM for containers). If you can overcome these problems in your deployment, Macvlan's performance with VEPA mode is the best for single-host container networking. For multihost container networking, Linux bridge with routing daemon offers the best performance and is the most ubiquitous. Kubernetes also prefers the use of Linux bridge. We look at Kubernetes' requirements next.

Container Network Interfaces

We discussed how Docker bridge automatically assigns an IP address to a newly spun up container. In many cases, more sophisticated solutions might be required to configure container network interfaces. Two examples of network interface configurations that are more sophisticated than the default one are Calico and Flannel. To support these extensions, Docker and other container runtimes provide the ability to add network plugins that provide functionality such as IP address management. Two popular and competing models for providing network plugins are Container Network Model (CNM) and Container Network Interface (CNI). Of these, CNI seems to have won the day. Kubernetes relies on CNI, which is also now a Cloud Native Computing Foundation (CNCF) initiative. CNCF is the main organization providing the critical components of the container and microservices landscape.

Discussions of CNI are beyond the scope of this book. The default bridge CNI with a routing suite provides a high performance container networking solution, especially for Kubernetes.

Kubernetes Networking

As of this writing, Kubernetes is the most popular way to deploy microservices using containers.

Some terminology first. In Kubernetes, two important terms are *pod* and *service*. A pod is a set of containers that are always spun up and scheduled for execution together. The containers in a pod also share the same Linux namespace and cgroup. A pod is ephemeral; thus, communicating with a pod directly is not the recommended practice in Kubernetes. Instead, a set of pods provide a service, the microservice presumably, and the service has a name and an IP address. Entities external to the service access the service via its name and IP address. For example, you can use DNS to load balance across the pods or alternatively use a mechanism such as Linux's iptables or IP Virtual Server (IPVS) to load balance access to the service across the pods providing the service. Kubernetes can also monitor the state of the pods and the incoming access load and use this to spin up more pods in case of high loads or shut down pods in case of lighter load or replace a failed pod.

Kubernetes imposes the following restrictions for pod-to-pod or pod-to-host communication (see Kubernetes Networking (*https://oreil.ly/PpqMB*)):

- All containers should be able to communicate with all the other containers in the pod without the use of NAT.

- All containers in any pod should be able to communicate with any of the hosts, and vice versa, without using NAT.

- A container's IP address is the same whether you look at it inside the pod or outside. In other words, no NAT outside a pod.

A Linux bridge in conjunction with a routing daemon serves these requirements well.

Kubernetes also has a routing daemon, Kube-router, as part of its package. As quoted on its website (*https://oreil.ly/IQusU*), "One of the key design tenet of Kube-router is to use standard Linux networking stack and toolset. There is no overlays or SDN pixie dust, but just plain good old Linux networking. So it's a lot leaner." Kube-router uses BGP to advertise container address reachability and uses IPVS to provide load balancing. I've heard of people using static routes, as well, instead of a routing suite in certain simpler scenarios.

When accessing the service virtual IP address, the load balancer in the form of IPVS or iptables ensures that the requests are load balanced to a specific pod by rewriting the destination IP address from the service IP address to the specific pod IP address. The load balancer, of course, ensures that all further traffic for the service from the node is routed to the same pod. Thus, the basic communication restrictions imposed by Kubernetes for pod-to-pod or pod-to-host cover the case for external entity to service communication, as well.

As we studied under container networking, the use of overlays in Kubernetes is not a performant solution. Using the default bridge with a routed model is the simpler, and more high-performance route (pun intended).

Summary

We covered various aspects of container networking because microservices and containers are an integral part of the cloud native ecosystem. As a network admin or engineer, you hopefully saw the benefits of using the default Linux bridge and no NAT to allow containers on the same host to communicate with one another. The use of a routing daemon allows an easy extension of the best single-host solution to multihost container networking. This enables fast and simple networking for Kubernetes. Furthermore, the use of basic Linux constructs along with routing allows the seamless communication between containers, bare-metal servers, and VMs. Routing again shows why it is a key foundational technology of cloud native data centers and applications.

## CHAPTER 8

Multicast Routing

Multicast is a zero-billion-dollar industry
—Fred Baker

Many years ago, when I was still a relative newcomer to the networking field, I heard Fred Baker, then chair of the IETF, declare, "multicast is a zero-billion-dollar industry." That declaration still holds in the modern data center. If you want your applications to run in the cloud, forget multicast. However, with enterprise networks beginning to embrace Clos topology, the need for multicast has reared its head again. This is especially true in some deployments involving EVPN (discussed in Chapter 6). The goal of this chapter is to explain the role of multicast routing in the context of the modern data center. We will not get into aspects of multicast routing that have less to do with its specific use case with EVPN.

This chapter helps answer questions like:

- What is multicast routing and how is it different from unicast routing?
- Why use multicast?
- Why is multicast routing frowned upon in the modern data center?
- How does the central routing protocol for multicast, Protocol-Independent Multicast Sparse Mode, work?
- What adaptations are required to deploy multicast routing in Clos topologies?

We begin with an overview of multicast routing and the fundamental problems multicast routing is designed to address.

Multicast Routing: Overview

Even though I presume that you understand what multicast is, let me take a few sentences to explain it. Consider Figure 8-1. There are seven routers: the leaves L1 through L4, the spines S1 through S3, and an external router R1. There are five hosts, H1 through H6.

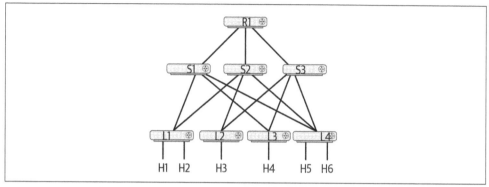

Figure 8-1. Sample topology to illustrate multicast

Imagine a scenario in which H1 wants to send the same packet to H3, H5, and H6. It can choose to replicate the packet three times, once to each of H3, H5, and H6. This is called *ingress replication* or *head-end replication* (we use the two terms interchangably in this book). Or it can choose to send a single copy addressed to a special address which is sent to L1. L1 sends a single copy of this packet to S2. S2 replicates the packet and sends one copy to L2 and one copy to L4. L4 further replicates the packet, sending a copy to H5 and H6; L2 meanwhile sends a copy of the packet to H3. This second model is called *multicast*. It differs from broadcast in that not everyone in the network gets a copy of the packet (H2 and H4 in this example).

Compared to the head-end replication example, the main benefit of multicast is the efficient utilization of network bandwidth in delivering packets destined for multiple entities. It is also more efficient in replicating packets only when it is really required.

Multicast addresses are different from unicast addresses. Multicast MAC addresses have the least significant bit of the first octet set to 1. IPv4 multicast addresses are identified by 1110 as the first four bits of the IPv4 address; that is, the first octet of the IPv4 multicast address is in the range 224 to 239. The total number of IPv4 multicast addresses is 2^{28} (ignoring the first four bits, which are fixed). In IPv4, addresses that start with 224 are considered link-local multicast and often used by control protocols such as routing protocol. For example, OSPFv2 uses 224.0.0.5 as the link-local multicast address to reach all OSPF routers on a broadcast link such as Ethernet. Link-local multicast is really bridged multicast because it is never routed.

IPv6 multicast addresses have the first eight bits set to 1. IPv6 multicast addresses also have an embedded scope: link-local, node-local, global, and so on.

Unicast packet forwarding has two models: bridging and routing. Similarly, multicast also has L2 or bridged multicast and routed multicast. As the name indicates, bridged multicast operates within a single subnet, whereas multicast routing works across multiple subnets. Because bridged networks build a spanning tree for packet forwarding, the same tree is used for forwarding both unicast packets and multicast packets.

Routing, on the other hand, is inherently a unicast forwarding mechanism. So multicast routing is an entirely different beast from unicast routing. To route multicast packets, multicast routing builds a *multicast distribution tree* over the unicast routing topology. In other words, with multicast routing, the unicast routing topology needs to be built before multicast can kick in.

Multicast groups connect *sources* (hosts sending multicast packets) with *listeners* (recipients of the packets). When a host joins a group, it can express interest in receiving packets from all sources or from particular sources. This leads to two kinds of multicast routes: (*,G) and (S,G). The first accepts packets from all sources in the group, whereas the second accepts packets from a single source.

In Chapter 5, we learned that unicast packet forwarding involves doing a longest prefix match of the packet destination address with the routing table entries. Multicast routing also uses lookups with longest prefix match to select the best route. Like the routing prefix term in the unicast routing world, the S and G in multicast routing are plucked from a packet and used in making a packet forwarding decision. The source comes from the source IP address and the group from the destination IP address. (S,G) entries are more specific (longer prefix) than (*,G) entries.

In switching silicon, multicast route entries take twice as much space a unicast entries. This is because the router must look up two addresses, the source address and the destination address (which carries the multicast group address). Multicast routing also involves doing what is called a Reverse Path Forwarding (RPF) check. We discuss RPF later in this chapter.

The Uses of Multicast Routing

Bridged multicast is used mostly for discovering members of a cluster and for heartbeat (keepalive) messages. Cloud native applications don't always rely on this mechanism, but many legacy applications do, as well as some newer applications.

Routed multicast is common in two scenarios: financial trading sites where the stock tickers come as multicase feeds, and broadcast media such as Internet Protocol Television (IPTV). In the data center, the use of routed multicast with EVPN is the only use case I'm aware of. Virtual networks use bridged or L2 multicast, but because of the routed overlay implementation of network virtualization, one implementation of the bridged multicast in the overlay network translates to routed multicast in the underlay network (see Chapter 6 for definitions of overlay and underlay).

Problems to Solve in Multicast Routing

Look again at Figure 8-1. There are two main questions that a multicast routing solution must address:

How do you prevent duplicate packet delivery?
>The topology has many loops, so packet duplication needs to be avoided. For example, let's assume L1 simply forwards a packet out all its router interfaces, to S1 and S2. What prevents S1 and S2 from both delivering a copy to L4? Following the same broadcast model, suppose S1 delivers the packet from L1 to all the routers connected to to S1 (L3, L4, and R1), and S2 delivers the packet to L2, L4, and R1. How does R1 know not to deliver S1's packet to S2, and similarly to deliver S2's packet to S1?

Where are the listeners for a multicast group?
>If H1 is the source of a multicast group G1, how do the routers know to whom to deliver the packet? If only H5 is the listener, how does L1 learn about this? From S1's perspective, how does it know to send the packet only to L3 and not to L4? How does L4 know to send the packet only to H5 and not H6?

The answer to both questions is to use a protocol that builds an acyclic directed tree connecting the listeners to the senders. The protocol also must allow listeners to express interest in specific groups and specific sources from those groups.

Before we continue, how does a listener know what multicast groups are available? That question is not addressed within the IP or L2 multicast framework. In most cases, this is part of the application; in other words, either the application uses predefined multicast groups or it is part of the application configuration.

Building a Multicast Tree

Figure 8-2 shows how the network of Figure 8-1 can be converted into a directed acyclic graph to avoid loops. Building a loop-free acyclic graph also avoids delivering duplicate packets (except maybe when the network topology changes).

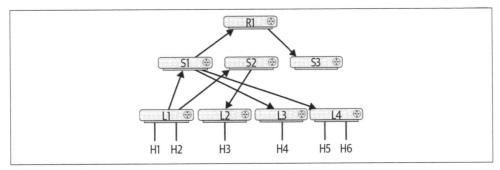

Figure 8-2. Converting a network into a multicast tree

You might have noticed that the tree has been built with L1 as the root. So Figure 8-3 is a redrawing of this topology, but from L1's perspective. The figure shows a logical view of the network from the point of view of multicasting instead of a physical view of the routers and their connections. The figure thus shows how the multicast overlay creates an acyclic graph for the efficient delivery of packets.

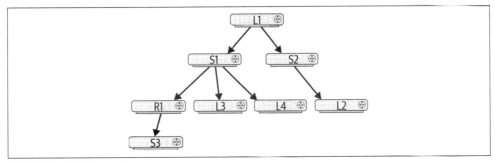

Figure 8-3. Converting a network into a multicast tree

Who elected L1 as the root of the tree? If the source of the multicast group is H3, will L2 become the root of the tree? What if both H1 and H3 are sources for the same multicast group G1? Will there be two trees now, one with L1 as the root and the other with L2 as the root? And does the graph need to be directed? After all, when the STP did the same thing with L2 networks, the tree was not directed. The answers to all of these questions rests with the nature of the multicast routing protocol.

Multicast Routing Protocol

A multicast routing protocol starts with a source and its listeners, and builds the most optimal acyclic graph for reaching the listeners; this constitutes the multicast distribution tree mentioned in "Multicast Routing: Overview" on page 162.

The multicast routing protocol has two pieces. The first piece, called *Internet Group Membership Protocol* (IGMP), allows a listener to express interest in a multicast group, either as a (*,G) or an (S,G) tuple. The other piece runs on routers to build the distribution tree and determine where the packets need to be delivered. The most popular multicast routing protocol inside enterprises is called Protocol-Independent Multicast (PIM).

A listener that wants to receive multicast traffic sends an IGMP Join message to create a multicast stream. In contrast, a listener sends an IGMP Leave message to stop receiving traffic from a multicast stream. The first-hop router for a listener is the last routing hop before delivery to the listener. Therefore, the first-hop router for a listener is called last-hop router (LHR) in the multicast distribution tree. The first-hop router for a source is called FHR in the multicast distribution tree. So, the LHR converts the IGMP Join message sent by a locally attached host into an appropriate multicast routing protocol specific message, for example PIM Join (we discuss PIM shortly).

One important concept in multicast routing is that the multicast routing state is soft state. Said differently, the protocols need to periodically assert interest in continuing to receive traffic for a multicast group. Without this periodic expression of interest, the nearest upstream router of the tree considers the receiver as either dead or as having lost interest and drops that listener from its distribution tree. The router will then prune the tree back if necessary. More specifically, if the listener stops sending IGMP Join packets and the LHR has no other listeners for that multicast group, the LHR will stop sending PIM Join packets altogether for that multicast group. This causes the LHR's upstream router for that multicast group to stop sending PIM Join for that multicast group if it has no other listeners and so on, all the way back to the FHR of the multicast distribution tree.

IGMPv3 is the version of IGMP most commonly found today, although for a very long time, IGMPv2 was popular. The primary difference is that IGMPv3 can specify interest in either (S,G) or (*,G), whereas IGMPv2 supported only the ability to specify interest in (*,G). In other words, IGMPv2 forced listeners to receive multicast traffic from all sources.

PIM is defined in RFC 7761 (*https://oreil.ly/RQEQW*). PIM offers many variations, each suited for a specific topology or use case:

PIM Sparse Mode (PIM-SM)
   Assumes that most receivers don't want to receive multicast and therefore records only participating routers (listeners).

PIM Dense Mode (PIM-DM)
   Used when most routers are interested in receiving all multicast traffic. The exceptions—the routers that don't want to receive certain (*,G) or (S,G) entries—

must send a message requesting that they be pruned out of the distribution of those multicast streams. This puts the onus on uninterested receivers to prevent delivery of unwanted packets.

PIM Source-Specific Multicast (PIM-SSM)
A simplified PIM-SM, useful in certain scenarios.

Bidirectional PIM (Bidir PIM)
Like PIM-SM, except that the multicast distribution tree is shared and nothing is source specific; there are no (S,G) routes.

PIM-SM is the most popular variation inside enterprises, with Bidir PIM being a distant second. In this chapter, we focus on PIM-SM as the multicast routing protocol.

PIM-SM Protocol Packets

PIM runs directly over IP; it does not use any transport protocol such as TCP or UDP. PIM protocol packets have the L4 Protocol Type in the IP header set to 103. PIM uses the reserved multicast address ALL-PIM-ROUTERS to send protocol messages that are not unicast, such as PIM Join and PIM Prune. The ALL-PIM-ROUTERS address for IPv4 is 224.0.0.13, whereas the IPv6 address is ff02::d. Table 8-1 lists the packet types.

Table 8-1. PIM protocol packet types

Packet type	Use	Periodicity	Destination address
PIM Hello	Sent by all PIM routers periodically on all PIM-enabled interfaces	30 secs	ALL-PIM-ROUTERS
PIM Register	Sent by FHR to RP for transmitting a multicast packet using the RP tree	60 secs	RP's IP address
PIM Register Stop	Sent by RP to FHR to stop sending packets for transmission down the RP tree	Sent in response to PIM Register	FHR's IP address
PIM Join/ Prune	Used to build (Join) or tear down (Prune) the multicast distribution tree for a multicast stream	60 secs	ALL-PIM-ROUTERS
PIM Assert	Sent to notify or rectify errors in the multicast packet distribution	—	ALL-PIM-ROUTERS

The IS-IS routing protocol can be used to build both unicast routing table entries and multicast table entries. This method was first adopted in the IETF standard, TRILL, and then later in proprietary solutions like Cisco's ACI. But there is no defined standard or interoperable implementations that supports using IS-IS as the IP multicast routing protocol. Multicast OSPF (MOSPF) was one of the first multicast routing protocols, but is not in use today. Other multicast routing protocols have also largely fallen by the wayside.

PIM Sparse Mode

In this section we examine in detail how PIM-SM works. The PIM-SM specification is in RFC 7761 (*https://oreil.ly/RQEQW*).

Rendezvous Point

The first term you need to understand with PIM-SM is the *rendezvous point* (RP), the root of a shared multicast distribution tree. This shared distribution tree is used to deliver packets from the senders to the receivers interested in (*,G) multicast streams. The RP is selected by an administrator and configured on all the PIM routers. An RP can be configured to serve only a set of multicast groups or all multicast groups.

The tree built from the RP toward all the listeners is a shared tree because it is common to all sources of a group. This shared tree is called the *RP Tree* (RPT). When a listener learns of a new source, the listener can also build a potentially more optimized path for the multicast stream from that source. Such a tree is a source group–specific tree and is called *Shortest Path Tree* (SPT). The SPT is obviously the optimal path from a source to a listener and so it's better to use the SPT over the RPT. But the SPT might not be available when the multicast traffic for a group begins to flow. So, when the traffic switches over from using the RPT to the SPT, the process is called *SPT switchover*.

Building a Multicast Distribution Tree

PIM-SM must address the following problems:

- Connecting a set of listeners to a group when the listeners express an interest before the source has started
- Connecting a set of listeners to a group when the source starts up before there are any listeners
- Handling endpoint failures gracefully
- Handling changes to a listener set for a given (*,G) or (S,G) multicast stream

- Handling topology changes

PIM is called "protocol independent" because it does not build its own unicast reachability topology. PIM expects unicast routing to be working correctly to identify unicast forwarding paths to sources. Let's use Figure 8-1 as the topology for the remainder of the discussion in this section.

One PIM session runs between the listener and its LHR, signaling an interest in a (*,G) or (S,G) tuple toward an RP. The other piece runs between the source and the sources FHR toward the RP to allow the RP to know about the source. The RP stitches the two endpoint interests together to allow the flow of multicast packets. The initial sequence of steps in the PIM-SM protocol is as follows:

1. The first step is to enable PIM-SM on all interfaces on a router that are on the path toward multicast sources, multicast receivers, or the RP. Enabling PIM-SM on an interface starts up the PIM machinery.

2. The next step is to configure the RP's IP address on all the routers, including the RP itself. Most implementations allow you to specify an RP and the multicast groups for which it is the RP. There are also solutions that attempt to autodiscover RPs. I'll ignore those details from our discussion. Let's just assume that R1 is the RP in our example.

3. PIM sends out Hello messages from the interface. The PIM Hello is a link-local multicast message, sent to the ALL-PIM-ROUTERS address, and so received by all PIM routers on that link.

4. The Hello messages are used to signal the presence of a PIM speaker. This is used in electing a designated router (DR) for a link. The DR is the only one to (1) send the multicast data received on to the bridged segment, (2) forward the PIM Join from the receivers onto the RP, and (3) send PIM Register messages for packets received on a link. This avoids multiple routers from forwarding packets onto a bridged segment, thereby causing duplication of packets.

Source starts first

We begin our study of how PIM-SM builds multicast distribution trees with the case in which a multicast source starts up before any listeners have registered interest in the multicast stream. The sequence of steps that follow is illustrated in Figure 8-4.

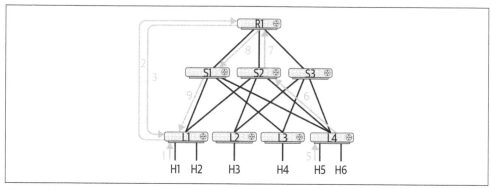

Figure 8-4. (*,G1) Tree setup via PIM-SM

1. Let H1 be the source for a group G1. A copy of H1's multicast packet is sent up to the control plane on L1 (we discuss how this is done later in the chapter).

2. The PIM process on L1 receives this packet. It encapsulates the packet as a PIM Register message, and sends it to the RP as a unicast packet. This Register message signals the presence of a new source, which could be either part of an already known multicast group or the beginning of a new multicast group. L1 also creates an (S,G) multicast routing entry for (H1,G1). Because there are no registered listeners at this point, the outgoing interface list (also called the *olist* or *OIF list*) for this group is empty. So the packet is not forwarded any further.

3. The RP receives this packet. The RP creates an (H1,G1) entry in its multicast routing table with an empty olist. This entry is what enables receivers that join later to rendezvous with the source and start receiving the multicast packets for the group. However, because no listeners are registered yet to receive this multicast stream, R1 sends a PIM Register Stop message to L1 to prevent further Register messages.

4. L1 receives the Register Stop message from the RP and stops sending Register messages for multicast packets from (H1,G1). Because there are no listeners, packets from H1 are simply dropped at L1. Thus, unlike L2 multicast, if there are no registered listeners in PIM-SM, no packet is delivered. In L2 multicast, even without any registered listeners, the multicast packets are flooded to all endpoints in the VLAN. (Many implementations provide a knob that can be enabled to send multicast packets only to registered listeners, just like L3.) No message is sent as a result of the activity in this bullet, so there is no step 4 in Figure 8-4. Remember we said that all state in multicast is soft state. Therefore, as long as the source continues to send packets, L1 will continue to send what are called PIM Null Register messages. These messages ensure the RP knows that the listener is still alive. They're called Null Register because they don't contain any data, just

the multicast source and group information for RP to know what multicast routing state to retain.

5. Now let's start up a listener. Let's assume H5 sends an IGMPv3 Join indicating an interest in the (*,G1) multicast stream. L4 traps this IGMP message and creates a (*,G1) multicast route on the box. The olist consists so far only of the interface toward H5. L4 consults the unicast routing table to identify the OIF to use to reach the RP, which is R1. In our case, there are three ways to get to R1: via S1, S2, and S3. If there are multiple interfaces, L4 picks one by hashing over the packet header of the multicast stream. This selection of an interface in the presence of multiple paths is similar to how an interface is selected from many equal-cost paths for unicast packets. Let's assume L4 picks the interface via S2 to reach R1.

6. L4 sends a PIM Join message indicating an interest in the (*,G1) multicast stream. L4 sends this message out the port to S2 because it selected S2 as the path to the RP. L4 also marks the interface toward S2 as the *RPF interface* for the (*,G1) route; that is, the interface on which it expects to receive the multicast data stream from the RP. Whenever a multicast data packet destined to this multicast group is received, the packet forwarding logic checks that this packet came in on the interface marked as the RPF interface. If it is, the packet is accepted. If it is not, the packet is dropped. This check on the incoming interface is called an *RPF check*. If the RPF check fails, a PIM Assert is usually sent out the incorrect interface.

7. S2 receives L4's PIM Join message. Because it has no entry for (*,G1), S2 creates a (*,G1) state in its multicast routing table. It sets the olist as the interface toward L4. S2 marks the RPF interface as the interface toward the RP S2 and then generates a PIM Join for the (*,G1) group and sends it to the RP.

8. R1 receives the message and sees that it does have state for (H1,G1) in its multicast routing table with an empty olist. It now has an interested listener, so it must ensure that the packets from the source H1 flow toward the listener. It has two paths to reach H1: via S1 and S2. It picks one of these based on flow hash, like in other cases, and sends a PIM Join message for the (H1,G1) stream. Let's assume that it picks S1. R1 sets the olist for (H1,G1) as going out of S2, the interface from which R1 received the PIM Join. R1 also sets the RPF interface to be the interface toward S1 given that it's the interface from which it expects to receive the multicast stream toward group G1 from source H1.

9. S1 receives the PIM Join message from R1 and creates a multicast route for (H1,G1) with the olist specifying the interface toward R1. S1 then does a lookup in the unicast routing table for source H1. It finds that this is the interface to L1. S1 sets the RPF interface to be the interface toward L1 for the (H1,G1) multicast group. Next, it originates a PIM Join message for the (H1,G1) multicast group and sends it to L1.

10. L1 receives the PIM Join message from S1 and updates its (H1,G1) multicast routing table entry with the updated olist specifying the interface to S1.

Now multicast packets sent by H1 flow from H1 → L1 → S1 → R1 → S2 → L4 → H5. Traffic is now flowing between the source and the listener H5, as shown in Figure 8-5.

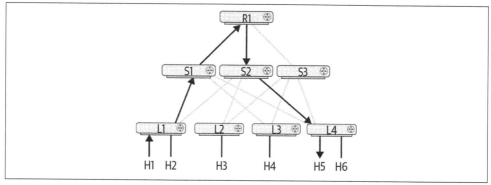

Figure 8-5. (*, G1) tree connecting the source H1 to the listener H5

However, this is a nonoptimal path between the source and the listener. There are two shorter paths between H1 and H5: (L1, S1, L4) and (L1, S2, L4). Therefore, even after a multicast distribution tree is set up, hosts and routers collaborate to optimize it. That's what we'll see happening now. The next sequence of steps is illustrated in Figure 8-6.

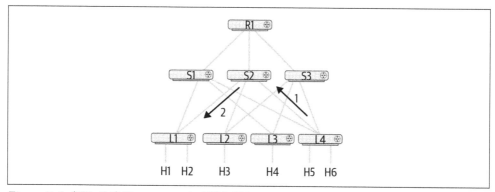

Figure 8-6. (H1, G1) Tree setup via PIM-SM

1. L4 doesn't know or care whether the path from L4 to L1 is shorter than its current (*,G1) tree. It knows that it has information about a specific source for (H1,G1). It consults the unicast routing table to identify the shortest path to H1. It discovers that it has two possible paths, via S1 and S2. L4 picks one of these two paths via the usual load-balancing method. Let's assume it picks S2. L4 sends a

PIM Join for the (H1,G1) message to S2. It creates a (H1,G1) multicast route with the olist as H5, and the RPF interface as the interface to S2.

2. S2 receives the PIM Join of (H1,G1). It consults the unicast routing table for the path to H1 and learns that it goes out the interface toward L1. S2 then builds a (H1,G1) multicast routing table entry with the OIF being the one toward L4 and the RPF interface being the interface toward L1. Next, because the multicast route entry for (H1,G1) is new, it generates a PIM Join of (H1,G1) to L1.

3. L1 receives the PIM Join of (H1,G1) and adds S2 to the multicast route table entry for (H1,G1).

At this point, multicast traffic from H1 on group G1 flows from H1 → L1 → S2 → L4 → H5. This is the optimal tree. We say that L4 has done an SPT switchover for (H1,G1). Figure 8-7 shows the routers involved in the multicast distribution route in gray, and the optimized traffic flow as blue lines. However, as shown by the black lines, there is still state for the larger (*,G1) route in the network. L1 is still sending the multicast stream for G1 from H1 to both S1 and S2, because S1 still has a valid PIM Join for (H1,G1).

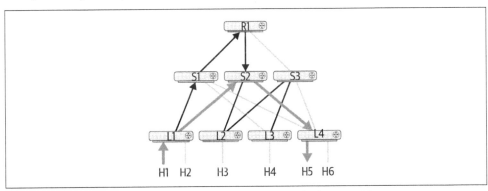

Figure 8-7. (H1, G1) tree connecting the source H1 to the listener H5

To avoid this wasted bandwidth to the RP, we need to notify the RP to stop sending traffic for (H1,G1) to S2. According to the rules of PIM-SM in section 4.5.6 of RFC 7761 (*https://oreil.ly/kolOx*), L4 cannot initiate the pruning of the tree, because L4 defined the same RPF interface for both the (S,G) and (*,G) interfaces. Both point to the interface from S2. Because S2 is the router with a different RPF interface for the (H1,G1) and (*,G1) interfaces, it is S2 that must do something. So, in the next PIM Join that S2 sends to the RP for its (*,G1) stream, it includes a special flag called the *(S,G,RPT) Prune* flag. The presence of the (S,G,RPT) Prune qualifier tells the recipient of the PIM Join that the sender of the PIM Join is still interested in receiving traffic for the (*,G1) group, but just not for streams originated by the specified source.

In our example, S2 sends the PIM Join for (*,G1) to R1 with the (S,G,RPT) Prune for source H1 to R1. In processing this message, R1 removes S2 from the olist for the (H1,G1) multicast route.

The sequence of steps that follow the pruning look as shown in Figure 8-8.

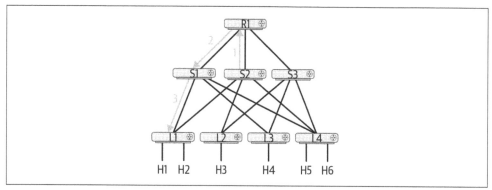

Figure 8-8. PIM (S,G,RPT) prune message flow for (H1,G1)

1. S2 notices that it has an (H1,G1) and a (*,G1) state, with a different RPF interface for each. It fires up an Override timer. The point of this timer is to prevent a flurry of Join messages from hitting the upstream router, all of them with the (S,G,RPT) bit set. If S2 receives a PIM Join for (*,G1) with the (S,G,RPT) bit set, it cancels the override timer because someone else already had the same idea and has sent that in the message. S2 can process the message right away and so the (S,G,RPT) message for (H1,G1) goes to the RP. In our example, no other node sends the (*,G1) Join with the (S,G,RPT) set for source H1. So, when the override timer expires, S2 will generate a PIM Join for the (*,G1) message with the (S,G,RPT) bit set for source H1 and send this toward the RP, in our case the interface to R1.

2. R1 receives this PIM Join, notices the (S,G,RPT) qualifier for the source H1, and removes the interface toward S2 from its olist for (H1,G1). At this point, the olist for (H1,G1) is empty at the RP. This triggers R1 to send a PIM Prune on the (H1,G1) tree toward its RPF interface, which is the interface to S1 in our case.

3. S1 receives the PIM Prune for (H1,G1) and removes the interface toward R1 from the olist for the (H1,G1) multicast route entry. At this point, it notices that the olist for (H1,G1) is empty. So it sends a PIM Prune for (H1,G1) to L1.

4. L1 receives the PIM Prune for (H1,G1) from S1 and removes S1 from the olist for its (H1,G1) multicast route entry. Now packets are flowing optimally between the source and the listener and there's no wasted bandwidth.

Let's summarize the control packet flow in this discussion:

- PIM Join/Prune messages of the (*,G) multicast stream flow toward the RP.

- PIM Join/Prune messages of the (S,G) multicast stream flow toward the source, S.

- An RPF check ensures that a multicast packet is accepted only on the one interface that it needs to be.

- In the presence of multipath, RPF interface selection picks one out of the many routes using the usual flow load-balancing mechanisms.

- PIM doesn't build its own copy of the topology, but relies on whatever built the unicast topology. This is why it is called "Protocol Independent."

- The RP maintains (*,G) and (S,G) state as appropriate to hook up sources and listeners independent of the order in which they join.

- PIM Join/Prune message processing is done independently by each node. These messages are never forwarded, their receipt might trigger the state machine in the recipient node to generate its own PIM Join/Prune message.

You might have noticed that the state machine is quite complicated with multiple moving parts, including processing even at intermediate nodes.

Let's consider next some other scenarios and the behavior in those cases.

R1 chooses S2 as the path to reach H1

In step 7 of Figure 8-4, if R1 chooses S2 instead of S1 to send the PIM Join of (H1, G1), S2 is now receiving two PIM Joins: one from L4 for (*, G1) and one from R1 for (H1, G1). These two do not conflict, but result in two separate multicast route entries: a (*, G1) entry with the olist toward L4 and the RPF being the interface toward the RP R1, and an (H1, G1) entry with the olist including the interfaces toward both R1 and L4 with the RPF being the interface toward L1. So, packets from the source H1 for the multicast group G1 hit the multicast route entry for (H1,G1). Similarly, packets for the group G1 from a different source than H1 hit the (*,G1) entry. This demonstrates the LPM lookup working also for multicast routing, just as it does for unicast routing.

H5 signals an interest in a specific source: (H1,G1) rather than (,G1)*

If H5 uses IGMPv3 to signal interest in only a specific receiver, H1, L4 sends a PIM Join directly for the (H1,G1) multicast stream. This means that the steps outlined in Figure 8-4 do not occur, and the protocol interaction proceeds directly to the steps outlined in Figure 8-7, with the obvious absence of any state associated with (*,G1).

Listener starts up first

Now let's consider the reverse of the scenario in the previous section. This time, a listener joins a multicast group before any source. Figure 8-9 illustrates the sequence of steps.

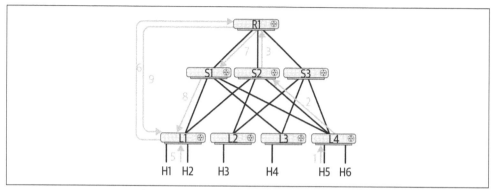

Figure 8-9. PIM control flow when listener starts up before source: (*,G)

1. The game starts this time with H5 expressing an interest in a (*,G1) group via an IGMP message.

2. L4 receives this IGMP message and sends a PIM Join on the (*,G1) group toward the RP, picking S2 as the choice from among S1, S2, and S3. L4 creates a multicast route for (*,G1) with an RPF interface consisting of the interface to S2 and an olist containing the interface pointing to H5.

3. S2 receives the PIM Join and creates a (*,G1) multicast route with the RPF interface as the interface pointing to R1 and the olist containing the interface pointing to L4. S2 then generates a PIM Join message for (*,G1).

4. R1 receives this Join and creates a (*,G1) state with the OIF being the interface pointing to S2. Because R1 has no information about any source, it has no RPF interface to set. At this point, the listeners and the RP are ready to spring into action if they hear about a source.

5. A source H1 starts sending traffic to group G1. As in the previous case, L1 traps this packet, encapsulates it in a PIM Register message, and sends it as a unicast packet destined to the RP, R1.

6. R1 receives this PIM Register message and, after looking at its state, realizes that there is an interested listener in this multicast group.

7. R1 generates a PIM Join for (H1,G1) toward the source, H1. Assume it picks S1 as the path to H1, like before. R1 sets the RPF interface as the interface to S1 and the olist containing the interface to S2, from which it had received the PIM Join for (*,G1).

8. S1 receives the PIM Join for (H1,G1) and creates a multicast route for (H1,G1) with an RPF interface consisting of the interface pointing to L1 and the olist containing the interface pointing to R1. It then generates a PIM Join for (H1,G1) and sends it to L1.

9. L1 receives the PIM Join and creates a (H1,G1) multicast route with the olist containing the interface toward S1 and the RPF interface being the interface toward H1.

The multicast data stream now flows from H1 → L1 → S1 → R1. When this stream hits R1, R1 sends a PIM Register Stop on (H1,G1) to L1, from which it had received the original PIM Register message.

At this point we've established state with traffic flowing from H1 to H5 via the shared RPT. L4 executes the SPT switchover just as described before to switch the path to the most optimal path from H1 to H5. The end result is the same whether the listener joins first or the source starts transmitting first.

What happens if H5 had sent an IGMP Join on (H1,G1) instead of (*,G1) before H1 had a chance to start? With no information about G1 anywhere in the network, because the behavior of a PIM Join for an (S,G) multicast stream is to flow toward the source, the result is that only L4, S2, and L1 have state for (H1,G1). However, it's possible that there are other listeners interested in a (*,G1) multicast stream. This information is known only to the RP. Therefore, when H1 starts sending the multicast data stream for G1, L1 still must do the logic of sending a PIM Register to the RP, which must handle it. If the RP has no registered (*,G1) listeners, it sends a PIM Register Stop right away. If it has registered listeners, it builds the (H1,G1) state like in steps 7 through 9 of Figure 8-9.

This sequence of operations, assuming no other interested listener, looks as shown in Figure 8-10. The multicast stream continues to flow toward H5 while L1 and the RP are working through the PIM Register process.

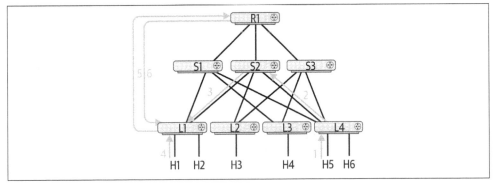

Figure 8-10. PIM control flow when listener starts up before source: (S,G)

Consider the case in which H5 sends an (H1,G1) IGMPv3 Join message and the sequence of operations in Figure 8-10 takes place. The RP is oblivious to the traffic flowing from L1 to L4 via S2. Now if H6 sends an IGMP Join message, but for the general (*,G1) route, if L4 merely follows the sequence of steps described for H5's (*,G1) message, L4 could get duplicate multicast packets. This is because the SPT tree would be delivering one copy, and the RPT would be delivering the other copy. The (S,G,RPT) Prune message kicks in again at S2, assuring the duplicate packets will stop.

In another example, if H3 opts in to receive the (H1,G1) multicast stream, the most optimal packet replication would be for L1 to send a copy to S2, which then sends one copy out the interface to L2 and another to L4. However, because each router independently decides the path to source for the (S,G) tree, L4 could pick S1 as the path to H1 while L2 picks S2 as the path to H1 (no other path is as short to H1 as via S2 from L3). In this situation, L1 would send one copy each to S1 and S2, and S1 would send a copy to L4 while S2 would send a copy to L2. So the multicast distribution tree is not always guaranteed to be predictable in the presence of multiple paths between the source and a set of listeners.

How is the first packet trapped to the CPU?

The previous discussions mentioned that copies of packets from the multicast data stream were sent to PIM for doing things like PIM Register, starting a PIM Join, and so on. How exactly does this trap happen?

Each FHR sets up a multicast route to catch all multicast packets. This entry sends the packet to the control plane only. The entry causes the switching silicon (or software packet forwarding stack) to send a packet belonging to a new source for a multicast group to the control plane, which then delivers the packet to the PIM process.

After an (S,G) entry is created on the FHR, the FHR sends periodic PIM Register messages. After the RP either has no need for the register packets or it sees multicast data flowing for the (S,G), it will send a Register Stop message. Then the FHR switches to sending PIM Null messages. The PIM Null Register message is sent without a copy of the multicast data packet. To trigger the PIM Null Register message from the router, the (S,G) entry is marked to send a copy of the multicast data packet to the control plane, besides forwarding the packet to interested listeners. Thus, if the source stops sending messages, the Null Register messages will also stop and the route can be removed.

On an LHR, the receipt of a multicast data packet triggers the creation of an (S,G) entry from the (*,G) entry present if an IGMP Join contained only a (*,G) entry. The IGMP Join will trigger the periodic sending of a PIM Join message. And an IGMP Leave causes the router to send a PIM Leave message. Prior to the reception of a multicast data stream, if the IGMP Join expresses interest in only a general (*,G) route, there is only a (*,G) multicast route entry on the last-hop router. This entry is also marked to send a copy to the control plane. A new source for a group triggers a copy to the control plane. After the (S,G) multicast route entry has been created for a specific source of the multicast group, the (*,G) entry will not be chosen, thanks to IP's LPM logic.

Multiple RPs and MSDP

A single RP is not a robust solution. What happens if that RP fails? To avoid this, it is recommended that you run more than one RP in a multicast routed network. Typically, in a PIM-SM network, RPs share an anycast address so that PIM speakers can use the closest RP. The RPs run a protocol called MSDP to synchronize the (S,G) state across the RPs. The benefit of anycast RP is the simplification in the configuration for the non-RPs. Specifying a single IP address for the RP and allowing unicast routing to pick the nearest PIM RP to process the packet enables all the RPs to share the burden of being an RP. It also helps with a robust switchover when one of the RPs fails, because the unicast routing will automatically route the packet to the next nearest RP.

With anycast RP, administrators get the benefit of a vastly simplified configuration without having to worry about deciding a priori how to spread the burden of an RP manually among the different RPs and how to pick the backup RP. The only missing piece is the synchronization of the PIM state across the RPs to enable minimal disruption when things do switch over. MSDP is the protocol that provides that synchronization.

MSDP was introduced to allow RPs running in different ISPs to synchronize multicast routing state information with one another for multicast distribution trees built across multiple different enterprises. Like BGP, MSDP supports internal and external MSDP peers, where the internal peers are the ones within the same routing domain. For our discussion, the internal peering is the only one that matters. MSDP synchronizes (S,G) state between the RPs, not (*,G).

MSDP runs over TCP and forms a full mesh by having every MSDP router peer separately with every other MSDP router running in the multicast routed network. MSDP is used only with PIM-SM in current usage. MSDP is an experimental IETF protocol and is unspecified for IPv6, primarily because there was a lack of need for this in IPv6. MSDP is specified in RFC 3618 (*https://oreil.ly/HQHiI*).

Why did we need a new protocol? Couldn't PIM itself have been used for this purpose? PIM's only job is to build and maintain multicast distribution trees, both shared (RPT) and source specific (SPT). PIM has no support for distributing or synchronizing state that doesn't affect in its primary purpose.

Alternately, couldn't BGP have been used instead of defining a new protocol? My speculation is that there was no strong reason for an independent protocol for this use case. Thus, MSDP is not a standard RFC, but an experimental one, and further work on it has been discontinued. Nevertheless, it is popular where multicast and anycast RPs are used. We don't discuss MSDP further in this book.

Cisco's NX-OS has a proprietary PIM extension to synchronize RP state, especially when used with anycast RP. This extension allows the RP receiving a PIM Register message to send it to all the other defined RP peers.

PIM-SM in the Data Center

Multicast in a Clos topology is an interesting beast. The widespread use of the Clos topology is a relatively new addition to packet-switching networks. The cloud native data center eschews the use of multicast because of the complexity it brings to maintaining a robust, reliable network. As we stated at the start of this chapter, the primary use case for multicast in the data center is in cases with network virtualization, where the amount of multicast in the overlay L2 network is quite substantial.

As a result, the use of multicast in Clos networks does not enjoy the maturity that comes from widespread deployment. With that said, let's look at the use of multicast, specifically the use of PIM, within the data center. Given that PIM-SM is the most popular multicast control protocol within an enterprise, we begin the discussion with the study of using PIM-SM in Clos topologies.

The first question that arises is where to locate the RP in a Clos topology: in the spines (for a two-tier Clos) or super-spines (three-tier), or on the leaves, incongruous as it sounds.

Let's begin with the simple case: two-tier Clos. If we pick the spine as the RP, we're violating a fundamental principle of Clos topology: the spine is merely a connective node, not one with services. If we decide to ignore that and proceed, we cannot ignore another fundamental principle of Clos topology: what you do to one spine, you must do to all spines. You cannot make a special case for only a subset of spines, for all the reasons we've discussed earlier.

Continuing this logic, if we make all the spines into RPs, we do get better resilience of the RP. However, this entails that we deploy MSDP to keep the (*,G) and (S,G) state synchronized on the RPs, because different leaves might end up registering with different RPs. In the data center, BGP is the most commonly used unicast routing protocol. However, the use of BGP prevents the spines from speaking with one another by default (see Chapter 15 for details). To ensure that the spines can speak to one another, you need to provide additional configuration (allowas-in 1, described in "Reason for allowas-in 1" on page 379). But using this actually creates the discouraged scenario of path hunting (discussed in Chapter 5). It's better to use a more constrained configuration that allows the spines to see only one another's IP address and not much more (allowas-in origin in FRR). But even with this we have a problem. In

Figure 8-1, if we make all the spines, S1 through S3, the RP, let's assume that when L4 sends a PIM Register for H5's interest in group (*,G1), it picks S3 instead of S2 because both are equal in L4's eyes. Now when H1 starts sending traffic in group G1, the PIM Register message from L1 goes to S1, which creates state for (H1,G1) and synchronizes this with the other spines via MSDP. However, there is no way for S3 to receive traffic from L1 with BGP. Thus, we've blackholed multicast traffic from a specific source to a listener in the event of a link failure (such as when the link between L1 and S3 fails). Using OSPF instead of BGP does help avoid this problem at the cost of increasing the number of protocols used in the case of EVPN. As a final reason to not use the spines as RP, consider that there are usually a large number of spines: commonly four or eight. In such a scenario, a full mesh of RPs synchronizing over MSDP seems to be overkill.

An alternate approach is to use one or more of the leaves as the RP. After all, if the listeners all switch to the SPT as quickly as possible, there should be no packets flowing via the RP. In other words, PIM-SM's normal behavior should not cause the leaves to have any additional traffic continuously flowing through it. This seems more logical and fits in with the model of Clos networks, where the services are pushed to the edge of the network rather than pulled into the core. Because the path from RP is rarely used because of SPT switchover, there is path optimization benefit to using the exit leaves as the RP.

In consideration of all these constraints and requirements, I advocate using exit leaves —in a two-tier Clos network or within a pod—as the RPs. There are commonly two to four exit leaves, and using them seems much more efficient and appropriate than running the RPs on spines. Figure 8-2 assumed this model, where R1 was an exit leaf, just drawn topologically differently. However, the use of exit leaves does lead to a problem of optimal paths, at least initially as we saw in "Building a Multicast Distribution Tree" on page 168, in which the multicast streams started out very inefficient and had to be gradually optimized.

In the case of EVPN (which we study more of in Chapter 17), every VTEP knows about every other VTEP and the virtual networks that they're interested in. As you might recall from Chapter 6, in the use of multicast with VXLAN, the operator defines a multicast group associated with each virtual network. Multidestination frames in a virtual network such as broadcast, multicast, and unknown unicast are sent as multicast, with the associated multicast group as the destination IP address.

In this scenario, PIM-SM and RP are useful for connecting sources and multicast groups that are unknown at the start. As discussed earlier, if the endpoint sends an IGMPv3 Join for an (S,G), the FHR of this endpoint builds an (S,G) tree toward the source, completely avoiding the RP. In the case of EVPN, the groups of interest and the sources in each of those groups is known ahead of time, as a result of the EVPN advertisements. Thus, each VTEP can automatically start building the (S,G) trees for all multicast groups that it cares about.

This leads to a much simpler, less-complicated configuration and maintenance of the multicast network. Although there's a proposal to implement this in FRR, this hasn't happened yet. The simplifications that result from such a proposal include the following:

- No need to configure RPs
- No need to use MSDP
- No worrying about switching from RPT to SPT
- Simpler troubleshooting, because there is much less configuration and protocols to get right for multicast to work right

PIM-SM and Unnumbered

We've discussed the use of OSPF and BGP with unnumbered interfaces as an efficient way to address the unnecessary complexity of configuring routing networks. The implementation of PIM with the use of unnumbered networks requires a few words.

When you use unnumbered OSPF, you assign the loopback (or appropriate Virtual Routing and Forwarding [VRF]) IP address to every interface. PIM picks the interface IP address as the source for sending its packets. However, with unnumbered BGP, there isn't even an IP address on the interface. So the PIM implementation must pick the loopback (or appropriate VRF) IP address for sourcing the packets.

Summary

"You think you know routing? Wait until you hear about multicast." This is an often-quoted saying among network practitioners and designers. We only touched upon the parts of the multicast protocol that are relevant to its use in the data center. I suspect that you are as boggled as most people are with multicast routing. This should also explain why cloud native data centers frown upon routed multicast and ban multicast in general from their networks. It can be an immense source of pain to troubleshoot when things go wrong.

CHAPTER 9

Life on the Edge of the Data Center

No man is an island, entire of itself; every man is a piece of the continent
—John Donne

Like men and women, data centers are not islands unto themselves. This chapter is about how they connect to the rest of world. It should help you answer questions such as these:

- In what ways can a Clos topology be connected to an external network?
- What are best practices for deploying a routing protocol at the edge?
- How does an enterprise handle connectivity in a hybrid cloud?

The Problems

Connectivity to the external world is a north-south traffic pattern, as described in Directionality in Network Diagrams. A fundamental driver for the selection of the Clos topology was its ability to handle east-west traffic patterns well. Let's now examine how to connect a network built using Clos topology to the external world. The answers to the following questions govern several factors that affect the connectivity of a data center to the external world:

- Why is the external connectivity required?
- What are the bandwidth demands of the connection to the external world?
- What upstream device will the data center network be connected to?
- What services are necessary for any traffic crossing the internal-to-external world?

The answer to the first two questions lead us to a choice between models for connecting to the external world. The next two questions guide the remainder of the edge connectivity discussion. The first question also leads us to consider the models by which you connect an on-premises data center with its cloudy brethren.

Connectivity Models

In this section, we examine three different ways the Clos topology can connect to an external network or the internet. We begin with a study of the first two questions raised in the previous section and then examine the models that provide the answers.

Why Connect to the External World?

There are many reasons to connect a data center to the external world. If you're providing a service, such as search, a recommendation system for advertising, or content delivery, connecting to the external world is how others access your application. Another increasingly common answer is connecting to access the part of the data center that is in the cloud. A third reason is that you're connecting to the external world to pull data, such as running a web crawler, which is then acted upon by the application running within the data center (building a search index, for example, or providing training data for your machine learning models).

Bandwidth Requirements for External Connectivity

Bandwidth inside the data center can be quite significant. For example, if you have a two-tier Clos with four spines and 16 leaves with a 100GbE connectivity between the leaf and the spine, you have 400GbE connectivity between the leaves. Each spine is terminating 1.6 Tbps (Terabits per second) of bandwidth (16 × 100GbE). A spine in a larger network, with, for example, 32 leaves or 64 leaves, terminates even higher bandwidths (3.2 or 6.4 Tbps). Because each leaf is connected to four or more spines, the total bandwidth capacity of the data center network can easily exceed 10 Tbps. High bandwidth capacity is one way the modern data center networks differ from those of the past.

Connections to the external world rarely demand that much bandwidth in most organizations. So the internet-facing routers of most enterprises have much lower capacity than the networks' internal network capacity. Another way to look at the network is that the interswitch links are lower-speed links (i.e., 40GbE instead of 100GbE), but pretty much the entire bandwidth coming from the servers is going out to the external world. This latter happens, for example, when the data center is serving high-bandwidth media delivery. Identifying the bandwidth requirements connecting to the outside world will determine the design of the network connecting a data center to the external world.

Connecting the Clos Topology to the External World

Figure 9-1 shows the most common way to connect a two-tier Clos topology to the external world. It shows the introduction of a new kind of leaf switch, called a *border leaf* switch or sometimes an *exit leaf*. This switch is similar to the other leaves except that instead of connecting to internal servers, it connects to internet-facing routers, which then connect to the external world.

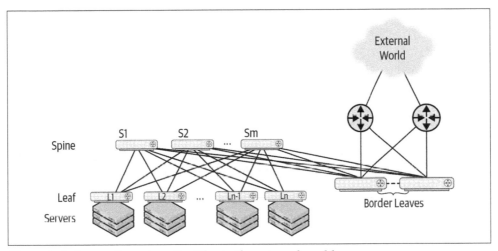

Figure 9-1. Connecting a two-tier Clos to the external world

The number of border leaves is determined by the oversubscription ratio expected between internal traffic bandwidth and external traffic bandwidth. The minimum is two border leaves, to avoid a single point of failure. Each border leaf is connected either to a single internet router, or more commonly, to a pair of internet routers so that a single link failure won't render a border leaf useless.

People used to the access-agg-core model of building networks automatically assume that the connectivity to the external world comes from the spines. They further make the mistake of having only a subset of spines connect to the internet routers as the amount of external bandwidth is small enough to not require the use of all the spines. As discussed many times before (see Chapter 2, for example), this is a bad idea and leads to all kinds of network problems. In the Clos design presented in this section, the border leaves are connected to all the spines, just like a normal leaf.

A larger network, such as a three-tier Clos network, follows a similar model, except that the connection is to super-spines instead of spines, as shown in Figure 9-2.

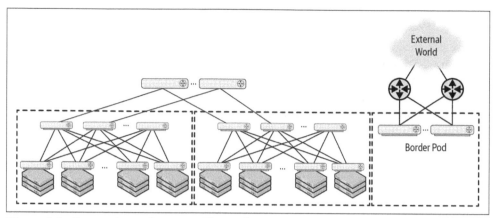

Figure 9-2. Connecting a three-tier Clos to the external world

In very large networks, if the number of spines exceeds the port count of a border leaf, it is no longer possible to connect the border leaves to all spines. In such situations, another tier of switches is added to the network to mitigate this problem. Given that you can easily find switches that are 64 ports of 100GbE, you need something approaching that many spines to run into this condition.

The final variation on connecting a Clos topology to the external world avoids defining border leaves. Instead, the spines connect to the internet routers. Figure 9-3 shows this variation. This model is used in very small networks or for networks where north-south traffic is close to the same amount as east-west traffic. When the operator has two to four spine switches and is very cost sensitive, they sometimes don't want to spend the money on extra edge switches. This is usually the case in small networks.

When the amount of traffic leaving the data center is higher than, or almost as much as, the east-west traffic, exiting the data center through the spines makes a lot of sense. But this is not a common case, and I've encountered only a couple of scenarios in which this was required.

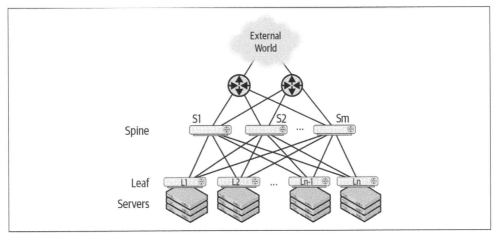

Figure 9-3. Connecting Clos to the external world via spines

Some operators also prefer this option because it saves an additional hop, which would be added by border leaves, in connecting to the external world. I don't see much justification for that reasoning these days. Switching silicon can forward packets in 300 ns or less. The 300 ns saved by avoiding border leaves isn't worth the possible additional expense. The extra cost comes about because the ports on an internet router are usually more expensive than the leaf and spine switches. For the reasons described earlier in this section, the operator must connect all the spines to the internet routers. If there are more than two spines, the cost adds up quickly.

The figures in this section have shown border leaves or spines connected to the external world via the internet routers. In rare occasions, border leaves can actually be the internet-facing routers, in which case the network reduces to the example shown in Figure 9-3. This happens in smaller enterprises with simple connectivity to the external world. By simple, I mean connectivity to a single ISP, or connectivity where there isn't even a routing peering session, just a static default route pointing to the ISP links.

Routing at the Edge

There is little need to expose all the details of the data center fabric to the external world. Thus, the border leaves are a logical place to provide route summarization. As discussed in Chapter 5, route summarization inside the data center cannot happen at the spines due to the way routing works, especially with BGP. Border leaves, because they connect to all the spines, ensure that a border leaf never loses connectivity to an internal prefix. A large number of failures must happen before the border leaf becomes isolated from a regular leaf.

If BGP is used as the Clos routing protocol, the border leaves also strip off the private ASN[1] before advertising the routes to the external world.

Services

The border leaves are also good places to string up various network services, such as firewalls and load balancers, to control access from the external world to the data center. Firewalls are typically deployed at the border leaves to ensure that only authorized traffic flows between the internal and the external network. This is depicted as the brick walls in Figure 9-4. We briefly described this scenario as one of the use cases of network virtualization in Chapter 6. Let's look at this scenario in a little more detail here.

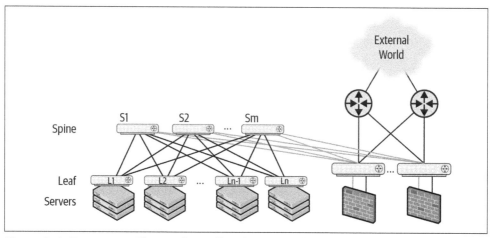

Figure 9-4. Connecting Clos via firewall to the external world

Figure 9-4 shows the border leaves using two VRFs, the green VRF for the internal network (shown by the lighter line), and the black VRF for the external network. The spines and the nonborder leaves do not need to know about this use of VRFs. As far as they're concerned, they use the default VRF to communicate with one another and with the border leaves. Similarly, the internet routers do not need to know anything about the use of VRFs by the border leaves. The border leaves learn the routes via BGP (or OSPF or IS-IS), which puts routes learned via the internal network in the green VRF and routes learned via the internet router (typically just the default route) in the gray VRF.

The firewalls are connected to the border leaves as shown in the figure. The border leaves have two (or more) interfaces to a firewall. The interfaces do not need to be

---

1 We discuss private ASN and how to strip it off in Chapter 15.

physical links, but can be VLAN tags over a single physical link to create multiple logical interfaces. The VLAN tag in such a situation is what is called an L3 subinterface. The border leaves tag the two interfaces as belonging to different VRFs. In our example, one belongs to the black VRF and the other belongs to the green VRF (represented by the lighter line). The firewalls have two BGP sessions: one over the green subinterface and one over the black subinterface.

Firewalls, like the spines and regular leaves, remain unaware of the VRFs. The firewalls just readvertise the routes learned via the green link to the BGP session over the black link, and vice versa. Thus, the default route learned by the border router via the internet router is sent to the firewall via the black link. The firewall readvertises this over the green link BGP session. From the perspective of traffic traversing from the internal to the external network, traffic now automatically flows through the firewall.

To illustrate this some more, let's trace traffic from servers to the internet:

1. Traffic destined to the external world, from the servers connected to L1, hit L1 because it is their default gateway.

2. L1 sees that the route matches the default route and sends the packet to one of the spines, based on the hash it builds using the packet header, as described in Chapter 5.

3. The spine delivers the packet to one of the border leaves based on a hash, as in the previous step.

4. The border leaf sends the packet out the green (or lighter colored) link to the firewall because that is the outgoing interface for the default route.

5. The packet thus reaches the firewall. If the packet is not authorized to be delivered to the outside world, the firewall drops the packet.

6. If the firewall considers the packet valid for delivery, it routes the packet over the black link (as that is where it learned the default route from).

7. The packet is now delivered back to the border leaf, but this time over the black link, which is in the black VRF.

8. The border leaf looks up the route, but this time in the black VRF, and dispatches the packet to the internet router.

The process is reversed for packets coming from the internet router to the internal network. In this case, the black VRF has the route for the internal network pointing the black interface to the firewall. Only if the firewall authorizes the packet does it deliver the packet back to the border leaf over the green (or lighter colored) link.

If other services such as load balancers are present, they can be chained in a similar way, going from the firewall to the load balancer before making their way to the inside or the outside.

We show the details of the configuration and additional configuration knobs that are necessary for configuring BGP on the border leaves in Chapter 17.

Hybrid Cloud Connectivity

A rising trend in data centers is the *hybrid cloud*. Hybrid cloud is defined as dividing a data center between the enterprise's on-premises servers and a cloud provider's servers. The two sets of servers are supposed to communicate with each other somewhat transparently. Many enterprises use the hybrid cloud model to dip their toes in the cloudy waters or as a way to move certain parts of the business to the cloud. In such a situation, how does communication occur between the on-premises data center and the public cloud instances?

This book focuses only on connectivity options and on the work to be done at the on-premises data center side of the equation. Hybrid connectivity solutions are evolving constantly, and anything written now is in danger of being out-of-date rather soon. So we focus on the parts that I expect to remain mostly unchanged as this rapid evolution progresses. Also, different cloud providers provide slightly different options. Rather than provide specific details about each, I touch upon these differences only where it affects the discussion pertinent to this book.

The most common model for running a service inside a public cloud is a *Virtual Private Cloud* (VPC) instance. A VPC consists of multiple compute nodes connected via an L3 network. Just like the cloud native data center networks we've been discussing so far, connectivity within a VPC is purely L3. I'm not aware of any cloud provider providing L2 connectivity inside a VPC. Furthermore, you cannot use multicast or broadcast inside a VPC. The VPC also doesn't run a routing protocol.

Each VPC contains one or more subnets. Each VPC has a virtual private router (called virtual private gateway in some cloud solutions) that routes between the subnets and controls access to the VPC from the external world. For example, the VPC can use NAT to access the internet, or provide publicly reachable IP addresses that are routed to the endpoints via the gateway. Each VPC can also communicate with other VPCs via the same gateway.

Connecting to a VPC from outside involves using either a VPN or a direct routed connection with the appropriate cloud service provider. The second option has two variations: one in which the customer's network is collocated with the cloud service provider's network, and the other in which the cloud provider provides a direct WAN connection to the customer's on-premises data center. Figure 9-5 shows these methods of connecting the on-premises data center to a VPC.

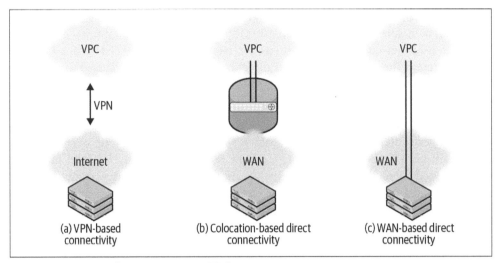

Figure 9-5. Ways of connecting to a VPC

Amazon, Microsoft, and Google all provide roughly equivalent solutions to the three methods: VPN-based connectivity and collocation-based direct connectivity, and direct connectivity via a WAN. The following criteria help to select which option to use:

VPN-based connectivity
This is the most common option, but also the least flexible and is not high capacity or high performance due to the encryption/decryption of traffic and the variability of traversing the internet. This is often chosen because it is cheaper than the other two.

Direct connectivity
This option is recommended if you need to transfer large amounts of data between the on-premises site and the VPC, or if your connectivity matrix is more complicated than a point-to-point VPN could provide. Different cloud service providers use different terminology to describe the service. AWS calls it Direct Connect, Microsoft Azure calls it ExpressRoute, and Google calls it Cloud Interconnect. All cloud service providers support either a direct connectivity via a collocation or via a service provider's WAN connection such as point-to-point Ethernet (via Q-in-Q, for example) or MPLS VPN connections.

All the options, including the ones that provide point-to-point Ethernet connectivity, provide only routed connectivity between the on-premises data center and the VPC. Thus, all connectivity is L3, both within the VPCs and between the VPCs, and the on-premises data center.

The direct connectivity options permit interconnect link bandwidth from 50 Mbps to 10 Gbps, with some supporting even 100 Gbps interconnection support. The point-to-point Ethernet connections are used for bandwidths of the order of 1 Gbps or more, whereas the MPLS VPN–based direct connectivity option is used when bandwidth requirements are lower than this, but still high enough to justify the need for direct connectivity.

When a VPN is used as in Figure 9-5(a), an IPsec tunnel is established between the on-premises router and the VPC gateway. A routing protocol is set up over this IPsec tunnel. In both Figure 9-5(b) and (c), one or more 802.1Q VLAN virtual interfaces are provided to peer with the VPC gateway. Each cloud service provider has a set of rules that need to be followed when the connectivity is direct and not over VPN. For example, Azure requires a redundant connection always, whereas AWS does not.

All the cloud service providers I've examined use BGP to establish connectivity between the on-premises data center and the VPC. This is because BGP is the default protocol for communicating routing information across administrative boundaries. A key advantage of BGP in such a context is its support for communicating routing policy information. This information is used, for example, to influence routing to follow the optimal path from the on-premises data center to the VPC.

Consider the example shown in Figure 9-6. An enterprise has offices in both NYC and SFO and corresponding VPC instances in the East Coast and West Coast regions of the cloud service provider. The routes of both VPCs show up in the routing tables at the routers on the NYC and SFO data centers. What you want to ensure is that packets from the NYC office to the East Coast VPC do not take the longer path shown in the figure, but rather the shorter, direct path. BGP allows you to make these sorts of policy decisions via route-maps, which we discuss in Chapter 15.

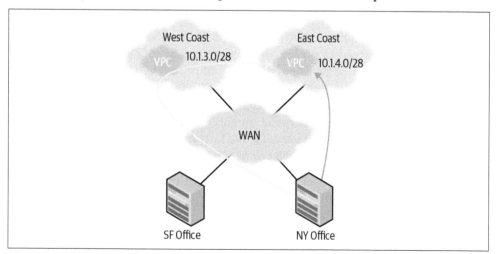

Figure 9-6. Nonoptimal routing scenario with direct-connect model

All cloud service providers allow you to advertise private and public IP addresses via the BGP session. BGP uses private ASNs in the peering session, and the version of BGP used is an external BGP (eBGP) multihop session.[2] If you're running IPv4 and IPv6 in the VPC and in your on-premises data center, you need to use separate BGP sessions, one for IPv4 and one for IPv6. This is currently true at all cloud service providers. When run from the cloud provider's network directly to a customer's on-premises data center, the BGP peering happens at the internet-facing routers.

They also prevent the use of the VPC gateway as a transit to reach the internet. In other words, with these peerings, VPC gateways can use the on-premises data center to reach the internet, especially if the on-premises router advertises the default route. But the on-premises data center cannot use the cloud as a transit to reach the internet.

To enable fast failure detection, the cloud service providers also recommend that you run BFD[3] over the interconnection links.

There are many more specifics to making all this work that are beyond the scope of this book. I refer you to the vendor-specific documents for more details in setting up the hybrid cloud connectivity.

Summary

In this chapter, we studied how to hook up the data center to communicate with the external world. We also studied the ways in which you can deploy hybrid cloud solutions to provide seamless routed connectivity between your on-premises data center and the VPC instances in the cloud.

---

2 We explain all of these concepts in Chapter 15.

3 See Chapter 5 for a description of BFD.

## CHAPTER 10

Network Automation

There's a lot of automation that can happen that isn't a replacement of humans but of mind-numbing behavior.
    —Stewart Butterfield

Skilled workers historically have been ambivalent toward automation, knowing that the bodies it would augment or replace were the occasion for both their pain and their power.
    —Shoshana Zuboff

With the ascent of artificial intelligence (AI) and machine learning in particular, the whole world seems to be taking a stand on automation. Books about automation abound; talks on the benefits and harms of automation are aplenty. I proffer that the question of network automation is far simpler than the discussion at large, though I believe it does reflect a little of the tension in that larger discussion—the tension to which Shoshana Zuboff alludes to. The view of network automation I'm discussing in this chapter is more of the Stewart Butterfield's kind, the freeing of network administrators' time and minds from dull, repetitive work.

This chapter aims to demystify network automation. As I've said before, a central concept that distinguishes cloud native data center networks from their older generation counterparts is the focus on efficient operations. Network automation is a key enabler of that goal. To that end, this chapter addresses questions such as the following:

- What is network automation and why should I care?
- Do I need to learn programming to learn network automation?
- Why is network automation hard?
- How can I try out automation in a gradual exploration of its benefits?
- What network automation tools are right for me?

- How can I make sure that my automated procedures work?

We will also provide a brief overview of Ansible (*https://www.ansible.com*) to help acquaint you with the broad strokes of the model for one popular automation tool. Reading the overview will allow you to understand the playbooks used later in this book.

What Is Network Automation?

Even though it might be obvious to you, I think it is worth defining what network automation is. Automation in the context of network administration refers to the process of allowing programs to perform the tasks that operators would otherwise need to perform manually, working on each individual box, one after the other. Consider the task of updating the box with a security update. The task is well defined, and so are the command(s) to perform the job. Having a program log in to every box that needs the update and performing the update without requiring manual intervention is an example of automation. Another example is checking the state of some service, for example the running state of BGP, across all boxes. Instead of running a show command box by box, if you can have a single program run the command across all the desired boxes, that would be automation. The program could also do more, such as rearrange the output in some meaningful way or only show the value of a certain field, and so on. At the other extreme of the network automation spectrum is the ability for the network to automatically fix problems that it detects.

So, what do you automate? Any task that is well defined and is repeatable across multiple boxes. If the repeatable steps are many and complicated, automation is even more clearly beneficial to take out the chance of errors introduced due to the laborious and involved process. Sadly, the networks in most enterprises are still manually managed. This is one of the leading causes for the inefficiency in running an on-premises data center. And network automation is one of the chief reasons (along with efficiencies of scale) why cloud operators are successful.

When it comes to network automation, configuration is as far as the practice has come. Cloud operators, especially the big two or three and a few others, have gone on to automate other aspects of managing the network, such as monitoring and alerting. Within configuration too, network automation use is often limited to zero-day configuration. Verification of this configuration, day two, and later configuration tasks are still largely manual.

Who Needs Network Automation?

If you're running or aim to run more than a handful of switches, you'll benefit from network automation. If you're designing a new greenfield network or managing an existing network, you'll benefit from network automation. If you're a small shop, mid-sized enterprise, or large enterprise, you'll benefit from network automation. If there's nothing else you remember from this chapter, I hope you remember that key takeaway. Unlike many networking fads you've lived through in your days in networking, automation makes sense. It helps you build predictable, scalable, and agile networks without losing your hair or your life. Let me use this section to explain why.

Network configuration in the older access-aggregation-core networks was complex, and nonrepetitive across the boxes. Also, most of the complex configuration occurred on a the large, chassis-based aggregation switches. These traits, combined with the appliance-like model of network equipment, made only manual operation possible.

However, with the rise of Clos topology and many small-form-factor switches, much of network configuration is repetitive. This numbs any human attendant and makes it difficult to not make mistakes. Such mistakes introduce random errors, and if there's one thing that's challenging to pin down, it's random errors. Data from various studies indicate that errors introduced by humans in configuration are the first or second biggest reason for network failures. Even if you consider yourself an inhabitant of the famous mythical city, Lake Wobegon (*https://oreil.ly/G8L_V*)—where everyone is above average and good looking—and thus above such data, the question must be asked: "Is the effort worth it?"

Time is the ultimate limited resource. Whatever time you've decided to devote to repetitive tasks or tracking down difficult-to-catch errors is time you won't be spending on getting perspective on problems, on a vision, and on getting ahead. You cannot build predictable networks without automating the tasks.

As the network grows, it becomes even more time consuming to roll in new equipment or to upgrade. A modern data center network contains many more boxes to manage, while managers emphasize the imperative to reduce the failure domain as much as possible. Even if you're running a smallish network with two spine switches and eight leaves, there are tens of interface addresses to configure and lots of duplication in the configuration. Without automating, it's difficult to keep track of all the information and add new equipment quickly.

At even slightly larger scale, the task quickly becomes really problematic: manual labor, typing commands over and over, logging in to one box after another. And at ever-larger scales, it is impossible to survive without automation.

Agility is the other dominant difference in modern data center networks. It is not just a matter of getting the job done—it needs to be done fast. In fact, it needed to be done yesterday. Automation combined with the proper architecture and technology can make changes fast. And they can be made with more confidence.

Thus, automation is an essential skill for the coming years, either directly applicable in your network itself, or potentially useful in the next job that you seek. Do not fear or resist automation as something too complex or unnecessary. As a network operator, you already have mastered more complex skills.

Does Network Automation Mean Learning Programming?

An often-asked question is whether network automation requires learning programming. Automation is letting a program do the task and so yes, in that sense you will be programming. But you can do quite a lot, learning just how to write in YAML and templating with Jinja2, neither of which I'd call programming as used in the feared sense of the word.

Learning Python is a definite plus and has the potential to ease up a lot of your tasks. Python is relatively easy to learn, and you don't need to learn much to put it to good use. Yes, you might need to get used to developers laughing at your code or writing so-called "spaghetti code." But for what you'll be doing, at least until quite late in the game, this will not matter.

Many network administrators mistake sysadmins for programmers, and they're most definitely not, at least not in the traditional sense of a developer. Just search the web for sysadmin and developer, and you'll run into quite a few articles that will tell you the same. But sysadmins can write Bash shell scripts and small programs to ease the monotony of repeating an operation. In the same sense, network administrators can be waist-high in automation without serious programming knowledge.

In any case, tools like Ansible makes it easy for you to start off the automation journey without requiring any programming knowledge. Later in this chapter, I show how many a network administrator took the plunge into network automation, starting with just file copying and YAML. (YAML, whose abbreviation jocularly stands for Yet Another Markup Language, is a very simple but structured format for providing configuration information.)

Why Is Network Automation Difficult?

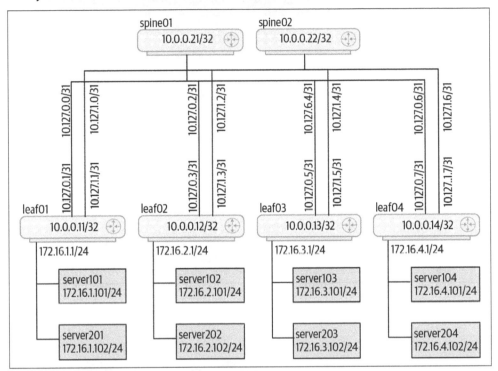

Figure 10-1. A two-tier example Clos network

We study in detail how to configure OSPF and BGP routing protocols for such a topology in later chapters. But for now, let's consider the following snippets of BGP configuration for a two-tier Clos network. For the sake of brevity, in Tables 10-1 and 10-2, we show configuration snippets for only two leaves—leaf01 and leaf02—as well as the two spines—spine01 and spine02.

Table 10-1. Sample BGP configuration for spines

spine01	spine02
! Configuration for spine01 ! interface lo ip address 10.0.0.21/32 ! interface swp1 ip address 10.127.0.0/31 ! interface swp2 ip address 10.127.0.2/31 ! interface swp3 ip address 10.127.0.4/31 ! interface swp4 ip address 10.127.0.6/31 ! router bgp 65000 bgp router-id 10.0.0.21 neighbor 10.127.0.1 remote-as 65001 neighbor 10.127.0.3 remote-as 65002 neighbor 10.127.0.5 remote-as 65003 neighbor 10.127.0.7 remote-as 65004 network 10.0.0.21/32	! Configuration for spine02 ! interface lo ip address 10.0.1.22/32 ! interface swp1 ip address 10.127.1.0/31 ! interface swp2 ip address 10.127.1.2/31 ! interface swp3 ip address 10.127.1.4/31 ! interface swp4 ip address 10.127.1.6/31 ! router bgp 65000 bgp router-id 10.0.0.22 neighbor 10.127.1.1 remote-as 65001 neighbor 10.127.1.3 remote-as 65002 neighbor 10.127.1.5 remote-as 65003 neighbor 10.127.1.7 remote-as 65004 network 10.0.0.22/32

Table 10-2. Sample BGP configuration for leaves

leaf01	leaf02
! Configuration for leaf01 ! interface lo ip address 10.0.0.11/32 ! interface swp1 ip address 10.127.0.1/31 ! interface swp2 ip address 10.127.1.1/31 ! interface vlan10 ip address 172.16.0.1/24 ! router bgp 65001 bgp router-id 10.0.0.11 neighbor 10.127.0.0 remote-as 65000 neighbor 10.127.1.0 remote-as 65000 network 10.0.0.11/32 network 172.16.0.0/24	Configuration for leaf02 ! interface lo ip address 10.0.1.12/32 ! interface swp1 ip address 10.127.0.3/31 ! interface swp2 ip address 10.127.1.3/31 ! interface vlan10 ip address 172.16.1.1/24 ! router bgp 65002 bgp router-id 10.0.0.12 neighbor 10.127.0.2 remote-as 65000 neighbor 10.127.1.2 remote-as 65000 network 10.0.0.12/32 network 172.16.1.0/24

The main thing that I hope leaps out at you is that the configurations are almost identical, except for the IP addresses and the 65xxx numbers. And it is these IP addresses and numbers that are a primary point of pain in network automation. You might have noticed patterns even in these numbers as used across the boxes, but that doesn't reduce the pain much. Let's dive a little deeper.

The Trouble with IP Addresses and Interfaces

In IP networks, interfaces have IP addresses. This is a fundamental fact of IP architecture. The structure and syntax of these addresses might have evolved with time, but an invariable fact is that each interface must have an IP address to participate in routing; in other words, packet forwarding based on IP addresses.

This model poses a chicken-or-egg problem for routing protocols. A routing protocol is used to dynamically learn about nonlocal destinations and update the path to these destinations based on network state. But how does a routing protocol communicate with its peer?

The most common answer has been to put the two ends of the link on a common subnet, typically a /31 or a /30. This allows one end to communicate with the other using bridging, given that the two ends are on the same subnet. For example, in Figure 10-1, the IP address on the spine end of the link and on the leaf end of the link must be in the same subnet. Indeed, the spine01 interface with address 10.127.0.0/31 links to the leaf01 interface with address 10.127.0.1/31. These two addresses belong to the same /31 subnet.

Even with IPv6, in which every interface automatically gets a link-local address, a protocol was invented[1] to ensure that one end got the other end's link-local IPv6 address.

After the other end's IP address is known (link-local or otherwise), ARP (or its IPv6 equivalent, NDP) can be used to determine its MAC address. As described in Chapter 5, obtaining this next-hop MAC address is fundamental to routing.

How do you automate the generation of a configuration for which the two ends of every interface are unique on every box? What's worse is that for this to be correct, you must know what the two ends of a link are. This pair-wise assignment of IP addresses is one of the primary reasons that network automation is technically difficult.

Scale

Some folks might think that they can fix the problem of IP addresses using some additional variables in their network automation tool. For example, with a tool like Ansible, they assume that they can just provide these additional IP addresses as

---

1 It is called Router Advertisement or rtadv.

variables in a file. Or that they can use a network address assignment tool such as Infoblox to come up with these addresses. But scale complicates this problem of configuring IP addresses on an interface. A 4-spine, 32-leaf Clos topology has $4 \times 32 \times 2 = 256$ interfaces that need IP addresses. In addition, if the configuration assumes a simple single subnet for each leaf and the servers to which it routes, an additional IP address needs to be assigned to the server subnet, plus an IP address for the loopback. If there is more than one subnet per leaf, which is not uncommon in enterprise networks, there are even more addresses. Writing out that many addresses as variables manually is painful, to put it mildly.

Network Protocol Configuration Complexity

Every routing protocol comes with its quirkiness, none more so than BGP, the most popular routing protocol in the data center. Not only does BGP require that the two peering ends have the correct IP addresses, but also that they be specified in the peering configuration. Furthermore, traditional BGP configuration requires you to uniquely and correctly pair the peering with another piece of information called the ASN.[2] Thus, Table 10-1 and Table 10-2 specified both IP addresses and ASNs for the system being configured and for every peer. This makes a difficult task even more difficult.

OSPF configuration traditionally comes with problems similar to those described for BGP. OSPF requires that we specify the IP addresses over which OSPF is to peer. In addition, it requires specifying the OSPF area[3] for each interface or address. A two-tier Clos topology has only a single area, so this part is somewhat simple compared to BGP. In addition, you need to specify passive interfaces, which are interfaces whose addresses you advertise but never peer over using OSPF.

IS-IS has somewhat different difficulties: you need to come up with a router ID in an obsolete address format.

When network virtualization is used, it raises the complexity of routing protocol configuration even more. Often, you must configure more arcane protocol knobs such as Route Distinguisher (RD)/Route Target (Target) or routemaps. Each part of this work is again box specific, resulting in the need for some basic programming.

L2 protocols often ride higher on the complexity curve. There are multiple protocols to configure, not just a single routing protocol. VLANs must be configured on every interface, and the values on either end must match. To keep the broadcast domain contained, administrators are often careful to configure only the VLANs on an

---

2 We study ASNs and BGP in Chapter 15.

3 We study OSPF configuration in detail in Chapter 13.

interface that matter to the other end. This also leads to box- and interface-specific configuration that doesn't lend itself to automation without the help of programming.

In the router configuration snippets in Table 10-1 and Table 10-2, we see that the same IP address is repeated multiple times. This duplication of information adds another vector for introducing errors.

Lack of Programmatic Access

The CLI has been the de facto model for accessing networking equipment. The CLI is fairly restrictive and lacks any programmatic access or features. There is often no way to access a programming language such as Python, and if there is way, it is only what the vendor provides; downloading extensions and libraries is not possible.

The CLI does not even provide valid error codes if a command fails. So textual output parsing has been the only way for a configuration tool to assess the success of a command. Furthermore, every vendor had a variation of the command's input and output for a specific task such as adding a VLAN or adding a route. Most server tools relied on some ability to run their own agent or code on the device.

Furthermore, SSH and SNMP were the only two supported modes of accessing any information on the device. Although conceived as a configuration and monitoring tool, SNMP today is used only for monitoring.

Think about tools such as Puppet or Chef or the granddaddy of them all, CFEngine. All of them were agent-based and required the OS to support standard programming languages such as Ruby or Python. This goes some way in explaining the success of Ansible as the network automation tool of choice: Ansible doesn't rely on running an agent on the network device.

Traditional Network OS Limitations

Traditional networking operating systems are designed not to be platforms, but appliances. This means that it is not possible for anyone but the vendor to extend or add to the device. Simplifications like globbing aren't supported.[4] Many operating systems, including Linux, provide information in an unstructured text format, not a structured format such as JSON. This is changing, but neither as fast nor as much as is necessary. Simplifications such as unnumbered interface support are missing in all the traditional networking software.

Open source routing suites such as FRR are far more advanced in this sense because they've added features that help simplify configuration or have completely rethought how configuration is done.

---

4 Given how IP addresses are unique for each interface, this is not a surprise.

What Can Network Developers Do to Help Network Automation?

No server software I'm aware of presents the headaches associated with network device configuration outlined in the previous section. Sysadmins are used to tools such as Sed and Awk, and even access to programming languages to overcome the limitations of the lack of structured input/output. Windows servers are rarely used, primarily because their designers largely ignore the pleas to make those boxes easy to manage. Some newfound interest in Windows is largely because it provides a shell: PowerShell.

There's a classic paper from the December 22, 2010, issue of ACM Queue (*https://oreil.ly/lmqX6*) titled "A Plea to Software Vendors from Sysadmins—10 Do's and Don'ts." I urge you to read the paper, it's quite short. The list in the article is a pretty good roadmap for network vendors to implement, as well as a vision for making the lives of network administrators easier through automation. I summarize the key requirements as follows:

- ASCII configuration files, not binary blobs
- Programmatic access, not just a graphical user interface (GUI)
- A crisp and simple backup/restore mechanism for all configuration, or at least the configuration of individual components
- A silent installation option; that is, don't make installations or updates manual
- An option to use system logs rather than individual log files
- Good instrumentation

To this original list, I add the following:

- Automation-friendly protocol configuration
- Structured input/output

Tools for Network Automation

Having studied the headaches associated with network automation and the requirements for good network administration, let us now turn to the tooling choices for network administration.

These tools fall into two broad categories:

The sysadmin toolkit
> Ansible, Salt, Puppet, Chef, and so on were developed first for configuring the OS and applications on an individual system, but found use for network configuration later.

The network administrator toolkit
> Options here include NETCONF, Yet Another Next Generation (YANG), and perhaps Restconf. NETCONF is the transport and can be used with flat-file configuration or YANG data models.[5]

The primary difference between the server administrator toolkit and the network administrator toolkit lies in the fundamental assumption made by the two models. The network administrator model assumes a uniform data model across all vendors for a component, whereas a sysadmin model does not make such an assumption. Unfortunately, the uniform data model is a mirage. It began with SNMP and continued with OpenFlow and now YANG. As anyone who has ever experienced those tools will tell you, the uniform data model is a myth that's busted right out of the starting blocks. Every network vendor modifies the "standard" data model in their own unique way to either extend it for new features or remove sections that are not applicable or just plain not implemented.

While the vendor architects and the draft writers haggle over what the data model ought to be,[6] network developers are left with no choice but to provide their own versions, and operators need to deal with the differences. In my opinion, this model is born of the appliance mentality and the preference to draft rather than code.

As a consequence, the uniform data model assumption provides just a veneer of a promise while making network administration difficult in practice. It also forces a rigid way of thinking. For example, the BGP data model does not support the unnumbered BGP model; the EVPN model doesn't support the FRR simplifications to configuration. Interface globbing or other forms of globbing are not supported, making for an inefficient remote access model. Innovation is either stifled or not recognized partly because of the myth of the uniform data model.

In comparison, consider the server model. Package and interface management are two functions that need to performed across Linux distributions. Red Hat and Debian are two prominent camps where these two functions are performed. Each camp provides its own coherent, consistent, and self-contained data model. Server administrator tools do not demand that the two camps provide a uniform model. In the plea by sysadmins, uniform data model is not an ask. Similarly, automation tools don't

---

5 Juniper and Cisco products typically use NETCONF, whereas every other data center box uses SSH or HTTP (for REST) as the transport.

6 By draft, I mean the things that are equivalent to IETF drafts, that eventually become standards.

attempt to paper over the configuration difference among PostgreSQL, MySQL, and Microsoft SQL Server, even though they're all traditional SQL databases.

How does this difference affect the network operator, you ask. Agreeing on a uniform model takes a long time, as anyone acquainted with SNMP or YANG will tell you. While the standards bodies are debating, networks are a-waiting. To get this going, each network vendor provides its version of the model. When the model is agreed upon—a year or two after your network is deployed—what is a network vendor to do? In their software releases, do they provide the standard version, thereby breaking your workflow if you upgrade, or do they keep both models? One road leads to code bloat and the other to operational pain.

To make the compatibility dilemma worse, the vendor hasn't been sitting still. More features have been added to the component, features that are not supported by the standard model. What happens to configuring those features?

You get the picture. In the server model, each vendor provides the model most sensible for its device. If vendor A provides much better abstractions and a more operator-friendly model, operators have the choice of using that as another deciding factor. A model that helps build a scalable, more predictable network is an advantage worth considering. The server administrator model just cuts to the chase and stops wasting time following a chimera.

My own personal experience is that the network administrator toolkit has always been a Neanderthal compared to the maturity, sophistication, and choice offered by server administrator toolkits. Unless you're dealing with a box that's not capable of working with one of the server administrator tools such as Ansible, my recommendation is to stay away from network administrator toolkits.

In terms of tools, if you have no preference, my recommendation is to use Ansible (*https://www.ansible.com*) for network automation. Here are the primary reasons for this recommendation:

- Ansible has probably the largest mindshare among network operators.
- Starting from version 2.2, the support for networking equipment has grown steadily. Just about every network vendor is supported.
- It is fairly simple for someone who knows the CLI to migrate to Ansible.
- Ansible uses a powerful and flexible templating tool called Jinja2 (*http://jinja.pocoo.org*).
- Almost zero programming knowledge is required. You can use Jinja2's control structures to do simple if/for/while control.
- Ansible runs on multiple platforms: Linux, of course, but also macOS and Windows.

- Last but not least, as befits cloud native solutions, Ansible is open source

Ansible isn't perfect. In fact, it has quite a few flaws, but it is the configuration automation tool with the largest momentum among network vendors and operators. For someone who's starting from scratch, that community support is critical. For example, there are plenty of Ansible playbooks to ogle over, and they're freely available on the internet.

Automation Best Practices

Automation is possible only when there are regular patterns that can be exploited. Typing the same command across multiple boxes is an example of such a pattern. At the very least, the desire to automate can help you clean up the network and make things more manageable, helping you bring some order to your network.

Seasoned practitioners of automation recommend the following best practices, which are independent of what tool you use:

Start simple
> Network automation can seem daunting if you attempt to bite off a large or complex task. The chances you'll stay on the automation path are higher if you start with simpler tasks. For example, automate the tasks of enabling routing and assigning loopback IP addresses.

Separate code from data
> As you become more sophisticated, you need to ensure that the code, which is what you do, is independent of the specific values for each of the devices. For example, if you start a very simple task such as assigning loopback IP addresses to routers, keep the IP addresses in a separate file (or files) from the command that does the assigning. Or, start by automating read-only commands such as getting the serial numbers or models of various devices. Ansible helps you in this by defining special files only for variables.

Validate
> The tools you use should provide you mechanisms to validate the entire configuration you're pushing before applying it. For example, Ansible has a validate keyword when pushing out files. Use a simulation tool such as one with Vagrant to validate the changes before actually pushing them out to real devices.

Git it in your soul
> Use a source code control system such as Git to save versions of your code. Do not be afraid to commit what works as quickly as possible. This allows you to revert back to working versions quickly.

Do rolling updates

The Clos topology helps you control the "blast radius" in case of errors. But you need to ensure you don't apply an erroneous change to all the nodes at once. Apply a change to a spine and a leaf and ensure that it works. Only then move on to applying it to other spines and leaves.

Pick consistent tooling and language

Ansible and Python go together. Puppet or Chef and Ruby go together. Don't mix languages and tools. It just means more headaches for you trying to fit one into the other. This does not mean you need to learn Python to use Ansible, but that should you choose to program in Python as you become more sophisticated, you'll be served well by Ansible, not so much if your tool is Puppet or Chef.

Iterate

As your skill improves, you'll find that you can improve the automation tasks by finding bigger patterns, a more efficient pattern, and so on. This is natural. Take the time to iterate to the solution that's right for your environment. As the famous software programmer Martin Fowler said, "You should use iterative development only on projects that you want to succeed."

Engage the community

Use tools that have a large, helpful community. For example, Ansible questions can be asked on multiple forums, including the popular Stack Overflow. The community can help you with the appropriate way to use the tool, even if they lack the domain expertise of networking itself. I've included a few online resources at the end of the chapter where you can get help on network automation.

Ansible: An Overview

This section provides an overview of Ansible. I am not trying to be comprehensive— there are entire books devoted to teaching Ansible. The point of this section isn't to teach Ansible as much as it is to familiarize you with some basic concepts that will allow you to follow the use of Ansible in the chapters on deployment.

Ansible is an automation tool providing a *push-based model* for automating the deployment of configuration on network and compute nodes, as demonstrated in Figure 10-2.

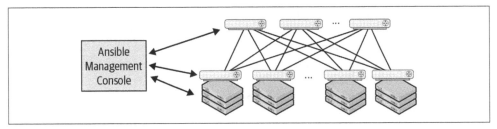

Figure 10-2. How Ansible works

Ansible is an application that runs on a Linux (or Mac) server. Its main inputs are:

- An inventory, which is a list of devices to which to push configuration
- Playbooks, which are a set of instructions indicating what the task is, whether it be generating a configuration or running a command

Following are the basic characteristics of Ansible:

Automation tool
  Ansible is largely used for configuration, though a more common starting point is to get an inventory report. You also can use it for validation after configuration, but not as well, because YAML and Jinja2 are just static definitions of formats, not programming languages. However, we demonstrate the use of Ansible for validation in Chapter 18.

Agentless
  Ansible works with any device without the need to install any Ansible-specific agent on the device. This makes it easier for network operators in a brownfield network. Changing versions of the network OS don't affect the usability of the tool. Ansible has added an agent-based model, but I've never heard of it being used.

Multiple native transport support
  By default, Ansible uses SSH natively to communicate with the device it's configuring. But it can use any transport the OS vendor provides. For example, Arista provides an Ansible module that uses the REST API of the OS to get more efficiency than SSH provides. Juniper and some of Cisco's operating systems provide NETCONF as the transport. But if no vendor-specific module is provided, SSH is assumed. To make the use of SSH painless, a password-less model is assumed via a key file or using a vault to store the passwords.

YAML
  Ansible uses YAML as its basic configuration language. YAML is used as the configuration language by many cloud native tools, such as Kubernetes. Thus, knowing YAML helps in more than just Ansible.

Templating to separate code from data

The basic model for Ansible is to use a template based on the templating tool Jinja2 (*https://oreil.ly/uknhE*) to allow operators to express the configuration in a generic template and then render the template with the device-specific parameters provided in a different file. The parameters for a device are automatically derived from separate files based on the device's hostname and what user-defined groups the device belongs to.

User extensible

Besides the standard modules provided by Ansible itself, a network operator can extend Ansible's functionality by writing their own customized module to perform certain actions. A lot of modules, for both networking equipment and servers, are developed and maintained by both Ansible and vendors. This makes for a feature-rich solution.

Ansible itself provides a rich set of resource modules. A resource module operates on a single resource such as a package manager or a service such as SSH or setting the banner displayed on login. The main advantage of these resource modules for network operators new to automation is that they require very little of even templating knowledge to accomplish a simple task, and so are an effective and efficient way to start.

Inventory

How does Ansible know which nodes to reach and how to reach them? For static entities such as network switches and physical servers, Ansible uses an inventory file. Typically the inventory file is in a well-defined place, */etc/ansible/hosts*. But you can change this location by providing the path using the -i option or via the *ansible.cfg* configuration file.[7] The inventory for the example shown in the rest of this section looks as follows:

```
vx ansible_host=192.168.121.154          ❶
eos ansible_host=192.168.121.109         ❶
server01 ansible_host=192.168.121.86     ❶
server02 ansible_host=192.168.121.82     ❶

[servers]                                ❷
server01
server02

[cumulus]                                ❷
vx
```

---

7 The Ansible documentation talks (*https://oreil.ly/aF1DC*) about the security risks associated with using *ansible.cfg* in the same directory as the playbooks, especially if the directory is writable by all users.

```
[arista]                                    ❷
eos

[linux:children]                            ❸
cumulus
linux

[routers:children]                          ❸
vx
eos

[all:vars]                                  ❹
ansible_port=22
ansible_user="vagrant"
ansible_ssh_private_key_file="/vagrant/machines/private_key"

[arista:vars]
ansible_network_os: "eos"
```

❶ This file indicates four devices: vx, eos, server01, and server02. Associated with each entry is a line with information about how to reach the device.

❷ The inventory also contains the various groupings associated with these four devices. For example, the servers group includes the server01 and server02 devices. There is a predefined group "all" that includes all the nodes.

❸ The groupings can include other groups so that you can avoid repeating the hostnames over and over again when a host is used in multiple groups. For instance, the group linux contains both cumulus routers and servers. The inventory also allows you to specify variables to use with each group.

❹ Although it's better to keep these variables elsewhere, you can define variables associated with either a group or host in this file as well. For example, the all group which includes every node listed has defined a bunch of variables under [all:vars]. It shows that the username to log in is vagrant for all nodes.

Besides these groups, you can have Ansible also create dynamic groups based on the device's distribution, version, or some other artifact. A dynamic group can usually be established only after Ansible manages to establish communication with the devices and retrieve the relevant information to create the grouping.

In the commands in the next section or two, when we refer to a device such as eos used with Ansible, the inventory file is consulted to retrieve the information to access the device.

The network operator has to build the inventory file by hand, especially for the physical devices such as network switches and compute nodes.

With the inventory in hand, the network operator can fire one-off commands or execute a well-defined workflow.

Playbooks

The second major piece in Ansible is executing well-defined workflows to execute well-defined tasks. This involves writing *playbooks*. These are sequences of tasks or *plays*. Here is a playbook, called *show-version.yml*, showing how to retrieve the version of the node:

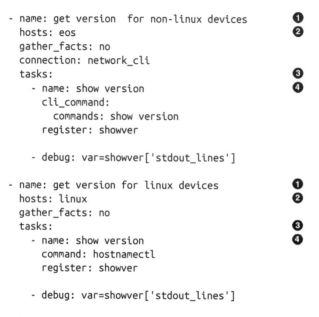

```
- name: get version  for non-linux devices    ❶
  hosts: eos                                   ❷
  gather_facts: no
  connection: network_cli
  tasks:                                       ❸
    - name: show version                       ❹
      cli_command:
        commands: show version
      register: showver

    - debug: var=showver['stdout_lines']

- name: get version for linux devices          ❶
  hosts: linux                                 ❷
  gather_facts: no
  tasks:                                       ❸
    - name: show version                       ❹
      command: hostnamectl
      register: showver

    - debug: var=showver['stdout_lines']
```

❶ This is a play. It groups all the tasks associated with each play. You can provide a meaningful name for the play.

❷ This is the list of hosts associated with the play. As the inventory file showed, linux here is the list of all native Linux hosts.

❸ This is the section that lists all the tasks associated with this play.

❹ This is the name associated with each task.

The output now looks like this:

```
$ ansible-playbook show-version.yml

PLAY [get version  for non-linux devices] ********************************* ❶

TASK [show version] ****************************************************** ❷
ok: [eos]
```

```
TASK [debug] **************************************************************
ok: [eos] => {
    "showver['stdout_lines']": [
        "vEOS",
        "Hardware version:     ",
        "Serial number:        ",
        "System MAC address:  5254.0072.ec50",
        "",
        "Software image version: 4.22.0F",
        "Architecture:           i386",
        "Internal build version: 4.22.0F-12170486.4220F",
        "Internal build ID:      2c34e816-9aa7-4c63-9a32-05140aec7dbd",
        "",
        "Uptime:                 1 weeks, 0 days, 3 hours and 4 minutes",
        "Total memory:           2014580 kB",
        "Free memory:            1258860 kB"
    ]
}

PLAY [get version for linux devices] ***************************************  ❶

TASK [show version] *******************************************************  ❷
changed: [server01]
changed: [server02]
changed: [vx]

TASK [debug] **************************************************************
ok: [vx] => {
    "showver['stdout_lines']": [
        "   Static hostname: cumulus",
        "         Icon name: computer-vm",
        "           Chassis: vm",
        "        Machine ID: 5bb87be8ca4449549db8947b5be70cfd",
        "           Boot ID: 3690e42cb1a74b9f87d89e76c4b2b914",
        "    Virtualization: kvm",
        "  Operating System: Cumulus Linux",
        "       CPE OS Name: cpe:/o:cumulusnetworks:cumulus_linux:3.7.0",
        "            Kernel: Linux 4.1.0-cl-7-amd64",
        "      Architecture: x86-64"
    ]
}
ok: [server01] => {
    "showver['stdout_lines']": [
        "   Static hostname: server01",
        "         Icon name: computer-vm",
        "           Chassis: vm",
        "        Machine ID: bf712b1790a50163052d66505719d284",
        "           Boot ID: 727291f8d1344e02bffaaf73d53cf623",
        "    Virtualization: qemu",
        "  Operating System: Ubuntu 16.04 LTS",
        "            Kernel: Linux 4.4.0-22-generic",
```

```
                "        Architecture: x86-64"
    ]
}
ok: [server02] => {
    "showver['stdout_lines']": [
        "    Static hostname: server02",
        "         Icon name: computer-vm",
        "           Chassis: vm",
        "        Machine ID: bf712b1790a50163052d66505719d284",
        "           Boot ID: d8b98e9a20904b1688166d161f5f203b",
        "    Virtualization: qemu",
        "  Operating System: Ubuntu 16.04 LTS",
        "            Kernel: Linux 4.4.0-22-generic",
        "      Architecture: x86-64"
    ]
}


PLAY RECAP ****************************************************************** ❸
eos                       : ok=2    changed=0    unreachable=0    failed=0
server01                  : ok=2    changed=1    unreachable=0    failed=0
server02                  : ok=2    changed=1    unreachable=0    failed=0
vx                        : ok=2    changed=1    unreachable=0    failed=0
```

The preceding output shows the list of devices on which the commands were run and what the results of those commands were.

❶ Each play is listed. If the play has a name, the name of the play is listed; otherwise, the line given by the hosts variable is listed. We see that this has two plays.

❷ Each play's task is executed. The playbook showed that each play has two tasks. As you might notice if you run this example, each task is completed for all hosts before the next task in the play is executed.

❸ A final recap is provided for all hosts on which the playbook was executed. For each host, it lists a set of status variables. ok=2 tells you that two commands were successfully executed. unreachable=0 tells you that the device against which this is listed was reachable to deliver and execute the commands. changed=0 tells you that no state on the device was changed as a consequence of the command. On the Arista device, a "show" command is treated as a "no change" command. On Linux, a command could execute anything. For example, it could be a script that internally changes the state. Therefore, Ansible always assumes that the state was changed as a consequence of using the "command" module. This is one reason why you don't want to execute commands directly on a Linux machine. A second reason is that executing commands directly does not cause the configuration to persist (survive restarts or reboots). Instead, every application provides a configuration file and a service file that abstracts the application start/stop/restart logic. So you update a configuration file and use Ansible's notify mechanism to have the application process the change. If the pushed change didn't really change the file, the application will not be notified.

For a network operator looking at the output of Ansible, the recap lines at the end provide the summary of what just happened. It is important to make sure that no commands failed and that no device was unreachable during any play. Ansible shows in red any host that has failed commands. When a task fails for a host, all subsequent tasks are ignored for that host.

There are several things to observe in this playbook:

- Using playbooks as a network-wide "show" command isn't very human friendly. This is not an indication of a flaw, but to point out the limitations of the "show" command.
- Tasks are broken down across hosts of a similar type. (The first part is for the host named eos, and the second part of the playbook is for all Linux hosts.)
- There is no attempt to paper over the differences between different operating systems in executing commands. *hostamectl* works on Linux machines, and *show version* on Arista's EOS. Non-Linux devices have different names for potentially the same task (`cli_command` instead of `command`, a connection specification, etc.).
- Traditional network devices need additional configuration, such as the parameter `connection`.
- By default, the command outputs of plays are not displayed. They need to be explicitly captured (via the `register` option) and displayed (via the `debug` option).

Ansible has a different model for network devices compared to Linux devices because traditional network devices often do not provide support for Python. On Linux hosts, Ansible pushes the Python template to execute for a task to the remote endpoint and executes the script on the device. For example, templates are rendered on each remote device independently and can be in parallel. On traditional network devices, Ansible assumes that it cannot execute Python locally on the remote node, and so executes the Python code locally for each remote node it's operating on, and then pushes the generated configuration output to the remote device. Network operating systems such as Cumulus Linux and SoNIC can be treated just like a Linux server, whereas most other network devices, including Arista and Cisco, cannot. This difference has consequences on performance, which we talk about later.

There is a clever playbook (*https://oreil.ly/6qjwf*) that shows how to use `cli_command` in a playbook coupled with variables to show the versions of various traditional network operating systems.

Ad Hoc Commands

Ansible also supports running ad hoc commands: commands that aren't saved anywhere, but executed using the parameters passed on the command line—a sort of glorified network-wide CLI. With Linux you can do the following to look at the parameters stored on the eos node:

```
$ ansible '!eos' -a 'cat /etc/lsb-release'
vx | SUCCESS | rc=0 >>
DISTRIB_ID="Cumulus Linux"
DISTRIB_RELEASE=3.7.0
DISTRIB_DESCRIPTION="Cumulus Linux 3.7.0"

server02 | SUCCESS | rc=0 >>
DISTRIB_ID=Ubuntu
DISTRIB_RELEASE=16.04
DISTRIB_CODENAME=xenial
DISTRIB_DESCRIPTION="Ubuntu 16.04 LTS"

server01 | SUCCESS | rc=0 >>
DISTRIB_ID=Ubuntu
DISTRIB_RELEASE=16.04
DISTRIB_CODENAME=xenial
DISTRIB_DESCRIPTION="Ubuntu 16.04 LTS"
```

You can use an ad hoc command to add a default route, for example (the -b option executes the command via sudo on a Linux host):

```
$ ansible '!eos' -b -a 'ip ro add 10.10.0.0/24 via 192.168.121.1'

vx | SUCCESS | rc=0 >>


server02 | SUCCESS | rc=0 >>


server01 | SUCCESS | rc=0 >>
```

Network devices that aren't Linux—which is just about every traditional networking device—have unique connection methods. Juniper uses NETCONF, whereas Arista and Cisco's NX-OS use a REST API. There are Python libraries specific to each vendor that wrap up the complexity of connecting to the devices. Ansible version 2.5 introduced a connection method called *network_cli* with the equivalent ad hoc command *cli_command* to standardize access to each of the devices. The commands themselves are not standardized, so you need to supply the device-appropriate command. Here is a simple cli_command for Arista and the corresponding output:

```
$ ansible eos -c network_cli -m cli_command -a 'command="show version"'
eos | SUCCESS => {
    "ansible_facts": {
        "discovered_interpreter_python": "/usr/bin/python"
```

```
    },
    "changed": false,

    ... snipped lines thay were too long

    "stdout_lines": [
        "vEOS",
        "Hardware version:     ",
        "Serial number:        ",
        "System MAC address:  5254.0072.ec50",
        "",
        "Software image version: 4.22.0F",
        "Architecture:           i386",
        "Internal build version: 4.22.0F-12170486.4220F",
        "Internal build ID:      2c34e816-9aa7-4c63-9a32-05140aec7dbd",
        "",
        "Uptime:                 1 weeks, 0 days, 2 hours and 56 minutes",
        "Total memory:           2014580 kB",
        "Free memory:            1264924 kB"
    ]
}
```

Structuring Playbooks

Ansible tries to enforce certain disciplines to both simplify the practice of automation for novices and ensure good practices such as avoiding duplication and separating code from data. The recommended directory structure for Ansible playbooks is shown in Example 10-1.

Example 10-1. Recommended Ansible directory structure

```
ansible.cfg                                        ❶
group_vars/                                        ❷
   routers.yml
   eos.yml
   server.yml
host_vars/                                         ❸
   vx.yml
   eos.yml

   ..
   server02.yml
inventory
roles/                                             ❹
   common/
        tasks/
        main.yml
   handlers/
   vars/
   files/
   templates/
```

```
routers/
    tasks/
      main.yml
handlers/
vars/
files/
templates/
servers/
    ...
site.yml
```

According to the Ansible documentation, "Roles are ways of automatically loading certain vars_files, tasks, and handlers based on a known file structure. Grouping content by roles also allows easy sharing of roles with other users." In the preceding example structure, we can observe the following:

❶ *ansible.cfg* lists the Ansible configuration specific to whatever is in this directory. I usually set this to contain the inventory file for the Vagrant simulation I'm running, for example.

❷ This directory contains the variables specific to each group. We had defined `linux`, `routers`, `arista`, and so on as groups in the inventory file.

❸ This directory contains the variables specific to each host. So you can have group-specific variables as well as variables that are specific to each host. If the same variable is defined in both the group- and host-specific variables file, the host-specific variable takes precedence.

❹ In Ansible, *roles* provides the equivalent of a function. Just like a function contains its own variables, a role contains things specific to the function the role performs. For example, if you have a role to render the BGP configuration across all nodes, you can have that defined as a template under the role's template directory. The difference between what's in the template directory versus the files directory is whether the output is to be passed through Jinja2 or it needs to be copied as is. An example of a file in this context is the daemons file that FRR requires that lists the routing daemons to launch, such as *bgpd*. You can stick that file under the files directory associated with configuring BGP.

I have not listed all the possible directories and files under each role. Ansible's recommended best practices are available in its documentation (*https://oreil.ly/sO8lc*).

In my experience, network administrators have a more difficult time when configuration is broken up into so much hierarchy. And in some ways, I don't blame them. Finding and collating information, knowing where to update something, and so forth all seem needlessly complicated. In my discussions with even nonnetwork adminis-

---

trators, roles is a difficult concept to manage for many. So if all of this seems too much to start with, I recommend at least the following two practices:

- Separate the code from the data. Using `host_vars` and `group_vars` makes sense and prepares you for a transition from a simpler model as you progress.
- Use Ansible's *include* option to break up the playbook into individual functional units that can be reused. You can then convert the include files into roles over time as you become more comfortable with Ansible.

A Typical Automation Journey

During my time at Cumulus Networks, I encountered many customers who were new to network automation. There was immense interest in network automation, and since the Cumulus Linux interface was the native Linux interface, all server automation tools automatically worked on Cumulus. Ansible had taken the lead mostly because it was the most friendly to people who didn't know programming. In this time, I watched the journey of many customers progress from a complete ignorance of network automation to making it part of their normal workflow.

The most common journey I saw involved the following progression. For the sake of brevity, I focus on only some aspects of the configuration because this is meant to highlight a possibility rather than demonstrate the complete configuration of a device.

There are more things to configure, such as setting up license keys, hostname, and locale. These tasks mostly follow the nondevice-specific pattern shown later. This Github repo (*https://oreil.ly/nf08_*) from Cumulus shows the playbooks for a bunch of common configuration tasks. There are other repos like this for other devices, such as Cisco and Arista. For example, Sean Cavanaugh and the Network Automation team of Ansible have some interesting repositories (*https://oreil.ly/Dxu11*), especially the one generating an inventory report in HTML and the network device–agnostic examples.

Glorified File Copy

In their first step on the network automation journey, operators crafted the configuration by hand for a few devices like before. They needed to do that anyway, because they did not know how to automate yet. After this, they used Ansible to push these handcrafted configuration files to the other devices. What this did was make them comfortable using Ansible. In the process, they also began to notice the patterns and the possibility of replacing completely handcrafted files with templates.

The directory structure in such a scenario resemble something similar to what is shown in Example 10-2.

Example 10-2. Sample directory structure of rudimentary automation

```
ansible.cfg
inventory
config/
     leaf01/
          interfaces
     frr.conf ❶
     daemons
     ntp.conf
     leaf02/
          interfaces
     frr.conf
     daemons
     ntp.conf
     ...
     spine01/
          interfaces
     frr.conf
     daemons
     ntp.conf
     ...
site.yml
```

❶ FRR didn't exist in those days; its predecessor was called quagga. So the file is called *quagga.conf*, not *frr.conf*.

The playbook, *site.yml*, might have resembled something like Example 10-3.

Example 10-3. The site.yml file for rudimentary automation

```
- hosts: network
  tasks:
    - name: copy interfaces
      copy: src=config/{{ansible_inventory_hostname}}/interfaces dest=/etc/network/
    - name: copy daemons
      copy: src=config/{{ansible_inventory_hostname}}/daemons dest=/etc/frr/
    - name: copy routing configuration
      copy: src=config/{{ansible_inventory_hostname}}/frr.conf dest=/etc/frr/
    ...
```

The whole thing was executed using a file named *ansible-playbook site.yml*. The device was rebooted because that was simpler than restarting the services associated with the modified files. This would involve understanding Ansible a bit more.

Automate the Configuration That Was Not Device Specific

All devices need to configure their timezone, the Network Time Protocol (NTP) server configuration, logging, and other such parameters. So instead of copying the same file over and over again for each host, the operators copied these files to a common directory. In our example, the FRR daemons file is common across the leaves and spines, and is node agnostic. The directory structure has the form shown in Example 10-4.

Example 10-4. Sample directory structure with common files

```
ansible.cfg
inventory
config/
     common/
            daemons
     leaf01/
           interfaces
     frr.conf
     leaf02/
           interfaces
     frr.conf
     ...
     spine01/
           interfaces
     frr.conf
     ...
site.yml
```

The playbook, *site.yml*, might resembled something like Example 10-5.

Example 10-5. The site.yml file for further device automation

```
- hosts: network
  tasks:
    - name: copy daemons
      copy: src=config/common/daemons dest=/etc/frr/
    - name: copy interfaces
      copy: src=config/{{ansible_inventory_hostname}}/interfaces dest=/etc/network/
    - name: copy routing configuration
      copy: src=config/{{ansible_inventory_hostname}}/frr.conf dest=/etc/frr/
    ...
    - name: Let the interface configuration take effect
      command: ifreload -a
    - name: restart frr
      service: name=frr state=restarted
```

It might no longer be necessary to restart the entire device, merely the appropriate services. But most operators rebooted the device after installing the day-zero configuration, and restarted or reloaded services for updates.

Template the Routing and Interface Configuration

When FRR introduced support for unnumbered interfaces, first with OSPFv2 and then with BGP, the only address associated with the interface was for the loopback. This worked at least for the spines, which had no other interface to assign addresses to (in contrast, the leaves had the VLANs associated with the server-facing ports). So the next step was to pull out the loopback IP address into a file and template the routing configuration. The Ansible directory structure looked like Example 10-6.

Example 10-6. Sample directory structure with common files

```
ansible.cfg
inventory
config/
      common/
              daemons
      spines/
      frr.conf.j2
      leaf01/
              interfaces
      frr.conf
      leaf02/
              interfaces
      frr.conf
      ...
      spine01/
              interfaces
      ...
host_vars/
          spine01.yml
     spine02.yml
   ...
site.yml
```

The playbook, *site.yml*, might resemble something like Example 10-7.

Example 10-7. The site.yml file considering loopback addresses

```
- hosts: network
  tasks:
    - name: copy daemons
      copy: src=config/common/daemons dest=/etc/frr/
    - name: copy interfaces
      copy: src=config/{{ansible_inventory_hostname}}/interfaces dest=/etc/network/
```

```
- hosts: leaf
  tasks:
    - name: copy routing configuration
      copy: src=config/{{ansible_inventory_hostname}}/frr.conf dest=/etc/frr/
      notify: restart frr
    - name: restart frr
      service: name=frr state=restarted

- hosts: spine
  tasks:
    - name: template out routing configuration
      template: src=config/spines/frr.conf.j2 dest=/etc/frr/
      notify: restart frr
    - name: restart frr
      service: name=frr state=restarted
```

The contents of *host_vars/spine01.yml* looked simply like this:

```
loopback_ip: 10.0.0.21/32
```

The same thing was done for other spines, each containing that spine's loopback IP address. The template file for the spine's routing configuration, *frr.conf.j2*, resembled Example 10-8 (for OSPFv2).

Example 10-8. FRR file for OSPFv2

```
interface lo
  ip address {{ loopback_ip }}
  ip ospf area 0.0.0.0
!
interface swp1
  ip address {{ loopback_ip }}
  ip ospf network point-to-point
  ip ospf area 0.0.0.0
!
interface swp2
  ip address {{ loopback_ip }}
  ip ospf network point-to-point
  ip ospf area 0.0.0.0
!
...
!
router ospf
  router-id {{ loopback_ip }}
  passive-interface lo
```

More Templating and Roles

From here, as their comfort with Ansible and automation grew, operators began to template more tasks, such as leaf configuration. Some even went ahead and embraced roles. To consider how we move the previous into roles, we can identify the following tasks:

- Copying the daemons file for FRR
- Copying the interfaces file
- Copying the *frr.conf* file for leaves
- Templating the *frr.conf* file for spines

You can create a role for each of these tasks. You could create just two roles, one to configure the interfaces and the other to configure FRR, but that'll prove more complicated given how we've divided the tasks so far. You could alternatively create a role for leaves and another one for spines and have a common role for the parts that are common to both. So you can replace the *site.yml* with the file shown in Example 10-9 using roles.

Example 10-9. The site.yml file considering roles done one way

```
- hosts: network
  roles:
    - copy_frr_daemons
    - copy_interfaces

- hosts: leaf
  tasks:
    - copy_leaf_frr
      notify: restart frr

- hosts: spine
  tasks:
    - copy_spine_frr
      notify: restart frr
```

Or carve it up as demonstrated in Example 10-10.

Example 10-10. The site.yml file considering roles done a second way

```
- hosts: network
  roles:
    - common

- hosts: leaf
  tasks:
    - leaf
      notify: restart frr

- hosts: spine
  tasks:
```

```
  - spine
    notify: restart frr
```

Notice how alike both are to the previous *site.yml*. However, the first set of roles feels easier to comprehend as to what is going on compared to the second. Nevertheless, Ansible seems to recommend (*https://oreil.ly/1HSsp*) the second model in its documentation. But proceeding with the first style of roles, the directory structure might resemble that shown in Example 10-11.

Example 10-11. Example directory structure with roles

```
ansible.cfg
config/
     leaf01/
          interfaces
     frr.conf
     leaf02/
          interfaces
     frr.conf
     ...
     spine01/
          interfaces
     ...
group_vars/
host_vars/
          spine01.yml
   spine02.yml
  ...
inventory
roles/
   copy_frr_daemons/
        tasks/
       main.yml
   files/
       daemons
   copy_interfaces/
        tasks/
       main.yml
   copy_leaf_frr/
        tasks/
       main.yml
   handlers/
        main.yml
   copy_spine_frr
       ...site.yml
```

The journey from this point on diverged depending on the organization's success with automation, its skill in increasing the sophistication, and its desire to continue the journey.

Some Observations from Fellow Journeymen

I had the opportunity and luck to speak to some of the large-scale practitioners of Ansible. These were operators in fairly large organizations who had decided to forge ahead in the automation journey. There were common threads across their experiences:

Ansible's good enough
> For network operators, they felt Ansible was the easiest automation tool to get into. Although Ansible continues to make network automation easier, these operators were content with the current feature set.

Performance needs improvement
> As described earlier, Ansible executes plays associated with traditional network devices locally on the server where Ansible is run rather than on the network device itself, as is the case with Linux. This translates to poor performance and the inability to scale automation to managing more than a hundred or a few hundred devices from a single server.

Embrace the common practice
> They felt that even though roles were somewhat more difficult to grasp, using roles as simple individual functions (copy FRR daemons file) instead of more complex function-based roles (router versus server versus web server, etc.) were easier to grasp and adopt.

Use tools to store inventory
> The sophisticated players used some software to be their "source of truth." Netbox (*https://oreil.ly/hPLUl*) is a popular, open source example of such a tool. Dropbox came up with NSOT (Network Statement of Truth) (*https://oreil.ly/-WOta*), another open source tool. I've also heard of one organization using Men & Mice (*https://oreil.ly/Y1h4T*), a proprietary software to handle their IP address management. The basic point I've heard about these tools is to use them to manage IP addresses rather than using *host_vars* files.

Lack of automated validation is scary
> For many of them, the lack of sophisticated verification tools to test the network post-deployment was scary. Pushing a configuration to hundreds of devices via Ansible and then not being able to run an automated tool to verify was a major reason to hesitate moving forward. Many of them had to write their own programs to make this happen.

They all insisted on starting simple and building on each little success to iterate their way to full automation.

Unnumbered Interfaces: The Secret to Network Automation

Without unnumbered interfaces, network automation would not have been as simple. Unnumbered interfaces are interfaces without a uniquely assigned IP address of their own (we discuss them in detail in "Unnumbered Interfaces" on page 98). In other words, with unnumbered interfaces, the only IP addresses you need on a device are on the loopback interface and on the server subnets. In the case of BGP, the use of "remote-as external"[8] coupled with the invention of unnumbered BGP made BGP configuration trivial. A similar simplification also helped with routing configuration for network virtualization.

To get an idea of the savings in the number of host variables covered by unnumbered interfaces, see Table 10-3. The list mentions only the host variables required for the loopback plus all the interfaces.

Table 10-3. The impact of unnumbered interfaces on host variables

Network	Minimum host vars (numbered)	Minimum host vars (unnumbered)
4 spines, 32 leaves	$36 + 4 \times 32 \times 2 = 288$	36 (one per router)
4 spines, 64 leaves	$64 + 4 \times 64 \times 2 = 580$	68 (one per router)
16 spines, 96 leaves	$112 + 16 \times 96 \times 2 = 3184$	112 (one per router)

The trouble with programmatically generating the configuration of these interface IP addresses is that any recabling or changes to the regular topology, which is not uncommon, will either renumber the entire network or require additional complexity in programming to handle the exceptions.

Sadly, no traditional routing stack supports unnumbered interfaces. As discussed before, this is one of the biggest reasons why network automation remains difficult. FRR, the open source routing suite, has been unique in pushing the envelope on making routing configuration simpler and easier, especially for network automation. As examples of this, it was the first routing suite to support BGP Unnumbered, provide sane defaults to eliminate needless clutter, and support OSPFv2 unnumbered on Ethernet interfaces.

---

8 We cover the meaning of this in Chapter 15.

Validating the Configuration

As the much-clichéd saying goes, "To err is human, to err a thousand times is automation." In this section, we examine the things that we can do to avoid this fate. We look at the following areas:

- Validating the configuration and reverting to a good state
- Testing the effect of the configuration before deploying it to production
- Automating the verification of the network state post-deployment

Single Source of Truth

In the age of automation, what is the source of truth about a device's state? Conventionally, you would look at the currently operational state on the device. But if the device were rebooted, the source of truth is its startup configuration. In the case of Linux (including Cumulus Linux), these are the various files stored in the */etc* directory. In most traditional network devices, it is stored in some vendor-specific format that is displayed in text form by *show startup-configuration*. In the case of Arista's EOS, for example, this blob is a text file called *startup-config* in */mnt/flash*.

If you use Ansible to format a device and reinstall its contents, the source of truth is the playbooks that regenerate the startup configuration.

In a correctly functioning infrastructure, there should be no disparity among the following aspects of configuration: the running or operational state, the startup configuration, and the automation scripts that generate the desired state of the device. But during the course of the network automation journey, it is not impossible for disparities to nevertheless arise among these three aspects. It is imperative to ensure that this disparity is addressed as soon as it is detected. Any laziness in this regard will only hurt your ability to provide a predictable network. More specifically, with automation, the Ansible playbooks, the templates, files, and so on are the source of truth. After you decide to automate something, resist the temptation to also manually tamper with it. If you do so, you're losing a key benefit of automation and you'll have a less predictable network.

Commit/Rollback in the Age of Automation

Many network devices provide a commit/rollback mechanism that tries to instate the configuration and then rolls back the staged configuration if it is not deemed appropriate. Typically, the staged configuration is checked for any errors that might have occurred due to typos or cut-and-paste errors. Some systems also perform syntax checking to ensure that the staged configuration is free of syntax errors.

The wisdom of sanity checks can be shown through a Juniper experience. Before Juniper introduced commit/rollback in its Junos OS, the network operating systems executed operators' commands immediately as they were typed. A typo or error in the middle of a long series of changes could break the network. Junos OS changed all that. Nowadays just about every network OS provides a commit/rollback option.

In the case of Linux, because the configuration comes from a text file, staging changes involves writing to a temporary file and then making this temporary file the new startup configuration file and reloading the appropriate service to use the new configuration.[9] Rollback involves discarding the temporary file.

Many services provide a syntax checker or dry run option to validate the configuration. Junos OS offers an additional knob to revert the applied configuration back to the previous working configuration if a key is not pressed within a specific time. This is useful to avoid completely losing access to the device due to a typo.

Ansible provides a validate option with the copy, template, and assemble modules, which can be used with Linux. Most traditional network devices provide a commit/rollback option in their specific module. For example, if you want to validate the FRR and interfaces configuration you're pushing, write the play as follows:

```
- name: copy FRR
  template:
    src: config/{{ansible_inventory_hostname}}/frr.conf
    dest: /etc/frr/
    validate: '/usr/bin/vtysh -C -f %s'
    backup: yes
  become: yes
  notify: restart frr

- name: copy interfaces
  template:
    src: config/{{ansible_inventory_hostname}}/interfaces
    dest: /etc/network/
    validate: 'ifup -a -s -i %s'
    backup: yes
  become: yes
  notify: restart interfaces
```

Because the file sets the backup option to yes, you can automatically revert to the older version on the device itself.

It is equally important to be able to revert the automation scripts back to their previously good state if the current version is no good. Source code control systems such as Git are fundamental to ensuring this. As mentioned in the section on best practi-

---

9 Reloading doesn't cause the service to hiccup as the new changes take effect, whereas restarting does.

ces, robust source control is an essential workflow item for a network administrator pursuing network automation.

In the same spirit, it is crucial to not make manual changes on individual devices. If you make a change, when an automation script reruns later, it can lead to a surprising result. The surprises that inevitably ensue when this happens make it difficult to troubleshoot because often the memory about the manual change has been lost to time and personnel changes. This makes for a less reliable and predictable network.

Ansible can verify that the running configuration or operational state is the same as the startup or desired configuration state for Arista and Cisco devices. It does this using the *intended_config* option with the configuration. As of this writing, Ansible did not support this check for any other network vendor or Linux.

Vagrant and Network Testing

One of the most useful tools in the modern sysadmin toolkit is Vagrant (*https:// oreil.ly/jgP9p*). The primary benefit of this tool is to use VMs to create a virtual copy of the real network, complete with the network devices and servers. It can then validate that the network functions as predicted by the configuration. It is not used to do datapath stress testing, such as pushing line rate traffic.

Vagrant uses *boxes* that are repackaged versions of the VMs of the network operating systems (including the routing suites and such) and server operating systems. Vagrant then uses one of the well-known hypervisors such as Virtualbox, KVM, or VMware to stitch these boxes together into a virtual infrastructure. More boxes are available for Virtualbox than for any of the other hypervisors.

Unfortunately, it is beyond the scope of this book to describe Vagrant and its use in much more detail. I recommend common web resources as well as *Vagrant: Up and Running* (O'Reilly) to explore this topic further.

I've used Vagrant to test and run all of the code in this book. The GitHub repo associated with this book gets you started. A Linux server or laptop or macOS machine with more than 16 GB memory is necessary to do something meaningful.

You can run the automation scripts on this virtual infrastructure and validate it before deploying it. Doing such a check, even in a rolling update fashion, on the production network goes a long way toward ensuring that the deployed configuration provides the desired behavior. If incompatibilities create errors in pushing the configuration to the switching silicon, this method will not catch them. But it does catch a wide variety of other kinds of problems. It has the potential to reduce the surprise factor and to significantly increase confidence in meeting the desired outcomes. Customers I know who started with this methodology have never looked back and use this method consistently to test upgrades and configuration changes.

I highly recommend that network administrators familiarize themselves with Vagrant, if your network vendor supports it. Arista, Cumulus, and Juniper currently do so. Every official Cumulus release is accompanied by a Vagrant box. This can be directly downloaded from Vagrant's website (*https://oreil.ly/-SpWq*) without requiring any interaction with Cumulus. Arista puts out a Vagrant box for its official releases too, but it is behind a registration wall. Juniper was probably the first network vendor to release a Vagrant box, though I don't know whether every Junos OS release has an equivalent Vagrant box.

Each of these vendors have differing levels of support for re-creating a virtual network. Cumulus has no restrictions beside the one imposed by the hypervisor in the number of switchports. Arista and Juniper restrict the number of switchports to a maximum of eight.

Automating Verification

Even if your configuration is correct, and you use something like Vagrant to validate the configuration before deploying it, verification of the network state is largely a manual operation. Servers have tools such as testinfra (*https://oreil.ly/p53EU*) and goss (*https://oreil.ly/P7sh7*) to verify their deployment, but network devices lack any support from such tools. Open source routing suites and other networking software are not supported by these tools. I've presented at various conferences and webinars about how we can use Ansible to do this kind of testing, but I haven't seen it being used in real life. Example 10-12 shows a sample playbook validating that BGP is working correctly in a two-tier Clos topology. We discuss validating the deployed configuration in greater detail in Chapter 18.

Example 10-12. Ansible playbook for validating a routing configuration

```
- name: Get bgp summary
  command: vtysh -c 'sh ip bgp summary json'
  register: cmd_out
  become: true

- name: Get the peer count
  set_fact:
    peer_count: "{{ ((cmd_out.stdout|from_json).totalPeers) }}"

- name: Get the peer list
  set_fact:
    bgp_peers: "{{ (cmd_out.stdout|from_json).peers }}"

- name: Validate peer count matches the expected number of leaves
  assert: { that: '(peer_count|int) == num_leaves' }
  when: "{{ 'spine' in group_names }}"

- name: Validate peer count matches the expected number of spines
```

```
  assert: { that: '(peer_count|int) == num_spines' }
  when: "{{ 'leaf' in group_names }}"

- name: Verify all BGP sessions are in established state
  assert: { that: 'bgp_peers[item]["state"] == "Established"' }
  with_items: "{{ bgp_peers }}"
```

There are startups such as Intentionet, Veriflow, and Forward Networks that are trying to fill this void in automated validation. Intentionet is based on the open source tool, Batfish (*https://oreil.ly/WNatZ*). Batfish does not require access to any running device. It validates the specified configuration *before* you deploy it. This adds an additional level of validation before you deploy the configuration. I don't have enough experience with them to comment on either their effectiveness or even their use. There are some online posts and examples for Cumulus (*https://oreil.ly/8DwT-*) and Arista (*https://oreil.ly/0RUKO*) that you can explore to get a taste for how predeployment validation works.

Summary

In this chapter, you learned about network automation, especially as it applies to configuration management: why it is essential in the modern data center, what makes network automation more difficult than its server counterpart, and how to go about the network automation journey. We dived briefly into the usage of what I think is the most popular network automation tool, Ansible. The goal of this chapter was not to teach you network automation, but give you enough information to plunge into books and online material that will. But this chapter hopefully empathized with the pain of a network administrator when it comes to network automation, and took a little of the sting out of the fear of network automation.

In closing, let me paraphrase the Chinese proverb:[10] "The best time to have started the network automation journey was three years ago. The second best time is now."

References

- Networktocode Slack channel (*https://oreil.ly/h5LHE*)
- Ansible Mailing lists (*https://www.ansible.com/community*)
- Free Ansible workshops (*https://oreil.ly/L1Pkb*)
- Stack Overflow (*https://stackoverflow.com*)
- Ivan Pepelnjak's Information Portal (*https://oreil.ly/iMbQ4*)

---

10 Here's the original: "The best time to plant a tree was 20 years ago. The second best time is now."

## CHAPTER 11

Network Observability

One of the dirtiest secrets in systems engineering is just how many outages are never really fully explained or understood. Or how many can't actually be explained or understood given existing telemetry.
—Charity Majors

A distributed system is one in which the failure of a computer you didn't even know existed can render your own computer unusable.
—Leslie Lamport

Two distributed systems experts, one a theoretician and the other a practitioner, separated by a generation, make the same observation. Distributed systems are hard to understand, hard to control, and always frustrating when things go wrong. And sandwiched in the middle between the endpoints is the network operator. "Is it the network?" is not too far down the list of universal questions such as, "What is the meaning of life, the universe, and everything?" Sadly, network operators do not even have the humor of a Douglas Adams story to fall back on.

The modern data center with its scale and the ever increasing distributed nature of its applications only makes it more difficult to answer the questions that network operators have been dealing with since the dawn of distributed applications. *Observability* represents the operator's latest attempt to respond adequately to the questions. Along with automation, observability has become one of the central pillars of the cloud native data center.

The primary goal of this chapter is to leave you with an understanding of the importance of observability and the unique challenges of network observability. You should be able to answer questions such as the following two questions:

- What is observability and why should I care?
- What are the challenges of network observability?

We begin the story with a definition of observability and how it is different from monitoring.

What Is Observability?

Observability can be defined as the property of a system that provides answers to questions ranging from the mundane (What's the state of BGP?) to the existential (Is my network happy?). More precisely, observability is a way for an operator to understand what's going on in a system by examining the outputs provided by the system. As a concrete example of this, without having examined BGP process' data structures, packet exchanges, state machine, and so on, we can use the show bgp summary command to infer the state of BGP as a whole on a node.

Twitter, which is credited with the use of the term in its current meaning, had this to say in its announcement (*https://oreil.ly/kjvDi*): "The Observability Engineering team at Twitter provides full-stack libraries and multiple services to our internal engineering teams *to monitor* service health, *alert* on issues, *support root cause investigation* by providing distributed systems call traces, and *support diagnosis* by creating a searchable index of aggregated application/system logs." (The emphasis is mine.)

Network operators today have a difficult time when it comes to their ability to answer questions. Alan Kay, a pioneering computer scientist once said, "Simple things should be simple, and complex things should be possible." Network operators have not seen network operations satisfy this maxim. Their *mean time to innocence*, to prove whether the network is at fault or what is the cause, has always been arduous. To describe why I say this with an example, think of what is needed to answer the question, "Are all my BGP sessions in Established state?" You can tell that by scanning a listing of the state of all BGP sessions. A better question might be "Which of my BGP sessions did not reach the Established state?" But you cannot answer this question unless the system provides you with a list of failed sessions. Providing a list of all peering sessions and using that to determine which peerings failed to establish successfully is not as good.

To understand why, consider a network with 128, or even 32, BGP sessions spread across multiple address families and VRFs. You can't list all these sessions on a single screen, and it takes time to eyeball it for a problem. Automating this also involves writing a more involved program, and let's face it, how many network operators automate this part of their life? If a system provides the option to list only the failed sessions, you can instantly focus on those. Even better is a command that lists failed sessions along with the reason for the failure. This saves you from examining logs or using some other mechanism to identify the cause of the failure. And now extend the problem to answering the question across tens to thousands of nodes, and you can understand the goal of a well-observed system.

How easily you can answer your question is a measure of how observable a system is. The more easily you can gather the information from the commands, the better you can grasp the crucial information, and the less information you need to keep in your short-term memory to build a map of the network as it is currently functioning.

Network operators have had some measure of monitoring, but not observability. One of the clearest descriptions of the difference between the two comes from Baron Schwartz, the founder and CTO of the popular VividCortex software. He once wrote (*https://oreil.ly/Dj6DF*): "Monitoring tells you whether the system works. Observability lets you ask why it's not working." For example, monitoring can tell you a BGP session is down, but observability can help you answer why. In other words, monitoring assumes we know what to monitor, implying also that we know the acceptable and abnormal values for the things we monitor. But the data center and the modern application architecture are large and complex enough to leave many things unknown. To reuse a popular cliché, "Monitoring is sufficient for capturing the known knowns, whereas observability is required for tracking down what went wrong when encountering the unknown unknowns."

The Current State of Network Observability

SNMP—one abbreviation for the tools available for network observability in most networks. Box-by-box—one phrase that describes the practice of network observability in most networks.

Let us examine this in more detail.

The Disenchantments of SNMP

Monitoring of switches (routers and bridges) arose in a time when those devices were appliances that only the networking vendor could modify. Therefore, accessing any information about the device required a protocol specifically developed for the purpose. That protocol was SNMP. It was one of the first technologies developed to allow for gathering data from remote systems.

In SNMP, the data model for reporting each feature—whether interface statistics, BGP information, or something else—is defined by a Management Information Base (MIB). Every feature has its own MIB. MIBs were designed to make discovery of the structure easy. By doing something called an *MIB walk*, you could visit every element of the MIB supported by a device and obtain its value. To support this, all the MIBs were tied together as a tree with support for both standard and private extensions. A MIB walk was thus essentially a traversal of a tree. Each element in the tree was numbered hierarchically, and that number never changed. For example, interface statistics were defined by the interface MIB (ifMIB), and ifMIB's name is encoded as 1.3.6.1.2.1.2. This encoded name is called the Object ID (OID).

This desire to keep things invariant also meant that each interface was given a unique unchanging number on the device. No matter how many times the device rebooted or the software was upgraded, the number associated with the device never changed. The protocol then defined what "next" meant when a management entity such as a Network Management System (NMS) asked a device for the next available element in the tree. This meant that if a device supported only OSPF but not BGP, the MIB walk would allow an NMS to automatically skip over BGP and return the next available element in the tree. Because this protocol was designed in the late '80s and early '90s, when the network bandwidth was four to six orders of magnitude lower than the current speeds, efficient encoding of all this data was essential. SNMP used Abstract Syntax Notation One (ASN.1) as the encoding scheme for transporting all this information.

So far, all of this sounds reasonable, if a bit dated. The trouble was the usual one associated with nascent technologies. The technology was evolving rapidly, with a new protocol or feature being added all the time. The vendors proudly considered most of these features to be value differentiators. SNMP itself was one such feature. Examination of the state of a device by telneting (yes, SSH had not yet been invented) into the device and typing commands was the normal way of operating the network.

Even as support for SNMP began to percolate through the networking industry, the definition of a MIB for each new feature took two if not more years to stabilize. So vendors started implementing their own versions of the MIB while the standards bodies hammered out an agreement. Because competing implementations had to agree, the MIB was often the lowest common denominator of the different implementations. Each vendor thus had vendor-specific extensions, along with earlier versions of a MIB that had to be supported for backward compatibility, side by side with support for the newer, standardized versions. The net result was that operators relied on SNMP to a varying degree, with reliance on the older standard interface and platform MIBs being the most ubiquitous.

SNMP was also defined with a pull model, where the NMS pulls the information rather than the device pushing it. With Godzilla-sized routers being the norm, there was a lot of information to retrieve. As a result, if you attempted a MIB walk too frequently, you risked overloading the CPU, either crashing it or starving other higher-priority processes such as routing protocols. This meant that monitoring affected network stability. So people learned to space out the walks, performing them no more frequently than a minute and no more frequently than five minutes.

What's the problem with this, you wonder. When data is gathered over such long intervals, problems that occur over more granular time are not reflected in the data.

Consider what happens when compute nodes gather data every second or every 15 seconds while switches gather data every minute or more. Network hiccups such as latency and drops that are visible to the compute endpoints are not visible in the view displayed by their networking counterparts. This sets up the classic war of the application versus the network, where each side shrugs and insists that the problem isn't because of them.

To this day, SNMP is shoehorned in or bolted on after a networking feature is developed, never developed in sync or as part of the feature. In practical terms, this means that router and bridge developers provide local CLI-based access to a lot more information for their debugging benefit, and only later consider SNMP-based access. But the SNMP approach to telemetry means that if there isn't an SNMP data model for providing information, the information cannot be provided. It is not uncommon for valuable information to be provided only by commands issued by the operator and lacking an SNMP data model.

Like the STP, SNMP is widely regarded as a technology whose time is done. Network operators have put up with the protocol and the data model it created mostly because of a lack of an alternative.

Box-by-Box Approach to Network Observability

A few years back, when I started to get deeply interested in network observability, I spent a little time talking to operators about their troubleshooting methodology. The thing that became immediately apparent was that it involved a lot of SSH'ing into boxes. Using *ping* and *traceroute* to determine the locus of the problem, the network operator typically opened multiple terminal windows, logging in to the box at the locus and its neighboring boxes. They then went about examining each router's configuration and the state of various components such as the routing table and the routing protocol state, box by box, trying to isolate the problem. Graphs and SNMP alerts were involved, but they didn't really help drill down the problem too quickly.

Take a simple example, in which you're trying to determine why an OSPF adjacency is down. The problem will most likely be caused by misconfiguration. Solving it involves looking at multiple pieces of information across the two boxes to identify the cause of the misconfiguration. Logs are sometimes useful in finding the cause faster, but not always (for example, if the subnets are misconfigured at the two ends).

As another example, I saw a customer struggle to identify the misbehavior of certain applications when network virtualization was enabled. In the end, the problem was caused by a misconfigured MTU on one of the transit links.

Why Is Observability Difficult with Networking?

A general observation is that observability has been more difficult with networking than with single-system programming. This is because of two primary reasons: the design of routers and bridges as appliances rather than as well-defined (and open) platforms, and the design of packet-switching silicon. Let me elaborate.

Compute nodes are general-purpose platforms. This means people other than the platform providers can write software that runs on the platform. This enables innovation at a faster pace and in ways that is more appropriate for an operator than a developer. So compute can innovate in terms of monitoring by providing multiple tools such as *statsd* and *collectd*. Because the generation of observability information is decoupled from its transport, an operator can gather the information in whatever way the developer provides it, package it in a way that's appropriate to the operator, and transport it using whatever protocol is appropriate at the time. The operator can choose to ship the raw data, massage the data into some other more appropriate form before shipping it, control how often and when it is gathered, and so on. None of this is possible on routers and bridges, even today. Some traditional vendors like Arista provide better support than others, but it is not like having Linux (even if Arista likes to talk about it this way).

On a compute node, you can single-step through a function. It is not possible to single-step through packet forwarding silicon. The speed and the capabilities of the switch have been the deterrents to this transparency. Chip vendors such as Barefoot Networks are trying to change this by providing detailed information about what happens to the packet as it is forwarded in a way that was not possible before. Although other merchant-silicon vendors are slowly starting to do the same, switching silicon remains relatively opaque. In addition, the tools to process whatever is produced by such switching chips are still evolving.

Observability in Data Center Networks: Special Characteristics

Networks have always been hard to observe. But the advent of the cloud native data center makes the problem worse. Here are some reasons why this is so:

Multipathing
> IP networks evolved in an age of sparse connectivity. The data center is by comparison a highly dense network. Multipathing is the norm, not the exception. Many operators use *ping* to check connectivity between endpoints, but *ping* does not test reachability over all paths. So operators have to change the way they look for connectivity. When it comes to that other common network troubleshooting tool, *traceroute*, many vendor versions of the tool do not support multipathing, as

far as I can tell. The versions of *traceroute* shipped by default with servers (mtr on Ubuntu, for example) need to be used with additional options (-u) to reveal multipathing.

Obscured by tunnels

When network virtualization is deployed, no popular implementation of the *traceroute* command can reveal the multiple paths via the underlay to get to the destination. Some vendors make this work if all the equipment is theirs, but not in the general case. An inability to see the network paths in a unified manner renders the most common network troubleshooting tools more difficult to use. Thus, using the standard *traceroute* tool as a way to fix the locus of a problem is no longer possible.

Containers and microservices

The advent of the microservice architecture makes the endpoints more ephemeral and the communication between the microservices even more critical. However, network observability tools today are siloed between compute and network (and storage). This, combined with the short lives of containers, makes it harder for network administrators to perform post-mortem analysis. One enterprise I worked with in my past life struggled to find the server on which a container was running, the essential prerequisite to isolating the problem.

Automation

Network automation is a fundamental skill for operational efficiency in the cloud native data center. Automation is at some level, code, and code has bugs. Mistakes made with automation can affect the entire network in more complicated ways. So the ability to validate and troubleshoot problems quickly is important.

Fixed-form-factor switches

The Clos topology frees up the network to be built entirely with a single kind (or at most a handful of kinds) of device. But the death of godboxes means there are far more devices to manage, so the classic box-by-box troubleshooting approach of networks doesn't work as well. There are lots of benefits to having simple and fixed-form-factor devices even for observability, but going beyond simple monitoring is important because of the number of devices.

Having considered the difficulties with observability in the data center, let us consider the ways in which observability is made easier by the cloud native data center:

Fixed-form-factor switches

Smaller boxes means that we can poll the device more frequently for information, because each box has a much smaller amount of information to gather and report. Having a single (or single handful) kind of device makes it more feasible to deploy a homogeneous telemetry solution.

Disaggregation

Network disaggregation and the requirements of the cloud native data center have elevated the need to build switches as platforms, not as appliances. As a result, the disaggregated switches run Linux as the network OS, permitting the unification of tooling and of gathering certain kinds of data such as interface statistics. "Streaming telemetry" is a big deal in networking today. Streaming contrasts with the previous generation, which gathered data using SNMP in intervals measured in minutes. Even traditional vendors such as Arista and Cisco have started offering the ability to gather data using non-SNMP methods.

Decomposing Observability

As the Twitter announcement in the previous section indicated, observability can be decomposed into the following pieces:

- Telemetry, or the gathering of data
- Storage: how the data gathered is stored
- Monitoring
- Alerting
- Data analysis and ad hoc queries

The Mechanics of Telemetry

Telemetry is the automated gathering of data from remote sites at a central location. The process of telemetry can be broken down into what (what is collected), when (when it is collected), and how (how it is transported). In networks today, SNMP controls the answer to all the questions. What is gathered is limited to the SNMP data models supported by the device. When is determined by the frequency that doesn't cause SNMP to overload and bring down the system. How is simply SNMP. However, even traditional network devices support some form of sending logs to a central location, usually via the syslog protocol.

Let's pay a closer look at each part and study the alternatives.

What Do We Gather?

Metrics and logs are well-understood constructs that we know we need to gather. In the microservices architecture, distributed call tracing is considered critically important to track down a poorly performing or failing component. In network switches, call traces can be replaced by packet traces. Until the advent of switching silicon such as Barefoot Networks' Tofino, packet traces were based on packet sampling and a technology called sFlow. In addition, state information about the device, such as the forwarding tables (MAC table, ARP/ND table, routes, etc.), along with the state of control protocols are all useful to gather.

There are two schools of thought on what data to gather. The first school of thought comes from Etsy, which was one of the pioneers of telemetry when it introduced *statsd*. In a seminal, humorous post (*https://oreil.ly/60lXR*), the company wrote, "If Engineering at Etsy has a religion, it's the Church of Graphs. If it moves, we track it. Sometimes we'll draw a graph of something that isn't moving yet, just in case it decides to make a run for it." You can't watch everything. Instrumentation and monitoring have costs, just like anything else." I subscribe to the Majors way of thinking.

Brendan Gregg at Netflix, another prominent thinker and practitioner in the design and architecture of distributed systems, provided an actionable description of what to gather. He's credited with the USE model (*https://oreil.ly/trwJB*) of gathering data about a resource. USE stands for Utilization, Saturation, and Errors. For example, in networking, links are a critical resource. Thus monitoring receive packets, transmit packets, and byte counts on the interface determines utilization, drop and error counts determine errors, and buffer utilization determines saturation. Thus, these parameters determine the USE metrics for an interface. Similar measures can be easily determined for other critical resources such as CPU, memory, temperature, and so on. In routing, you can consider a measure of how full the routing table is and the distribution of prefixes as examples of useful statistics to gather. You can also gather the state of all the hardware tables such as ACL tables, MAC table, and the tunnel table to monitor how full they are.

One additional and important parameter for operators to derive from the captured interface statistics is what I call the *polarization ratio* between the uplinks of the leaves. In a Clos topology, high capacity is achieved when the bandwidth used on each uplink is about the same. If this isn't happening, it could be an indication that either flow hashing isn't working as well as necessary or that there are lots of elephant flows that have ended up getting hashed onto the same link. You can identify this condition partly by looking at the ratio of packet counts across the links. If the polarization ratio isn't very close to 1, applications could be suffering suboptimal performance as a consequence. It might be necessary to tweak the flow hashing algorithm parameters (typically the hashing seed) to fix the problem.

Google's famous book *Site Reliability Engineering* (*https://oreil.ly/8UpPj*) (O'Reilly) adds latency as another important metric to gather. All large cloud service providers that I know of measure latency across the network and use anomalous variations in this latency to detect problems.

Packet captures using sFlow are another kind of useful data for tracking what sort of traffic is flowing through the network. I have heard of sFlow packet sampling using 1 in 30,000 packets in certain large networks.

How Do We Gather?

After you have identified a set of information to gather data about, you need to determine how to gather it. For a long time, SNMP was the only answer on network equipment. On compute nodes, tools such as *collectd* (*https://oreil.ly/MHvXD*) and *statsd* (*https://oreil.ly/GooIL*) have been popular for a long time. But both are being supplanted by newer tools such as Prometheus (*https://oreil.ly/1gT-3*) and InfluxDB (*https://oreil.ly/XN7AQ*). The popularity of these tools has also spread to network equipment, where their use is clubbed under the marketing moniker of streaming telemetry. Big data tools such as Kafka (*https://oreil.ly/5KYpl*) are also increasingly being used to stream the data from various endpoints to a collector.

When it comes to logging, the most common model is to use *syslog* to push data to a remote *syslog* server. From there, people push the data into powerful log analyzers such as Splunk or the open source equivalent, ELK (*https://oreil.ly/kvERG*) (which stands for Elastic, Logstash, and Kibana, the three components of the product).

A popular debate that rages when it comes to the mechanics of gathering data is whether the pull model or push model is better. Specifically, operators argue whether it is more useful to push data from the endpoints (which run data gathering agents) to a collector or to have the collector poll the agents at a specified polling interval. For a long time, the compute folks were focused on pushing the data, whereas the network operators were pulling the data. With the advent of Prometheus, the pull model became popular even with the compute folks. The Prometheus folks even put out a blog post (*https://oreil.ly/mki6k*) to address this contentious issue.

In terms of the principles of computer science, I liken push to an interrupt, whereas pull is like a poll. Polling is generally frowned on because it tends to be wasteful and causes the CPU to busy-wait. However, well-regarded solutions such as DPDK for packet forwarding work on the poll model for various reasons, including the disruptive impact of interrupts when their frequency is too high.

In my opinion, the question as to which is better, pull or push, generates the classic engineering answer: it depends. We can use key characteristics to gauge the strengths and weaknesses of the system. Here are the primary differences between the models:

Just-in-time monitoring
> With the push model, agents can push the the data to the collector as soon as events occur, allowing for timely alerting and information capture. In a pull model, the collector knows of an event only when it decides to pull the information. If the system running the agent suffers a catastrophic failure, the event might not even be captured at all because the poll came around too late. This, I think, is the central difference between a pull and push model. The rest can be engineered away.

Need for agents

The pull model can be designed to use existing transport and commands to pull the data. For example, you can use the REST API available with a system to pull the relevant data at the frequency you desire. With push, you need NOS-specific agents for each telemetry solution. Given the closed nature of network equipment, this has been a deal breaker. But the advent of network disaggregation has opened up vendors to start addressing this issue.

Making changes is complex

If you need to change the frequency of data gathering or what is gathered, you must touch every affected agent. In a pull model, the collector is the only one that has to change. For example, adding new commands or changing what fields in a command are gathered can be made once at the collector. Of course, pull solutions such as SNMP or even Prometheus need changes on the agent end too, so this difference is largely specific to the solution used.

To address the unassailable difference between push and pull models, SNMP responded with "and," not "or." SNMP used a push model using what it called *traps* to notify the collector of critical, time-sensitive events while using the pull model for gathering data that was less time-sensitive. An example of critical, time-sensitive data is link-up or link-down events, whereas interface statistics is an example of data that isn't time-critical.

When Do We Gather?

As we discussed in "The Disenchantments of SNMP" on page 235, compute and network should gather data at the same frequency—much more often than is currently common in networking. Gathering data too infrequently makes it difficult to catch problems and understand your system well. But gathering data too frequently can also be unnecessary. For example, if the NOS pulls up statistics from the hardware every 30 seconds, polling for statistics faster than that is not useful. Checking for disk failures every 15 seconds is another example of unnecessary frequency. In general, a default period of 15 seconds seems appropriate across both network and compute for most of the cases. It is the default time used in Prometheus too. Whatever the frequency, it is important to make the measurement interval for a specific service uniform across all nodes: compute and network.

Storing the Data

The model used for gathering determines how the data is stored, often. Most tools use a time-series database. In the past, when storage was expensive and systems were simpler, the data was frequently *rolled up* or aggregated within an hour or so. In other words, if a metric was gathered every minute, at the end of an hour, the metric was rolled up for the hour by storing the average for the hour along with some other information such as min, max, and sometimes standard deviation. With this, the data for each individual minute was lost. Similarly, the hourly data was rolled up into the day, the day's data was rolled up into a week, and so on. The idea was based on the observation that older data is less useful and that therefore, rolled-up data was sufficient information. On compute nodes, *statsd* rolled up data it gathered every second into five-second or larger intervals before pushing it to the collector.

However, with cheap storage and more experience in troubleshooting systems, rolling up data is now frowned upon. Operators often want to troubleshoot noncritical, but unexpected behavior that might have occurred over the weekend when they return to work on Monday. So raw data, captured say every 15 seconds, is often stored for days and rolled up only after a week or two. This is the new norm.

The Uses for Multiple Data Sources

So we gather all this different data. Is one type better suited for answering certain kinds of questions than the others? I notice that network operators are called in for two distinct classes of problems: one where the communication has failed, and the other when the communication is suboptimal. The first class is when A can't talk to B, whereas the second class is when A's communication with B is very slow and lossy. Besides this, observability is also needed for capacity planning.

That A cannot talk to B is almost always the result of incorrect or inconsistent state, either in the network or at either of the endpoints, A and B. For example, if A is using B's hostname to reach it, the problem could be a misconfigred DNS server address or just plain inability to reach the DNS server. The problem could also be that B's hostname is misconfigured in DNS, or on A or B itself. Handling complete communication failures is a complex process that involves examining the state across multiple nodes to track the problem down. However, in some cases, the problem is entirely caused by a bad cable. If you examine the metrics and see that the error count or drop count is continuously increasing anywhere along the path from A to B, you'll be able to isolate the problem.

Suboptimal communication between A and B similarly could be due to congested links or to transient but persistent routing loops. So examining metrics for congested links is important, as is examining logs to see whether there is some persistent routing loop.

Packet captures are useful more for compliance and security than for observability. It's quite expensive to capture even just the headers on a modern data center router, which transfers anywhere from 3.2 to 12.8 terabytes per second of data. Using sFlow is better to get a statistical sampling of the data flowing through the network. Packet captures of control protocols can be useful when debugging certain control protocol issues. These usually involve running *tcpdump* or Wireshark.

The moral of the story is that you'll need all kinds of tools and information to isolate a problem.

Of Alerts and Dashboards

All this data gathering has traditionally been used for alerting and building dashboards.

Alerting involves notifying the operator proactively of critical events, hopefully before the effects of the problems become widespread or catastrophic. The definition of what is critical, what the threshold values are, the alerting mechanism, who is alerted, and such are customizable, because each system needs to choose highly specific values in order to fulfill the mission of noticing and recovering from serious problems. With the increasing use of tools such as HipChat, PagerDuty, and Slack, any modern alerting framework must interact with these tools instead of merely sending email or lighting up a dashboard.

Sadly, alerting is one of the weakest tools in the operator's observability toolkit. It leads to "alert fatigue" like the boy who cried wolf once too often. Operators start ignoring alerts because the alerting system is too simple and the alerts turn out to be false positives. Many surveys and studies confirm this problem. An example of such a false positive is when a CPU spikes momentarily but drops back to normal levels. An alerting system that allows you to watch for an anomaly to persist over a few cycles before triggering an alert would be better at generating fewer false positives. Another example of a bad alerting system is notifying too many people. A third way to function poorly is an alerting system that generates duplicate alerts. Google's SRE books, referenced at the end of this chapter, provide good ideas on how to build a good alerting system.

The other thing that the data is used for is to build dashboards of the distributed system. The dashboard consists of graphs that are supposed to reveal at a glance whether something is wrong with the system, and some hint of how to look for the source of the problem. For example, a simple red/yellow/green block could indicate whether BGP is working properly across the network. Typically, the network dashboard is different from the application monitoring dashboard, and different teams are responsible for each. Furthermore, different tools each have their own dashboards. Logging tools come with dashboards that differ for the tools that gather statistics, the tools that do packet sampling, and so on.

Modern tools try to overcome some of this fragmentation by integrating other kinds of data along with their core competence. For example, the logging favorite ELK has Beats for gathering statistics. Modern graphing tools such as Grafana (*https:// grafana.com*) allow you to pull data from multiple backends and customize your own dashboard. Beyond that, people are using tools such as Plotly and Bokeh to develop their own sophisticated dashboards. But all this is unavailable for the vast majority of network operators, because they're not used to deploying dashboards like this.

However they're assembled, dashboards are better at indicating the existence of a problem than at pinpointing the cause. As Charity Majors once said, "You cannot debug with a dashboard." You can follow her argument about the state of alerts and dashboards on this Twitter thread (*https://oreil.ly/wNef_*).

With the advent of cheap storage and the ability to store raw data for longer periods of time, how can we move beyond dashboards and alerts to create highly observable, informative systems? Data analysis tools such as Python's pandas, and data query languages such as SQL, are emerging to help operators ask questions of the gathered data and look for correlations in ways that the network developer did not intend. In other words, they provide a step toward a true querying platform to ask unanticipated questions up front, in a manner similar to a debugger. However, no open source tool exists that provides such a functionality.

Summary

In this chapter, we examined what observability is and why it is so important in the cloud native data center. Sadly, the dearth of multivendor or open source tools that help address the troubleshooting and ad hoc queries aspects of network observability prevents me from writing about the practical use of this aspect of observability. I don't cover the deployment of monitoring and alerting in this book largely because of the increase in the size of this book and the lack of time. Hopefully, the information presented in this chapter will help guide what is useful to gather and why.

References

- Schwartz, Baron. "See the Details with 1-Second Resolution Data" (*https://oreil.ly/WsM9v*).

- Majors, Charity. "Observability—A 3-Year Retrospective" (*https://oreil.ly/w64Yc*).

- Volz, Julius. "Pull doesn't scale—or does it?" (*https://oreil.ly/xwPH5*).

- Google's SRE books (*https://oreil.ly/q18ao*), *Site Reliability Engineering* and *The Site Reliability Workbook* (O'Reilly).

## CHAPTER 12

Rethinking Network Design

Most of our assumptions have outlived their uselessness.
—Marshall McLuhan

The cloud native data center network comes in many different sizes and shapes, ranging from the ones run by the hyperscalars such as Amazon, Google, and Microsoft to the networks of much smaller organizations, anywhere from 20 to 50 switches. But the common goals across all of them are reliability and cost efficiency. Operational cost efficiency is much harder to achieve than cost efficiency of purchasing a router. In my experience in dealing with a wide swath of organizations, cloud native data center networks achieve reliable, cost-efficient networks by adhering to the following design principles:

- Standard, simple building blocks
- A reconsideration of network failures
- Ruthless focus on simplicity

Each of these principles overturned fundamental network design principles on which enterprise and data center networks had thus far been built. I touch upon these aspects many times over in the course of this book. However, dedicating a short chapter to these principles before we move from the architecture and technology to actual deployment will, I predict, serve you well. Missing one or more of these principles trips up organizations that are trying to evolve and lands them back in the old morass.

To be sure, these three concepts draft off one another to paint a more complex picture than the way I present them as separate concepts. Also, not having been an employee at any of the cloud service providers when the new architecture was taking shape, I can't tell whether these principles evolved organically (although I suspect they did) as opposed to having been conceived in a fully mature form.

We'll conclude this chapter by considering the constraints preventing network operators from adopting the principles.

Standard, Simple Building Blocks

This principle markedly differentiates the cloud native data center operators from those of the previous era. The Clos topology, along with network disaggregation, allow new operators to select less than a handful of types of boxes, say one each for spine and leaf, and build out a network of any size with these boxes. The leaf boxes usually support one set of high-speed ports to connect to the spines, and another set of lower-speed ports to connect to the servers. For example, a leaf switch might have a recent chipset that offers either 8 100GbE ports and 48 25GbE ports or 6 100GbE ports with 48 10GbE ports. The spines in turn might have 32 to 128 100GbE ports, depending on the anticipated size of the network.

As discussed earlier, a key advantage of using these simple standard building blocks is inventory management. In the server world, the use of the PC based on Intel (or AMD) and Linux allowed operators to keep their inventory management simple. The same applies to routers now.

In contrast, the previous era networks were built using small access boxes and much bigger aggregation boxes. The access and aggregation boxes worked much better if they were from the same vendor. The switching chips used in these boxes were specific to each vendor. Each aggregation box consisted of control cards and switching linecards. As the boxes evolved, keeping track of which linecards went with which box meant a more complicated inventory. If you had a multivendor strategy, you needed to manage inventory across these different vendors separately.

Another advantage of these simple fixed-form-factor boxes is the ability to automate their configuration. In the access-agg network, the aggregation box had a fairly complex configuration. To make matters worse, it often housed a linecard that functioned as a firewall or a load balancer. This made configuring the box a lot more complicated, not to mention providing another avenue for vendor lock-in. So why did people buy these boxes? Among other factors, a key benefit of the Swiss Army knife model box was that you could configure multiple functions on a single management console. In other words, it provided a simplified management model. This was necessary in the absence of network automation. With the advent of network automation, and a scale-out model with Clos topology, it is far more efficient to focus on simple, standard boxes that perform one function.

Vendor lock-in is always a threat, even with the move to clouds or with network disaggregation. But the question is, how easy is it to fall into vendor lock-in? Some solutions, such as OpenFlow, can lead to as much vendor lock-in as the access-agg era, maybe even more. So mere use of network disaggregation or merchant silicon isn't sufficient to avoid this problem. On the other hand, it is more difficult to fall into the trap of deploying vendor-specific solutions in these situations because the software and hardware come from different vendors. The use of vendor-specific solutions such as Cisco's FabricPath or Juniper's QFabric is much harder when simple and standard network devices are used.

One way operators fall into the trap of old-world design is by trying to reduce the number of boxes to limit the complexity and cost of cabling. In pursuit of this goal, operators end up buying chassis switches from vendors as spine switches. These chassis switches have changed somewhat, but preserve many of the negative traits of earlier generations. They often contain proprietary silicon, complicate failure handling, and reduce the power of simplified inventory management.

Chassis switches from Facebook's OCP, such as Minipack, are better suited to limiting the number of cables while preserving the properties of the new design. First, the internal backplane connecting the linecards in these OCP switches is just a Clos network built with the same merchant silicon as the cards for the front panel. Second, each linecard functions independently from the other linecards, and there is no central control processor attempting to make the entire chassis look like a single box. Both of these characteristics help such a chassis switch preserve the characteristics of a standard, simple building block.

On the other hand, the rise of merchant-silicon chips that support 64 to 128 ports of 100GE calls into question even the use of these OCP-approved chassis switches. As we discuss next, keeping the boxes relatively small in size, 128 ports instead of 512 ports, for example, also plays a role in the effect of failure in the network.

The use of simple, standard boxes plays a key role in the application of the other principles in this chapter.

Network Disaggregation

Network disaggregation makes inventory management even simpler.

Without network disaggregation, a multivendor strategy usually requires that operators be trained in the use of two different appliances and their user interface. Some attempt to paper over the differences using tools such as OpenConfig. The hyperscalars and an increasing number of others are moving instead to network disaggregation. With network disaggregation, you can retain the same OS, but to prevent running into issues of supply chain or vendor lock-in, operators source these boxes from different hardware vendors. For example, buying switches from Dell and Edgecore is a common pattern I have encountered. With the use of a network OS that works across these vendors and box types, network architects adhere to the server market's model of standardizing on a few different types of servers and a common OS: Linux.

Failure: Missing the Forest for the Trees

The other fundamental shift in network design was the return to the original model of IP networks: networks don't fail; individual components will. To ensure that the network keeps running in the face of individual component failures, the network designer must use the natural redundancy that comes with smaller building blocks. Smaller routers lead to limiting the scope of failures to be as restricted as possible. In other words, the "blast radius" of what's affected by a failure is kept as small as possible.

The use of the Clos topology encourages a scale-out model in which the core is kept from having to perform complex tasks and carry a lot of state. It is far more scalable to increase scale by pushing complex functionality to the leaves, including into the servers, where the state is distributed. Because the state is distributed among many boxes, the failure of one box has a much smaller blast radius than a single large box that carries a lot of state.

When operators buy large spine switches in an effort to reduce the number of boxes they have, they also automatically increase the blast radius of a failure. This is often not factored into the thinking of the operator. With a spine switch of 512 ports, you can build a two-tier Clos topology of 512 racks. But now the effect of a failure is much larger. If instead you broke this up into a three-tier Clos network with eight pods of 64 racks each, you get a far more reliable network.

Network failures of the hyperscalar cloud providers are very public. That they fail as infrequently as they do despite their massive scale and the resulting complexity is something that is less frequently commented upon.

Let's delve a bit more into other aspects of failure handling in cloud native data center networks.

L2 Failure Model Versus L3 Failure Model

L2 networks were the bedrock of networks until the recent past. The primary problem of L2 networks is that they're unreliable at anything but a very small scale. STP has the fundamental problem of becoming promiscuous when it fails rather than falling politely silent. In other words, when STP times out on a port waiting for a Hello, it assumes the other end is a host and so starts sending traffic out that port. If this port were in a blocked STP state (blocked to break loops and create an acyclic tree, which is what STP does), the result would be a loop that causes the entire network to fail, as discussed in Chapter 1. The switch that failed to send the Hello might have done so because it had an overloaded control plane. That networks can fail completely as a result of a single failure is in the DNA of STP.

L3 networks, the bedrock of the cloud native data center, fail closed, instead. In other words, if a router doesn't hear from a neighbor within a specific period of time, the router marks the node as dead and removes it from all its paths. This means that a node that is either overloaded or down stops receiving traffic as the other nodes route around it.

Thus, an L3 network is inherently more stable than L2.

Simple Versus Complex Failures

Simple boxes tend to experience simple failures. Fixed-form-factor switches use a single switching chip, a single CPU, and so on. This means that hardware failures can be isolated fairly quickly. The large aggregation boxes of the access-agg era failed in complex ways because there were so many moving parts: multiple switching chips, multiple CPUs, dual backplanes connecting the linecards to the central control card, and so on.

When a piece of hardware failed in the access-agg era, the inventory management and the cost of the box usually encouraged network operators to troubleshoot the problem while the box continued to live in the network. This approach put enormous pressure on the network operator because the clock continued to tick on the network downtime as they raced to identify the problem. Resolving the failure required, for example, determining whether the linecard was merely not connected properly or whether it failed only in some specific slot. Even if the entire card failed, the operator had to ensure that the problem was specific to the linecard, as opposed to something on the control processor or the backplane itself that would soon affect all other linecards.

With simple, standard, and inexpensive boxes, it is easy to replace one box with another of its kind. This means that the faulty box can be removed from the network and debugged offline while a substitute box lets the network come back to full operational state. Automation and the use of well-defined, simple functions ensured that changing boxes was neither laborious nor time consuming. This method is far healthier for both the network and the operator.

Handling Upgrades

L2 protocols do not allow traffic to drain gracefully from a node for a scheduled maintenance or replacement. For example, the Link Aggregation Control Protocol (LACP) has no support for gracefully retiring a link without affecting traffic flowing through it. It is not possible to notify the peer to stop sending traffic on a link, allowing the currently flowing traffic to drain completely before shutting down the link.

STP similarly has no method to gracefully withdraw a node from the tree. This means that existing traffic is affected unnecessarily even when the event can be planned. Routing protocols, on the other hand, support graceful withdrawal from the network, maintaining reliability.

The principle of making a network reliable by making individual nodes reliable led to disastrous ideas such as In-Service Software Upgrade (ISSU). ISSU was also touted as the antidote to system upgrades because it allowed existing traffic to flow unaffected by the upgrade. As just about anyone who has worked with ISSU will tell you, it is anything but reliable. When I worked at Cisco, ISSU was reliable only as the cause of high-priority bugs. It almost single-handedly slowed down releases.

The cloud native data centers, almost to a person, eschewed ISSU. They used the ability of L3 routing protocols to withdraw the node from the network and upgrade in peace. It seems traditional vendors are also coming around, if only very recently, to recognize the bad design of ISSU. An indication of this understanding comes through in Figure 12-1, a tweet from Joe Onisick, who was a technical marketing director until recently at Cisco's data center switches.

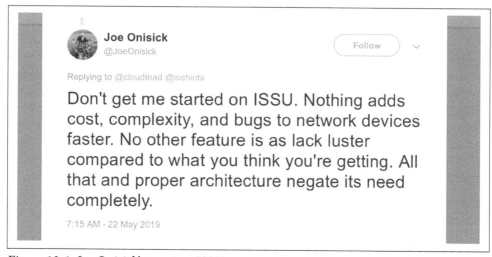

Joe Onisick
@JoeOnisick

Follow

Replying to @cloudtoad @ioshints

Don't get me started on ISSU. Nothing adds cost, complexity, and bugs to network devices faster. No other feature is as lack luster compared to what you think you're getting. All that and proper architecture negate its need completely.

7:15 AM - 22 May 2019

Figure 12-1. Joe Onisick's tweet on ISSU

The Pursuit of Less

Traditionally, network operators were trained in the school of Gordon Gecko, "Greed, for lack of a better word, is good." Thus, the more features a box has, the better the box must be. When I first began engaging with customers during my time at Cumulus, I often ran into the dreaded feature list. Many network operators required a list of features to be supported even to consider a vendor. The list was a mishmash of the important, the useful, and the just plain irrelevant or redundant. For example, they had IS-IS on it as a routing protocol we had to support, even though they used OSPFv2 at that time and had no plans for switching to IS-IS. When asked why they needed it, what I heard was post-hoc rationalization. Some realized that the list came from a different era, and went away to come back with a more appropriate list.

The ethos of the cloud native network operators, on the other hand, is best captured in a saying by Marissa Mayer, "What you want, when you want it. As opposed to everything you could ever want, even when you don't." Let's compare and contrast the difference in the perspectives that arise from these two different ways of approaching networks.

How the Right Architecture Helps

At the highest level, the new operators embraced the architecture of Clos topology. This freed them from the ills that plagued the access-aggregation networks. A main reason why operators relied on long feature lists was that L2 technology has many inherent limitations that prevent it from being a bedrock for stable, reliable networks. So individual vendors built in many features to fix these problems. The trouble was that the enhancements were vendor specific: sometimes built into the hardware, at other times built into extensions of a standard protocol, and at other times spawning entirely new protocols. The implementation of fail-safe, vendor-specific features was merely a function of historical evolution; that is, they were conceived in an environment vastly different from the one encountered by the cloud native operators.

L2, as the rubric of a network, also meant a plethora of protocols. You had STP and LACP, both mentioned earlier. You also had a FHRP and various STP enhancements, some standard and some proprietary. Then you had a protocol such as Unidirectional Link Detection (UDLD), multicast protocols, and of course, routing protocols. All this meant a lot of complexity, which led to complex failures and interactions, as dio cussed earlier.

Relying solely on an L3 network and eliminating multicast from the network freed operators to run the entire network on essentially two protocols: the routing protocol and BFD. This simplified configuration and protocol complexity significantly.

Feature Set Essentialism

A rather popular book of recent times is Greg McKeown's *Essentialism* (Virgin Books). In it, he writes, "Essentialism is not about how to get more things done; it's about how to get the right things done. It doesn't mean just doing less for the sake of less either." Approach network design and the use of features in this manner. Rather than seeking a plethora of vendor-driven options, go back to first principles and design the network that serves your needs based on the maxim of "what you want, when you want it." Even within a single protocol, for example, do not attempt to use as many knobs as possible; use as few as possible. In every case, if you see simpler options among other vendors, consider pushing your incumbent to provide the same functionality.

For example, ask your vendor why they don't support unnumbered interfaces with OSPF and BGP, especially as those technologies are standards based and not subject to any vendor-specific patents. When you use EVPN, don't accept a vendor's spin on why you need multiple BGP sessions; push the vendor for a single one. (We discuss EVPN in Chapter 17.) Alternatively, ask whether you can get away with doing head-end replication rather than deploy multicast. In many cases, I've noticed vendors push for solutions that are far more complex than necessary or desirable because either they don't support the simpler option or the complex solution leads to vendor lock-in. If your configuration is so compact that you can eyeball it for errors, chances are your network will be more reliable.

Moving up another level, the new network design keeps out of the network what never belonged in the network. Traditional network vendors added more and more features into switches as a way to have the boxes play a more important role in the data center rather than providing efficient, high-speed connectivity. This method also leads to the lumping of unnecessary and unnatural features into switches. This in turn leads to more complicated boxes and a network that is far less reliable because of the inherent complexity of an individual box.

Constraints on the Cloud Native Network Design Principles

Of course, principles often bite the dust in the face of practical realities on the ground. In the case of rethinking network design, practical considerations at a particular organization might limit adoption of the design principles described in this chapter.

The first and foremost constraint comes from the applications deployed on the network. The hyperscalars and many cloud native data center operators had the luxury of working with a clean slate, writing and owning the applications that ran on their network. For instance AWS, Microsoft Azure, and Google can all refuse to provide L2 functionality or multicast in their VPC offerings. However, many financial institutions and mature organizations might be saddled with old "legacy" applications that either can't be rewritten at all or present a prohibitive cost to rewrite. In such cases, they cannot help but bend the network to the will of these applications.

Many of these older applications made assumptions about the network, such as the use of multicast and broadcast in clustering or discovery; here, eliminating L2 would be hard. But newer applications, especially in the area of storage, also continue to make these erroneous assumptions. Restricting these applications to older networks is one way some organizations I know dealt with this problem. They discouraged the running of such applications by charging more to run such networks so that the newer applications were constructed to not make these old erroneous assumptions.

Another constraint is when you're saddled with older equipment and not able to deploy the new network design.

Summary

This chapter laid out the design principles underpinning the new cloud native data center network, and explained how they help build networks that are stable, scalable, and easy to manage. Table 12-1 summarizes the principles and how they differ from those of the previous generation. These principles create a virtuous cycle of network design that leads to far greater scalability, cost efficiency, and reliability. Keep the principles in mind as we now delve into the actual deployment of various technologies, such as routing and network virtualization within the data center. Remember the maxim from Essentialism: "Weniger aber besser." In English: "Less but better."

Table 12-1. Difference in network design between cloud native and access-agg networks

Cloud native networks	Access-agg networks
Standard, simple building blocks	Vendor-specific, complex building blocks
Reliability of network, not nodes	Reliability of networks via reliable nodes
Essential feature set	Complex, long feature sets

## CHAPTER 13

Deploying OSPF

It was 20-minute invention...I designed it without pencil and paper. Without pencil and paper you're forced to avoid all avoidable complexities.
—Edsger Djikstra

This chapter begins the actual deployment details in a Clos topology: here, the link-state rubber meets the OSPF road. We explore configuration of the OSPF routing protocol for use in a Clos topology. I picked OSPF because within the data center, it is more popular than its older and better-designed cousin, IS-IS. Both protocols, however, use the shortest path algorithm—invented by the Dutch computer scientist, Edsger Djikstra—to build the routing table. As he states in the opening quote, it is a simple and elegant algorithm and the cause of much of his fame.

The goal of this chapter is to help network engineers determine the ideal OSPF configuration for their networks. This chapter should help answer the following questions:

- When is OSPF useful in the data center?
- What are the key design principles for configuring OSPF?
- What are the differences between OSPFv2 and OSPFv3, and how should I use them?
- How do I configure OSPF in my routing stack?
- How do I configure OSPF on servers, for example, to provide a routed environment for containers?
- How do I use OSPF to help upgrade the router software?

We begin by describing the problems we need to solve. We then map these problems into OSPF concepts that address them, before finally describing the actual configuration. If you're already versed in OSPF, you can skip the section on OSPF concepts. There are several books out there that describe OSPF's inner workings in great detail. In this chapter, we introduce only those concepts relevant to the problems at hand and provide a brief introduction to the protocol. As described in Chapter 12, the new network design ethos should be as simple as possible. Also, the Clos topology is a regular topology, and therefore you shouldn't need some of the more complicated parts of OSPF. For instance, we won't bother studying OSPF virtual links or designated router election in this chapter, because they're not used in a Clos topology.

The examples used in this chapter employ the open source routing suite, FRR, primarily because of my familiarity with it. I use it also because in the spirit of cloud native design, FRR is an open source routing suite. However, I also show how equivalent configurations will look on a Cisco or Arista box.

Why OSPF?

BGP is the most popular routing protocol used within the data center. Why then would someone consider OSPF? In what scenarios is OSPF appropriate and in what scenarios is it not?

OSPF is actually the more familiar choice for enterprise network administrators to use as a routing protocol. BGP is steeped in the myth that it is very complex (although at its core, in my opinion, BGP is far simpler than OSPF), and its users are mostly the administrators dealing with the backbone or WAN side of an enterprise network. OSPF belongs to a class of protocols called Interior Gateway Protocol (IGP), and it is the most popular IGP at the time of this writing. So the primary reason people choose OSPF over BGP is because they are more familiar with it.

OSPF is also sometimes used instead of BGP to build the underlay network in network virtualization solutions such as EVPN. Outside of FRR, not many proprietary or open source routing stacks support the clean and efficient use of a single BGP session with a neighbor to do both overlay and underlay networks. The traditional model, coming from the service provider world, is to use an IGP to configure the underlay network, and BGP to configure the overlay network. Network administrators more familiar with this model will often turn to OSPF. In this case, they use OSPFv2 rather than OSPFv3, because most VXLAN networks use an IPv4 underlay exclusively.

As the size of the network increases, and/or the number of prefixes to be advertised increases, BGP becomes the go-to routing protocol. For advertising fewer than 32,000 prefixes, OSPF is a fine choice as a routing protocol. That said, I know of OSPF's use in a substantially large data center, though the number of prefixes advertised is within the limits described.

As discussed in Chapter 5, OSPF runs a separate protocol for IPv4 (called OSPFv2 or just OSPF) and IPv6 (called OSPFv3). If your network uses only IPv4, OSPF is adequate. When you add IPv6, the most common model is to use both OSPFv2 and OSPFv3 protocols to administer the network. If your network vendor supports running only OSPFv3 with multiprotocol support, I recommend using that instead of running both OSPFv2 and OSPFv3 because such a choice gives you a single point for configuring, troubleshooting, and understanding your network.

The Problems to Be Addressed

Figure 13-1 illustrates two basic Clos network architectures that we use for examples.

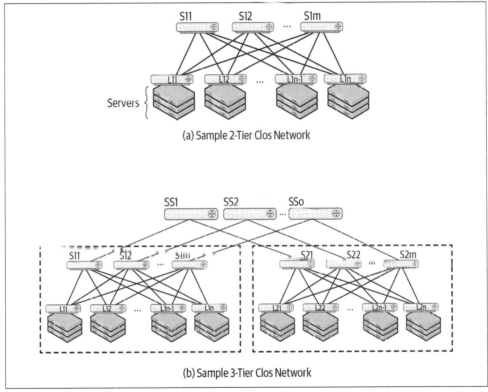

Figure 13-1. Clos topologies used for OSPF configuration

As described in Chapter 5, if you use a link-state routing protocol, all the routers in a routing domain know the local link-state information of every other router in the domain. The route to all destinations is computed using this link-state information. Because a router can be accurate in the knowledge of its local link state, using this knowledge to compute forwarding paths allows a network to rapidly converge to a stable state in the event of link or node failures.

In this chapter, we use OSPF for enabling routing in the topologies shown in Figure 13-1. The problem is broken up into the following:

- Configuring OSPF for IPv4
- Configuring OSPF for IPv6
- Configuring OSPF on the server
- Configuring OSPF with VRF

Determining Link-State Flooding Domains

A router communicates only with its configured neighbors. In Figure 13-1(a), for example, L1 exchanges information only with the spine routers, S1 through Sm. To ensure that every router in the network has the local information about every other router, a router must propagate the information received from one neighbor to all of its other neighbors. Therefore, S1 propagates L1's information unmodified to all of its neighbors, L2 through Ln. This process of forwarding unmodified routing information received from one router to other neighbors is called *flooding* in OSPF parlance.

In large networks, storing the link state of every router in the network can take up a lot of memory on every node. So all link-state protocols restrict the spread of unmodified information throughout the routing domain by breaking the domain up into smaller segments or groups. OSPF uses the term *areas* to describe this smaller segment. The scope of the flooding is limited to a contiguous area. Every router interface is assigned to an area. Different router interfaces can be assigned to different areas.

OSPF supports two levels or hierarchies. The *backbone area* is the top level of the routing hierarchy and is the primary area. Every OSPF routing domain, however trivial, must have a backbone area. The second level in the hierarchy is called the *nonbackbone area*. There can be multiple nonbackbone areas, but only a single backbone area. Multiple nonbackbone areas are connected together via the backbone area. The backbone area cannot be partitioned; that is, it has to be one contiguous segment. In other words, OSPF will not work if traffic from one part of backbone area has to traverse through a nonbackbone area to reach another part of the backbone area.[1]

The area is identified by a 32-bit number that can be written as either a single-digit string such as 0 or 1, or an IPv4 dotted-decimal string such as 0.0.0.1. The backbone area has the area identifier of 0 or 0.0.0.0.

---

1 This is why virtual links were invented.

The first question for our sample network is to map OSPF areas to the topologies shown in Figure 13-1. In Figure 13-1(a), this mapping is simple because OSPF runs only between the routers: all the inter-router links are in the backbone area. In Figure 13-1(b), the possible choices are to run a single area across the entire network, or to create a separate area for each pod and one backbone area across the pods; in other words, between the spine routers and super-spine routers. In the latter case, the backbone area covers the spine routers and the super-spine routers, and each pod is in a nonbackbone area.

Numbered Versus Unnumbered OSPF

The most common OSPFv2 deployment model assumes that the interface at either end of an OSPF link is numbered; for instance, each end of the link is assigned a valid IP address. More specifically, they're assigned IP addresses from the same subnet. Typically, this address is from the /30 or /31 subnet in the case of IPv4. Because the addresses are shared only between the two ends of a single link, I recommend the use of /31 to avoid wasting IPv4 addresses. In the initial days of network disaggregation, when merchant-switching silicon had small routing tables, the pioneering network operators turned off advertising for these interface-only routes. IPv6 introduced link-local addresses (addresses starting with fe80) to specifically handle such scenarios.

As discussed in Chapter 5, unnumbered interfaces makes for a smaller routing table, a smaller vector for security attacks, and less churn in the routing table when links or nodes come up or go down. Furthermore, as we discussed in Chapter 10, automating the assignment of IP addresses on interfaces is painful without resorting to programming. Avoiding the use of interface IP addresses would therefore be a good thing.

OSPFv2 has supported *unnumbered interfaces* from its early inception. In OSPFv2, if an interface has a /32 address, it is treated as an unnumbered interface. Typically, this /32 address is that of the loopback interface. To advertise this address beyond the neighbors, you need to add this address to the loopback interface (or any other interface that does not go down, such as the master VRF interface in Linux). Thus, with OSPFv2 unnumbered, we assign the loopback's IP address to every link on which we want to run OSPF. This use of a single address, independent of what's on the other side, vastly simplifies network automation.

Sadly, outside of FRR, most network routing stacks do not support unnumbered OSPFv2. The missing support for this vastly useful and simple feature in traditional routing stacks is an example of why hyperscalar network operators considered networks difficult to manage.

Support for IPv6

As mentioned earlier, IPv6 support required a complete overhaul of OSPF and resulted in a new protocol called OSPFv3. The upshot of this is that most routing stacks have two separate implementations of OSPF: the original one implementing OSPFv2, and a new one implementing OSPFv3. Even with this, fewer implementations supported both IPv4 and IPv6 over OSPF. Cisco NX-OS and Juniper have supported it for a while, and Arista added support for it in its 4.17.0F release. FRR does not support multiple address families with OSPFv3. The open source routing suite, BIRD (*https://bird.network.cz*), not only supports multiple address families with OSPFv3, but even uses a single code base to support both OSPFv2 and v3.

Because this chapter uses FRR as the basic routing suite for which we're showing the configuration, we use the multiple protocols model to show support for IPv6. We include an example to show how to do the same configuration using Cisco's NX-OS.

Support for VRFs

OSPFv2 and v3 support VRF, specifically running separate instances of the protocol, one per VRF. In FRR, only OSPFv2 supports VRF as of release 7.0.[2] Use of VRFs with OSPF is not very common. When used to construct the underlay in EVPN, the underlay runs in the default VRF.

Requirements for Running OSPF on Servers

Some network operators want to run a pure routed network, starting from the endpoints. For example, operators deploying Kubernetes find it simpler to just run a routing protocol on the host to advertise either individual container or pod addresses as well as Kubernetes service addresses. These operators handle connections from the servers to multiple switches through ECMP instead of an L2 solution such as bonding.

Most often, I've run across operators using BGP in such a scenario. Kuberouter, the Kubernetes network module that handles routing, uses BGP as well. But I've met several operators using OSPF in such a scenario. Using OSPF on servers raises the following additional questions:

How do you define areas, given that the servers add another layer of hierarchy?
    With servers running OSPF, in a two-tier Clos topology such as the one shown in Figure 13-1(a), the servers are assigned to a nonbackbone area. In a three-tier Clos topology, the servers are assigned to the nonbackbone area and all the routers from the leaves to the super-spines are assigned to the backbone area. With FRR, it is also possible to use multi-instance OSPF to run two separate instances of OSPF on the pod spine routers. One instance (a separate OSPF process in case of FRR) is used to connect servers, leaves, and spines. A second instance is used

---

2 VRF support is different from the multi-instance OSPFv2 support in FRR.

to connect the spines and the super-spines. You can redistribute the routes learned from one instance of OSPF into the other.

How do you ensure that the servers are shielded from the chattiness of link-state protocols?

Link-state protocols can be quite chatty in their effort to update the network of changes in the local state information of every router in the area. A server with only one way out to the external world has little need to be made aware of all these updates. OSPF defines a nonbackbone area as being a *totally stubby* area to shield routers in an area from knowledge about changes in the rest of the network. By placing the servers in such an area, they can be shielded from seeing fluctuations in other parts of the network. This also prevents the servers from having a large routing table or dealing with the protocol overhead of running OSPF. We cover how this configuration works later in the chapter.

OSPF Route Types

In this section, we delve into some OSPF details that will help us in understanding how OSPF constructs the world and the implications of such a construction for our Clos topologies in Figure 13-1. To understand how OSPF constructs the world, refer to Figure 13-2.

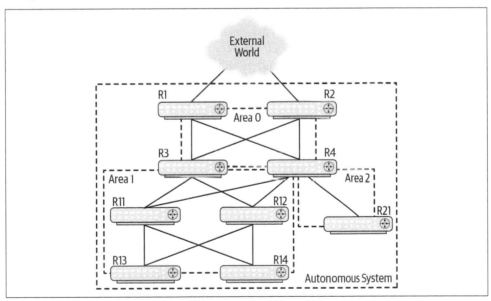

Figure 13-2. Sample topology to illustrate OSPF concepts

In routed networks, an *Autonomous System* (AS) represents an autonomously managed collection of networks. For example, the enterprise network of a single organization is considered an AS. In Figure 13-2, the entire network in the large dotted box is an AS.

As defined earlier, in OSPF, each interface of a router can belong to a different area. The backbone area of the AS in Figure 13-2 consists of the interfaces between the routers R1 and R4 shown in the topmost boxed rectangle. Area 1 consists of the four routers R11 through R14 and their connections to R3 and R4. Area 2 consists of a single router R21 and its connection to R4.

R1 and R2 are connected to the external world, which we have simplified to a blob. In reality, R1 might be closer to some destinations in the external world than R2, and similarly, R2 might be closer to some external destinations than R1. So preferably, R3 (and R4) will send to R1 traffic that ends up closer to R1, and other traffic to R2 that ends up closer to R2.

Often in such networks, R1 and R2 run multiple routing protocols. R1 and R2 run OSPF toward the routers internal to the AS: R3 and R4. R1 and R2 also typically use BGP to communicate with routers outside the AS. By running both protocols, R1 and R2 can seamlessly stitch the external world with the internal. They use BGP to learn about destinations in the external world and to advertise about the destinations in its own AS. They use OSPF to learn about the destinations internal to this AS and to inform the internal network about the external destinations.

In small networks, R1 and R2 can be statically configured with a default route pointing to the next-hop router in the external world, and the external routers can be statically configured with a single subnet (or very few subnets) that covers the entire internal network. In such cases, the routers still need to advertise in OSPF the default route that has been configured statically. Thus, routing protocols need the ability to advertise about routes populated via means other than OSPF itself (such as statically programmed or via BGP).

Advertising routes learned via one protocol in another protocol are called *redistributing routes*. Redistributing routes also applies to routes learned statically (administratively). In OSPF, redistributed routes are refered to as *external routes* because they were learned external to OSPF. In contrast, routes learned between the routers in the areas of an AS are called *internal routes* because they were learned via OSPF. OSPF calls R1 and R2 Autonomous System Border Routers (ASBRs) because they are the border between this AS and the external world. OSPF generalizes this concept and calls any router that advertises external routes an ASBR. Thus, if R13 redistributes a static route or a connected route, R13 is an ASBR even though it is part of the same AS.

The routes learned via OSPF by R1 and R2 will be advertised to the external world, because that is how the world knows how to communicate with this network. Those advertisements will typically hide the details of the internal network and advertise only *summarized routes*. For example, if the internal network takes a /24 subnet and divides it into two /25 subnets between areas 1 and 2, R1 and R2 will advertise only the /24 subnet, not the individual /25 subnets.

R3 and R4 have links in more than one area. They are connected to the backbone area (via links to R1 and R2) and to nonbackbone area 1 (via links to R11 and R12). Additionally, R4 is connected to nonbackbone area 2 (via links to R21). OSPF calls R3 and R4 Area Border Routers (ABRs). Routers in area 1 learn about one another's routes via normal OSPF flooding within area 1. They also learn about R21's routes and potentially the external routes via R3 and R4. Routes learned within an area are called *intra-area routes*, whereas routes learned from an ABR are called *inter-area routes*. External routes learned via an ABR are still external routes. When computing paths, OSPF's algorithm chooses intra-area routes over inter-area routes, and both over external routes. In the case of Clos networks, the preference of intra-area routes over inter-area routes is irrelevant because two areas are not connected. For instance, in Figure 13-2, traffic between the areas has to pass through R3 and R4.

The Messiness of Stubbiness

Inter-area and external routes are additional information to store and process for an OSPF router. In older times, many routers could not handle a lot of information, either because they had smaller memory or low-power CPUs. Such low-power routers are used even today in places like branch offices, where they do not process any information about the external world except the path to everything not local to the branch. Such routers need only a simple default route leading them out of the branch office. Servers can be considered to be the equivalent of low-powered or branch routers, in the sense that they need only a single default route leading out to everywhere else but themselves.

OSPF defines multiple types of nonbackbone area to address these conditions. When an ABR advertises just the default route as a way to reach everything outside the area, the area is called a *totally stubby* area. To keep the computation simple, this default route is advertised as an inter-area route. OSPF's rather messy rules prohibit such an area from advertising any external route. In other words, you cannot use the *redistribute* command to redistribute routes on the routers inside a totally stubby area.

Because this is very restrictive and problematic in many cases, Cisco introduced a new kind of stubby area called *not-so-stubby area* (NSSA). OSPFv2's inflexible LSA structure made this rather simple operation into a complex mess at an ABR. An ASBR in a stubby area advertises external routes via an LSA of type 7. The ABRs of such an area convert the type 7 routes into the well-understood type 5 routes for everybody else's consumption.

The upshot of all this for a network operator running OSPF on servers is to put the servers in a totally stubby area and to not use route redistribution. Alternatively, you can define the area to be NSSA, but it leads to unnecessary messes when you need to troubleshoot a problem.

OSPF Timers

Like any other protocol, OSPF has timers that affect convergence and various other aspects of OSPF's functioning. A good routing stack should provide sensible defaults for a given environment so that you don't usually have to worry about configuring these timers. FRR, for example, sets defaults for various environments in which it is deployed. One of these environments is a data center. Nevertheless, it's useful to understand the various timers that OSPF uses and how to determine their values:

Hello Interval

This is OSPF's keepalive timer; it determines how often OSPF sends out packets to its neighbors to indicate that it is alive. Typically, it is set to 10 seconds. If there are faulty cables, such as unidirectional cables, this timer can bring OSPF peering down and allow the network to route around such cables. The other reason for this timer is to ensure that the OSPF process itself hasn't died.

Setting this timer to a low value forces the OSPF process to process the keepalive packets of all the peers at a fairly rapid rate, which adds to the CPU load. By default, administrators use Bidirectional Fault Detection (BFD) to catch faulty cables, so the only reason to use a lower value for the Hello timer is to catch buggy processes. Assuming you're dealing with a good routing stack, leaving this value at its default is best.

Dead Interval

This is the amount of time to wait before declaring the peer to be dead. It is typically set to four times the Hello Interval. In other words, four consecutive Hello packets must be lost for a peer to bring down a peering. This timer ensures that a peer is declared dead only after four consecutive hello interval windows. If one or two hello packets are lost due to packet drop or because the process was busy with something like SPF computation, peers will not declare a router dead. The default value is 40 seconds and, as with the Hello Interval, the default is a fine value. If you change the Hello Interval, change this timer as well to keep the desired ratio of failures.

Retransmit Interval

This is the amount of time to wait for an acknowledgment of a packet containing link-state information before retransmitting it. Examples of such packets include LSA packets, Link-State Request packets, and Database Description packets. The default value is five seconds. This is another timer best left to its default value. Increase this if you're peering with a low-powered router that takes a much longer time to process and acknowledge link-state packets.

Transmit Delay

Every OSPF LSA packet contains the age of the packet. There is a maximum age associated with the LSA, and if the LSA's age exceeds this maximum value, the LSA is deleted and the paths are recomputed. To keep the LSA age accurate, every OSPF router increments the age of the LSA by a configured amount to account for the processing and propagation delay by the router. This configured amount is governed by the Transmit Delay timer. By default, this is set to one second, and I recommend leaving the value at the default.

SPF Computation Timers

OSPF uses a set of timers to decide on the optimal time to start recomputing paths after learning about a change in the network state. Recomputing paths can be compute intensive, especially in large networks. Furthermore, in the days when OSPF was designed, the routers had comparatively wimpy CPUs compared to the modern ones, so the OSPF implementers wanted to optimize recomputation. Optimization required striking a balance between waiting too long after learning about a change (such as when a router comes up or goes down) and not waiting long enough to let the changes build up. Traditional routing stacks used to wait 200 ms (called the *SPF delay timer*) from the time of receiving the first change to start computing the paths. Subsequent runs would hold off recomputing by as much as 10 seconds (called the *max SPF hold timer*), increasing in increments of one second (called hold timer) if the changes continued to be received.

A newer algorithm, called *incremental SPF*, is now used to recompute only the paths that are affected rather than for the entire network. So FRR changes the defaults to be 0 for the SPF delay timer, 5 seconds for the max SPF hold timer, and 50 ms for the hold timer. In the age of faster CPUs and support for incremental SPF, these decreased timers seem sensible. Unless you have a reason to change these values, I recommend leaving them alone.

Peering neighbors must have the same Hello Interval timers and the same Dead Interval timers. Otherwise, OSPF refuses to establish the peering relationship between those neighbors.

Besides these timers, OSPF has a bunch of other timers, such as one limiting how quickly you can send LSAs to the neighbor to avoid overwhelming it in the presence of a large number of updates. I recommend leaving all these timers alone.

OSPF States

Table 13-1 presents a brief description of the OSPF states when an interface is trying to establish an OSPF routing session on an interface. I assume point-to-point interface. The states listed here are useful to troubleshoot OSPF peering sessions that don't come up, which we discuss in Chapter 18.

Table 13-1. OSPF neighbor states and their meaning

State	Meaning
One-way	Node has sent a Hello on interface
Two-way	Node has sent and received a Hello on interface
ExStart	Node is negotiating with peer on how to exchange link-state database
Exchange	The two peers are synchronizing each other's link-state database
Full	The peers have completely synchronized the link-state database with each other

Dissecting an OSPF Configuration

In this section, we examine the actual configuration of OSPF in the various scenarios we described at the beginning of this chapter. In the process, we also consider the effects of configuration style and design choice on network automation. The OSPF commands covered in this section are as follows:

- *ospf router-id* `router-id` and *ospf6 router-id* `router-id`
- *ip ospf area* `area` and *interface* `ifname` *area* `area`
- *ip ospf network point-to-point* and *ipv6 ospf6 network point-to-point*
- *area* `area` *stub no-summary*
- *area* `area` *range* `prefix`
- *max-metric* and *stub-router*
- *passive-interface* and *ipv6 ospf6 passive-interface*
- *network* `prefix` *area* `area`
- *redistribute connected*

Configuration for Leaf-Spine in a Two-Tier Clos Topology: IPv4

Let's now look at two ways to write OSPF numbered configurations. As we do so, it will be clear that the numbered model, which is the most common one, is not conducive to network automation. We gradually progress toward the unnumbered model, including an Ansible snippet, to automate configuration.

For our examples in this section, we use the network architecture in Figure 13-3, but narrow our focus to leaf01 and spine01 for brevity. The IP addresses inside each router are the router's loopback IP addresses. The servers are connected as a bridged network to their associated leaf router. The subnet of the bridge is shown in Figure 13-3 along with the individual IP addresses of each of the interfaces on the bridge. I've tried to follow a pattern in the creation of these addresses, knowing full well that not everyone is fortunate enough to have as many IP addresses to play with.

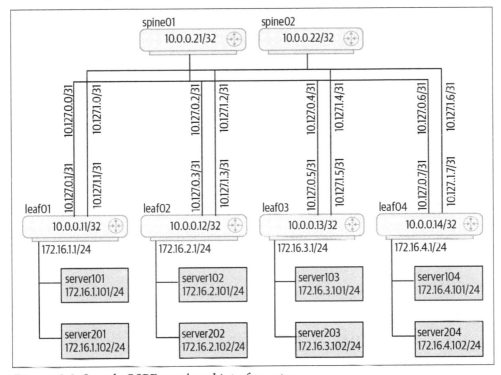

Figure 13-3. Sample OSPF numbered interface setup

Example 13-1 shows how most people I've encountered configure OSPF. The IP addresses of the interfaces are specified along with the area they're assigned to.

Example 13-1. Common OSPF config style

```
! Configuration for spine01
!
interface lo
 ip address 10.0.0.21/32
!
interface swp1
  ip address 10.127.0.0/31
  ip ospf bfd ❶
!
interface swp2
  ip address 10.127.0.2/31
```

```
  ip ospf bfd
!
interface swp3
  ip address 10.127.0.4/31
  ip ospf bfd
!
interface swp4
  ip address 10.127.0.6/31
  ip ospf bfd
!
router ospf
  ospf router-id 10.0.0.21
  network 10.127.0.0/31 area 0
  network 10.127.0.2/31 area 0
  network 10.127.0.4/31 area 0
  network 10.127.0.6/31 area 0
  redistribute connected

! Configuration for leaf01
!
interface lo
 ip address 10.0.0.11/32
!
interface swp1
  ip address 10.127.0.1/31
  ip ospf bfd
!
interface swp2
  ip address 10.127.1.1/31
  ip ospf bfd
!
! This next statement is for the servers subnet
!
interface vlan10
  ip address 172.16.0.1/24
!
router ospf
  ospf router-id 10.0.0.11
  network 10.127.0.1/31 area 0
  network 10.127.1.1/31 area 0
  redistribute connected
```

❶ This enables the use of BFD (see "Bidirectional Forwarding Detection" on page 107) with the specific OSPF peer.

The problems with this configuration, basic as it is, include the following:

- The configuration is not easy to automate, because the configuration of every node looks different. spine01's configuration will look different from that of the other spines, leaf01's configuration will look different from all the other leaves, and so on.

- Errors are easy in this configuration because we're duplicating the IP address in the specification of the interface and in the network statement.

- Errors cannot be caught easily (such as by eyeballing) because they probably stem from the interactions between multiple lines, so multiple pieces of information need to be verified.

- OSPF takes additional time to exchange routes because the links are not declared to be point-to-point links. By default, OSPF assumes that the link between the routers is a bridged link with more than two routers on the link. This causes OSPF to run what is called the Designated Router election, which is unnecessary in this scenario and adds to the time it takes to exchange information.

- Redistributing connected information merely duplicates all the interface IP address information, because we already exchanged that information via the *network* statement. If a lot of VLANs are routed, using *redistribute connected* is an easy way to escape typing a lot of lines in the configuration. But this labor savings comes at the cost of duplicating some route information, adding some time (even if minimal) to the path computation step.

The first step to fixing the information is to replace the previous configuration with the equivalent shown in Example 13-2.

Example 13-2. A cleaner numbered OSPF configuration

```
! Configuration for spine01
!
interface lo
  ip address 10.0.0.21/32
  ip ospf area 0
!
interface swp1
  ip address 10.127.0.0/31
  ip ospf network point-to-point
  ip ospf area 0
  ip ospf bfd
!
interface swp2
  ip address 10.127.0.2/31
  ip ospf network point-to-point
  ip ospf area 0
  ip ospf bfd
!
interface swp3
  ip address 10.127.0.4/31
  ip ospf network point-to-point
  ip ospf area 0
  ip ospf bfd
!
```

```
interface swp4
  ip address 10.127.0.6/31
  ip ospf network point-to-point
  ip ospf area 0
  ip ospf bfd
!
router ospf
  ospf router-id 10.0.0.21
  passive-interface lo

! Configuration for leaf01
!
interface lo
  ip address 10.0.0.11/32
  ip ospf area 0
!
interface swp1
  ip address 10.127.0.1/31
  ip ospf network point-to-point
  ip ospf area 0
  ip ospf bfd
!
interface swp2
  ip address 10.127.1.1/31
  ip ospf network point-to-point
  ip ospf area 0
  ip ospf bfd
!
! This next statement is for the servers subnet
!
interface vlan10
  ip address 172.16.0.1/24
  ip ospf area 0
!
router ospf
  ospf router-id 10.0.0.11
  passive-interface default
  no passive-interface swp1
  no passive-interface swp2
```

You might notice that this configuration is quite a bit simpler than the previous version; specifically:

- We don't duplicate the interface address information in *network* statements.

- We declare the interfaces to be point-to-point from OSPF's perspective, thus avoiding unnecessary designated router computation and speeding up convergence.

- We eliminate distributing duplicate information by removing the redistribute statement. This also eliminates external routes. Doing so further decreases convergence time due to the way OSPF handles external routes in its path computation logic.

- Because we need to specify the interface address information anyway, we automatically add the routed VLAN interfaces to OSPF. The *passive-interface* statements instruct OSPF to merely announce those interfaces as being connected to it, without attempting to form an OSPF peer over that interface. I show two different styles to both instruct and to keep the size of the configuration file. When there are lots of routed VLAN interfaces—in other words, a lot of passive interfaces—using the *passive-interface* model as shown in the case of leaf01 will lead to a smaller configuration file. In the case of a spine when only the loopback interface is the passive interface, the model shown for spine01 leads to a smaller configuration. You might prefer one style over another and use that for both scenarios. That is fine.

Despite these improvements, this configuration does not make automation of this configuration easy. The configuration fails in that regard because every node looks different and every inter-router link needs to be properly assigned an IP address. Automation tools such as Ansible fail to make this issue simple for the user. Specifically, the problem for automation is to ensure that the two ends of the link belong to the same subnet. If the network administrator can write code, say in Python or any other language, they can simplify this task. But most network administrators are not programmers, even in a script-writing sense.

Let's now consider simplifying the configuration even more, using unnumbered OSPF. The address assigned to each interfaces is the same as the loopback IP address on the router, as shown in Figure 13-4. We show this configuration snippet in Example 13-3.

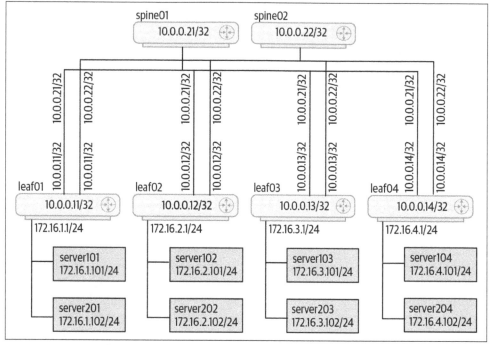

Figure 13-4. Sample OSPF unnumbered interface setup

At first glance, Figure 13-4 might look similar to Figure 13-3. But a closer look reveals that just one address is used for all inter-router links, and that it is the same address as the loopback address. The loopback address is also the router ID. All in all, just a single address suffices for everything except the subnets exposed to the servers. Example 13-3 presents the associated configuration.

Example 13-3. An OSPF unnumbered configuration

```
! Configuration for spine01
!
interface lo
  ip address 10.0.0.21/32
  ip ospf area 0
!
interface swp1
  ip address 10.0.0.21/32
  ip ospf network point-to-point
  ip ospf area 0
  ip ospf bfd
!
interface swp2
  ip address 10.0.0.21/32
  ip ospf network point-to-point
```

```
  ip ospf area 0
  ip ospf bfd
!
interface swp3
  ip address 10.0.0.21/32
  ip ospf network point-to-point
  ip ospf area 0
  ip ospf bfd
!
interface swp4
  ip address 10.0.0.21/32
  ip ospf network point-to-point
  ip ospf area 0
  ip ospf bfd
!
router ospf
  ospf router-id 10.0.0.21
  passive-interface lo

! Configuration for leaf01
!
interface lo
  ip address 10.0.0.11/32
  ip ospf area 0
!
interface swp1
  ip address 10.0.0.11/32
  ip ospf network point-to-point
  ip ospf area 0
  ip ospf bfd
!
interface swp2
  ip address 10.0.0.11/32
  ip ospf network point-to-point
  ip ospf area 0
  ip ospf bfd
!
! This next statement is for the servers subnet
!
interface vlan10
  ip address 172.16.0.1/24
  ip ospf area 0
!
router ospf
  ospf router-id 10.0.0.11
  passive-interface default
```

```
no passive-interface swp1
no passive-interface swp2
```

The Missing Interface Ranges

Sadly, most router stack configurations do not support the ability to glob or specify interface ranges. If interface ranges were available, you could do something like the following on a spine with 64 leaves, depending on unnumbered interfaces:

```
! Configuration for spine01
interface lo
  ip address 10.0.0.11/32
interface swp[1-64]
  ip address 10.0.0.11/32
  ip ospf network point-to-point
  ip ospf area 0
  ip ospf bfd
router ospf
  ospf router-id 10.0.0.11
  passive-interface lo
```

Catching problems in such a trivial configuration is easy. In some of my presentations, I deliberately introduced errors in this configuration and viewers immediately caught them.

If you use Ansible for your network automation, you can define a simple configuration, as shown in Example 13-4.

Example 13-4. Templating spine01's config with Ansible

```
{# frr.j2 #}
interface lo
  ip address {{ loopback_ip }} ❶
{% for i in range({{isl_start}}, {{isl_end+1}}) %} ❷
interface swp{{ i }}
  ip address {{ loopback_ip }}
  ip ospf network point-to-point
  ip ospf area 0
  ip ospf bfd
{% endfor %}
!
router ospf
  ospf router-id {{ loopback_ip }}
  passive-interface lo

hosts: spines
tasks:
  name: Generate config for router
  template: ❸
```

```
            src: frr.j2
            dest: /etc/frr/frr.conf
```

❶ loopback_ip is a variable defined in the *host_vars* file of spine01.

❷ isl_start and isl_end are variables defined in the spine *group_vars* file.

❸ The template module expands the template specified into the *frr.conf* file and stores it in the location specified by the "dest" variable on the spine node.

The complexity of using numbered interfaces instead of unnumbered interfaces was discussed in Chapter 10. If your vendor's routing stack doesn't support it, ask them why and demand that it be supported. You'll build more reliable networks this way, at least in the data center.

Configuration for Leaf-Spine in a Two-Tier Clos Topology: IPv6

IPv6 did some things right in its basic design. There is no longer a need to assign IP addresses to individual interfaces in IPv6. IPv6 automatically derives a link-local IPv6 address. In other words, the basic routing model in IPv6 uses unnumbered interfaces. FRR, among other routing protocol suites, uses a different configuration block for OSPF with IPv6. For the same topology, the OSPFv3 configuration looks as shown in Example 13-5.

Example 13-5. An OSPFv3 configuration

```
! Configuration for spine01
!
interface lo
  ipv6 address 2001:10::21/128
  ipv6 ospf6 passive
!
interface swp1
  ipv6 ospf6 network point-to-point
  ipv6 ospf6 bfd
!
interface swp2
  ipv6 ospf6 network point-to-point
  ipv6 ospf6 bfd
!
interface swp3
  ipv6 ospf6 network point-to-point
  ipv6 ospf6 bfd
!
interface swp4
  ipv6 ospf6 network point-to-point
  ipv6 ospf6 bfd
!
```

```
router ospf6
  ospf6 router-id 10.0.0.21
  interface lo area 0
  interface swp1 area 0
  interface swp2 area 0
  interface swp3 area 0
  interface swp4 area 0

! Configuration for leaf01
!
interface lo
  ipv6 address 2001:10:0::11/128
  ipv6 ospf6 passive
!
interface swp1
  ipv6 ospf6 network point-to-point
  ipv6 ospf6 bfd
!
interface swp2
  ipv6 ospf6 network point-to-point
  ipv6 ospf6 bfd
!
! This next statement is for the servers subnet
!
interface vlan10
  ipv6 address 2001:172:16::1/24
  ipv6 ospf6 passive
!
router ospf6
  ospf6 router-id 10.0.0.11
  interface lo area 0
  interface swp1 area 0
  interface swp2 area 0
  interface vlan10 area 0
```

The improvements in comparison to IPv4's configuration are obvious. IP addresses are completely missing from the configuration on inter-router links.

Let's compare FRR's routing configuration with Cisco's NX-OS configuration. Here is what Cisco's NX-OS configuration for the same two nodes looks like:

```
! Configuration for spine01
!
interface loopback 1
 ipv6 address 2001:10::21/128
 ospfv3 passive-interface
 ipv6 ospfv3 201 area 0
 !
interface ethernet 1/1
  ospfv3 network point-to-point
  ipv6 ospfv3 201 area 0
 !
interface ethernet 1/2
```

```
  ospfv3 network point-to-point
  ipv6 ospfv3 201 area 0
!
interface ethernet 1/3
  ospfv3 network point-to-point
  ipv6 ospfv3 201 area 0
!
interface ethernet 1/4
  ospfv3 network point-to-point
  ipv6 ospfv3 201 area 0
!
router ospfv3 201
  router-id 10.0.0.21

! Configuration for leaf01
!
interface loopback 1
 ipv6 address 2001:10::11/128
 ipv6 ospfv3 201 area 0
 ospfv3 passive-interface
!
interface ethernet 1/1
  ospfv3 network point-to-point
  ipv6 ospfv3 201 area 0
!
interface ethernet 1/2
  ipv6 ospf6 network point-to-point
  ipv6 ospfv3 201 area 0
!
! This next statement is for the servers subnet
!
interface vlan10
  ipv6 address 2001:172:16::1/24
  ospfv3 passive-interface
  ipv6 ospfv3 201 area 0
!
router ospfv3 201
  router-id 10.0.0.11
  log-adjacency-changes detail
```

Configuration with Three-Tier Clos Running OSPF

When you want to configure a three-tier Clos network with OSPF, as discussed earlier, there are two possible cases: one with OSPF running on the servers and the other
without. In the latter case, each pod is a separate nonbackbone area and the links
between the spine switch of each pod and the super-spine switch become the backbone, area 0. You can assign every pod the same nonbackbone area, area 1. We discuss route summarization after we discuss configuring OSPF on servers.

Configuration with Servers Running OSPF: IPv4

When used with containers, some customers use OSPF on the host to advertise the container IP addresses or the specific container bridge IP subnet. In such a scenario, as we discussed earlier, the leaf router advertises only a default route to the server by treating the servers as belonging to a totally stubby area. We look at the configuration of leaf01 and a server named server101 attached to it. We reduce the options we have to consider by assuming the use of unnumbered interfaces.

The first task is to connect the servers. This requires converting the server-facing ports on leaf01 to routed ports. In the examples so far, the server-facing ports were part of a VLAN; that is, they were bridged ports. If you use a bridge to hook up leaf01 and the servers attached to it, the behavior of OSPF in such a scenario is for every OSPF router on the bridged segment to peer with every other router on the same bridged segment. In the example figure, leaf01 would set up OSPF peering relationships with server101 and server102. But server101 and server201 would also OSPF peer with each other, which is unnecessary and just adds complexity and overhead to running OSPF on the servers.

To appreciate the overhead, consider the common deployment in which there are 40 servers per rack. In such a scenario, leaf01 would have 40 OSPF peers, one with each of the servers. Each of the 40 servers would also OSPF peer with each other. Thus, every server has 40 OSPF peers: one with the other 39 servers and one with leaf01. This leads to a total of 1,600 peering sessions, which adds a lot of chattiness and overhead in the area. What makes this really bad is that none of it is required, because updates flow only from leaf01, the designated router. (Additional configuration is required to make sure it always becomes the designated router.)

Instead, if you make the server-facing ports pure routed ports on the switch (leaf01 in this example), all the servers peer only with the leaf they're connected to and things become sane again. Figure 13-5 shows the result. The containers within each server are connected to a docker bridge which is shown inside each server with IP addresses in the subnet 192.168.x.x. The server's NIC itself is in the 172.16.x.x subnet.

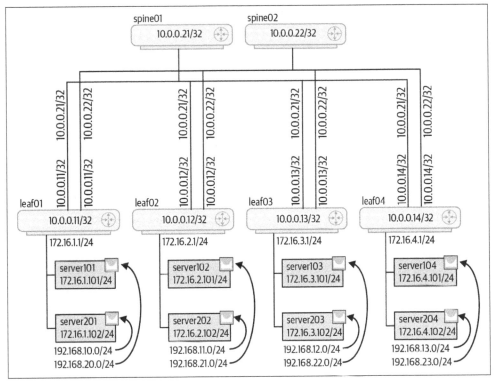

Figure 13-5. Sample setup with servers running OSPF

As per the discussion in "The Messiness of Stubbiness" on page 265, the next configuration choice is to put all the servers in a single different, totally stubby, non-backbone area. Assuming a docker0 bridge, Example 13-6 is the configuration from the perspective of leaf01 and host server101.

Example 13-6. OSPF unnumbered configuration for leaf01 and server101

```
! Configuration for leaf01
!
interface lo
 ip address 10.0.0.11/32
 ip ospf area 0
!
interface swp1
  ip address 10.0.0.11/32
  ip ospf network point-to-point
  ip ospf area 0
  ip ospf bfd
!
interface swp2
  ip address 10.0.0.11/32
```

```
  ip ospf network point-to-point
  ip ospf area 0
  ip ospf bfd
!
! Now the server connections
!
interface swp3
  ip address 10.0.0.11/32
  ip ospf network point-to-point
  ip ospf area 1
  ip ospf bfd
!
interface swp4
  ip address 10.0.0.11/32
  ip ospf network point-to-point
  ip ospf area 1
  ip ospf bfd
!
router ospf
  ospf router-id 10.0.0.11
  passive-interface lo
  area 1 stub no-summary

! Configuration for server101
!
interface lo
 ip address 172.16.0.101/32
 ip ospf area 1
 !
interface eth1
  ip address 172.16.0.101/32
  ip ospf network point-to-point
  ip ospf area 1
  ip ospf bfd
!
interface docker0
  ip ospf area 1
  ip ospf bfd
!
router ospf
  ospf router-id 172.16.0.101
  passive-interface lo
  passive-interface docker0
  area 1 stub no-summary
```

The main difference from the version without OSPF running on the server is, of course, the specification of the additional ports—the server-facing ports—which are now running OSPF. An additional difference is the declaration of area 1 as a totally stubby area, through the command *area 1 stub no-summary*. It is important to note that this declaration of a totally stubby area needs to be on both the server and the leaf. If you don't do this, OSPF will not bring up the peering. The no-summary keyword indicates that not even summary routes from other areas are to be provided to this area, just the default route. That change makes it a totally stubby area. Because a totally stubby area cannot be an ASBR, you cannot use *redistribute connected* or any other redistribute on the servers.

The configuration also announces the IP address of the default docker0 bridge.[3] You need to ensure that Docker does not NAT the IP address of the containers as it leaves the server. You can do this as described in "Suppressing NAT in Docker" on page 157.

Running the configuration, let's take a look at the routing table on spine01:

```
vagrant@spine01:~$ ip ro
10.0.0.11 via 10.0.0.11 dev swp1  proto ospf  metric 20 onlink
10.0.0.12 via 10.0.0.12 dev swp2  proto ospf  metric 20 onlink
10.0.0.13 via 10.0.0.13 dev swp3  proto ospf  metric 20 onlink
10.0.0.14 via 10.0.0.14 dev swp4  proto ospf  metric 20 onlink
10.0.0.22  proto ospf  metric 20
        nexthop via 10.0.0.11  dev swp1 weight 1 onlink
        nexthop via 10.0.0.12  dev swp2 weight 1 onlink
        nexthop via 10.0.0.14  dev swp4 weight 1 onlink
        nexthop via 10.0.0.13  dev swp3 weight 1 onlink
172.16.1.101 via 10.0.0.11 dev swp1  proto ospf  metric 20 onlink
172.16.1.102 via 10.0.0.11 dev swp1  proto ospf  metric 20 onlink
172.16.2.101 via 10.0.0.12 dev swp2  proto ospf  metric 20 onlink
172.16.2.101 via 10.0.0.12 dev swp2  proto ospf  metric 20 onlink
172.16.2.102 via 10.0.0.12 dev swp2  proto ospf  metric 20 onlink
172.16.3.101 via 10.0.0.13 dev swp2  proto ospf  metric 20 onlink
172.16.3.102 via 10.0.0.13 dev swp2  proto ospf  metric 20 onlink
172.16.4.101 via 10.0.0.14 dev swp4  proto ospf  metric 20 onlink
172.16.4.102 via 10.0.0.14 dev swp4  proto ospf  metric 20 onlink
```

Compare the output to the output of the same command without running OSPF on the servers:

```
vagrant@spine01:~$ ip ro
10.0.0.11 via 10.0.0.11 dev swp1  proto ospf  metric 20 onlink
10.0.0.12 via 10.0.0.12 dev swp2  proto ospf  metric 20 onlink
10.0.0.13 via 10.0.0.13 dev swp3  proto ospf  metric 20 onlink
10.0.0.14 via 10.0.0.14 dev swp4  proto ospf  metric 20 onlink
10.0.0.22  proto ospf  metric 20
        nexthop via 10.0.0.11  dev swp1 weight 1 onlink
        nexthop via 10.0.0.12  dev swp2 weight 1 onlink
        nexthop via 10.0.0.14  dev swp4 weight 1 onlink
        nexthop via 10.0.0.13  dev swp3 weight 1 onlink
172.16.1.0/24 via 10.0.0.11 dev swp1  proto ospf  metric 20 onlink
172.16.2.0/24 via 10.0.0.12 dev swp2  proto ospf  metric 20 onlink
172.16.3.0/24 via 10.0.0.13 dev swp2  proto ospf  metric 20 onlink
172.16.4.0/24 via 10.0.0.14 dev swp4  proto ospf  metric 20 onlink
```

---

3 Docker assigns the IP address for the docker0 bridge via the */etc/docker/daemon.json* file.

You can see, in the latter output, that the spines see only the summarized subnet route rather than the individual routes to each server. The summarized routes clearly scale better than every node carrying each individual server IP address.

So in summary, what should you do? This is a question also when we have a large three-tier Clos network. Should each pod see all the routes in every other pod or can we get away with defaults? Where shall we summarize in such a situation? We tackle that next.

Summarizing Routes in OSPF

In the case of the servers, the leaves are the ABRs. So they can summarize the routes of the individual servers back into the subnet route that was present before the servers started running OSPF. Here's the command to summarize:

```
area <area> range <ip-summary-route> advertise
```

For example, on leaf01, the command is as follows:

```
area 1 range 172.16.1.0/24 advertise
```

In a three-tier Clos topology, the only place summarization is possible is on the pod spines, because they're the only ABR when the servers are not running OSPF. If the routes from all the pod leaves can be summarized into a few subnets, the *area* command can be used to summarize on the spines.

When summarizing, it is important to consider the behavior in case of failures, as discussed in "Route Summarization in Clos Networks" on page 105. With servers running OSPF, the problem of summarizing at the leaves happens only when the hosts are dual-attached to two switches and the link dies between one of the switches and a server.

OSPF and Upgrades

It is useful to be able to upgrade a box without affecting the traffic flowing through it. The primary method to do this is by first draining all traffic from the box, and then upgrading it. Unlike L2 protocols such as LACP or spanning tree, routing protocols come with built-in support for draining traffic from a router. The network OS has to do additional work to ensure that the traffic is fully drained before upgrading the box after the appropriate routing commands have been issued.

In OSPF, there are two methods to drain traffic from a router: one is used in OSPFv2 and the other in OSPFv3.

In OSPFv2, the command used is called *max-metric*. In link-state protocols, the path computation logic uses the cost (or metric) of each of the links between the source and the destination to pick the path with the smallest cost. The *max-metric* command changes the cost of every link on a router to be the maximum possible value. So every router in the network will compute the path excluding that router. Traffic in transit due to the previous path computation will be delivered without a problem. But no new traffic will use the path via that router. The router can monitor its links and, when the traffic drops to a sufficiently low value, decide that it is safe to upgrade.

OSPFv3 offers a more direct method to drain traffic, called a *stub router*. When you set a router to be stub router, it advertises its LSAs with the "R" bit and "V6" bits cleared. This indicates to all the other routers to exclude such a router from IPv6 and other path computations. Some routing stacks provide the *max-metric* command, even if using OSPFv3, to make the commands between the two protocols look similar. FRR supports only the *stub-router* command as of this writing.

Best Practices

Here are the best practices in deploying OSPF in the data center. This is based on the use cases I've encountered in production. It is designed to simplify the configuration, make it automation friendly, and help troubleshoot when problems occur.

- Use unnumbered interfaces, if supported.
- Area number for a pod, or area number for servers can be reused. In other words, two different leaves can use the same area number to address the servers connected to them. Similarly, two different pods can use the same area number. This area number can be 1, for example. So you only ever have two areas, area 0 and area 1.
- Use `ip ospf area` instead of `network` statements in the numbered interface configuration. This helps avoid duplicating the IP address in multiple places. With unnumbered, you have to use the `ip ospf area` model in any case.
- When using unnumbered interfaces, either on servers or on routers, always assign the IP address to the loopback interface also, and ensure that the loopback interface is declared as a passive interface and in the correct area.
- Use BFD and leave the default timer values unchanged. This leads to a more robust and simpler configuration.
- Always enable the detailed logging of OSPF adjacency changes via the `log-adjacency-changes detail` configuration knob. FRR enables this by default, and so is missing from the FRR examples earlier in the chapter.
- Avoid the use of *redistribute connected*. It might look like a simplification to the configuration, but you end up advertising unnecessary and duplicate information. Avoiding external routes also simplifies OSPF processing on routers.
- Keep OSPF configuration to the minimum necessary to ensure a robust network.

Summary

This chapter explored the use of OSPF as a routing protocol within the data center. Although BGP remains the most popular routing protocol within the data center, OSPF is still a valid choice in certain situations. We looked at designing OSPF appropriately for various scenarios, including running OSPF in three-tier Clos networks and on servers themselves. We saw the benefits of using unnumbered OSPF, including reducing the attack vector and easing network automation. The goal of this chapter was to give a network administrator all the appropriate information to configure OSPF in the data center. In the next chapter, we look at using BGP as the routing protocol in the data center. We examine validating the OSPF configuration and displaying OSPF's state in Chapter 18.

## CHAPTER 14

BGP in the Data Center

Would it save you a lot of time if I just gave up and went mad now?
—Douglas Adams

BGP is like a mythical beast: respected but also greatly feared. From its birth in 1989 as the replacement for a routing protocol called the Exterior Gateway Protocol (EGP) to the present, BGP has evolved into a sophisticated, mature, rich (and therefore, some would say, complex) routing protocol, which still is responsible for piecing together the internet as we know it today. Besides this, it has been applied to solve routing in new areas (the data center) which are far from its roots. Furthermore, it has also morphed to support new ideas such as SDN controllers. To its detractors, Douglas Adams probably perfectly captures their sentiments about understanding BGP.

I'd like to save you a lot of time not going mad. So, we begin with a brief overview of only those basic BGP concepts that are required to understand its use inside the data center. After that, we examine the specific adaptations to make BGP work in the data center. This chapter is a concise introduction to the protocol. Readers interested in more details are welcome to peruse either the standard or other books on the subject matter.

By the end of this chapter, a reader should be able to answer questions such as these:

- What do the BGP terms such as ASN, community, attribute, and best path mean?
- Should I use eBGP or iBGP in the data center?
- What is the ASN numbering scheme when using BGP in the data center?
- How are BGP timers modified for use in the data center?

This chapter sets the stage for the next two chapters, which cover how BGP is configured for a Clos network, without and with network virtualization.

Basic BGP Concepts

If you're new to BGP, or maybe want a refresher, this section is for you. This is a Cliff Notes description of BGP, as befits a book like this.

BGP Protocol Overview

BGP is called a *path vector routing protocol*. A *vector* is an array or list of objects. Therefore, a path vector routing protocol is one that builds and distributes a vector of objects, each object defining the path from one network (usually IP) address to another. I write "objects" and not "routers" because the object is something called an AS, about which I have more to say later.

As of this writing, BGP's version number is 4, also known as BGP-4. It is defined in RFC 4271 (*https://oreil.ly/CO7Zj*), although some specifications in that document have been overridden by later RFCs (for example, the Capabilities Advertisement RFC).

BGP runs over TCP. This allows BGP to ignore problems such as fragmentation, reassembly, handling acknowledgments, retransmissions, and other such issues that other routing protocols typically deal with. In fact, BGP is the only routing protocol that runs over TCP. Every other common protocol either runs on IP, or even further below, as an L2 packet. BGP accepts new connections and sends connect requests to TCP port number 179.

The notorious complexity of BGP follows from its versatility. For instance, BGP peers exchange routing information for multiple network types, including IPv4, IPv6, and network virtualization technologies including MPLS and VXLAN. Thus, BGP is called a *multiprotocol routing protocol*. And because BGP exchanges routing information across administrative domains, it supports the ability to apply complex routing policies. These policies govern multiple aspects of BGP's behavior, including computing the best path to reach a destination, the routes that are advertised, and the attributes they're advertised with. BGP supports ECMP, which was defined in Chapter 5, as well as Unequal-Cost Multipath (UCMP), though not all implementations support UCMP.

BGP peering between speakers in different administrative domains (or autonomous systems in BGP parlance) is called *external BGP* (eBGP). BGP peering between speakers within an administrative domain (or within the same autonomous system) is called *internal BGP* (iBGP). BGP has different rules for eBGP peering and iBGP peering.

BGP is an extremely extensible protocol. People come up with new ideas for it all the time. In many ways, BGP is the HTTP protocol for routing developers. It is used to carry all kinds of information between routers that might have nothing to do with routing and that BGP was not originally designed for. BGP's extensibility makes it very adaptable and powerful, but it also makes it difficult to understand if you attempt to use all the myriad knobs it provides. This is why it's crucial to be minimalistic in the use of BGP. Don't use something just because you can.

BGP Peering

BGP peering is not a client-server relationship but a peer-to-peer relationship. Figure 14-1 shows a sample timeline sequence in the life of a BGP peering session.

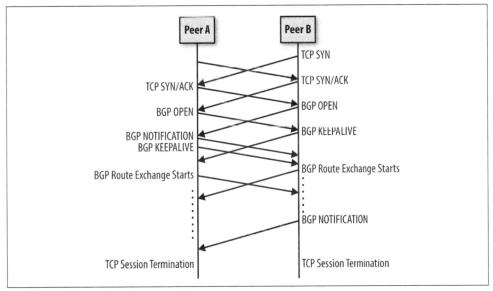

Figure 14-1. BGP peering timeline sequence diagram

As peers, both ends of a BGP connection can initiate the TCP connection. Both connections typically succeed, leaving the two sides with two separate TCP connections for communicating with each other. This condition is called *connection collision* in the BGP standard. BGP reduces these two TCP connections to a single TCP connection by resolving the collision. The winning TCP connection is the one initiated by the speaker with the higher router-id, where each router-id is treated as an unsigned 32-bit number. A router-id is the unique identifier of the BGP speaker. Unlike some other protocols, BGP doesn't define a priority field during session initiation, because the specifics of which side's connection is picked up are a minor detail that doesn't affect any other part of the BGP decision making.

The BGP standard also defines the possibility of a "passive" connection, in which one side never initiates the TCP connection but just responds when another node requests a connection. This is used, for example, when endpoints running Kube-router or other such solutions peer with BGP running on a router. We discuss passive connections in Chapter 15.

BGP State Machine

The BGP state machine is fairly simple. It consists of three main phases: TCP connection establishment, the elimination of connection collision along with capability exchange, and route exchange. These phases pass through a few more specific states, as shown in Figure 14-2. The dashed lines in the figure indicate the state transitions in case of an error, and the solid lines indicate the state transitions under normal circumstances. The names of these states are worth learning, because when you look at BGP neighbor information, the command output shows the state a peering session is in.

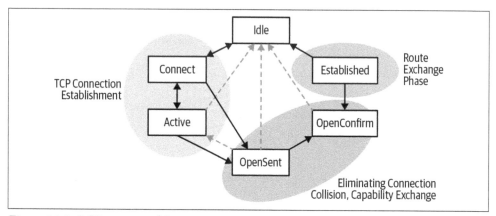

Figure 14-2. BGP state machine

Autonomous System Number

Every BGP speaker is assigned an ASN that identifies the organization represented by that speaker. In the context of BGP, an organization is defined as a network that is controlled by a single entity and has a well-defined routing policy. Typically, service providers such as Verizon, AT&T, and T-Mobile are each assigned a unique ASN, and so are major enterprises such as ExxonMobil, Apple, and Amazon. In some cases, an organization might have several ASNs (for example, as a result of acquisitions). For example, Apple has three ASNs, whereas Amazon has 14.

The path vector of a network address is the list of ASNs traversed by that address. As such, the list of ASNs is used to identify routing loops, determine the best path to a prefix, and associate routing policies with networks. On the internet, each ASN is allowed to speak authoritatively about only particular IP prefixes.

ASNs come in two variations: two-byte and four-byte. The two-byte cousins are more popular because they've been around longer and are also just easier to read (for instance, the two-byte ASN 64000 is much easier to take in visually than the four-byte ASN 4200000000). Most routing protocol suites today support both variants.

ASNs also have a private number space for use in internal networks, without the global internet being aware of these numbers. Data centers commonly use the private ASNs for internal use. We discuss this in more detail later in the chapter.

BGP Capabilities

As a continuously evolving protocol, BGP allows the negotiation of capabilities on every peering session to ensure that the two sides exchange only information that is supported by both sides. This negotiation is defined by RFC 5492 (*https://oreil.ly/ _Nrro*). The kinds of capabilities exchanged (in the BGP Open message) include what address families are supported by each side.

BGP Attributes, Communities, Extended Communities

As my friend and noted BGP expert Daniel Walton says, BGP route advertisements carry little Post-it notes. These Post-it notes are called *BGP path attributes*. There are different kinds of attributes, depending on their use and semantics. Attributes are encoded using the well-known Type, Length, and Value (TLV) model.

The base BGP-4 RFC defines seven path attributes that every compliant implementation must support. These attributes are used in BGP's best path computation. For example, one of the attributes, AS_PATH, is what carries the path vector associated with a route.

Some attributes are mandatory; in other words, they must be always transmitted, whereas others might not always appear in a message. But if any of the seven base path attributes is present, the recipient must be able to process it. Other attributes defined outside the base RFC are called *optional attributes*. Not all implementations might support them. For example, the MP_REACH_NLRI attribute is used to advertise MPLS labels, but not all implementations need to support this. The only requirement for a receiver to process an optional attribute is to forward an attribute flagged as *transitive*, even if it does not understand that attribute.

BGP also allows user-extensible grouping of routes via an attribute called *communities*. Communities are transitive optional attributes. Communities are used by operators to group together a set of advertised routes to apply a routing policy to. A routing policy influences the semantics of BGP Update message processing and best-path computation for those routes. Operators can use configuration commands specific to their routing stack to configure the tagging of routes with communities and to influence BGP's behavior based on the value of a community. A single Update message can carry multiple communities.

Communities are four-byte values, not arbitrary text strings. The first two bytes are always the ASN of the BGP speaker that originated the community, whereas the remaining two bytes are left up to the network operators to use as they want. Like much of BGP, communities were designed in the early dawn of the internet. With the advent of 4-byte ASNs and the desire for more than 2 bytes of operator stuffing, we now have *extended communities* (8 bytes instead of 4), and *large communities* (12 bytes). Network virtualization routing information with two-byte ASNs uses extended communities, whereas the information with four-byte ASNs uses large communities.

BGP Best-Path Computation

A BGP router computes the best path for each advertised route, starting from itself. BGP's best-path selection is triggered when a new UPDATE message is received from one or more of its peers. Implementations can choose to buffer the triggering of this computation so that a single run will process all updates instead of triggering rapid route updates by running the computation too frequently. BGP advertises a route only if the computation changes (adds, deletes, or updates) the best path for a given network destination.

OSPF, IS-IS, and other routing protocols have a simple metric by which to decide the specific path to accept. BGP has eight! You can use this pithy mnemonic phrase to remember the priority in which these metrics are used when computing the best path:

```
Wise Lip Lovers Apply Oral Medication Every Night.
```

Denise Fishburne, a Cisco engineer, invented this phrase and was kind enough to let me use it in this book. Table 14-1 illustrates the correspondence between the mnemonic and the actual metrics. The best path is considered one that is better in the value of the metric in the order specified (see section 9.1 of RFC 4271 (*https://oreil.ly/Fk1FK*) for details on the best path computation). If the values are equal for a metric between a new update and the existing best path, the next metric is compared to break the tie.

Table 14-1. BGP best-path metrics

Mnemonic	BGP metric name
Wise	Weight
Lip	LOCAL_PREFERENCE
Lovers	Locally originated
Apply	AS_PATH

Mnemonic	BGP metric name
Oral	ORIGIN
Medication	MED
Every	eBGP over iBGP
Night	Nexthop IGP Cost

That said, in the data center, only two of these metrics are used: locally originated and AS_PATH. In other words, a prefix that is local to a node is preferred to one learned via BGP, and a shorter AS_PATH length route is preferred over a route with a longer AS_PATH length. If the AS_PATH lengths are equal, the paths are considered equal cost. In reality, the default BGP implementation not only requires the AS_PATH lengths to be the same to be considered equal cost, but the individual ASNs in the AS_PATH must be identical. You need to turn on a knob that relaxes this restriction and only uses the AS_PATH length in determining equal cost.

Support for Multiple Protocols

BGP can advertise how to reach not just IP addresses, but also other information such as MPLS labels and MAC addresses. The basic standard that defines support for multiple kinds of addresses is RFC 4760 (*https://oreil.ly/xZ-ub*). Each network protocol supported by BGP has its own identifier, called the Address Family Indicator (AFI). The AFI identifies the primary network protocol. For example, IPv4 and IPv6 each have their own AFI. However, even within an AFI, there is a need for further distinctions. For example, unicast and multicast reachability information differ significantly. BGP distinguishes these cases by using separate Subsequent Address Family Indicator (SAFI) numbers for unicast and multicast addresses. The IPv4 Unicast AFI-SAFI is the one assumed in the base RFC. So when no AFI/SAFI is specified, it is assumed to apply to IPv4 Unicast.

The AFI/SAFI list that is of interest to a BGP speaker is advertised using BGP capabilities in the BGP OPEN message. Two BGP peers exchange information about a network address only if both sides advertise an interest in its AFI/SAFI.

BGP Messages

Table 14-2 lists the different message types sent by BGP and their specific uses.

Table 14-2. BGP message types and their use

Message type	Use	Periodicity
Open	Sent on session establishment to identify router and exchange capabilities	Once
Update	Used to exchange route advertisement and withdrawal	Only when information changes
Keepalive	Heartbeat, used to signal the remote peer that we're alive and kicking	Configured, usually 60 seconds

Message type	Use	Periodicity
Notification	Sent on error or when administratively closing the session	On error or close
Route Refresh	Request remote peer toresend all the routes	Only as needed

Each BGP message is encoded as a TLV. Every BGP message carries a fixed BGP header that also includes the type of BGP message.

The workhorse BGP message is Update, which carries the list of advertised routes and the list of withdrawn routes. Unlike OSPF and IS-IS, which withdraw information by aging out the link-state information, BGP has an explicit withdraw mechanism. The format of the BGP Update message is shown in Figure 14-3(a). BGP uses the term Network Layer Reachability Information (NLRI) to mean the advertised routes. Communities are encoded in the "Path Attributes List" section.

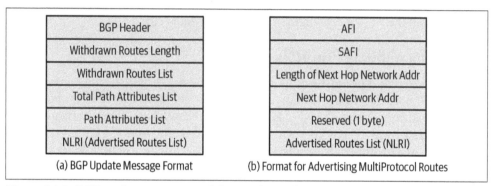

Figure 14-3. BGP update message and format for multiprotocol network addresses

Figure 14-3(b) shows how the NLRI is encoded for non-IPv4 address families. This is called MP_REACH_NLRI. It is an optional, nontransitive Path attribute. When present, it is in the "Path Attributes" part of Figure 14-3(a). Key information, such as the next hop for the prefixes listed in the NLRI, can be encoded differently for IPv4 and other protocols. In IPv4, the next hop is present as a well-known path attribute called NEXTHOP, encoded in the "Path Attributes List" section of the message. However, if you're advertising IPv6 routes, the next hop and the advertised routes are encoded as shown in Figure 14-3(b). A single BGP Update message can carry information about more than one AFI/SAFI. For example, a single BGP update message can carry updates for both IPv4 and IPv6. In such a scenario, the MP_REACH NLRI and the standard NLRI are both present in the message. If no IPv4 prefix is being advertised, the NEXTHOP attribute will not be present in the path attributes list and only the relevant MP_REACH NLRI will contain the appropriate next-hop information.

Adapting BGP to the Data Center

Before its use in the data center, BGP was primarily, if not exclusively, used in service provider networks. Because of this history, BGP deployment needs some modifications that are not discussed in the most common BGP books because they were written for service provider networks. If you're a network operator, understanding these differences and their reason is important in preventing misconfiguration.

The dense connectivity of the data center network is a vastly different space from the relatively sparse connectivity between administrative domains. Thus, a different set of trade-offs are relevant within the data center. BGP's usage in the data center can be summarized as follows:

- eBGP is used as the sole routing protocol
- eBGP is used with private ASNs
- BGP's ASN numbering scheme must be such that you don't run into BGP's path hunting problem
- BGP's timers are adapted to update more aggressively than in service provider networks

Let's examine each of these points in some more detail now.

eBGP Versus iBGP

Given that the entire data center is under the aegis of a single administrative domain, iBGP seems like the obvious answer. But eBGP is chosen in just about every deployment inside the data center.

The primary reason for this is that eBGP is simpler to understand and deploy than iBGP. iBGP can be confusing in its best path selection algorithm, the rules by which routes are selected, advertised, and which prefix attributes are acted upon or ignored. There are also limitations in iBGP's multipath support under certain conditions: specifically, when a route is advertised by two different nodes. Overcoming this limitation is possible but cumbersome.

A newbie is also far more likely to be confused by iBGP than eBGP because of the number of configuration knobs that need to be twiddled to achieve the desired behavior. Many of the knobs are incomprehensible to newcomers and only add to their unease.

A strong nontechnical reason for choosing eBGP is that there are more full-featured, robust implementations of eBGP than iBGP. The presence of multiple implementations means a customer can avoid vendor lock-in by choosing eBGP over iBGP. This was especially true before about mid-2012; until then many iBGP implementations tended to be buggy and lacked features required to operate within the data center.

eBGP: Flying Solo

In the traditional model of deployment, BGP learns of the prefixes to advertise from another routing protocol, usually OSPF, IS-IS, or Enhanced Interior Gateway Routing Protocol (EIGRP). These are called internal routing protocols because they are used to control routing within an enterprise. However, in the data center, eBGP *is* the internal routing protocol. No additional one is required.

Private ASNs

Private ASNs are ASNs that are not visible in the global internet. They're internal to an enterprise, similar in a fashion to the private IP addresses such as those in the 10.0.0.0/8 IPv4 subnet. Private ASNs come in both the two-byte and four-byte ASN variants. The two-byte ASNs support 1,023 private ASNs (64512–65534), whereas four-byte ASNs come with support for almost 95 million private ASNs (4200000000–4294967294), more than enough to satisfy a data center of any size in operation today.

Nothing prevents an operator from using global ASNs inside the data center, as long as they're stripped before communicating with the outside world. However, there are two reasons why this is not a good idea. The first is that using global ASNs might confuse operators and tools that attempt to decode the ASNs into meaningful names. Because many ASNs are well known to operators, an operator might very well become confused, for example, on seeing Verizon's ASN on a node within the data center.

The second reason is to avoid the consequences of accidentally leaking out the internal BGP information to an external network. This can wreak havoc on the internet. For example, if a data center used Twitter's ASN internally, and accidentally leaked out a route claiming, say, that Twitter was part of the AS_PATH for a publicly reachable route within the data center, the network operator would be responsible for a massive global hijacking of a well-known service. Misconfigurations are the number one or number two source of all network outages, and so avoiding this by not using public ASNs is a good thing.

BGP's ASN Numbering Scheme

As discussed in Chapter 5, BGP's ASN numbering scheme is as follows:

- Each leaf gets its own ASN
- All spines in a two-tier Clos get a single ASN. In a three-tier Clos, all spines within a pod get the same ASN, but the ASN is different for each pod.

- In a three-tier Clos, all super-spines get the same ASN.

Figure 14-4 illustrates this numbering scheme.

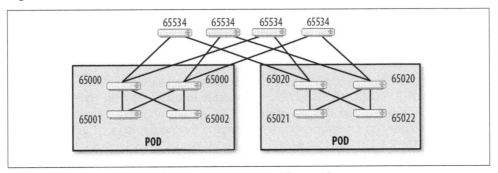

Figure 14-4. BGP ASN numbering in a three-tier Clos topology

As discussed in Chapter 5, this numbering scheme results in a simple up-down routing.

BGP's Path Hunting Problem

Path-vector protocols suffer from a variation of a problem called count-to-infinity, which afflicts distance vector protocols. Although we cannot get into all the details of path hunting here, you can take a look at a simple explanation of the problem from the simple topology shown in Figure 14-5.

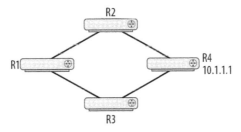

Figure 14-5. Sample topology to illustrate path hunting

In this topology, all of the nodes have separate ASNs. Now, consider the reachability to prefix 10.1.1.1 from R1's perspective. R2 and R3 advertise reachability to the prefix 10.1.1.1 to R1. The AS_PATH advertised by R2 for 10.1.1.1 is [R2, R4], and the AS_PATH advertised by R3 is [R3, R4]. R1 does not know how R2 and R3 themselves learned this information. When R1 learns of the path to 10.1.1.1 from both R2 and R3, it picks one of them as the best path. Due to its local support for multipathing, its forwarding tables will contain reachability to 10.1.1.1 via both R2 and R3, but BGP's best path selection internally still uses only one of R2 or R3 as the best path.

Let's assume that R3 is picked as the best path to 10.1.1.1 by R1. R1 now advertises that it can reach 10.1.1.1 with the AS_PATH [R1, R3, R4] to R2. R2 accepts the advertisement, but does not consider it a better path to reach 10.1.1.1, because its best path is the shorter AS_PATH R4.

Now, when the node R4 dies, R2 loses its best path to 10.1.1.1, and so it recomputes its best path via R1, with the AS_PATH [R1, R3, R4]. R2 also sends a route withdrawal message for 10.1.1.1 to R1. R3 does the same. However, if R3's route withdrawal comes before R2's, R1 switches its best path to R2 and advertises the route to 10.1.1.1 with the AS_PATH [R1, R2, R4]. R3 now switches to using the path via R2 as being the best path and thinks that the route 10.1.1.1 is still reachable. When R2's withdrawal to route 10.1.1.1 reaches R1, R1 withdraws its route to 10.1.1.1 and sends its withdrawal to R3. The exact sequence of events might not be as described here due to the timing of packet exchanges between the nodes and how BGP works, but it is a close approximation.

The short version of this problem is this: because a node does not know the physical link state of every other node in the network, it doesn't know whether the route is truly gone (because the node at the end went down itself) or is reachable via some other path. And so, a node proceeds to hunt down reachability to the destination via all its other available paths. This is called *path hunting*.

In the simple topology of Figure 14-5, this didn't look so bad. But imagine R1 and R4 are leaves in a Clos topology, and R2 and R3 are the spines. Consider a normal Clos topology in which there are 32 or 64 leaves and four to eight spines. Each leaf can pick a different spine as its best path. When R4 dies, each spine hunts for the path to R4 via each of the leaves, with some additional hunting as each leaf picks a different spine as the best path. The problem can become quite significant, with a surfeit of additional message exchanges and increased loss of traffic due to misinformation propagating longer than necessary.

Multipath Selection

As described earlier, two paths are considered equal if they are equal in each of the eight criteria mentioned. One of the criteria is that the AS numbers in the AS_PATH match exactly, not just that they have equal-length paths. This breaks multipathing in two common deployment scenarios within the data center.

The first deployment scenario, in which the same route might be announced from different ASNs, is when a server is dual attached, with a separate ASN for each top of rack switch, as shown in Figure 14-6. In the figure, the oval shapes represent a bond or port channel; that is, the two links are made to look as one higher-speed logical link to upper-layer protocols.

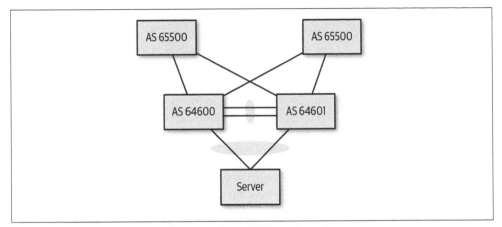

Figure 14-6. The need for looking at AS_PATH lengths only

Let's assume that both leaves announce a subnet route to 10.1.1.0/24, the subnet of the bridge to which the server is attached. In this case, each spine sees the route to 10.1.1.0/24 being received, one with AS_PATH of 64600, and the other with an AS_PATH of 64601. As per the logic for equal-cost paths, BGP requires not only that the AS_PATH lengths be the same, but that the AS_PATHs contain the same ASN list. Because this is not the case here, each spine will not multipath; instead, they will pick only one of the two routes.

In the second deployment scenario, when virtual services are deployed by servers, multiple servers will announce reachability to the same service virtual IP address. Because the servers are connected to different leaves to ensure reliability and scalability, the spines will again receive a route from multiple different ASNs, for which the AS_PATH lengths are identical, but the specific ASNs within the path itself are not.

There are multiple ways to address this problem, but the simplest one is to configure a knob that modifies the best-path algorithm. The knob is called *bestpath as-path multipath-relax* in FRR and in other routing stacks. What it does is simple: when the AS_PATH lengths are the same in advertisements from two different sources, the best-path algorithm skips checking for exact match of the ASNs, and proceeds to match on the next criteria.

Fixing BGP's Convergence Time

There are four timers that typically govern how fast BGP converges when either a failure occurs or when it is recovering from a failure (such as a link becoming available again). Understanding these timers is important because they affect the speed with which the information propagates through the network, and tuning them allows an operator to achieve convergence speeds with BGP that match other internal routing protocols such as OSPF.

Advertisement interval

When working in routing traffic in the internet, stability is far more important than rapid change. In the data center, the opposite is true. The primary BGP timer responsible for making sure updates are made is the *advertisement interval*. BGP waits the duration configured for advertisement interval between sending successive updates to a peer. By default, this is 30 seconds. In the data center, this value must be set to 0. This change alone can bring eBGP's convergence time to that of other IGP protocols such as OSPF.

Keepalive and Hold timers

A BGP speaker sends a Keepalive message every configured period on every established session. If the remote peer doesn't receive a Keepalive message for a duration that is equal to a value called *Hold timer*—usually three times the Keepalive time—it declares the peer dead and terminates the peering session. By default the Keepalive time is 60 seconds. This means that it takes three minutes to detect that a peer is down. By default, for eBGP sessions for which the peer is a single routing hop away, a session is reset immediately on link failure. What the Keepalive and Hold timers do is catch any software errors whereby the link is up but has become one-way due to an error, such as in cabling. Some operators enable a protocol called BFD to detect errors due to cable issues in less than a second, or at most one second. However, to catch errors in the BGP process itself, you need to adjust the Keepalive and Hold timers. Inside the data center, three minutes is a lifetime. The most common values configured inside the data center are three seconds for Keepalive and nine seconds for the hold timer.

Connect timer

This is the least critical of the four timers. When BGP attempts to connect with a peer but fails due to various reasons, it waits for a certain period of time before attempting to connect again. This period by default is 60 seconds. In other words, if BGP is unable to establish a session with its peer, it waits for a minute before attempting to establish a session again. This can delay session reestablishment when a link recovers from a failure or a node powers up. Within the data center, the value of this timer is usually set to 10 seconds.

Summary

This was a whirlwind tour of BGP and its adaptation for use within the data center. Keep in mind that a lot of BGP's complexity as used in service provider networks is irrelevant when used within the data center. BGP in the data center is a far simpler and faster beast than its service provider setting. The fundamentals of the protocol in either use case are the same, nevertheless. Armed with this knowledge, we can now set out to study the mechanics of BGP deployment in the data center.

## CHAPTER 15

Deploying BGP

Tell me what you need, and I'll tell you how to get along without it.
—Scott Adams

This chapter delves into administering the BGP routing protocol. The goal of this chapter is to help network engineers configure BGP in their data center network.

This chapter should help answer the following questions:

- What are the core configuration concepts of BGP?
- How do I configure BGP for a Clos network?
- How does unnumbered BGP work?
- How do I configure BGP to peer with BGP speakers on hosts such as with Kube-router?
- How do I configure BGP to gracefully leave the network for scheduled maintenance?

This chapter should also help the network engineer compare and contrast administering BGP across various routing stacks. I'm assuming that you have either read Chapter 14 or are familiar with the concepts presented in that chapter.

Core BGP Configuration Concepts

We begin our journey by studying the basic concepts of BGP configuration. It consists of the following basic parts:

- Global BGP configuration, which includes:
  — router-id configuration

— Neighbor (or peer) configuration

— Routing policy definitions

— Timer configuration

- Neighbor-specific configuration, which includes:

  — Non-global Timer configuration

  — Non-address-family-specific configuration

- Address-family-specific configuration, which includes:

  — Neighbor-specific activation of AFI/SAFI

  — Route advertisement specification

  — Application of routing policy to specific neighbors

Part of the complexity of BGP configuration is figuring out which of the sections contains a specific knob.

For the discussion in this chapter, we use the topology from Chapter 13, reproduced here in Figure 15-1.

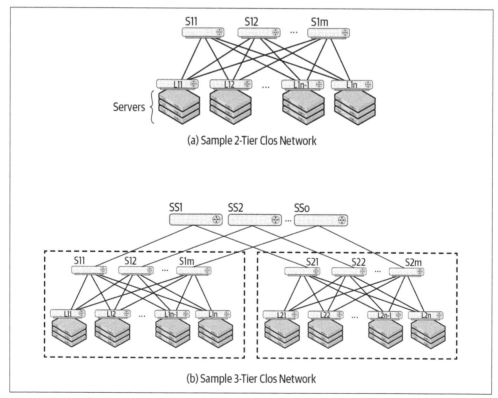

Figure 15-1. Clos topologies used for BGP configuration

Just as in the case of OSPF in Chapter 13, we consider each of the following cases, going from the simplest to the more complicated:

- Configuring BGP for IPv4
- Configuring BGP for IPv6
- Configuring BGP with VRF
- Configuring BGP on the server

We tackle using BGP to configure network virtualization in the next chapter. Because we've already discussed the concepts behind configuring BGP in a Clos network in Chapter 14, let's dive right down to the configuration. We begin by looking at a traditional BGP configuration using numbered interfaces and then move to examining the configuration using unnumbered interfaces. After we're done with this, we examine configuring BGP for the remaining cases.

The configuration shown in the following sections is based on the open source routing suite, FRR. People working with traditional vendor stacks such as Arista and Cisco's NX-OS can easily adapt this FRR configuration to their stack-specific configurations.

Traditional Configuration for a Two-Tier Clos Topology: IPv4

As in the case of OSPF, we begin with the traditional BGP configuration using numbered interfaces for distributing IPv4 routes. We use the specific version of a two-tier Clos topology shown in Figure 15-2.

As discussed in Chapter 14, we're using eBGP. The ASN associated with each router is shown inside the router, at the upper left, and is part of a series beginning with 65000. The spines both have the same ASN, 65000, whereas the leaves each have a different ASN, starting from 65011 for leaf01 and ending with 65014 for leaf04. As before, the IP address inside each router in the figure is that router's loopback IP address. The servers are connected through a bridged network to their associated leaf router.

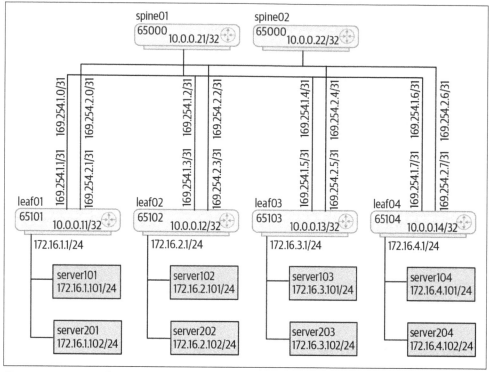

Figure 15-2. A traditional BGP setup

Example 15-1 shows the traditional BGP configuration for spine01 and leaf01.

Example 15-1. Traditional BGP configuration for spine01 and leaf01

```
! Configuration for spine01
!
interface lo
 ip address 10.0.0.21/32
!
interface swp1
  ip address 169.254.1.0/31
!
interface swp2
  ip address 169.254.1.2/31
!
interface swp3
  ip address 169.254.1.4/31
!
interface swp4
  ip address 169.254.1.6/31
!
router bgp 65000
```

```
bgp router-id 10.0.0.21
bgp log-neighbor-changes
timers bgp 3 9    ❶
no bgp default ipv4 unicast ❷
neighbor 169.254.1.1 remote-as 65011
neighbor 169.254.1.3 remote-as 65012
neighbor 169.254.1.5 remote-as 65013
neighbor 169.254.1.7 remote-as 65014
neighbor 169.254.1.1 advertisement-interval 0 ❶
neighbor 169.254.1.3 advertisement-interval 0
neighbor 169.254.1.5 advertisement-interval 0
neighbor 169.254.1.7 advertisement-interval 0
neighbor 169.254.1.1 bfd
neighbor 169.254.1.3 bfd
neighbor 169.254.1.5 bfd
neighbor 169.254.1.7 bfd
bgp bestpath as-path multipath-relax ❸
address-family ipv4 unicast
    neighbor 169.254.1.1 activate ❹
    neighbor 169.254.1.3 activate
    neighbor 169.254.1.5 activate
    neighbor 169.254.1.7 activate
    redistribute connected ❺
    maximum-paths 64          ❻
exit-address-family

! Configuration for leaf01
!
interface lo
 ip address 10.0.0.11/32
!
interface swp1
  ip address 169.254.1.1/31
!
interface swp2
  ip address 169.254.2.1/31
!
! This next statement is for the servers subnet
!
interface vlan10
  ip address 172.16.1.1/24
!
router bgp 65011
  bgp router-id 10.0.0.11
  bgp log-neighbor-changes
  timers bgp 3 9                ❶
  no bgp default ipv4 unicast ❷
  neighbor 169.254.1.0/31 remote-as 65000
  neighbor 169.254.2.0/31 remote-as 65000
  neighbor 169.254.1.0/31 advertisement-interval 0 ❶
  neighbor 169.254.2.0/31 advertisement-interval 0
  neighbor 169.254.1.0/31 bfd
  neighbor 169.254.2.0/31 bfd
```

```
address-family ipv4 unicast
   neighbor 169.254.1.0/31 activate ❹
   neighbor 169.254.2.0/31 activate
   redistribute connected ❺
   maximum-paths 64        ❻
exit-address-family
```

The configuration looks remarkably similar to the one shown in Example 13-1. The main points to note are:

❶ The default BGP timers need tuning because the default values are unsuitable for the data center.

❷ BGP assumes a bunch of default behavior for the IPv4 Unicast address family. The most critical one is its automatic enabling of the advertisement of IPv4 routes by default. But many operators prefer to activate it explicitly. So via this line, they specify turning off the default activation for the IPv4 Unicast address family.

❸ See "Multipath Selection" on page 298 for an explanation of this option.

❹ An address-family must be activated for each neighbor to make BGP advertise that address-family's routes to the neighbor. activate causes BGP to advertise the capability for that address-family in the BGP OPEN message. Only if the other side also supports processing the address-family will the routes be advertised.

❺ The specification of the redistribute command is under a specific address-family section. Because BGP is a multiprotocol routing protocol, using the redistribute command under a specific address-family only redistributes information of that address-family. If you need to redistribute connected routes for more than one address-family, you need to specify the redistribute command under each address-family section.

❻ Unlike OSPF, which automatically uses ECMP, BGP needs to be explicitly told to do so via the maximum_paths command. Like the redistribute command, you can configure BGP to use ECMP only for a specific AFI/SAFI.

The problems with this configuration are similar to OSPF, but a shade more difficult:

• The configuration is not easy to automate, because the configuration of every node looks different. spine01's configuration will look different from that of the other spines, leaf01's configuration will look different from all the other leaves, and so on.

- The configuration requires us to use each remote peer's IP address in the neighbor configuration because that is the address the BGP process tries to establish a connection to or accept a connection from. This requirement of needing the peer's IP address information makes BGP configuration a little more complicated than OSPF's when it comes to automation and troubleshooting.

- The configuration also requires the use of the remote peer's ASN. This is easy from the leaves' point of view because all spines have a single ASN, but you must do it carefully in the case of spines to associate the ASN with the right IP address.

- Errors cannot be caught easily (such as by eyeballing) because they probably stem from the interactions between multiple lines, so multiple pieces of information need to be verified.

- The `neighbor` command must be repeated to configure various parameters such as advertisement interval, activation, and so on.

- Because interfaces have IP addresses, the `redistribute connected` command advertises the IP addresses of the interfaces along with those of the loopback and the server subnets. The interface IP addresses add overhead (BGP messages, the RIB and FIB sizes, and so on) to the state and are unnecessary, as we discussed in Chapter 13.

- BGP also supports a `network` configuration knob we can use to specify the prefix we want to advertise. We could use that to advertise merely the loopback and server subnet instead of using `redistribute connected`. But that takes us away from deriving a configuration that is as homogeneous across the routers as possible.

We start the journey of simplifying this configuration by using a feature called *peer groups* to create templates. After that, we examine removing the advertisement of the interface IP addresses by adding a routing policy to the `redistribute connected` statement.[1]

Peer Group

To simplify repetition when configuring multiple neighbors, most routing suites support a form of templating called *peer group*. The user creates a peer group with a name and then proceeds to configure the desired attributes for neighbor connection (such as `remote-as`, connection timers, and the use of BFD). In the next step, the operator assigns each real neighbor to the created peer group, thus avoiding the need to type the same boring stuff over and over again. Many implementations, including

---

1 In OSPF, we didn't use `redistribute`, so we didn't need to discuss using a routing policy.

FRR, Cisco, Juniper, and Arista, support some form of peer group. Cisco's NX-OS supports a more flexible templating model called template.

Example 15-2 shows spine01's configuration from Example 15-1 with the use of peer groups.

Example 15-2. Traditional BGP configuration with peer groups

```
router bgp 65000
  bgp router-id 10.0.0.21
  bgp log-neighbor-changes
  timers bgp 3 9
  no bgp default ipv4 unicast
  neighbor peer-group ISL                                    ❶
  neighbor ISL bfd                                           ❷
  neighbor ISL advertisement-interval 0                      ❷
  neighbor 169.254.1.1 remote-as 65011                       ❸
  neighbor 169.254.1.1 peer-group ISL                        ❹
  neighbor 169.254.1.3 remote-as 65012
  neighbor 169.254.1.3 peer-group ISL
  neighbor 169.254.1.5 remote-as 65013
  neighbor 169.254.1.5 peer-group ISL
  neighbor 169.254.1.7 remote-as 65014
  neighbor 169.254.1.7 peer-group ISL
  bgp bestpath as-path multipath-relax
  address-family ipv4 unicast
      neighbor ISL activate
      redistribute connected
      maximum-paths 64
  exit-address-family
```

❶ This defines a peer-group called ISL.

❷ These assign attributes that all members of the ISL peer-group share.

❸ The remote-as value is different for each peer and so we cannot have a common one defined in the peer-group.

❹ This adds this neighbor to the peer-group already defined. This is when the neighbor inherits all the attributes associated with that peer-group.

Routing Policy

Routing policy, at its simplest, specifies when to accept or reject route advertisements. Based on where they're used, the accept or reject could apply to routes received from a peer, routes advertised to a peer, and redistributed routes. At its most complex, routing policy can modify metrics that affect the bestpath selection of a prefix, and add or remove attributes or communities from a prefix or set of prefixes. Given BGP's use primarily in connecting different administrative domains, BGP has the most sophisticated routing policy constructs of any routing protocol.

A routing policy consists of a sequence of if-then-else statements, with matches and actions to be taken on a successful match.

For example, to avoid the problem of advertising the interface IP addresses, as described in the previous section, the pseudocode for the routing policy would look like the following (we develop this pseudocode into actual configuration syntax by the end of this section):

```
if prefix equals '169.254.0.0/16' then reject else accept
```

In a configuration that redistributes connected routes, as we have done in previous examples, a safe policy would be to accept the routes that belong to this data center and reject any others. The configurations we've seen so far contain two kinds of prefixes: 172.16.0.0/16 (assuming there are lots of host-facing subnets in the network) and the router's loopback IP address, for example 10.0.0.11/32. We also see the interface address subnet, 169.254.0.0/16, which must not be advertised. So a first stab at a routing policy would be the following:

```
if prefix equals 172.16.0.0/16 then accept
else if prefix equals 10.0.0.0/24 then accept
else reject
```

But this would accept anyone accidentally announcing the subnet 10.0.254.0/26, as an example. We want to accept only prefixes that are the precise addresses of the router loopbacks, all of which are /32 addresses. How can we do this? By adding more qualifiers:

```
if prefix belongs to 172.16.0.0/16 then accept
else if (prefix belongs to 10.0.254.0/24 and
          address mask equals 32) then
      accept
else reject
```

The qualifier we added, `address mask equals`, allows us to match addresses more precisely by accounting for not just the address, but the address mask, as well.

Because multiple such routing policies are possible, let's give this policy a name and make it a function thus:

```
ACCEPT_DC_LOCAL(prefix)
{
    if prefix belongs to 172.16.0.0/16 then accept
    else if (10.0.254.0/24 contains prefix and
              subnet equals 32) then
    accept
    else reject
}
```

Just about every network configuration I've seen uses all caps for route-map and prefix-list names. Although this is just a name, and operators are free to choose their conventions—all caps, camelCase, or anything else—but it is useful to be aware of convention.

Route Maps: Implementation of Routing Policy

Route maps are a common way to implement routing policies. FRR, Cisco's IOS, NX-OS, Arista, and many others support route maps. Junos OS uses a different syntax which, some would argue, is more intuitive and powerful. The open source routing suite BIRD goes a step further and uses a simple domain-specific programming language instead of this combination of route-maps and prefix-lists. The details of describing that are beyond the scope of this book, but if you're interested, you can find the details on BIRD's web pages (*https://bird.network.cz*).

Each `route-map` section has the following syntax:

```
route-map NAME (permit|deny) [sequence_number]
  match classifier
  set action
```

This assigns a name to the policy, indicates whether the matched routes will be permitted or denied, and then matches inputs against a classifier. If a `match` clause successfully matches a classifier, the `set` clause acts on the route. The optional sequence number specifies the order in which the route-map sections are executed when there is more than one of them with the same name.

The `permit` keyword applies the action when the match succeeds, whereas the `deny` keyword applies the action when the match fails. In other words, `deny` functions as a "not" operator: if there's a match, reject the route.

Route maps have an implicit "deny" at the end. Thus, if no entry is matched, the result is to reject the input.

Classifiers in route maps

Route maps come with a rich set of classifiers. You can use an extensive variety of traits as classifiers, and different implementations support different subsets of these classifiers (some support all the standard classifiers plus some of their own). Table 15-1 is a subset of the classifiers that I think are most useful in the data center, although I've seen cases in which other classifiers have been used as well.

Table 15-1. Classifiers in route maps

Classifier name	Description
as-path	Match value from BGP's AS_PATH
ip	Match IPv4 information such as IP address, next hop, or source

Classifier name	Description
ipv6	Match IPv6 information such as IP address, next hop, or source
interface	Match name of interface
peer	Match session peer's information

As an example of a routing policy using IP prefixes as classifiers, let's begin by looking at how two prefixes are defined:

```
ip prefix-list DC_LOCAL_SUBNET seq 5 permit 172.16.0.0/16 ge 24
ip prefix-list DC_LOCAL_SUBNET seq 10 permit 10.0.0.0/24 ge 32
```

These commands together define a single list called DC_LOCAL_SUBNET that contains two prefixes: 172.16.0.0/16 and 10.0.0.0/24. In both cases, matching any prefix against this list checks whether the prefix either matches exactly or is contained in the prefixes provided. In this case, `10.0.0.0/24 ge 32` specifically states that any match must be on a subnet that is /32. Even though it says "greater than or equal to," /32 is the highest-numbered mask in IPv4 and indicates the smallest possible subnet consisting of a single host, so this functions as an exact match for /32 prefixes only.

`seq <number>` is used to identify the order of matches. For example, if you wanted to reject 10.1.1.1/32 but permit every other address in 10.1.1.0/24, the right way to order the prefix-lists using sequence numbers would be as follows:

```
ip prefix-list EXAMPLE_SEQ seq 5 deny 10.1.1.1/32
ip prefix list EXAMPLE_SEQ seq 10 permit 10.1.1.0/24
```

Now, we can define a route-map to match the two prefixes with the DC_LOCAL_SUBNET name. The following is the route-map equivalent of the if-then-else route policy pseudocode described earlier in the routing policy section, and includes the `redistribute` command that takes this policy into account:

```
ip prefix-list DC_LOCAL_SUBNET seq 5 permit 172.16.0.0/16 ge 26
ip prefix-list DC_LOCAL_SUBNET seq 10 permit 10.0.0.0/24 ge 32
route-map ACCEPT_DC_LOCAL permit 10
  match ip-address DC_LOCAL_SUBNET

redistribute connected route-map DC_LOCAL_SUBNET
```

There is no `set` clause in the `route-map` section in the preceding example because we're merely allowing or denying a set of prefixes; there is no other action to be performed.

Instead of IP prefixes, we can use interface names. For example, if all we need to do is advertise the router's primary loopback IP address, the configuration lines are as follows:

```
route-map ADV_LO permit 10
  match interface lo
```

```
        redistribute connected route-map ADV_LO
```

Note that this will not advertise the host-local 127.x.x.x address associated with the loopback interface, but only the globally reachable IP addresses. The benefit of this approach is that it allows you to change interfaces freely and use noncontiguous IP addresses for them, without changing the route-map or modifying the BGP configuration. Some operators prefer to use IP prefixes instead of interface names because they want to ensure that an incorrect address assignment doesn't lead to bad route advertisements.

If we wanted to advertise both loopback and vlan10's IP addresses, we'd do the following in FRR:

```
route-map ADV_LO permit 10
    match interface lo

route-map ADV_LO permit 10
    match interface vlan10

    redistribute connected route-map ADV_LO
```

Note that `match interface` is supported in FRR, specifically in use with `redistrib ute connected`, but not all routing suites support it.

Writing secure route maps

There are two ways of writing a route map. The first is to write what is explicitly permitted, and leave everything else implicitly denied. The second is the opposite: write what is explicitly denied, and then permit everything else. The first method is more secure and is the recommended method. To illustrate this, the ADV_LO route map was written to explicitly permit loopback and the server subnet interface; everything else was rejected/ignored. If we redo that route map by adding explicit deny clauses and permitting everything else, we get the EXCEPT_ISL_ETH0 route map that follows. swp1 and swp2 are interswitch links and eth0 is the management interface, all of which are to be rejected. We're assuming that the only other interfaces left are the loopback and server subnet:

```
route-map EXCEPT_ISL_ETH0 deny 10
    match interface swp1
route-map EXCEPT_ISL_ETH0 deny 20
    match interface swp2
route-map EXCEPT_ISL_ETH0 deny 30
    match interface eth0
route-map EXCEPT_ISL_ETH0 permit 40

    redistribute connected route-map EXCEPT_ISL_ETH0
```

The final permit configuration allows through any interface that didn't match one of the deny route maps.

Following is the pseudocode equivalent of this route-map:

```
EXCEPT_ISL_ETH0(interface)
{
    if interface is not swp1 and
        interface is not swp2 and
        interface is not eth0 then
        redistribute connected
}
```

The disadvantage of this approach is that any new interface that comes up with a valid IP address will have its IP address immediately advertised, whether the administrator intended it or not. Therefore, this is considered an insecure approach that you must never use in configuring routing policy.

The alternative is the one we showed earlier in which only loopback and vlan10 interface addresses were advertised and the rest were not. In other words, you explicitly permit only the ones you want to and deny the rest. This can be tedious if there are lots of interfaces whose addresses need to be announced. Typical routing suite implementations do not allow the specification of multiple interfaces via a syntax such as swp1-49 (include all interfaces from swp1 through swp49). In such cases, resorting to using IP addresses that might be a smaller list might be an option if the IP addressing used on the interfaces comes from only a few subnets.

Route maps in BGP

Besides redistributed routes, you can apply route maps in multiple other places during BGP processing. Here are some examples:

Filter out the prefixes to accept in an advertisement from a neighbor
```
neighbor 169.254.1.1 route-map NBR_RT_ACCEPT in
```

Filter out the routes to advertise to a neighbor
```
neighbor 169.254.1.1 route-map NBR_RT_ADV out
```

Filter out the routes considered for advertisement via a network statement
```
network 10.1.1.1/24 route-map ADV_NET
```

Effect of route maps on BGP processing

BGP is a path-vector routing protocol, so it doesn't announce route updates until it runs the best-path algorithm. Route-maps are applied on packet receive and on packet send. If a BGP speaker has tens or hundreds of neighbors with route maps attached, running the route-map for each neighbor before advertising the route becomes CPU intensive and slows down the sending of updates. Slow update processing can result in poor convergence times, too.

Therefore, peer groups often are used with route maps to drastically reduce the amount of processing BGP needs to do before advertising a route to its neighbors. Instead of relying on just user-configured peer groups, implementations typically build up these groups dynamically. This is because even within a single peer group, different neighbors might support different capabilities (for example, some might support MPLS; some might not). This information can be determined only during session establishment. So user configuration either doesn't help or places an undue burden on the user to ensure that it sets up all neighbors in a peer group support with exactly the same capabilities.

Some implementations support the dynamic grouping and ungrouping of peers that have the same outgoing route policy and the same capabilities to enhance the performance of route processing in the presence of routing policy. BGP runs the policy once for a prefix that encompasses the entire peer group. The result is then automatically applied to each member of that peer group. This allows implementations to scale to supporting hundreds or even thousands of neighbors. This feature is called *dynamic update group* or *dynamic peer group*. Not all implementations support this, and so it's worth checking whether the implementation you're considering does.

Providing Sane Defaults for the Data Center

When crossing administrative and trust boundaries, it is best to explicitly configure all of the relevant information. Furthermore, given the different expectations of two separate enterprises, almost nothing is assumed in BGP, with every knob needing to be explicitly configured.

When BGP is adapted for use in the data center, this behavior of explicitly configuring everything isn't necessary. Every knob that must be configured strikes terror (or at least potentially sows confusion or adds to the cognitive load) in the minds of newbies and intermediate practitioners. Even those who are versed in BGP feel the need to constantly keep up because of the amount of work required to configure BGP.

A good way to avoid all of these issues is to set up good defaults so that users don't need to know about the knobs they don't care about. The BGP implementation in many proprietary routing suites originated in the service provider world, so such an option is not typically available. With open source routing suites that are geared toward the data center, such as FRR, the default configuration saves the user from having to explicitly configure many options. Good defaults also render the size of your configuration much more manageable, making it easy to eyeball configurations and ensure that there are no errors. As your organization becomes more familiar with

BGP in the data center, sane default configurations can provide the basis for reliable automation.

FRR supports the option of defining the defaults to be used depending on the use case. The option `frr defaults datacenter` sets up the defaults for the data center. The option is unfortunately available only at build time at this point, but it should be a configurable option soon. Here are the default settings in FRR for BGP when you choose `frr defaults datacenter`, based on the collective experience of seeing the network configurations of hundreds of organizations:

- Multipath enabled for eBGP and iBGP
- Advertisement interval set to 0
- Keepalive and Hold timers set to three seconds and nine seconds, respectively
- Logging adjacency changes enabled

With the use of peer groups, route maps, and sane defaults, the spine configuration from Example 15-2 can be simplified to that shown in Example 15-3.

Example 15-3. Numbered BGP configuration in FRR for spine01

```
router bgp 65000
  bgp router-id 10.0.0.21
  no bgp default ipv4 unicast
  neighbor peer-group ISL
  neighbor ISL bfd
  neighbor 169.254.1.1 remote-as 65011
  neighbor 169.254.1.1 peer-group ISL
  neighbor 169.254.1.3 remote-as 65012
  neighbor 169.254.1.3 peer-group ISL
  neighbor 169.254.1.5 remote-as 65013
  neighbor 169.254.1.5 peer-group ISL
  neighbor 169.254.1.7 remote-as 65014
  neighbor 169.254.1.7 peer-group ISL
  bgp bestpath as-path multipath-relax
  address-family ipv4 unicast
      neighbor ISL activate
      redistribute connected route-map ADV_LO
  exit-address-family

  route-map ADV_LO permit 10
    match interface lo
```

BGP Unnumbered: Eliminating Pesky Interface IP Addresses

To make BGP truly easy to automate requires us to eliminate the remaining two sources of configuration that make BGP configuration specific to each router. Example 15-4 presents the configuration we aim to end up with when we're done.

Example 15-4. Unnumbered BGP configuration in FRR

```
! Configuration for spine01
!
interface lo
 ip address 10.0.0.21/32 ❶
!
router bgp 65000
  bgp router-id 10.0.0.21 ❶
  no bgp default ipv4 unicast
  neighbor peer-group ISL
  neighbor ISL remote-as external
  neighbor ISL bfd
  neighbor swp1 interface peer-group ISL
  neighbor swp2 interface peer-group ISL
  neighbor swp3 interface peer-group ISL
  neighbor swp4 interface peer-group ISL
  bgp bestpath as-path multipath-relax
  address-family ipv4 unicast
      neighbor ISL activate
      redistribute connected route-map ADV_LO
  exit-address-family

  route-map ADV_LO permit 10
     match interface lo

! configuration for leaf01
!
interface lo
 ip address 10.0.0.11/32 ❶
!
! This next statement is for the servers subnet
!
interface vlan10
  ip address 172.16.1.1/24 ❷
!
router bgp 65011
  bgp router-id 10.0.0.11 ❶
  no bgp default ipv4 unicast
  neighbor peer-group ISL
  neighbor ISL remote-as external
  neighbor ISL bfd
  neighbor swp1 interface peer-group ISL
```

```
neighbor swp2 interface peer-group ISL
address-family ipv4 unicast
    neighbor ISL activate
    redistribute connected route-map ADV_LO_SRVRS
exit-address-family

route-map ADV_LO_SRVRS permit 10
    match interface lo
route-map ADV_LO_SRVRS permit 20
    match interface vlan10
```

❶   router-id definition is the only difference across all BGP configurations.

❷   The server subnet definitions will be different per leaf.

As shown in Example 15-4, the BGP configurations differ only in the value of the router-id. Any configuration that involves knowledge of the peer's IP address and ASN has been eliminated.

Let's see how FRR accomplishes this magic. We begin with the simple one first, the use of "remote-as external."

A remote-as by Any Name

There are two primary uses for specifying a peer's ASN in the neighbor specification:

- To indicate explicitly which ASN to connect to, when connecting across administrative domains, where harm on a large financial and global scale is possible by connecting to the wrong administrative domain accidentally

- To identify whether the BGP peering is to be governed by iBGP rules or eBGP rules

In the data center, the only real reason for the use of an ASN is for BGP's loop detection via AS_PATH. (iBGP does this via a cluster-id that is automatically generated, but iBGP has more complex processing, as discussed in Chapter 14, and so isn't used in the data center as the primary routing protocol for the Clos fabric.) So we can ignore the need to specify the peer's specific ASN.

Based on this reasoning, FRR added two new choices to the remote-as keyword: *external* and *internal*. "External" means that you expect to set up an eBGP connection with this neighbor (the peer's ASN must be different from mine), whereas "internal" means that you expect to set up an iBGP connection (the peer's ASN must be the same as mine). In reality, you can even ignore this specification because a BGP speaker can identify iBGP versus eBGP by the ASN received in the BGP OPEN message. However, the remote-as command helps kick off creation of the BGP peer data structure given that it's easy to make a typo in the neighbor specification in one of the commands and accidentally create a new BGP peer. For example, if there were a peer 169.254.1.11 and there was a typo in one of the neighbor commands—neighbor 169.254.11.1 timers connect 9 instead of neighbor 169.254.1.11 timers con nect 9—you don't want BGP to begin spinning up a new neighbor session.

The old method of specifying the exact ASN of course remains available.

How Unnumbered Interfaces Work with BGP

Getting BGP to work with an interface that has no explicitly assigned IP address relies on four well-defined features:

- The use of IPv6's link-local address on an interface
- The use of IPv6's Router Advertisement protocol to learn the peer's link-local address
- The use of RFC 5549 to announce an IPv4 address with the IPv6 link-local address as the next hop
- Populating the routing table to use the information obtained via the RFC 5549 address announcement

We examine each of these pieces in a little more detail next.

IPv6 link-local address

IPv6 stack is now available on all network operating systems, whether it be Linux or a traditional vendor stack. When enabled on a link, IPv6 automatically generates an IPv6 address that is valid only on that link, a *link-local address* (LLA). Most often, the interface MAC address is used to generate the address. IPv6 LLAs have a well-defined format: they start with fe80. An example of an IPv6 LLA is fe80::5054:ff:fe6d:4cbe.

Unnumbered BGP uses this LLA to set up the TCP connection. Instead of asking the user to specify this, FRR uses the interface name to understand that the user wants to use the IPv6 LLA to establish the BGP peering. So, if fe80::5054:ff:fe6d:4cbe is the IPv6 LLA of the interface, FRR expects to receive a connect request on that address from the peer on that interface. Alternatively, it uses that address to send the connect request to the peer.

However, to establish a connection with a remote entity, BGP needs the IPv6 LLA of the interface on the other end of the link. How does a node get that automatically? Via IPv6 router advertisement.

IPv6 router advertisement

To allow hosts and routers to automatically discover neighboring routers, IPv6 designers added router advertisement (RA). RA is one of the messages used in IPv6's

NDP (*https://oreil.ly/J_IYR*). IPv6 NDP is the IPv6 equivalent of IPv4's ARP. When enabled on an interface, RA periodically announces the interface's IPv6 addresses, including the LLA. Thus, one end can automatically determine the other end's IPv6 address. Like IPv6, RA is universally implemented these days on both hosts and routers.

To be crystal clear, the use of IPv6 LLA does not require operators to begin deploying IPv6 as the network addresses in their networks. The IPv6 LLA is used only to establish a TCP connection for starting a BGP session. Besides enabling IPv6 on a link, which is typically enabled automatically, and the enabling of the IPv6 router advertisement on the link, no other knowledge of IPv6 is expected of the operator.

RFC 5549

Establishing a TCP connection over IPv6 LLA isn't enough. To exchange IPv4 routes, we need a next-hop IPv4 address. But the interface on which BGP peering has been established has no IPv4 address and there is no other reachable IPv4 address for the router to advertise. So how does this work? There are two parts to this: a control-plane part and a packet forwarding (or data plane) part. The control-plane part involves implementing a standard, well-defined extension to encoding BGP's next-hop value. That standard is defined in RFC 5549 (*https://oreil.ly/FUjps*), which is titled "Advertising IPv4 Network Layer Reachability Information with an IPv6 Next Hop." Remember, an IPv4 NLRI is just the route. So, this RFC defines how to advertise an IPv4 route with a next-hop IPv6 address. Exactly what we need!

In Chapter 14, we said that the encoding in Figure 14-3(a) is used with the NEX-THOP attribute for IPv4 routes, and that Figure 14-3(b), the MP_REACH_NLRI attribute, is used for non-IPv4 routes. The AFI/SAFI fields of the MP_REACH_NLRI attribute define the network address family of the advertised route. The Nexthop Network Address belongs to the same AFI/SAFI. RFC 4760 (*https://oreil.ly/CzNqY*), which defines the form and function of MP_REACH_NLRI, said that if the Nexthop Network Address field could have different encodings, the encoding of the field must allow for easy identification of the encoding used. Here's what RFC 5549 says:

- You can use MP_REACH_NLRI for IPv4 (and VPN-IPv4) routes as well.
- You use the length field of the Nexthop Network Address field to identify whether the field carries both link-local and global IPv6 addresses or just one.

In other words, use Figure 14-3(a) for IPv4 routes with IPv4 next hop, and use Figure 14-3(b) for IPv4 routes with an IPv6 next hop.

As with any other BGP extension, the support for encoding and processing an IPv4 route with an IPv6 next hop is first negotiated as part of the capability exchange in the BGP OPEN message. Only if both sides of a peering session support this capability is this method of advertising IPv4 routes with IPv6 next hop used. The BGP capability to indicate support for RFC 5549 is called *extended next hop*.

Packet forwarding with RFC 5549

With the control-plane problem addressed, how does packet forwarding work? Do the routing tables have to be extended to support an IPv6 next hop for an IPv4 route? Does the packet-switching silicon need to support this functionality as well? Let's study this to understand why supporting RFC 5549 *does not* require changes to packet-switching silicon.

In "Routing Overview" on page 82, we explained how the next-hop router's IP address is used only to determine the MAC address of the next-hop router's interface. This MAC address is used as the destination MAC address in the packet being routed so that the packet can be accepted by the router. The next-hop router's IP address is not used anywhere in the packet.

The IPv6 RA gives us not only the link-local IPv6 address of the peer router, but also the MAC address of the peer interface on that router. So, for any given IPv6 link local address, we have its corresponding MAC address. Packet-switching silicon typically has a route pointing to a group of next hops, and each entry in the next hop only contains the MAC address (and VLAN). So the packet-switching silicon's routing table can be populated with an IPv4 route with the next-hop MAC address with this information. Thus, the information from the RFC 5549 encoding can be used to populate the packet-switching silicon just as if we had received an IPv4 route with an IPv4 next-hop address.

FRR and RFC 5549

The next-hop router's IP address is needed for only one trivial thing: it appears in the output of commands displaying the route, as discussed in "Linux Routing Table Display" on page 88. You can work around this by using a dummy IPv4 address. FRR uses 169.254.0.1 as this dummy IPv4 address (and you cannot change it via configuration as of this writing). 169.254.0.0/16 is defined by convention to be an IPv4 LLA subnet, although IPv4 LLAs are not automatically assigned to an interface the way IPv6 LLA is. Consider the following output of FRR's show ip route:

```
$ sudo vtysh -c 'show ip route'
Codes: K - kernel route, C - connected, S - static, R - RIP,
       O - OSPF, I - IS-IS, B - BGP, E - EIGRP, N - NHRP,
       T - Table, v - VNC, V - VNC-Direct, A - Babel, D - SHARP,
       F - PBR,
       > - selected route, * - FIB route

C>* 10.0.0.11/32 is directly connected, lo, 20:04:01
B>* 10.0.0.12/32 [20/0] via fe80::5054:ff:fe92:a7dd, swp4, 20:03:52
  *                     via fe80::5054:ff:fef5:ca97, swp2, 20:03:52
```

```
       *                      via fe80::5054:ff:feb6:d927, swp1, 20:03:52
 B>* 10.0.0.13/32 [20/0] via fe80::5054:ff:fe92:a7dd, swp4, 20:03:52
       *                      via fe80::5054:ff:fef5:ca97, swp2, 20:03:52
       *                      via fe80::5054:ff:feb6:d927, swp1, 20:03:52
```

Here, each IPv4 route has a next-hop IPv6 LLA (the addresses start with fe80::). We also see that this route was learned via BGP. When you look at the Linux kernel side for the same route, you see the code shown in Example 15-5.

Example 15-5. Linux FIB output for routes advertised using RFC 5549

```
$ ip ro show
10.0.0.12  proto bgp  metric 20
        nexthop via 169.254.0.1  dev swp4 weight 1 onlink
        nexthop via 169.254.0.1  dev swp2 weight 1 onlink
        nexthop via 169.254.0.1  dev swp1 weight 1 onlink
10.0.0.13  proto bgp  metric 20
        nexthop via 169.254.0.1  dev swp4 weight 1 onlink
        nexthop via 169.254.0.1  dev swp2 weight 1 onlink
        nexthop via 169.254.0.1  dev swp1 weight 1 onlink
```

And the `ip neighbor` table entry looks like this:

```
$ ip neighbor
169.254.0.1 dev swp2 lladdr 52:54:00:f5:ca:97 PERMANENT
169.254.0.1 dev swp1 lladdr 52:54:00:b6:d9:27 PERMANENT
169.254.0.1 dev swp4 lladdr 52:54:00:92:a7:dd PERMANENT
fe80::5054:ff:fe92:a7dd dev swp4 lladdr 52:54:00:92:a7:dd router REACHABLE
fe80::5054:ff:fef5:ca97 dev swp2 lladdr 52:54:00:f5:ca:97 router REACHABLE
fe80::5054:ff:feb6:d927 dev swp1 lladdr 52:54:00:b6:d9:27 router REACHABLE
```

You can see that the entry for 169.254.0.1 on every interface has the same MAC address (for instance, 52:54:00:f5:ca:97) as the corresponding IPv6 entry for the interface. Further, the entry has been marked as PERMANENT, which is an indication to the kernel that the entry is a static entry. In other words, the kernel must not attempt to refresh this ARP entry.

Tying all the pieces together, FRR implements unnumbered BGP as follows:

1. FRR implements IPv6 RA natively. FRR's RA when enabled on an interface announces its own LLA and MAC address. RA packets are used with a link-local multicast address and so they're never forwarded.

2. On receiving an RA packet from a peer router on an interface, FRR's RA extracts the MAC address and the associated IPv6 LLA.

3. Now that the interface's peering address is known, FRR kicks BGP into action to start connection establishment using the learned IPv6 LLA.

4. After a successful BGP connection establishment, BGP uses capability negotiation to ensure that both sides of the peering session support RFC 5549.

5. BGP receives a route advertisement for a route, say 10.0.0.11/32, from the peer with the peer's IPv6 LLA (and global IPv6 address if one is configured).

6. If BGP selects this path as the best path to reach 10.0.0.11/32, it passes this route down to the RIB process[2] (called zebra in FRR), with the next hop set to the IPv6 LLA received in the BGP UPDATE message.

7. Let's assume the RIB picks this BGP route as the best route with which to populate the FIB. The RIB process now consults its database to see whether it has the information for the MAC address associated with this IPv6 LLA. It sees that there is such an entry.

8. The RIB process now adds a static ARP entry for 169.254.0.1 with this MAC address, with the peering interface as the outgoing interface.

9. The RIB process then pushes the route into the kernel routing table with a next hop of 169.254.0.1 and an outgoing interface set to that of the peering interface. So, the final state in the FIB looks as shown in Example 15-5. At this point, everything is set up for packet forwarding to work correctly. More specifically, the packet forwarding logic remains unchanged with this model.

If the link goes down or the remote end stops generating an RA, the local RA process yanks out the LLA and its associated MAC from the RIB. This causes the RIB process to decide that the next hop is no longer reachable, which causes it to notify the BGP process that the peer is no longer reachable. RIB also tears down the static ARP entry that it created. Terminating the session causes BGP to yank out the routes pointing out this peering interface.

The packet sequence timeline for the BGP route exchange in Unnumbered BGP looks as shown in Figure 15-3.

---

2 See "RIB and FIB" on page 87 to learn what a RIB does.

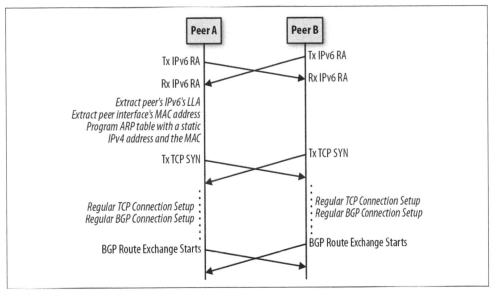

Figure 15-3. Packet sequence timeline for unnumbered BGP in FRR

Interoperability

So, does the use of 5549 imply that every router in the network needs to support it for it to work? Is it possible to have one BGP peering session with a 5549-capable router and another with a non-559 capable router and exchange routes that both see? Yes.

Every eBGP peer sets the NEXTHOP to its own IP address before sending out a route advertisement. Figure 15-4 shows a hypothetical network in which routers B and D support RFC 5549, whereas routers A and C do not. So the links between B and A and between B and C have explicitly configured interface IP addresses. When A announces reachability to 10.1.1.0/24, it provides its peering interface's IPv4 address as the next hop. When B advertises reachability to 10.1.1.0/24, it sets its IPv6 LLA as the next hop when sending the route to D, and sets its interface's IPv4 address as the next hop when sending the route to C.

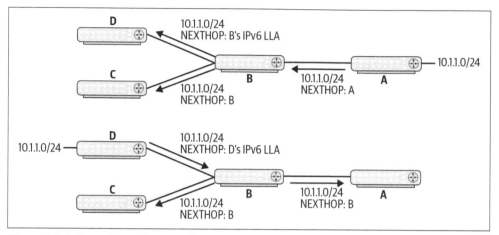

Figure 15-4. Sample topology to illustrate interoperability with RFC 5549

In the reverse direction, if D announces reachability to a prefix 10.1.2.0/24, it uses its interface's IPv6 LLA to send it to B. When B announces this to A and C, it sets the next hop to be that of the IPv4 address of the peering interface.

Final Observations on BGP Configuration in FRR

As discussed earlier, unnumbered BGP requires that we enable IPv6 RA and support for RFC 5549. Both these capabilities are not enabled by default in FRR. Enabling these on an interface looks as shown in the following snippet:

```
! Enable RA on an interface and advertise it every 5 seconds
interface swp1
  no ipv6 nd suppress-ra  ❶
  ipv6 nd ra-interval 5  ❷
!
...
router bgp 65011
  bgp router-id 10.0.0.11
  neighbor ISL peer-group
  neighbor ISL remote-as external
  neighbor ISL bfd
  neighbor ISL capability extended-nexthop  ❸
  neighbor swp1 interface peer-group ISL
  neighbor swp2 interface peer-group ISL
...
```

❶ Enable RA.

❷ Set the advertisement interval for RA; the default is one hour.

❸ Advertise the capability that says we support RFC 5549.

FRR eliminates the need to explicitly specify the extended-next-hop capability and to enable RA. When you specify `neighbor swp1 interface...`, FRR assumes that you're using unnumbered BGP, enables RA automatically on that interface, and advertises the capability in the BGP peering session over that interface. The knobs are present for you to twiddle if you so choose, but they're unnecessary for the common case. This is another example of FRR's design of choosing sane defaults and removing complex knob twiddling from users. This is how we end up with a BGP configuration shown in Example 15-4.

Unnumbered BGP Support in Routing Stacks

The first implementation of unnumbered BGP was in FRR. Subsequently, many other routing stacks have started supporting it. goBGP and BIRD, two other open source routing suites, support unnumbered BGP. A commercial routing stack startup called RtBrick has support for it as well. No traditional vendor routing stack supports unnumbered BGP as of this writing, though Brocade put out an implementation using a different model from the one described in FRR. Arista supports RFC 5549, but not the unnumbered BGP way of configuring BGP. Cisco's NX-OS added support only to pull it out, cause unknown. All of these statements are, of course, qualified by "as of this writing."

Summary

This section showed that unnumbered BGP works and demonstrated the dramatic simplification in the configuration that results from this feature. For the rest of this chapter and the next, we assume the use of unnumbered BGP in all configuration snippets.

Configuring IPv6

Adding support for IPv6 in BGP involves merely activating the AFI/SAFI and advertising the relevant routes. The configuration snippet for adding it to the configuration shown in Example 15-4 is as easy as:

```
address-family ipv6 unicast
    neighbor ISL activate
    redistribute connected route-map ADV_LO
```

This snippet applies to the BGP part of the configuration (the one under `router bgp`). The `route-map` use indicates this is for a spine. The addition to the leaf configuration is similar except that a different route map is used because a leaf must advertise the loopback and locally attached server subnets.

In the early days of multiprotocol BGP, buggy implementations led people to configure separate BGP sessions for IPv4 and IPv6. This ensured that IPv4 connectivity was not lost when a BGP session flapped due to a bug in the IPv6 support. These days, most implementations handle IPv6 fairly well, so a single session for carrying both IPv4 and IPv6 routes is perfectly acceptable.

As discussed in Table 14-2, IPv6 routes are advertised by the MP_REACH_NLRI attribute. IPv6 routes can be carried with only an LLA address, or with both an LLA and a global IPv6 address. IPv6 was explicitly designed to use LLAs for routing. So advertising with just the LLA is sufficient. Global IPv6 addresses are useful in peering that spans multiple hops, something that is not common inside the data center.

BGP and VRFs

When used without MPLS or VXLAN in a non-VPN context, using BGP to advertise VRF-specific routes involves configuring multiple instances of BGP, one per VRF. Consider the classical two-tier topology of Figure 15-1 and assume that we have two VRFs, private and public. Assume that each inter-router link has two VLANs, 100 and 200, which are used to separate private and public VRFs, respectively. Although the respective VLAN numbers are irrelevant and have only a link-local scope, the VRFs are plumbed across all the leaves and spines. On the leaves, let's assume servers in the private VRF are in the 172.16.10.0/24 subnet and associated with VLAN 10, whereas servers in the public VRF are in the 172.16.20.0/24 subnet and associated with VLAN 20. Consider the BGP peering between leaf01 and spine01. The configuration looks as follows with the use of the VRFs:

Example 15-6. BGP VRF configuration snipppet in FRR

```
! BGP configuration for spine01
router bgp 65000 vrf private
   bgp router-id 10.0.0.21
   neighbor peer-group ISL
   neighbor ISL remote-as external
   neighbor ISL bfd
   neighbor swp1.100 interface peer-group ISL
   neighbor swp2.100 interface peer-group ISL
   neighbor swp3.100 interface peer-group ISL
   neighbor swp4.100 interface peer-group ISL
   bgp bestpath as-path multipath-relax
   address-family ipv4 unicast
      neighbor ISL activate
      redistribute connected route-map ADV_VRF_PVT
   exit-address-family
!
!
router bgp 65000 vrf public
   bgp router-id 10.0.0.21
   neighbor peer-group ISL
   neighbor ISL remote-as external
```

```
      neighbor ISL bfd
      neighbor swp1.200 interface peer-group ISL
      neighbor swp2.200 interface peer-group ISL
      neighbor swp3.200 interface peer-group ISL
      neighbor swp4.200 interface peer-group ISL
      bgp bestpath as-path multipath-relax
      address-family ipv4 unicast
         neighbor ISL activate
         redistribute connected route-map ADV_VRF_PUB
      exit-address-family
!
!
route-map ADV_VRF_PVT permit 10
   match interface private
!
route-map ADV_VRF_PUB permit 10
   match interface public
!

! BGP configuration for leaf01
router bgp 65011 vrf private
   bgp router-id 10.0.0.11
   neighbor peer-group ISL
   neighbor ISL remote-as external
   neighbor ISL bfd
   neighbor swp1.100 interface peer-group ISL
   neighbor swp2.100 interface peer-group ISL
   address-family ipv4 unicast
      neighbor ISL activate
      redistribute connected route-map ADV_VRF_PVT
   exit-address-family
!
!
router bgp 65011 vrf public
   bgp router-id 10.0.0.11
   neighbor peer-group ISL
   neighbor ISL remote-as external
   neighbor ISL bfd
   neighbor swp1.200 interface peer-group ISL
   neighbor swp2.200 interface peer-group ISL
   address-family ipv4 unicast
      neighbor ISL activate
      redistribute connected route-map ADV_VRF_PUB
   exit-address-family
!
route-map ADV_VRF_PVT permit 10
   match interface private
route-map ADV_VRF_PVT permit 20
   match interface vlan10
!
route-map ADV_VRF_PUB permit 10
   match interface public
```

```
route-map ADV_VRF_PUB permit 20
   match interface vlan20
```

This shows that we have two BGP configuration sections, one for each VRF. This configuration style is common across most routing stacks. The creation of the VRF itself must be done outside of FRR as of this writing. You create the VRF interface using the Linux *ip* command or using a tool like *netplan* or *ifupdown2*. The association of an interface to a VRF is also done outside of FRR.

Let's examine the answers to some of the common questions that arise when looking at this configuration:

What should I use as the router-id?
> The non-VRF instance of BGP used the loopback IP address as the router-id. Each VRF has a loopback-like interface that is the name of the VRF itself. That interface is assigned an IP address that can be used as the router-id for the VRF.

What should I use as the ASN?
> Though most implementations support using different ASNs with different VRFs, using the same ASN is simpler. ASNs are not scoped by VRF like IP addresses are, and so there is no reason to use a different one per VRF.

If I have 32 VRFs, do I need 32 of these individual BGP sections?
> Unfortunately, yes.

Can I reuse the peer-group definitions across VRFs?
> Unfortunately, not in FRR. Cisco's NX-OS template model allows you to do this.

Peering with BGP Speakers on the Host

With solutions such as Kube-router and Calico, BGP peering between leaves and servers is coming to the fore. I focus on Kube-router in this section. The setup of Kubernetes pods and the network is shown in Figure 15-5. This is just a segment of the usual two-tier Clos topology that we showed in Figure 15-2. We're assuming the use of unnumbered BGP; thus, we don't have any interface IP addresses. Also, we show only leaves (leaf01 and leaf02) and servers (server11 and server21) for focusing on the details. Clearly, there is more than just one server behind each of the leaf01 and leaf02 leaves.

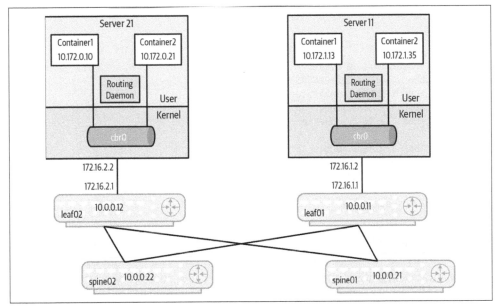

Figure 15-5. Sample topology to illustrate Kube-router and leaf BGP peering

As shown, each of the servers has two containers connected to the Kubernetes bridge, cbr0. server11 has assigned the address 10.172.1.0/24 to cbr0, and server12 has assigned the address 10.172.2.0/24 to cbr0. The individual container IP addresses are shown. The servers themselves are assigned IP addresses out of the subnet assigned to their respective leaves. server11 has the IP address 172.16.1.2, while server21 has the address 172.16.2.2, with the corresponding .1 address being assigned to the leaf itself. The leaf is the first-hop router to the servers and the gateway address is the appropriate .1 address (172.16.1.1 for leaf01, for example).

When Kube-router is run on the servers, BGP requires that the nodes be assigned an ASN. All nodes in the Kubernetes cluster get the same ASN, and this ASN is from the private ASN space, like everything else within the data center. Let's assign the private ASN 64512 for Kube-router's use. First the Kube-routers set up an iBGP mesh so that they can learn the pod subnet IP addresses of one another. So via the iBGP session between server11 and server21, server11 learns of the subnet IP address of 10.172.2.0/24 and server21 learns of 10.172.1.0/24. An examination of the routing table on server11 will reveal something like this:

```
$ ip route show
default via 172.16.1.1 dev eth0
10.172.2.0/24 via 172.16.1.1 dev eth0
```

By configuring Kube-router to also peer with the leaf, BGP will allow these pods to be externally reachable as well. A trivial way to configure BGP on the leaf to peer with

Kube-router would be to have a snippet that looks like this (from leaf01's perspective):

```
router bgp 65011
    bgp router-id 10.0.0.11
    neighbor peer-group SERVERS
    neighbor SERVERS remote-as external
    neighbor 172.16.1.1 peer-group SERVERS
    neighbor 172.16.1.2 peer-group SERVERS
    ...
    neighbor 172.16.1.40 peer-group SERVERS
    address-family ipv4 unicast
        neighbor SERVERS activate
        redistribute connected route-map ADV_LO_SRVRS
    exit-address-family
```

We've assumed that there are 40 servers connected to leaf01. Listing out 40 servers like this is long and tedious. Furthermore, not all the servers might be online yet. Simply specifying the neighbor even if it's not present leads to a lot of clutter in the output and false positives about errors in BGP because some of the sessions will not be in Established state; the other end may not even be up. This sort of configuration also complicates the renumbering of the IP address if need be.

BGP provides a simpler option for handling this case, called *dynamic neighbors*.

BGP Dynamic Neighbors

Because BGP runs over TCP, as long as one of the peers initiates a connection, the other end can remain passive, silently waiting for a connection to come, just as a web server waits for a connection from a client such as a browser.

The BGP dynamic neighbors feature is supported in some implementations where one end, the listening end, is passive. It is just told what IP subnet to accept connections from, and is associated with a peer group that controls the characteristics of the peering session.

Recall that the servers within a rack typically share a subnet with the other servers in the same rack. So the leaf in our case is assumed to be the listening end. A typical configuration of BGP dynamic neighbors on a leaf will look as follows:

```
router bgp 65011
  bgp router-id 10.0.0.11
  ...
  neighbor SERVERS peer-group
  neighbor SERVERS remote-as 64512
  bgp listen range 172.16.1.0/24 peer-group SERVERS
  ...
```

The *listen* command notifies BGP to accept any BGP connection that is received on the 172.16.1.0/24 subnet and treat the configuration for this peering session to be taken from the peer-group template, SERVERS. We explicitly defined the ASN to be used because servers and network typically belong to different organizations within a data center and this forces the connection to be accepted only from the predefined ASN. You can limit the number of peers that the dynamic neighbor model supports via the command neighbor listen limit *limit-number*. For example, by configuring bgp listen limit 20, you allow only 20 dynamic neighbors to be established at any given time. Limits are usually set to protect the router from taking on more load than planned.

On the server side, the switch's peering IP address is typically that of the default gateway. In the case of leaf01, this is 172.16.1.1, and in the case of leaf02, it is 172.16.2.1.

Kube-router can also advertise the service's IP address when it becomes available. goBGP, which is used by Kube-router internally, doesn't support the use of BFD. Calico uses BIRD as the routing protocol suite which supports BFD.

BGP and Upgrades

As discussed in Chapter 13, when upgrading a router, it is useful for the router to gracefully take itself out of the forwarding paths. In other words, traffic must be drained from the router to be upgraded before the router is upgraded. OSPF offers max-metric to enable a node to take itself out of all routed paths (except what was uniquely connected to it only). In the same way, BGP supports the same functionality using a few different methods. Let's begin with the most common one.

AS_PATH Prepend

In the data center, AS_PATH is the main parameter that affects the selection of a path in BGP's best-path computation. Therefore, to take a router out of contention for being in the best path toward a destination, we can increase the AS_PATH length. This is done via an option called *as-path prepend*. This adds the specified ASN once to the AS_PATH attribute before advertising the routes to the neighbors. The recommended ASN to prepend is the router's own ASN. Just like OSPF's max-metric, if there is no other path to a destination except via the router trying to take itself out, the as-path prepend still makes packets flow through the router.

The following snippet demonstrates how as-path prepend is used:

```
router bgp 65011
  ...
  neighbor ISL route-map MAINT out
  ...

route-map MAINT
  set as-path prepend 65011
```

This command prepends the ASN 65011 to the AS_PATH before advertising it to all the neighbors defined by the peer-group ISL.

GRACEFUL_SHUTDOWN Community

A relatively recent addition to the BGP standards list is a well-known BGP community called GRACEFUL_SHUTDOWN, which allows a router to take itself out of the forwarding paths gracefully. RFC 8326 (*https://oreil.ly/oOk7o*) defines this community and the behavior to make this work correctly. After a BGP speaker receives a route with the GRACEFUL_SHUTDOWN community set, it lowers the LOCAL_PREF attribute to 0, making it less preferable than the routes with the default LOCAL_PREF of 100. FRR (and other implementations) assigns a default value for the LOCAL_PREF if it is not defined in the received BGP UPDATE message. This default value in FRR is 100. By changing the LOCAL_PREF to be lower than 100, we end up not selecting the path that goes through the router that advertised the community GRACEFUL_SHUTDOWN. I have not seen the LOCAL_PREF attribute used inside the data center for any other purpose than the graceful shutdown.

FRR automatically changes the LOCAL_PREF without any further configuration required. Other implementations require the use of a route map or equivalent routing policy to effect this change.

Enabling a node to transmit this community string is via the `bgp graceful-shutdown` command.

Max-MED

A third, but much less preferred way to advertise that a node wants to take itself out of the path is by changing the MED attribute in the advertised route. FRR supports a BGP configuration knob called `max-med` (similar to `max-metric` in OSFP) to change the MED to a significantly higher value. MED is another attribute not used within the data center, but is part of the BGP bestpath computation. Enabling this parameter, however, requires that all routers have an additional knob enabled. MED is considered in the bestpath computation only if the LOCAL_PREF and AS_PATH lengths are the same. Otherwise, they take precedence over the MED metric. Enabling this knob is shown in the following snippet for FRR:

```
router bgp 65000
  bgp router-id 10.0.0.21
  ...
  bgp max-med administrative
  ...
```

Best Practices

Here are the best practices for deploying BGP, based on my experience with various customer networks over the past 10 or so years. As in the case of OSPF, these suggestions aim to simplify the configuration, make it automation friendly, and help troubleshooting when problems occur:

- Follow the ASN-numbering model described.
- Use unnumbered BGP if you can. Many more routing suites support it now, both open source and proprietary. I strongly recommend pushing your vendor to support this.
- Ensure that the loopback has a valid IP address (besides the one in the 127.0.0.0/8 subnet). Ensure that this address is advertised.
- On non-FRR suites, enable multipathing. This is automatically enabled in FRR.
- Enable the `bgp bestpath as-path multipath-relax` knob.
- On non-FRR suites, always enable the detailed logging of peering session changes. FRR enables this by default.
- Use a single eBGP session to advertise reachability of multiple address families.
- Use BFD to catch issues with cables such as unidirectional links, besides catching other kinds of connection errors fast.
- Use route maps when interfacing with servers to ensure you never accept prefixes for which they're not responsible.
- Use dynamic neighbors with limits to simplify peering with servers.
- Do not summarize anywhere except the leaves.
- Keep the configuration to the minimum necessary. This makes for a robust network that is easy to understand, manage, and troubleshoot.

Summary

In this chapter, we dived deep into configuring BGP for the underlay—base Clos topology. We studied how unnumbered BGP works and the simplifications it brings to the configuration. We also studied concepts such as peer groups and routing policy configuration. We looked at how Kube-router uses BGP to advertise pod subnets and service IP addresses and how best to configure BGP on a leaf to peer with BGP on servers. We examine troubleshooting BGP and looking at the various show commands in Chapter 11.

## CHAPTER 16

EVPN in the Data Center

Simplicity does not precede complexity, but follows it.
—Alan Jay Perlis

Before we study how to configure network virtualization in the data center, we need to acquaint ourselves with the basics of EVPN. As defined before, EVPN is a solution that provides the control plane for network virtualization. In the simplest of terms, EVPN is a technology that connects L2 network segments separated by an L3 network. EVPN accomplishes this by building the L2 network as a virtual Layer 2 network overlay over the Layer 3 network. It uses BGP as its control protocol, and in the data center it uses VXLAN for packet encapsulation.

In this chapter you should find answers to questions such as these:

- What is EVPN and why is it popular?
- What are the control-plane models for deploying EVPN?
- What BGP constructs support EVPN?
- How does EVPN bridging differ from traditional 802.1Q bridging?
- How do I support dual-attached hosts?

EVPN is a fairly complex solution born out of the desire to find an alternative to Virtual Private LAN Service (VPLS) in the service provider network. I find that a lot of the work is not directly relevant to EVPN's use in the data center, though vendors won't ever stop trying to complicate a solution. I will not be discussing the pieces that I find irrelevant to the data center. Some of this is a matter of opinion, but hopefully one born out of designing network technologies and working on network designs for many years.

We already discussed how VXLAN bridging and routing works in Chapter 6. VXLAN provides the data-plane encapsulation for an L2 point-to-multipoint virtual network over a routed underlay, whereas EVPN defines the technology for the control plane. The specifications in this are created by the Network Virtualization Overlay over L3 (NVO3) working group of the IETF. In this chapter we focus only on the control-plane aspects of EVPN.

Why Is EVPN Popular?

I once penned a blog post[1] titled "Network Virtualization and the End-to-End Principle" in which I argued that network virtualization was just an application that ran on top of a routed network. SDN could be used to provide the control plane for network virtualization. This way, the network fabric could stay aloof from network virtualization. However, an SDN controller-based solution never took off the way many predicted it would. Enterprises instead began to look seriously at EVPN.

EVPN is a mature technology that has been available in MPLS networks for some time. It uses BGP as the control protocol to exchange reachability information for virtual networks. A draft standard that adopted this to VXLAN has been available and relatively stable with multiple vendor implementations. There has been a lot of additional work in progress at the IETF, the standards body that governs IP-based technologies. In short, EVPN already had the chops to be the alternative to controller-based VXLAN solutions. And by the summer of 2017, its moment in the data center had come.

Companies adopted VXLAN and the world of network virtualization, but wanted native VXLAN routing (or RIOT, as it is often called, for Routing In and Out of Tunnels). Merchant-switching silicon with RIOT support began to arrive in volumes in the middle of 2017 to support real deployments. The confluence of mature technologies (VXLAN and EVPN) combined well with support in merchant-switching silicon that allows the deployment of production-quality data centers with network virtualization support. And this is what makes EVPN in the data center relevant today.

The Problems a Network Virtualization Control Plane Must Address

An overlay network virtualization control plane must solve the following problems:

- Provide a mapping of the inner to the outer address
- Identify the virtual network to which an inner address belongs

---

1 Alas, the blog is no longer available.

- Identify the encapsulation used given that there can be multiple encapsulations available

Beyond this, VXLAN needs to know which VTEPs[2] are interested in which virtual networks, so that multidestination frames such as Broadcast, Unknown unicast, and Multicast (BUM) traffic can be delivered only to the interested endpoints.

EVPN goes even further and also provides support for the following:

- ARP/ND suppression
- Routing
- Multihomed nodes
- L3 multicast

Besides this, you need to perform individual, device-specific configurations such as:

- The creation of a VTEP
- Associating a VXLAN virtual network with its local version of a virtual network, typically VLANs
- Specifying the method for handling multidestination frames: ingress replication (also called head-end replication) or underlay multicast
- Handling the configuration associated with using underlay multicast

We deal with the device-specific configuration in Chapter 17.

Where Does a VTEP Reside?

The VTEP, as a memory refresher, is the edge of the network virtual overlay, the place where the nonvirtual network meets the virtual network; the place where packets are encapsulated on their way into the overlay and decapsulated on their way out of the overlay. The closer to the endpoints the VTEP functionality resides, the more the core of the network can be kept unaffected by changes in network virtualization state. Making the host endpoints as the VTEPs allows the routers that comprise the Clos topology to function just as routers and nothing more. This keeps the network immutable, and network virtualization looks more like an application rather than a function of the network. Cloud providers such as Amazon and Microsoft use this model in their VPC solutions, except that forwarding within a VPC is via routing, not bridging. The encapsulation they use is also specific to each cloud provider, and they don't use VXLAN. They also use a proprietary control plane to distribute the map-

---

2 Another common name for VTEP is NVE.

ping of the inner to outer addresses. Cloud service providers offer neither L2 connectivity nor multicast. So they do not need to worry about issues of handling multidestination frames.

Some private cloud solutions using EVPN are using FRR to start EVPN from the host itself. This is a standards-based, controller-less solution that, coupled with host-based solutions such as eBPF and iptables, provide a solution equivalent to those provided by companies such as VMware. For further details, see "iBGP Characteristics".

In the case of a Clos topology, besides the host, the next ideal location for a VTEP is the leaf. It makes no sense to do VTEP at the spine or super-spine, because EVPN connects virtual L2 network segments separated by a routed underlay, whereas in a two-tier Clos network, the L2 networks terminate at the leaf. Leaf VTEPs are the most common deployment model of EVPN in the data center.

One Protocol to Rule Them All, Or…?

As discussed earlier, NVO3 consists of two parts: a routed underlay and the overlay. We discussed how we can use OSPF and BGP as the routing protocols to build the routed underlay. BGP, specifically eBGP, is far more popular than OSPF in the data center. However, when it comes to EVPN, given its use in the service provider world as a VPN solution, traditional vendors push for a solution that looks similar to how it is deployed in the service provider world. There, OSPF (or IS-IS) is used to build the routed underlay, and iBGP is used to exchange virtual network information.

Just as FRR innovated the configuration of BGP via unnumbered BGP, it was also the first to use a single eBGP session for building both the routed underlay and the exchange of virtual network information. In other words, exchanging MAC addresses is as simple as enabling another AFI/SAFI, like IPv6, in BGP. I suspect that in time, others will follow in the footsteps of FRR again, seeking simpler alternatives to the more complex, traditional options. We consider both models in this section. But before doing that, we need to understand two basic characteristics of iBGP.

iBGP Characteristics

iBGP peering usually takes place between peers that are separated by a routed network. This is very unlike eBGP peering, which is almost always between peers on either side of a physical link. For example, iBGP peering is between leaves for the use case of NVO3 in a Clos topology. This means that each leaf sets up an iBGP peering session with every other leaf. This full-mesh iBGP peering quickly becomes unscalable and fragile. To overcome this problem, two separate solutions were invented: *BGP confederations* and *Route Reflectors* (RRs). Of the two, RR is by far the most popular solution and the way people consider deploying iBGP with NVO3.

RR follows a hub-and-spoke model, in which all the iBGP speakers connect to a group of central RR servers. The job of the RRs is to compute the best path for a route and advertise that to each of the RR clients. However, unlike eBGP, the RR doesn't modify the next-hop network address for a route; instead, it leaves it to be whatever the value was in the advertisement that the RR received.

To illustrate, consider Figure 16-1, which illustrates how eBGP and iBGP differ in their propagation of the next hop from routes they learn. In the case of eBGP, the next hop is always modified to be the advertising router. This is called *next-hop self*. In case of iBGP, the next hop associated with a route is not modified when advertised to a peer. In the example shown, A can then choose a data path to, for instance, 10.1.1.0/24, completely bypassing B. If you assume B as an RR, it is only offloading the computational duplication and the full-mesh connection scalability between the iBGP speakers. For this reason, it is not uncommon to find compute nodes functioning as RRs. If there are multiple RRs, the RRs do not even have to communicate amongst themselves to fulfill their job as an RR. As shown in Figure 16-2, this means that you can use the Clos network merely as a connectivity layer; that is, just as the underlay and keep it simple. However, this is not common. Yet.

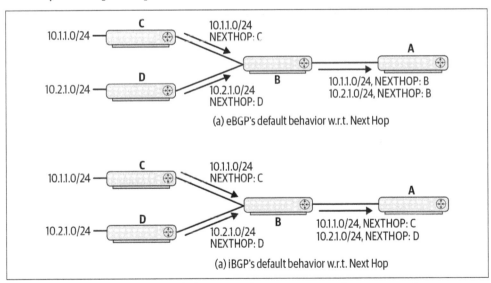

Figure 16-1. eBGP versus iBGP behavior with respect to next-hop propagation

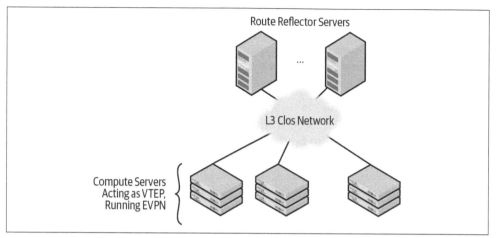

Figure 16-2. RRs as servers and pure L3 underlay

In a more typical deployment, the spines in a Clos topology act as RRs. The spines are part of the underlay and have no knowledge of the virtual networks. They're also the nodes to which all leaves connect. So it seems a natural fit for the spines to function as RRs. The only requirement is that all the spines can act as RRs to ensure that all spines share the same performance characteristics, and that the failure characteristics of the RRs remain the same as for the underlay and packet forwarding.

To summarize, iBGP deployment uses RRs. In a Clos topology, spines are a natural shoe-in to be the RRs.

Separate Underlay and Overlay Protocols

As mentioned earlier, traditional network vendors use different routing protocols for the underlay network (OSPF or IS-IS) and the overlay network (iBGP). The spines are used as iBGP RRs. Cisco's ACI solution utilizes this model too, with IS-IS as the basic underlay routing protocol. Here are the main disadvantages of this model:

- Rip-and-replace of the routing underlay is disruptive if you're already running the underlay with eBGP today.
- More protocols mean more complexity and are more difficult to troubleshoot when things break.

To address the first problem, one vendor promotes the use of eBGP as the routed underlay and iBGP for the overlay. Most routers run a single BGP process to handle both eBGP and iBGP sessions. So this adds additional BGP sessions between leaves and spines, for little added benefit. The separate sessions mean that things can still go out of sync between the two sessions.

One vendor advocates using two eBGP sessions: one on the interface IP address for the underlay, and another between the loopbacks of a leaf and spine for the overlay. Although their official claim is that this is more robust, what I hear from internal sources is that this is recommended because of a buggy implementation that results in long convergence times if a link flaps.

eBGP Only

An alternative approach, first implemented in FRR, is to use a single eBGP session to exchange both underlay and overlay routing information. In my own opinion, and after speaking with many BGP experts, this option is the simpler and more elegant solution for the Clos topology in the data center.

To simplify the configuration for an eBGP session that transports both underlay and overlay information, FRR automatically avoids modifying the next-hop address for virtual network routes while continuing to do so for the underlay routes. Other implementations that use a single eBGP session require the use of something akin to the following snippet (shown as a route map, discussed in "Route Maps: Implementation of Routing Policy" on page 310):

```
route-map NH_UNCHANGED permit 10
    set ip next-hop unchanged

router bgp ...
    ...
    neighbor 169.254.0.1 route-map NH_UNCHANGED out
    ...
```

The BGP process on the spines needs to retain information it receives about both the overlay and the underlay. It uses the underlay information to build the underlay packet forwarding table. It needs to retain the overlay information it receives from a leaf to pass it to the other leaves (functioning like a RR). However, the spines don't know anything about virtual networks and will drop the information about them unless otherwise instructed. FRR automatically makes the spines keep that information when it recognizes that the same session is used for carrying both underlay and overlay routes. In other vendor implementations that support a single eBGP session model, additional configuration might need to be added. For example, with Cisco routers, you must add `retain-route-target-all` to the EVPN configurations.

BGP Constructs to Support Virtual Network Routes

BGP added a few constructs to support advertising virtual network routes. These first arose in the context of MPLS L3VPNs in service provider networks. The first issue is what AFI/SAFI to use. EVPN uses the AFI/SAFI of *l2vpn/evpn*. This is because EVPN is considered to be a kind of an L2 VPN. Next, BGP must handle the model allowing addresses to be duplicated across virtual networks. Here's an analogy I came up with to explain the problems this causes BGP.

Imagine Santa Claus is like BGP. Come Christmas, a lot of kids will be getting the exact same present, the viral toy for that year. Worse still for poor Santa, some kids will receive multiple copies of the same toy, thanks to their large, extended family. Santa has multiple responsibilities. First, he must keep copies of this identical toy separate. So Santa asks each gift-giver to stamp their copy with a unique ID to avoid mixing up the same gifts for different kids. Santa's second responsibility is to not play favorites among the relatives. He must not decide to (wittingly or not) give a child exactly a single copy of a toy or choose which copy from which relative a child receives. Why is this a risk? Because Santa is like BGP, he runs the best-path algorithm on each toy and picks only one. However, it is up to each kid to decide which copy of a toy they choose to keep. Maybe the kid wants to keep the gift from his favorite aunt. How does an excited youngster know which copy is from which relative? So Santa asks for a family-specific unique identifier for each gift as well. In other words, every toy has an identifier that is across all gifts and another identifier that is specific to each family. Convert toys to addresses, and you have *Route Distinguisher* (RD) as the first identifier and *Route Target* (RT) as the second identifier. How do these two interact in a BGP UPDATE message processing?

Every BGP implementation I know of maintains two kinds of routing tables: a global one and one per virtual network. BGP runs the best-path algorithm on the global table to pick a single path to advertise for each prefix to its peers. Because the RD is unique to each originator, all copies of a route will be advertised to a neighbor. To install routes into a virtual network's routing table, BGP first uses the import RT clause to select specific candidate routes from the global table to import into this virtual network. Then, it runs the best-path algorithm again on the imported candidate routes, but this time within the context of the virtual network's routing table. If the same address is advertised with multiple RTs, the best-path algorithm selects the best one. Multiple RTs can be imported into a single virtual network routing table.

Route Distinguisher

As explained in the previous section, an RD is an eight-byte value that is added to every virtual network address to keep the address globally unique. Section 4.2 of RFC 4364 (*https://oreil.ly/EK2Wk*) defines the RD, its formats, and its use. There are three different RD formats. The RD format used in EVPN is defined by RFC 7432 (*https://oreil.ly/eiQpW*) and shown in Figure 16-3.

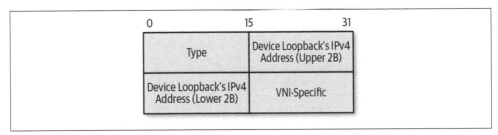

Figure 16-3. Format of RD for use with EVPN

If you're wondering how the Virtual Network Instance (VNI) is three bytes long but can be encoded in a two-byte space in the RD, this is not an issue, because it is assumed that no VTEP will, in practice, host more than 64,000 VNIs. Most switching hardware doesn't support this many VNIs on a single device today. Even if they could or did, supporting this many VNIs on a single device is not considered acceptable because of the number of customers who would be affected by a failure of the device. It is the combination of the router's IPv4 loopback address plus the VNI that makes the RD unique across the network. Thus, the value of the VNI-specific part of the RD is a device-local encoding of the VNI, not necessarily the absolute value of the VNI.

Because the router's loopback IP address is part of the RD, two nodes with the same virtual network will end up having different RDs. This solves the problem of distinguishing sources with the same IP address.

The RD is encoded as part of the NLRI in the MP_REACH_NLRI and MP_UNREACH_NLRI attributes.

Route Target

RT is an additional path attribute added to virtual network NLRIs. As mentioned earlier, RT encodes the virtual network it belongs to. A BGP speaker advertising virtual networks and their addresses uses a specific RT called the *export RT*. A BGP speaker receiving and using the advertisement uses this RT to decide which local virtual network to add the routes to. This is called the *import RT*. In a typical VPN configuration, the network administrator must configure both import and export RTs.

The definition and use of RT is specified in section 4.3.1 of RFC 4364 (*https://oreil.ly/w1tfk*). The encoding of the RT for EVPN with VXLAN is described in section 5.1.2.1 of RFC 8365 (*https://oreil.ly/km7lk*) and is shown in Figure 16-4 below.

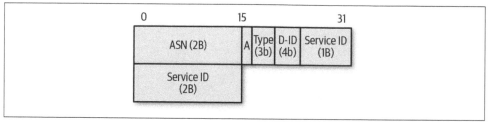

Figure 16-4. Format of RT for use with EVPN-VXLAN

The definitions of the different fields are as follows:

ASN
> The two-byte ASN of the BGP speaker advertising the address.

A
> A bit indicating whether the RT is autoderived or manually configured.

Type
> A three-bit field indicating the encapsulation used in EVPN. For VXLAN, it is 1, and for VLAN, it is 0.

Domain-ID (D-ID)
> Four bits that are typically zero. In certain cases, if there is an overlap in the VXLAN numbering space, this field is used to qualify the administrative domain to which the VNI belongs.

Service ID
> Three bytes containing the virtual network identifier. For VXLAN, it is the 3-byte VNI; for VLAN it is 12 bits (the lower 12 bits of the 3-byte field).

FRR's use of RD and RT

The EVPN standard specifies that the RT can be automatically derived, if desired. Not all implementations support this model yet, but FRR does. It encodes RT as described earlier, assuming VXLAN as the encapsulation. Most other implementations require you to state this objective via a configuration such as `route-target import auto`.

FRR maintains a bitmap in which each bit represents a separate VNI. The VNI-specific two bytes in the RD come from the value of this bit position. FRR also allows an administrator to manually configure the RT for a specific virtual network, but this is not recommended because of the potential to make mistakes.

EVPN Route Types

As we have previously discussed, non-IPv4 unicast routes are advertised via the MP_REACH_NLRI and MP_UNREACH_NLRI attributes. For most AFI/SAFI combinations, the structure and content of the reachability information carried in an UPDATE message is the same across that AFI/SAFI. This is not the case with EVPN. There are disparate pieces of information to be exchanged. For example, the update can be reachability to a specific MAC address, or it could be reachability to an entire virtual network. Also, unlike IPv4 and IPv6, because EVPN has already consumed both an AFI and a SAFI, there is no way to separate information about unicast and multicast addresses. To accommodate these additional subdivisions, EVPN NLRI encodes different types of information via a Route Type. Table 16-1 lists the types applicable in the data center.

Table 16-1. EVPN Route Types

Route Type	What it carries	Primary use
RT-1	Ethernet Segment Auto Discovery	Supports multihomed endpoints in the data center, used instead of MLAG
RT-2	MAC, VNI, IP	Advertises reachability to a specific MAC address in a virtual network, and its IP address
RT-3	VNI/VTEP Association	Advertises a VTEP's interest in virtual networks
RT-4	Designated Forwarder	Ensures that only a single VTEP forwards multidestination frames to multihomed endpoints
RT-5	IP prefix, VRF	Advertises IP prefixes, such as summarized routes, and the VRF associated with the prefix
RT-6	Multicast group membership	Contains information about which multicast groups an endpoint attached to a VTEP is interested in

A few more route types have sprung up in EVPN besides the ones listed here.

FRR version 7.0, the latest release at the time of this writing, supports only Route Types 2, 3, and 5.

Communicating Choice of BUM Handling

As explained in "Multidestination frame handling in VXLAN" on page 135, there are a couple of choices when handling BUM traffic: head-end replication or routed multicast in the underlay. Therefore, each VTEP must inform the other VTEPs of what it can support. RT-3 EVPN messages can carry a BGP attribute called Provider Multicast Service Interface (PMSI), which identifies the kind of BUM packet handling supported by this device. The PMSI attribute is defined in a completely different standard (RFC 6514 (*https://oreil.ly/Scbyn*)) from the usual EVPN standards. The values suggested by the EVPN draft for signaling the replication model follow. Most are variants of Protocol-Independent Multicast (PIM), described in "Multicast Routing Protocol" on page 165:

- 3 for PIM-SSM

- 4 for PIM-SM
- 5 for Bidir PIM or Bidirectional PIM
- 6 for ingress replication

Many implementations advertise the use of ingress replication, but not the use of multicast. This might have to do with the implementation doing something other than the options listed. For example, Cisco's ACI solution uses IS-IS to build the multicast trees, and IS-IS isn't even a defined bit in RFC 6514. The bottom line is if you use a routed multicast underlay, there is no way to detect misconfiguration across VTEPs, because the information is not advertised by most implementations.

EVPN and Bridging

We already delved into the packet flow in VXLAN bridging and routing in "Illustrating VXLAN Bridging and Routing" on page 131. In this section, we explore how 802.1Q's flood-and-learn model is supplanted by EVPN. The primary difference is that EVPN uses BGP to distribute reachability to MAC addresses and IP routes along with the associated virtual network. Also, STP is not used. To understand how bridging works with EVPN, consider the topology shown in Figure 16-5.

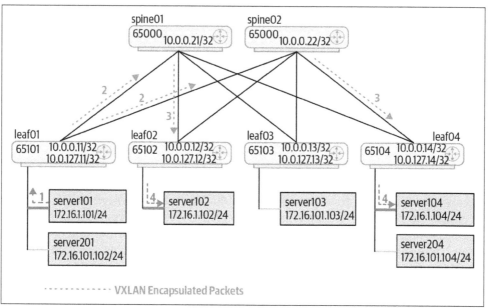

Figure 16-5. Sample EVPN bridging topology

Remember that the underlay is routed; that is, packets between leaves and spines are always routed, never bridged. The leaves are the VTEPs, as explained earlier. To function as a VTEP, they need an IP address to source and receive packets. Typically, a single IP address is used across all VNIs. EVPN has also been enabled on all the leaves. 802.1Q bridging is enabled only on the ports between a leaf and the servers locally attached to it, as in a Clos network.

The spines are only part of the underlay. We're assuming a single eBGP session peering in the following sequence, but the behavior is not that different if the spines are acting as RRs.

Device-local configuration also defines the mapping of the local VLAN to the global VNI. In Figure 16-5, assume that the red VLAN (represented by the thick line) is mapped to the red VNI, and the blue VLAN (represented by the thinner line) to the blue VNI.

The first thing to notice is that unlike previous Clos network illustrations, the subnets in this figure are not confined to a single rack. Subnet 172.16.1.0/24 is in the red VNI, no matter where the red VNI is, and subnet 172.16.101.0/24 is in the blue VNI. Different leaves can associate a subnet with different VLAN IDs as long as all those different VLAN IDs map to the same global VNI. All information exchanged in EVPN is about the global VNI, not the local VLAN instantiation of it. Thus, the subnet is also associated with the global VNI because it spans multiple routers.

Next, every leaf has a second IP address, the VTEP IP address, associated with it in the 10.0.127.0/24 subnet; all VXLAN-encapsulated packets will have the source and destination IP address from this subnet. The network administrator must also ensure that this VTEP IP address is advertised via BGP; otherwise, the other VTEPs will not know how to reach this address.

Each leaf learns about the virtual networks every other leaf is interested in via RT-3 routes. So leaf01 knows that leaf02 and leaf04 are interested in the red VNI, and leaf03 and leaf04 are interested in the blue VNI. Similarly, other leaves learn this information from the BGP UPDATEs.

EVPN Bridging with Ingress Replication

Now, let's follow the sequence of packets to understand how EVPN bridging works with head-end replication. Let's have server101 send a packet to server104. Because server101 and server104 belong to the same subnet, server101 sends an ARP request packet asking for server104's MAC address. This goes in the form of a Ethernet broadcast packet with the destination MAC of FF:FF:FF:FF:FF:FF and a source MAC address of MAC_{101}:

1. The packet sent from server101 to leaf01 is no different in this case from traditional bridging. leaf01 receives this packet and, just as in traditional bridging, learns that MAC_{101} is reachable via the port attached to server101. leaf01 understands that the packet is a broadcast packet and so needs to be sent to all the

recipients of the red VNI. leaf01 uses head-end replication to flood the packet to all the interested leaves—in this case leaf02 and leaf04. Most merchant silicon requires you to program the list of next hops for each tunnel endpoint in head-end replication. So implementations can choose to spread the load of head-end replication across the spines.

2. leaf01 VXLAN encapsulates the packet and sends one copy to spine01 (destined to leaf02) and one to spine02 (destined to leaf03). The packet to leaf02 has the destination IP address of leaf02's VTEP—for instance 10.0.127.12—and the source IP address of leaf01, 10.0.127.11. Similarly, the packet to leaf04 has the destination IP address of 10.0.127.14 and the source IP address of 10.0.127.11.

3. When spine01 receives the packet, it does a routing lookup of the IP in the VXLAN header, which is that of leaf02. It then routes the packet out the port to leaf02. spine02 does the same for the packet destined to leaf04.

4. When these VXLAN-encapsulated packets reach leaf02 and leaf04, they each know that they are the egress VTEP because the destination IP address in the packet is their IP address and the UDP destination port says that this is a VXLAN packet. They decapsulate the packet and use local 802.1Q bridging to determine the locally attached ports to which to send the packet out. Neither leaf02 nor leaf04 attempt to send this packet in VXLAN-encapsulated form to any other node. Thus, they avoid flooding a VXLAN-encapsulated packet after decapsulation back into the VXLAN overlay, the equivalent of the self-forwarding check in IP. In EVPN, the check is referred to by its routing protocol name, *split-horizon check*. Now server104 and server102 both receive the packet.

Neither leaf02 nor leaf04 learn anything about MAC_{101} from this flooded packet. However, leaf01 has a new local entry in its MAC forwarding table. So leaf01 advertises the reachability to MAC_{101} in the red virtual network via a BGP UPDATE message. Specifically, it uses an EVPN RT-2 message, which carries the {VNI, MAC} advertisement. The message says that MAC_{101} in the red virtual network is reachable via the VTEP leaf01. leaf01 delivers this information to its BGP peers, spine01 and spine02. spine01 and spine02 in turn deliver this message to their peers, which are leaves leaf02, leaf03, and leaf04. The leaves receive multiple copies of the updates, one from each of the spines. These leaves now populate their MAC forwarding tables with information about MAC_{101}. They note that MAC_{101} is remote and reachable via the leaf01's VTEP IP address, 10.0.127.11. leaf03, which has no red VNI, simply stores this message (or can discard it). Because the spines have no knowledge of virtual networks, they don't know that leaf03 has no red VNI and so is not interested in this message.

If server104's ARP reply to server101 arrives before the MAC table update on leaf04, the return packet can be flooded just like the broadcast packet because leaf04 doesn't know about MAC_{101} yet. If the ARP reply arrives after leaf04 has updated its MAC table based on the BGP UPDATE from leaf01, the reply can be sent directly only to leaf01. If the packet is unicast to leaf01 only, the hash of the packet header of the frame received from server104 determines randomly whether leaf04 sends the packet to spine01 or spine02.

leaf04 also learns that MAC_{104} in the red VNI is attached to the local port pointing out to server104. leaf04 sends a BGP UPDATE message with an EVPN RT-2 type indicating that MAC_{104} in the red VNI is reachable via leaf04. This message is delivered to both spine01 and spine02. They deliver this BGP UPDATE to all the other leaves. At the end of the BGP processing, leaf01, leaf02, and leaf04 know that MAC_{101} in the red VNI is reachable via VTEP leaf01 and that MAC_{104} in the red VNI is reachable via leaf04.

Thus, here are the primary differences between EVPN bridging from traditional 802.1Q bridging:

- Inserting the remote MAC address into the MAC table is done via BGP UPDATEs in EVPN, instead of learning from the data packet itself in 802.1Q.
- The path of the reply from server104 to server101 can take a different path compared to the packet from server101 to server104 in EVPN, whereas they're the same in 802.1Q bridging.

The parts that remain common to EVPN bridging and 802.1Q bridging include the following:

- Locally attached MACs are populated in the MAC table via standard 802.1Q learning.
- Flooded packets are delivered to all end stations in the virtual network.
- Each {virtual network, MAC address} tuple is associated with a single egress port.

EVPN Bridging with Routed Multicast Underlay

Let's consider the same example as in the previous section, but with a routed multicast underlay. The packet sequence assumes the use of PIM-SM with the RPs being located on the spines. Even though we mentioned in "PIM-SM in the Data Center" on page 180 that the use of spines as RP is problematic, we use it in this case to reduce the packet sequences that need to be described and simplify the explanation. We assume the use of OSPF to construct the routed unicast underlay. We use anycast RP to allow any of the spines to provide the appearance of a single RP (as explained in "Multiple RPs and MSDP" on page 179). But we ignore MSDP in the rest of this discussion. I presume that you are familiar with the PIM-SM behavior as described in Chapter 8.

Let's assume that assignment of multicast groups to VNI is a device-specific configuration. It is not communicated via BGP. For the sake of simplicity, let's assign the red multicast group (G_{red}) for BUM traffic in the red VNI, and the blue multicast group (G_{blue}) for BUM traffic in the blue VNI. This assignment is done on each of the leaves.

Figure 16-6 shows the packet sequence. The complexity of the packet sequence with multicast compared to ingress replication should make it abundantly clear how complicated the routed multicast underlay option is.

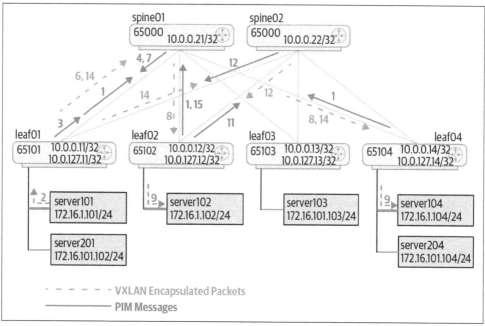

Figure 16-6. EVPN bridging packet sequence with routed multicast underlay

1. When the red multicast group is assigned to the red VNI, each of the leaves sends a PIM Join message with interest in the $(*, G_{red})$ multicast route to the RP. Different leaves can pick different spines to send this message to.

2. server101 sends the ARP request for server104 as usual. leaf01 gets this packet.

3. leaf01 sends a PIM Register packet to the spine it decides is the RP closest to it. Let's assume it picks spine01.

4. spine01 receives the PIM Register message. Consulting its state, spine01 realizes that it has interested listeners, leaf02 and leaf04. It sends a PIM Join for (leaf01,G_{red}) to leaf01. It creates a multicast entry for (leaf01,G_{red}) with the RPF interface being the one toward leaf01, and the olist being the interfaces toward leaf02 and leaf04. Implementations often have the RP send the data packet received via PIM Register on the $(*, G_{red})$ tree.

5. leaf01 receives the PIM Join from the spine and sets the multicast entry for (leaf01,G_{red}) with an olist that points to spine01.

6. The ARP requests need to keep coming because these requests have really not gotten to any of leaf02 or leaf04 yet. On the next ARP packet received by leaf01, leaf01 encapsulates the packet in a VXLAN header with the destination IP address set to G_{red} and the source IP address set to its VTEP IP address, 10.0.127.11. The lookup on this packet in the multicast routing table sends the packet to spine01.

7. spine01, on receiving this packet, sends a PIM Register Stop message to leaf01, because leaf01 will otherwise continue to send a PIM Register packet on every new ARP packet received in the red VNI.

8. spine01 also forwards the packet as per its multicast routing table to leaf02 and leaf04.

9. leaf04 receives the packet and notices that it has no (leaf01,G_{red}) state in its multicast routing table. It does have a (*,G_{red}) state pointing out the interface to server104. The packet is delivered to server104. The same occurs at leaf02 and the packet is delivered to server102.

10. leaf04 creates a multicast routing table entry for (leaf01,G_{red}) and looks up the unicast path to reach leaf01. It has two paths, via spine01 and spine02. Let's assume it picks the path via spine01. It now sets the RPF interface for (leaf01,G_{red}) to the interface being toward spine01 and the olist being the interface toward server104. At this point packets are flowing from leaf01 to leaf04 using routed multicast underlay.

11. Now leaf02, like leaf04, also decides to create a multicast entry for (leaf01,G_{red}). It also looks up the unicast path to leaf01 and discovers it can use spine01 or spine02. Let's assume it picks spine02. It sets the RPF interface for the multicast entry to the interface toward spine02, and sets the olist for the entry to be server102. It sends a PIM Join for (leaf01,G_{red}) to spine02.

12. spine02 receives the PIM Join for (leaf01,G_{red}). It sees that the path to leaf01 is via the interface to leaf01. It creates the multicast route entry for (leaf01,G_{red}) with the RPF interface set to the interface toward leaf01 and the olist being the interface toward leaf02. It sends a PIM Join for (leaf01,G_{red}) to leaf01.

13. leaf01 receives the PIM Join from spine02 and sets the olist for the (leaf01,G_{red}) entry to point to both spine01 and spine02.

14. BUM packets in the red VNI from leaf01 will now go to both spine01 and spine02. spine01's packets to leaf02 will be dropped because leaf02 has set the RPF interface for that group to be the interface toward spine02.

15. leaf02 now sends a (leaf01,G_{red},RPT Prune) message to spine01 since it no longer needs packets from the RPT tree, and it finishes its SPT switchover.

16. spine01 receives the (leaf01,G_{red},RPT Prune) message from leaf02 and removes leaf02 from its (leaf01,G_{red}) multicast route entry olist.

Some implementations choose to speed up the tree setup by starting the configuration immediately when the multicast group is assigned to a VNI on a leaf. Let's examine the packet sequence in such an implementation. To simplify the packet flow, we examine the setup from the perspective of leaf01 only.

1. When the red multicast group is assigned to the red VNI, each of the leaves sends a PIM Join message with interest in the (*,G_{red}) multicast route to the RP. Different leaves can pick different spines to send this message to.

2. leaf01 knows that it is possibly a source if it receives any BUM packet from the servers attached. So, leaf01 sends a PIM Null Register for the (leaf01, G_{red}) group to the RP. Other leaves do the same.

3. The RP uses this Null Register to build a (leaf01, G_{red}) tree toward leaf01. It sends a PIM Join for (leaf01, G_{red}) to leaf01 and sets the RPF interface to be the interface toward leaf01. The olist is leaf02 and leaf04.

4. leaf01 receives the PIM Join and creates a (leaf01, G_{red}) multicast route entry with the olist being spine01.

5. server101 sends an ARP request.

6. Because there's an (leaf01, G_{red}) multicast route entry already, the VXLAN-encapsulated packet flows to spine01. leaf01's PIM process, however, also gets a copy of the packet, which it then sends to spine01 as a PIM Register message.

7. Upon receiving the VXLAN-encapsulated packet for (leaf01, G_{red}), spine01 sends a PIM Register Stop message to leaf01.

8. The VXLAN-encapsulated packet also flows toward leaf02 and leaf04 which were in the olist for (leaf01, G_{red}).

The rest of the packet sequence looks similar to the previous multicast packet sequence.

What happens if leaf02 sends the PIM Join for (*,G_{red}) to spine02, and leaf04 sends it to spine01? This is possible because both spines are functioning as anycast RP and different leaves can pick different spines to send their PIM Join to. leaf01 will send the PIM Register (or the PIM Null Register) message to only one of the spines, say spine01, and only spine01 will create the (leaf01,G_{red}) tree. How will leaf01's packets ever reach leaf02?

This part is handled by MSDP. As soon as spine01 creates the (leaf01,G_{red}) multicast route, MSDP synchronizes that information to spine02. spine02 uses this information to send a PIM Join for (leaf01,G_{red}) group because it is connected to leaf02 and that leaf has expressed interest in the (*,G_{red}) multicast stream. spine02 sends the Join request over the RPF interface to leaf01, which is the link toward leaf01. It marks the multicast route as having an olist pointing to the interface to leaf02. On receiving the PIM Join from spine02, leaf01 adds the interface to spine02 to the olist for the (leaf01,G_{red}) multicast route. Now packets will flow to both leaf02 and leaf04.

Handling MAC Moves

Providing L2 connectivity comes with a whole host of additional complications that a protocol must deal with. Handling MAC moves is one such issue.

In Figure 16-5, let server101 host a VM with a MAC address of $MACVM_{101}$. After it first speaks, using the model of EVPN bridging, all leaves learn that $MACVM_{101}$ is being associated with VTEP leaf01. Now consider what happens if the VM now migrates to server102. When it first speaks after the move, leaf02 learns that $MACVM_{101}$ is locally attached to itself. It also has an entry that states that $MACVM_{101}$ is associated with leaf01 populated via BGP. Because locally attached entries take precedence over entries learned via BGP, leaf02 switches its MAC table to have $MACVM_{101}$ point out the port to server102. It then sends out a BGP EVPN RT-2 UPDATE message indicating that others should switch their association for $MACVM_{101}$ to leaf02. leaf04 does so without a problem. But leaf01 thinks that MAC address is locally attached to itself. Because locally attached entries take precedence over entries learned via BGP, leaf01 will not switch its association for $MACVM_{101}$ to leaf02, but continues to think it is locally attached. This is wrong.

To fix this issue, EVPN defines a new BGP extended community called MAC Mobility, the format of which is shown in Figure 16-7.

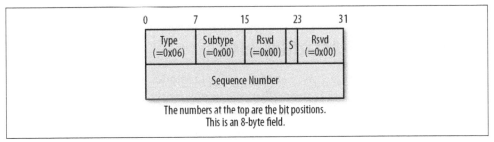

Figure 16-7. Format of MAC Mobility extended community

The first basic rule about using this extended community is that it must be used for advertising a MAC address that is locally learned, if the MAC address is already associated with a remote VTEP. The sequence number indicates the number of times this MAC address has moved. For instance, the first time this attribute is attached to an RT-2 advertisement of a MAC address, the sequence number is bumped to 1. The second basic rule is that if you receive an advertisement for a MAC address in a virtual network with this extended community, you must accept this advertisement as the best path either if you don't hold an entry with this extended community or if the sequence number in the new advertisement is higher than the one currently in your database. In case multiple updates are received with the same sequence number but from different VTEPs, the one with the lower VTEP IP address wins.

Static MAC addresses are MAC addresses that are not allowed to move. When advertising such MAC addresses, the route must be tagged with the MAC Mobility extended community with the "S" bit in the community set. When any VTEP receives a MAC advertisement with such a tag, it must ignore any locally detected changes in that MAC address in the associated virtual network.

Sometimes, messages indicating that a MAC address moved are incorrect. One reason is lax security in L2 networks, making it possible to spoof a MAC address and make it move from a safe host to a compromised host. Another reason for spurious moves is that a problem in a connected 802.1Q network can cause the STP to continuously update its tree. When the tree is updated, a MAC address might appear in a different location in the tree, making it look like the MAC address moved.

To handle all of these cases, if a VTEP detects that a MAC address is updating too frequently, it can stop sending or handling further updates to that MAC address. It must also notify the administrator that this is happening. There is no clearly defined way to get out of this situation.

FRR's EVPN implementation supports MAC Mobility as defined by the standard. If it detects that a MAC address has moved too many times within a specified time period, it ignores MAC address updates associated with the MAC address for some time, before restarting the MAC Mobility timer. The number of moves and the time periods can all be specified.

Support for Dual-Attached Hosts

As discussed earlier, in enterprise networks, compute nodes are frequently attached to more than one switch. This is primarily done to ensure that a single link failure or a single switch failure doesn't leave a compute node disconnected from the network. This also allows the center to upgrade a switch without taking down all the compute nodes associated with that switch during the upgrade window. As an enterprise network solution, EVPN is also frequently deployed with dual-attached hosts. We don't discuss a variation of the same idea: multisite attachments in which geographically dispersed data centers are hooked up via some form of a WAN connection. The problems associated with such sites are more intricate, and we don't have room to discuss it in this book.

Figure 16-8 shows the usual topology, but with hosts server101, server201, and server102 dual attached to both leaf01 and leaf02. Even though the common case is where all hosts are dual attached, I've come across deployments in which some nodes are dual-attached and some are singly attached. This happens when the deployment is hosting multiple workloads, such as a modern Hadoop cluster and a more traditional application or even OpenStack.

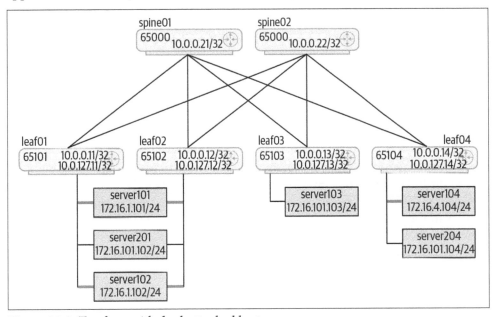

Figure 16-8. Topology with dual-attached hosts

The following subsections address the problems of dual-connected hosts and how to address them. Following are the problems to be addressed:

- How are the dual-attached hosts connected to the switches?

- How is the dual-attached node seen by the other VTEPs? In other words, how do VTEPs leaf03 and leaf04 in Figure 16-8 view server101, server201, and server102?

- What happens when some of the hosts lose their connection to one of the switches? For example, what happens if server102 loses its link to leaf01?

- How does packet delivery work for a multidestination frame, such as a BUM packet? Do the dual-attached servers get duplicates because leaf01 and leaf02 each deliver a copy? Duplicates can confuse certain applications if they're not running over a reliable stream protocol such as TCP.

Host-Switch Interconnect Model

In the most common deployment, the host treats the two links as being in a bond (aka link aggregation). The two main advantages of a bond are that both links are usable at the same time and that as a bond, the link needs a single IP address instead of two. Using both links at the same time is also referred to as active–active mode.

A bond is created using the standard LACP. LACP ensures that the host is properly connected to the proper devices. For example, if server102 accidentally hooks up a cable to leaf03 instead of leaf02, this is caught by LACP because server102 will discover that it is not communicating with the same entity on both the links. LACP supports bonding only if the links are connected to the same pair of devices on all links. LACP also catches problems such as unidirectional link failures.

Some host vendors charge extra for enabling LACP, so many switch implementations support the notion of a static bond in which the administrator configures the two ends of the link as being in a bond without using LACP.

Some customers use the dual-switch interconnect only to handle failure. In this case, one of the links is in standby mode. It comes alive only when the active link dies. This is called NIC teaming or active–standby mode. This mode makes some assumptions similar to the bond mode. It assumes that when the standby link comes alive, it has the same IP address as the recently deceased link. It also assumes that the default gateway is the same on this link as on the other link.

We discuss these two cases in which the links are bonded (with or without LACP) for the rest of this discussion because that is the most common deployment.

VXLAN Model for Dual-Attached Hosts

Most packet-switching silicon implementations as of this writing assume that a MAC address is behind a single VTEP. In Figure 16-8, there are two different switches associated with each of the dual-attached hosts. So how do the remote VTEPs (leaf03 and leaf04 in the figure) handle this case?

There are two possibilities: each VTEP has its own IP address or both VTEPs share a common IP address. The shared VTEP IP address is the most common deployment. The main reason for this is that the common implementation of a MAC forwarding table supports only a single port of exit. In traditional bridging, there was never a reason for a MAC address to have multiple ports of exit. STP explicitly eliminates multiple paths to eliminate loops. Bonds are represented as a single logical port to avoid this problem; additional logic after the logical port selection allowed the implementations to pick a single outgoing physical port to transmit the packet.

As of this writing, the Linux kernel and most switching silicon that I'm aware of support the single common IP address model. So even if you have a vendor that supports the alternate model, using the common IP address model ensures interoperability with other vendors.

Following this model, in the example topology of Figure 16-8, leaf01 and leaf02 will both transmit packets for all dual-attached hosts with a source VTEP IP address that is common to them both. Most implementations verify that the switches have the same common IP address configured via a protocol such as the Multichassis Link Aggregation (MLAG), described shortly. I'm not aware of any implementation that uses the information from the EVPN messages to verify the common IP address. The network administrator must also ensure that this common IP address is advertised via BGP; otherwise, the other VTEPs will not know how to reach this VTEP IP address.

Switch Peering Options

Before we proceed to look at the other problems and how they are handled, we must examine the model adopted by the pair of switches to which the dual-attached hosts are connected. There are essentially two answers: MLAG and EVPN.

MLAG

The standard LACP does not support creating a bond when the links are split at one end across multiple devices. In other words, the standard does not support a model where dual-attached hosts connect to two different switches (leaf01 and leaf02). Therefore, every networking vendor has their own proprietary solution to provide that illusion. The generic name for this solution is MLAG, but each vendor has a brand name for their solution, and the specific implementation and deployment details vary across implementations. For example, Cumulus and Arista require a separate peer link (shown as a dotted line between L1 and L2) to be present between the MLAG pair of switches. Cisco's NX-OS does not require the peer link to be present.

A entire book can be written about MLAG. Here, we skip all the details and focus on how it solves the problems at hand in the next few sections.

EVPN support for multihoming

EVPN supports dual-attached devices natively. It calls them *multihomed* nodes. The main details of this solution are described in section 8 of RFC 7432 (*https://oreil.ly/RdzVG*) and section 8 of RFC 8365 (*https://oreil.ly/bB86m*). Primarily, EVPN uses RT-1 and RT-4 message types to handle multihomed nodes. RT-1 tells the network which switches are attached to which common devices or Ethernet segments. An Ethernet segment in a data center is defined as either the bridged network to which a VTEP is connected or a bonded link. When connected to a bond, the RT-1 advertisement carries the LACP identifier of the remote node (i.e., the host in our case) as the Ethernet segment ID (ESI). When other VTEPs receive the BGP updates of this RT-1 advertisement, they can determine which of their peers are attached to the same host.

RT-4 elects one of the peers as the designated forwarder for multidestination frames. The RT-4 advertisement carries the mapping of the Ethernet segment to the router servicing the segment. From all the advertisements received for an Ethernet segment, each VTEP selects the segment with the lowest VTEP IP address as the designated forwarder for a virtual network. In this case, a common VTEP IP address is not required across the two peers.

Let's break this down using our sample topology. First, the standard allows leaf01 to be the designated forwarder for one set of nodes—say server101 and server201—and leaf02 to be the designated forwarder for another set of nodes—say server102. In Figure 16-8, each host carries only a single VLAN. But if the hosts supported multiple VLANs, the standard further allows leaf01 to be the designated forwarder for a node —say server101—for one set of VLANs, and leaf02 as the designated forwarder for that node for a different set of VLANs.

Handling Link Failures

What happens if one of the hosts—for example, server102 in Figure 16-8—loses a link to leaf01? The answer to this is also implementation specific. Even if the solution involves MLAG, two different implementations might do different things.

In the case of MLAG, using the peer link to reach the host via the other switch is the most common implementation. In our example, both leaf01 and leaf02 advertise reachability to server102 via a common VTEP IP. The underlay multipaths traffic addressed to the common VTEP IP between leaf01 and leaf02. When leaf01 loses its connectivity to server102, it withdraws its advertisement of server102. However, because leaf02's advertisement is still valid, leaf03 and leaf04 see that MAC_{102} is still reachable via the common VTEP IP. So, a packet to server102 can still end up at leaf01, even though the link between them is down and leaf01 cannot deliver the packet directly. In such cases, leaf01 decapsulates the packet and uses the peer link to send the packet unencapsulated to leaf02, which then delivers the packet to server102.

Is it possible to avoid the use of the peer link by, for instance, readvertising the MAC address of server102 and indicate that it is singly attached to leaf02? After all, both leaf01 and leaf02 have unique IP addresses that belong only to them. Alas, most packet-switching silicon support only a single IP address as the source of a VXLAN VNI, even though a VNI can have both dual-attached and singly attached hosts. Thus, implementations cannot indicate that server102 uses leaf02's unique VTEP IP while server101 uses the common VTEP IP. So even if a dual-attached host has lost a link to one of the VTEP peers, its address is announced using the common VTEP IP address; the peer link is used to deliver the packet to this host.

Without a peer link, most implementations will reencapsulate and send the packet to the other switch. In our example, leaf01 decapsulates the VXLAN packet, adds a new VXLAN header with the destination IP of leaf02, and sends the packet.

In EVPN multihoming implementations, the switch that lost the connectivity to the host will also withdraw reachability to the ESI identified by the LACP of the host. This is done for both RT-1 and RT-4 routes. The other switch eventually receives these withdrawals. On receiving the RT-4 withdrawal, the remaining switch appoints itself the designated forwarder for server102. Receiving the RT-1 withdrawal tells the switch that the host is singly attached to it. The switch cannot attempt to forward the packet to its peer when it loses connectivity to the host. In our example, when leaf02 receives the withdrawal originated by leaf01, it knows that if it loses the link to server102, it cannot forward a packet to leaf01. However, reencapsulating a VXLAN packet without routing violates the split-horizon check. Thus, this model needs additional support from the underlying switching silicon.

Avoiding Duplicate Multidestination Frames

When the common VTEP IP model and ingress replication are used, only one of the pair of switches gets a packet. This is because the other VTEPs represent the pair with a single common VTEP IP address, and one is chosen at random to get an anycast packet. However, in the model without a shared common VTEP IP address, both switches will get a copy of multidestination frames (BUM packets, for example).

To ensure that only one of the pair sends a packet to the end station, the two nodes use the RT-4 message to pick only one of them to deliver a multidestination frame in a virtual network. However, control protocol updates take time, and during the process of electing a designated forwarder or during transitions, the host can either receive no multidestination frames or receive duplicates. There's nothing that can be done about it.

ARP/ND Suppression

ARP requests and gratuitous ARP (GARP) packets are BUM packets because these packets are sent to the broadcast address. In the sample topology, if server101 had ARP'd for server104's MAC address and obtained it, it seems unnecessary to have server201's ARP request for server104's MAC address behave the same way as server101's request. leaf01 can cache server104's ARP information and respond directly. This has the good effect of reducing BUM traffic in the network.

NDP is the equivalent of ARP for IPv6 addresses. As a result, ND would benefit from the same caching and response by leaf01. This function of caching a remote host's ARP/ND information and responding to ARP/ND requests for this information is ARP/ND suppression.

ARP/ND suppression uses RT-2 messages to convey the IP address associated with a MAC address in a virtual network. It is up to the implementation to decide whether it wants to send separate MAC and MAC/IP advertisements or use a single message for both. FRR uses a single message update model when ARP/ND suppression is enabled.

Just as the MAC forwarding table marks when entries are learned via a control protocol, entries in the ARP cache (or IP neighbor table in the Linux kernel) are marked as having been learned via a control protocol. The kernel does not attempt to run ARP refresh for such entries. The kernel also does not age out entries that have been marked as learned via a control protocol. The protocol is responsible for removing these entries when the remote entries, advertisements are withdrawn. FRR also removes them on graceful shutdown or on recovery from a crash.

This functionality must be enabled via configuration. Some implementations allow this configuration only if the VTEP is also the gateway router for that virtual network. Cisco's is an example of such an implementation. Linux (and hence Cumulus) allows you to configure this independently of whether the VTEP is the gateway router for that network.

ARP/ND suppression support is available in Linux kernels starting with version 4.18, thanks to the work done by Cumulus engineers.

A Little RT-2 Note

RT-2 is a tricky little route advertisement because it can be used in so many ways that people can become confused by it. I've provided this brief note in the hope that it reduces the confusion.

Figure 16-9 shows the message format of RT-2. This is defined in section 7.2 of RFC 7432, the base EVPN standard (*https://oreil.ly/qb2nm*). In the use case of the data center with VXLAN, the Ethernet Tag ID is ignored; that is, set to 0. The Ethernet Segment Identifier is useful when EVPN is also used for multihomed hosts (FRR does not support this in version 7.2).

When ARP/ND suppression or routing is disabled, only the RD, MAC address, and MPLS Label1 fields in the message are used. The MAC address length field is always set to six, the MAC address field carries the MAC address, and the MPLS Label 1 field carries the L2 VNI associated with the MAC address.

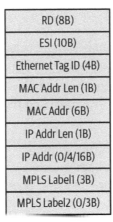

| RD (8B) |
| ESI (10B) |
| Ethernet Tag ID (4B) |
| MAC Addr Len (1B) |
| MAC Addr (6B) |
| IP Addr Len (1B) |
| IP Addr (0/4/16B) |
| MPLS Label1 (3B) |
| MPLS Label2 (0/3B) |

Figure 16-9. EVPN RT-2 message format

When ARP/ND or routing is enabled, the IP address associated with the {VNI, MAC} is also advertised. Implementations might choose to send two separate RT-2 advertisements, one for just the MAC and the other for the MAC/IP, or just a single MAC/IP advertisement. FRR sends a single MAC/IP advertisement. The IP address length is set to 4 for IPv4 and 16 if it's an IPv6 address. If a MAC address has both an IPv4 and an IPv6 address, two (or three) separate RT-2 advertisements are sent since RT-2 can hold only one IP address.

When only asymmetric routing is used, MPLS Label1 carries the L2 VNI associated with the MAC/IP binding, and MPLS Label2 is not used. When symmetric routing is used, MPLS Label2 field carries the L3 VNI.

EVPN and Routing

We already studied the packet flow in case of routing the overlay packets in "Illustrating VXLAN Bridging and Routing" on page 131. This section, like the one on bridging, focuses on the parts specific to EVPN. At the risk of repeating myself ad nauseam, when we talk about routing with EVPN, we're talking about routing the packet that is underneath the encapsulation—the original packet received by the VTEP.

Centralized Versus Distributed Routing

We discussed two possible options for routing the overlay packets in "Illustrating VXLAN Bridging and Routing" on page 131: centralized and distributed routing. When does deploying one make sense over the other? Distributed routing should be the preferred approach unless:

- You have a lot of routers that don't support RIOT and the cost of upgrading the boxes is prohibitive. Adding two or more newer routers that support RIOT and using distributed routing might be a more palatable solution.

- You need routing only when leaving the data center—for instance, for north-south traffic—so using the exit leaves as the routers makes centralized routing easy. This also preserves the recommended model of deploying services such as firewalls at exit leaves.

If you do choose to deploy centralized routing, you can choose from a few possible deployments. In the first method, both routers are active for all VNIs. In the second, each is active for one subset of the VNIs and is configured to be on standby for the other VNIs.

In the first method, when both are active for all VNIs, you must guard against the risk that any flooded packet results in duplicate routed packets. To understand this better, consider when server101 sends a packet to its first-hop router. If leaf01 does not know the router's MAC address, it will replicate the packet to all VTEPs interested in the red VNI (because server101 is in the red network). If two or more exit leaves are acting as the router, all of them receive a copy of this flooded packet, and they will all route the packet, resulting in duplicate packets. As explained earlier, this can cause trouble in some kinds of network traffic.

Using a model such as the VTEP anycast IP address with ingress replication can ensure that only one of the dual interfaces gets the packet. Alternatively, a protocol such as Virtual Router Redundancy Protocol (VRRP) can ensure that only one of them routes the packet for a network. A third way to ensure that only one of them routes a packet is to use the designated forwarder model described for bridging in "EVPN support for multihoming" on page 357.

My recommendation is to use the VTEP anycast IP model with ingress replication owing to its simplicity (no additional protocols and minimal configuration).

The main point to consider with distributed routing is to rethink the ways services such as firewalls and load balancers are deployed. In the centralized routing model, services were located at the border leaves. If these services are needed only for traffic in and out of the data center, deploying the services at the border leaves still works. But if the services are needed for traffic within the data center itself, the best way to deploy the services is on each host itself. Another way to address the services problem is via the use of VRFs, as described in "Services" on page 188.

Symmetric Versus Asymmetric Routing

"VXLAN and Routing: H1 to H6" on page 136 covered the different models of routing in EVPN: asymmetric and symmetric. The primary reason to choose the asymmetric routing model is if you have interoperability concerns. All the main vendors in the data center space support the symmetric model. Juniper and Cumulus also support the asymmetric routing model. If you're deploying centralized routing, asymmetric routing is the natural choice. If you advertise non-EVPN routes such as the default route or other non-MAC related routes, then symmetric routing is the obvious choice. I recommend choosing the symmetric model of routing unless you have specific reasons why you cannot use it.

Route Advertisements

An EVPN RT-2 advertisement contains the IP address associated with a {MAC, VNI} tuple. This information is used to populate the routing table. But there are cases for which we need a summarized route or a route to be advertised that has been learned as an IP route. Consider where the routing table needs to be populated with the default route that leads to the outside world. Typically, the exit leaves advertise this route. A new route type, RT-5, was introduced to advertise IP routes. IP routes are not advertised automatically; they must be configured. IP routes are always advertised with an L3 VNI. Every device maps the L3 VNI to a local VRF before populating the routing table.

We also discussed symmetric and asymmetric routing in "Illustrating VXLAN Bridging and Routing" on page 131. Asymmetric routing works just fine with RT-2 advertisements. Symmetric routing needs additional support.

There are three additional pieces of information required for symmetric routing: the VNI to use between the ingress and egress VTEPs, the next-hop IP address (which is the egress VTEP's IP address), and the router MAC address of the egress VTEP. These need to be conveyed in some BGP UPDATE message. The egress VTEP's IP address is always carried in the NEXTHOP attribute of the BGP advertisement. The RT-2 message has provisions allowing it to carry the other two pieces of information.

RT-2 supports carrying two VNIs (or Multiprotocol Label Switching [MPLS] labels in the original EVPN standard). With asymmetric routing, only one of the two VNI fields is used to announce the L2 VNI. With symmetric routing, both VNI fields are used, one for L2 VNI and the other for the transit or L3 VNI.

The route also needs to carry the egress VTEP's MAC address, because this address is used as the destination MAC address on the inner packet. This MAC address is carried as a new BGP Extended Community in the advertisement. This new extended community is called the Router MAC Extended Community.

The Use of VRFs

In EVPN, routing is assumed to occur within the context of a VRF. The underlay routing table is assumed to be in the default or global routing table, whereas the overlay routing table is assumed to be in a VRF-specific routing table. It is possible to have asymmetric routing (discussed in "Illustrating VXLAN Bridging and Routing" on page 131) work without the use of VRFs. But VRFs are necessary if the endpoints have to communicate to the external world, because RT-5 advertisements are involved. RT-5 advertisements always occur in the context of a VRF: the L3 VNI signaled in the advertisement. Thus, to preserve a uniform routing model, I strongly recommend always using VRFs with EVPN routing.

Deploying EVPN in Large Networks

As we've learned, except for RT-5, routes in an EVPN network are largely /32 routes. This is OK in typical two-tier Clos networks that scale to about 50,000 to 80,000 endpoints. (That number is more my comfort zone for a single-failure domain in enterprises than a hardware or software limitation; it is not vendor specific.) However, as networks become larger and we move into three-tier Clos networks, the lack of summarization begins to affect the deployment. This inability to summarize affects not just how big the forwarding tables become, but also the number of nodes to which ingress replication needs to replicate and the total number of VNIs in the system. All this negatively affects the robustness of the entire system. If a systemic failure can take down the entire network or render it less adaptable than you need it to be, you must reconsider the design. For these reasons, I don't think a two-tier Clos with more than 128 leaves can be robust. For bigger networks, I highly recommend a three-tier Clos design.

A three-tier Clos network that provides merely L3 connectivity cannot be directly adapted to an EVPN network. This is because of the answer to the question: Where do you summarize? We cannot summarize at the spine layer within each pod (see "Route Summarization in Clos Networks" on page 105). In a pure L3 Clos, each rack already summarizes all locally attached subnets, because a subnet can be attached only to a single leaf (or pair of leaves) and so the network can scale more effectively than with EVPN which advertises endpoint addresses (/32 or /128 routes). Making the super-spine the point of summarization defeats the primary design of a Clos network, which is to scale out the network by spreading the load to the edges, not suck it up into the center of the network. The scale and complexity of design and functionality of the super-spines becomes quite large. Furthermore, providing services such as firewalls for traffic in and out of pods becomes difficult in this design.

To preserve the efficient distribution of tasks in the network, I recommend adding pod exit leaves, using them as the points of summarization and as locations to hook up pod-level services such as firewalls. Each pod is now quite self-contained, as shown in Figure 16-10.

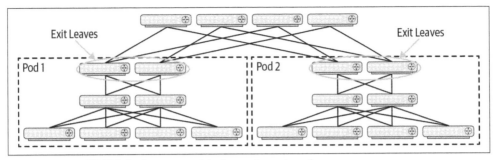

Figure 16-10. EVPN deployment with three-tier networks

Let me first say that if this looks to you like a four-tier Clos network, it is not. I've just switched the position of the exit leaves in the figure from being next to the other leaves to being on top, mostly to fit onto the screen.

In this network, the exit leaves primarily summarize the prefix routes specific to the pod, advertise it to the super-spines, and advertise a default route to the pod. The exit leaves receive prefix routes of the other pods from the super-spine.

How does this model handle the case where a VNI spans multiple pods? The exit leaves in a pod cannot summarize for those VNIs. Furthermore, BUM handling has to deal with sending packets across pods. This complicates the multicast processing even more for groups that are stretched across pods because these groups have to find a more optimal RP than the RP for groups restricted to a pod. Although solutions are always possible, my recommendation is to avoid stretched VNIs as much as possible due to the additional stresses they bring.

Summary

In this chapter, we covered the pieces important to deploy EVPN, as well as the control plane for network virtualization. This chapter, in combination with the packet forwarding described in "Illustrating VXLAN Bridging and Routing" on page 131, lays the groundwork for understanding the theory behind network virtualization deployment in the data center. In the next chapter, we discuss the actual configuration of EVPN.

## CHAPTER 17

Deploying Network Virtualization

The unavoidable price of reliability is simplicity.
—Tony Hoare

In this chapter, we explore administration of the different network virtualization solutions described in earlier chapters. Specifically, we examine the configuration of overlay virtual networks. EVPN, covered in Chapter 16, is assumed to be the control protocol, and VXLAN is the encapsulation protocol. Configuration of OSPF and BGP for VRF was covered in "Support for VRFs" on page 262 and "BGP and VRFs" on page 326, respectively.

The following key questions are addressed in this chapter:

- How do I configure EVPN bridging and routing in my network?/
- How do I configure the key routing protocols (eBGP, iBGP, and OSPF) for network virtualization?

The Configuration Scenarios

EVPN provides a few configuration choices, especially the choice of routing protocol in the underlay and the handling of multidestination frames. To this end, I cover the following three high-level configurations:

- Single eBGP session for underlay and overlay
- OSPF for underlay, iBGP for overlay with ingress replication
- OSPF for underlay, iBGP for overlay with routed multicast underlay

The configurations for the underlay have been laid out in the previous chapters, so I won't be discussing them further here, especially OSPF's. Besides this, we also have noncontrol protocol configuration such as creating VXLAN VNIs, mapping VNIs to VLANs, and so on. As per the recommendations I provided in Chapter 16, the configurations assume a distributed, symmetric routing model for EVPN. However, I will point out differences in configuration between symmetric and asymmetric routing, between centralized and distributed routing, and between routing and bridging. Because routed multicast underlay is not supported on native Linux yet (only on Cumulus Linux), I won't show its configuration in the device local configuration. The PIM-SM configuration is helpful for other reasons, and so I include it.

We use the topology shown in Figure 17-1 to write out the configurations. We also assume the use of MLAG to have the servers dual attached to the leaves. The exit leaves are shown here to provide input on how the connectivity to the external world looks in an EVPN network. We'll use unnumbered BGP and OSPF everywhere possible. The interfaces to the firewall and the edge router from the exit leaves are numbered interfaces because edge routers and firewalls most likely do not support unnumbered BGP.

The use of VRFs bears some mention here. All IP routes within EVPN are within the context of a VRF. All MAC addresses are within the context of a VNI. A set of VNIs is mapped to a VRF and the VRF is associated with a unique VNI. VRF is similar to a VLAN in this regard: it has only local significance, VLANs and VRFs are mapped to their own unique VNIs for global scope. The VRF is associated with an L3 VNI, and a VLAN is associated with an L2 VNI. The underlay operates in the default VRF.

The internal network is in the black VRF, called evpn-vrf. Connectivity to the external world is via the red VRF, called internet-vrf. Traffic has to pass through the firewall to go from one VRF to the other. The underlay is in the default VRF. The black VRF and default VRF look indistinguishable on a link. This is because the black VRF packets are VXLAN encapsulated, whereas the underlay packets are not.

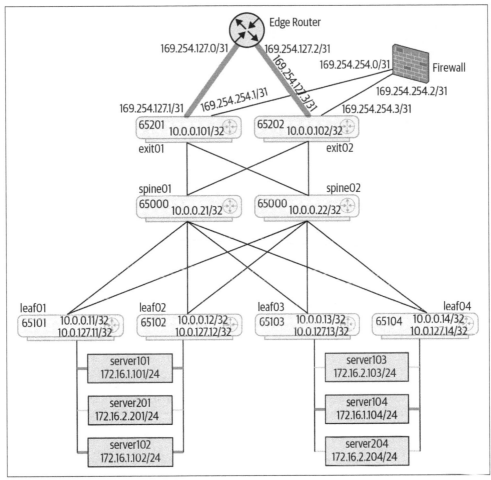

Figure 17-1. Topology used for EVPN configuration examples

Device-Local Configuration

Let's begin with the simplest of the lot: device-local configuration that is not specific to the routing protocol used. Using ifupdown2, for example, on a Debian-based distribution (such as Cumulus Linux and Ubuntu) results in the following snippet of configuration on leaf01:

```
auto all
iface lo inet loopback
  address 10.0.0.11/32                          ❶
  clagd-vxlan-anycast-ip 10.0.0.112             ❷
  vxlan-local-tunnelip 10.0.0.11                ❸

iface vni13                                     ❹
```

```
    mtu 9164                                                    ❺
    vxlan-id 13                                                 ❻
    bridge-access 13                                            ❼
    bridge-learning off                                         ❽

iface vni24                                                     ❹
    mtu 9164                                                    ❺
    vxlan-id 24                                                 ❻
    bridge-access 24                                            ❼
    bridge-learning off                                         ❽

iface vlan13                                                    ❾
    mtu 9164
    address 172.16.1.11/24                                      ❿
    address-virtual 44:39:39:ff:00:13 172.16.1.1/24            ⓫
    vlan-id 13                                                  ⓬
    vlan-raw-device bridge
    vrf evpn-vrf                                                ⓭

iface vlan24
    mtu 9164
    address 172.16.2.11/24                                 ❿
    address-virtual 44:39:39:ff:00:13 172.16.2.1/24       ⓫
    vlan-id 24                                             ⓬
    vlan-raw-device bridge                                 ⓭
    vrf evpn-vrf                                           ⓮

#
# This is the L3 VNI definition that we need for symmetric configuration.
# This is used to transport the EVPN-routed packet between the VTEPs.
#
iface vxlan4001                                                 ⓯
    vxlan-id 104001
    bridge-access 4001
#
iface vlan4001                                                  ⓰
    hwaddress 44:39:39:FF:40:94
    vlan-id 4001
    vlan-raw-device bridge
    vrf evpn-vrf
#
```

Following are some observations on this configuration that might not be obvious:

❶ If you define the IP address in ifupdown2, as done here, don't also define it in the FRR configuration.

❷ This configures the Cumulus-specific MLAG implementation, CLAG, by defining the shared VXLAN source tunnel's IP address. Other vendors will provide their own version of this configuration for their specific MLAG implementation. This is required because of the dual-attached servers.

❸   This specifies the local source tunnel IP address to be used when CLAG isn't operational. When CLAG is operational, the address specified in point 2 is used as the tunnel source IP address.

❹   Each VXLAN VNI is represented by a device in the Linux kernel. There is support for using a single device for all VNIs starting with Linux kernel version 4.14. But this model isn't supported by the rest of the ecosystem (no way to configure vlan-vni mapping, for example) and so I don't show it.

❺   VXLAN tunnel interfaces recommend using jumbo frames, so we set the MTU of the interface to 9164.

❻   This defines the VNI associated with this device.

❼   This maps the VNI to a local VLAN ID. In this case, the mapping is an identity function.

❽   We don't want to enable learning of remote MAC addresses because we have EVPN. So we disable learning on the VNIs.

❾   This defines the SVI for the VNIs—these are the VNIs for which the node supports routing.

❿   This is the unique IP address of this leaf on the specified VNI.

⓫   This is the secondary gateway IP address for the VNI. The address is shared across all the leaves that carry this VNI. Servers are configured to use this IP address as the default gateway address to allow a server to be attached to any rack and not have to change its default gateway configuration.

⓬   This indicates the VLAN for which this interface is the SVI.

⓭   Linux allows the presence of multiple 802.1Q bridges on the same device. An interface is assigned to only one of the bridges and so there is no ambiguity on the link about the use of a VLAN. For example, we saw in Chapter 7 how containers use this model of having multiple bridges. As a consequence, an SVI needs to be associated with a specific bridge. This line accomplishes that function.

⓮   This indicates the VRF that the SVI is a part of.

⓯   This is the L3 VNI used in symmetric routing.

⓰   This is merely the local instantiation of the L3 VNI.

The same configuration on an Arista looks as follows:

```
interface Loopback1
  ip address 10.0.0.112

interface vxlan1                                    ❶
  vxlan source-interface Loopback1
  vxlan-udp-port 4789
  vxlan vlan 13 vni 13
  vxlan vlan 24 vni 24
  vxlan vrf evpn-vrf vni 4001

interface vlan13
  mtu 9164
  vrf evpn-vrf
  ip address 172.16.1.1/24

interface vlan24
  mtu 9164
  vrf evpn-vrf
  ip address 172.16.2.1/24
```

Most of the configuration should be obvious as this looks quite a bit similar to the previous ifupdown2 variant. The only difference is in the VNI specification.

❶ Arista already follows a model of defining a single VXLAN device for all the VNIs, and therefore can use a single VXLAN device configuration to map the VLAN to the VNI and assign the VRF to an L3 VNI. As of this writing, Arista didn't support the use of a routed multicast underlay.

Single eBGP Session

We begin with the complete configurations for one of the leaves, one of the spines, and one of the exit leaves. Example 17-1 shows the configuration in FRR as in the rest of the book.

Example 17-1. Sample FRR configuration for symmetric routing with single eBGP session model

```
!
! ==========================
! Configuration for spine01
! ==========================
!
interface lo
  ip address 10.0.0.21/32
!
router bgp 65000
    bgp router-id 10.0.0.21
```

```
    bgp bestpath as-path multipath-relax
    neighbor peer-group ISL
    neighbor ISL remote-as external
    neighbor swp1 interface peer-group ISL
    neighbor swp2 interface peer-group ISL
    neighbor swp3 interface peer-group ISL
    neighbor swp4 interface peer-group ISL
    neighbor swp5 interface peer-group ISL
    neighbor swp6 interface peer-group ISL
    address-family ipv4 unicast
        neighbor ISL activate
        redistribute connected route-map LOOPBACKS
    address-family l2vpn evpn
        neighbor ISL activate                                      ❶
!
route-map LOOPBACKS permit 10
    match interface lo
!

!
! ========================
! Configuration for leaf01
! ========================
!
interface lo
    ip address 10.0.0.11/32
!
! This VRF definition is needed only for symmetric EVPN routing configuration
vrf evpn-vrf                                                       ❷
        vni 104001
!
router bgp 65011
    bgp router-id 10.0.0.11
    bgp bestpath as-path multipath-relax
    neighbor fabric peer-group
    neighbor fabric remote-as external
    neighbor swp1 interface peer-group fabric
    neighbor swp2 interface peer-group fabric
    address-family ipv4 unicast
        neighbor fabric activate
        redistribute connected route-map LOOPBACKS
    !
    address-family l2vpn evpn
        neighbor fabric activate
        advertise-all-vni                                          ❸
  advertise-svi-ip                                                 ❹
    !
!
route-map LOOPBACKS permit 10                                      ❺
    match interface lo
!
```

```
!
! ========================
! Configuration for exit01
! ========================
!
interface lo
  ip address 10.0.0.101/32
!
interface swp3
  ip address 169.254.127.1/31
!
interface swp4.2
  ip address 169.254.254.1/31
!
interface swp4.3
  ip address 169.254.254.3/31
!
interface swp4.4
  ip address 169.254.254.5/31
!
vrf evpn-vrf
   vni 104001
!
! default VRF peering with the underlay and the firewall
!
router bgp 65201                                                    ❻
    bgp router-id 10.0.0.101
    bgp bestpath as-path multipath-relax
    neighbor fabric peer-group
    neighbor fabric remote-as external
    ! These two are peering with the spine
    neighbor swp1 interface peer-group fabric
    neighbor swp2 interface peer-group fabric
    ! This is peering with the firewall to announce the underlay
    ! routes to the edge router (via the firewall) and receive the
    ! default route from the edge router (also via the firewall)
    neighbor swp4.2 interface remote-as external
    address-family ipv4 unicast
        neighbor fabric activate
  neighbor swp4.2 activate
        neighbor swp4.2 allowas-in 1                               ❼
        redistribute connected route-map LOOPBACKS
    !
    address-family l2vpn evpn
        neighbor fabric activate
        advertise-all-vni                                          ❸
    !
!
route-map LOOPBACKS permit 10
    match interface lo
!
! evpn vrf peering to announce default route to internal net
```

```
!
router bgp 65201 vrf evpn-vrf                                        ❽
    bgp router-id 10.0.0.101
    neighbor swp4.3 interface remote-as external
    address-family ipv4 unicast
        neighbor swp4.3 activate
        ! The following two network statements are for
        ! distributing the summarized route to the firewall
        aggregate-address 172.16.1.0/24 summary-only               ❾
        aggregate-address 172.16.2.0/24 summary-only
        neighbor swp4.3 allowas-in 1
    exit-address-family
    !
    ! This config ensures we advertise the default route
    ! as a type 5 route in EVPN in the main BGP instance.
    ! The firewall peering is to get the default route
    ! in the evpn-vrf from the internet-vrf. Firewall
    ! does not peer for l2vpn/evpn.
    !
    address-family l2vpn evpn                                       ❿
      advertise ipv4 unicast
!
! internet vrf peering to retrieve the default route from the
! internet facing router and give it to the firewall.
!
router bgp 65201 vrf internet-vrf                                   ⓫
    bgp router-id 10.0.0.101
    bgp bestpath as-path multipath-relax
    neighbor internet peer-group
    neighbor internet remote-as external
    neighbor swp4.4 interface peer-group internet
    neighbor swp3 interface peer-group internet
    address-family ipv4 unicast
        neighbor internet activate
        neighbor swp4.4 allowas-in 1
  neighbor swp3 remove-private-AS                                   ⓬
        redistribute connected route-map INTERNET
    !
!
route-map INTERNET permit 10
    match interface internet-vrf
!----
```

It's worth noting a few possibly obscure or not obvious points about this configuration:

❶ The spine activates the l2vpn evpn address family to signal to its peers that it can process EVPN routes. This is not an indication that the spine is participating in the overlay. This line is required on all nodes that exchange EVPN information.

❷ This VRF definition is what distinguishes symmetric routing configuration from asymmetric routing in the configuration. This definiton specifies the L3 VNI used by a VRF. Think of this mapping as the equivalent of the VLAN-VNI mapping. This configuration line is necessary for symmetric routing, as described in "Route Advertisements" on page 363.

❸ This single-line configuration on the leaf enables the advertisement of EVPN information, specifically RT-2 and RT-3 routes. This is present only on leaves (exit or normal).

❹ You need this line to allow the individual leaves to run *ping*, *traceroute*, and similar networking administration commands from the leaves on the evpn-vrf. Remember that in the distributed routing scenario, all leaves share a common gateway address for the locally attached VLANs. In this example, all leaves have 172.16.1.1/24 and 172.16.2.1/24 as the default gateway addresses for VLANs 13 and 24 that are local to all the leaves. In addition to this, each leaf has its own individual, unique IP address on those subnets. For example, leaf01 has 172.16.1.11, leaf02 has 172.16.1.12, and so on in VLAN 13. It is this unique IP address and its MAC address that are advertised via this line of the configuration. The common IP address across all leaves is not advertised.

❺ Unlike the simple routed Clos network, there is no server subnet to advertise via redistribute connected because the subnet route is no longer localized to a single rack/leaf. Individual /32 routes for the server subnets are advertised as RT-2 EVPN routes.

❻ This is the first of the three BGP sections on the exit leaves. This section deals with the underlay and the receiving of EVPN routes from the rest of the leaves. It also peers with the firewall to ensure that the underlay gets the default route. If the underlay is to be completely isolated from the edge router, you can do so by eliminating the peering with the firewall and/or by adding the appropriate rules in the firewall.

❼ This is a new configuration line, discussed later in this chapter. But one additional point to note is the use of the interface name even when the device is assigned an IP address and is peering potentially with a neighbor that doesn't support unnumbered BGP. FRR has the smarts to look at the interface IP address and, if the address belongs to subnet /31 or /30, know the peer's IP address. This is because both the /30 and /31 subnets have only two usable endpoint IP addresses, so if you know one of them, you automatically know the other. For example, 169.254.254.0/31 has the usable addresses: 169.254.0.0 and 169.254.0.1.

❽ This VRF configuration on the exit leaf is required to advertise the default route in the evpn-vrf VRF. The default route is learned from the internet via the firewall.

❾ This line instructs BGP to announce only the summarized route 172.16.1.0/24, and do so only if there's at least one route in that subnet. The external world doesn't need to know how to reach each of the specific hosts. Because exit leaves are leaves, they can summarize routes without a problem, as discussed in "Route Summarization in Clos Networks" on page 105. Lines like this still contain specific IP addresses, but that is necessary because such information is part of a policy and not easy to automatically determine. Furthermore, it is not a big administration burden because the lines are used only on the exit leaves. As an additional aid to automation, these lines are common across all the exit leaves.

❿ This advertises the default route as an RT-5 EVPN route. There is no activate statement in this section because there are no neighbors with whom EVPN routes are to be exchanged in this VRF. Remember, the RT-5 route is announced in the underlay BGP session. In my opinion, this is an example of a configuration that hints at the implementation (and is derived from it) instead of being constructed from the user perspective.

⓫ This is the VRF configuration to interface with the edge router in the internet-vrf for connectivity to the outside world. The internet-vrf has no EVPN configuration, so there is no need to define an L3 VNI for the internet-vrf like we do for evpn-vrf in the second bullet earlier.

⓬ This configuration strips off all private ASNs before advertising the routes to the edge router.

When VXLAN is the virtual network overlay, BGP doesn't require any per-VRF peering, because the VNI in the packet encodes this information. On the exit leaves, however, the peering between the exit leaves and the edge router, as well as the peering between the exit leaves and the firewall, are not VXLAN encapsulated, but use the hop-by-hop VRF model. The ingress interface defines the VRF of the packet. Therefore, BGP peering is VRF specific on the exit leaves. The BGP configuration for a hop-by-hop VRF model was described in "BGP and VRFs" on page 326.

Asymmetric routing configuration recently added support for the use of an L3 VNI to allow distribution of IP prefixes, such as default routes. If you want only EVPN bridging on the leaves, the configuration looks the same as the one shown, but without defining an SVI for the subnets of the VNIs on the leaves and the definition of the VRF-VNI mapping. Also, advertise-svi-ip also has no place when all you need is EVPN bridging. If you use centralized routing with the exit leaves acting as the routers, in conjunction with only EVPN bridging in the leaves, exit01's configuration looks as shown in Example 17-2.

Example 17-2. exit01's FRR configuration for centralized routing

```
router bgp 65201
    bgp router-id 10.0.0.101
    bgp bestpath as-path multipath-relax
    neighbor fabric peer-group
    neighbor fabric remote-as external
    neighbor swp1 interface peer-group fabric
    neighbor swp2 interface peer-group fabric
    ! This is peering with the firewall to announce the underlay
    ! routes to the edge router (via the firewall) and receive the
    ! default route from the edge router (also via the firewall)
    neighbor swp4.2 remote-as external
    address-family ipv4 unicast
        neighbor fabric activate
        neighbor swp4.2 allowas-in 1
        redistribute connected route-map LOOPBACKS
    !
    address-family l2vpn evpn
        neighbor fabric activate
        advertise-all-vni
        advertise-default-gw                                        ❶
    !

!
route-map LOOPBACKS permit 10
    match interface lo
!
! evpn vrf peering to steer internal traffic through firewall
! for external connectivity
!
router bgp 65201 vrf evpn-vrf                                       ❷
    bgp router-id 10.0.0.101
    neighbor swp4.3 remote-as external
    address-family ipv4 unicast
        neighbor swp4.3 activate
        ! The following two network statements are for
        ! distributing the summarized route to the firewall
        aggregate-address 172.16.1.0/24 summary-only
        aggregate-address 172.16.2.0/24 summary-only
        neighbor swp4.3 allowas-in 1
    exit-address-family

router bgp 65201 vrf internet-vrf
    bgp router-id 10.0.0.101
    bgp bestpath as-path multipath-relax
    neighbor internet peer-group
    neighbor internet remote-as external
```

```
    neighbor swp3 interface peer-group internet
    neighbor swp4.4 interface peer-group internet
    address-family ipv4 unicast
        neighbor internet activate
        neighbor swp4.4 allowas-in 1
        redistribute connected route-map INTERNET
!
route-map INTERNET permit 10
    match interface internet-vrf
!
```

Here are the things to note in this configuration:

❶ This line causes the default router MAC to be advertised to the leaves via an RT-2 route. This MAC route carries the Router MAC Extended Community, discussed in "Route Advertisements" on page 363.

❷ Because routing takes place only at the exit leaves, there is no need to announce any EVPN routes learned from the evpn-vrf via the firewall to the internal network. Therefore, there is no L2 VPN/evpn address-family configuration in this peering session.

Reason for allowas-in 1

Let's talk about why we need the new BGP option, allowas-in 1. Recall that there are multiple connections between the firewall and an exit leaf, one in each VRF. However, the firewall itself is VRF-unaware and merely sees multiple BGP sessions. When the firewall reflects the routes learned from a neighbor in one VRF to the neighbor in the other VRF, the exit leaf's BGP rejects these routes due to BGP's ASPATH loop detection. To understand this better, see Figure 17-2.

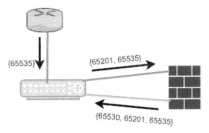

Figure 17-2. Illustrating the AS_PATH loop with VRFs

The arrows show the AS_PATH on a route that is advertised first by the edge router, received by the exit leaf in the internet-vrf. This AS_PATH is then passed to the firewall in the internet-vrf and received back in the evpn-vrf. As shown, the AS_PATH

---

starts off with just the edge router's ASN, 65535. When the router returns to the exit leaf from the firewall in the evpn-vrf, the ASN of the exit leaf, 65201, is already present in the AS_PATH. exit01 will therefore reject this because it detects a loop. If you enable debugging on exit01, you'll see a message like this in the logs:

```
2018-04-13T06:19:04.101100+00:00 exit01 bgpd[4112]: 169.254.253.0
rcvd UPDATE about 0.0.0.0/0 -- DENIED due to: as-path contains our own AS;
2018-04-13T06:19:04.101380+00:00 exit01 bgpd[4112]: 169.254.253.0
rcvd UPDATE w/ attr: , origin ?, mp_nexthop
fe80::4638:39ff:fe00:4a(fe80::4638:39ff:fe00:4a)(fe80::4638:39ff:fe00:4a),
path 65530 65201 65535
```

To avoid this route being dropped, add the option `allowas-in 1`. This option tells BGP to ignore a single occurrence of its own ASN in the ASPATH loop detection. Because we want this specific configuration only with the firewall peering, we use this specifically only with the firewall sessions and not against the peer group as a whole.

An alternative solution is discussed in "allowas-in Versus Separate ASN" on page 385.

You might observe that the route going on to the spine and the leaves will contain the AS_PATH {65201, 65530, 65201, 65535}. Why won't the spines and the leaves reject this route, when they see the loop? It's because BGP's AS_PATH loop check tests to see only whether the receiving BGP router's ASN is already present in the AS_PATH. It doesn't attempt to check for duplicates for other ASNs.

OSPF Underlay, iBGP Overlay

For this case, we use the OSPF unnumbered configuration for the underlay described in Chapter 13, Example 13-3. The main difference from that configuration is that we don't advertise the server subnet addresses in OSPF, as we did in the case of a pure underlay. We advertise only the loopback IP addresses. This includes the VTEP IP address. Some routing suites assign the VTEP IP address to a different device than the loopback, in which case you must ensure that OSPF advertises reachability to this IP address as well.

Example 17-3 shows iBGP configuration on leaf01 and spine01.

Example 17-3. FRR configuration for leaf01 and spine01 with iBGP

```
!
! =========================
! Configuration for spine01
! =========================
!
interface lo
  ip ospf area 0
  ip address 10.0.0.21/32
!
```

```
interface swp1
  ip ospf network point-to-point
  ip ospf area 0
  ip address 10.0.0.21/32
!
interface swp2
  ip ospf network point-to-point
  ip ospf area 0
  ip address 10.0.0.21/32
!
interface swp3
  ip ospf network point-to-point
  ip ospf area 0
  ip address 10.0.0.21/32
!
interface swp4
  ip ospf network point-to-point
  ip ospf area 0
  ip address 10.0.0.21/32
!
interface swp5
  ip ospf network point-to-point
  ip ospf area 0
  ip address 10.0.0.21/32
!
interface swp6
  ip ospf network point-to-point
  ip ospf area 0
  ip address 10.0.0.21/32
!
router ospf
  ospf router-id 10.0.0.21
  passive-interface lo
!
router bgp 65000
  bgp router-id 10.0.0.21
  bgp bestpath as-path multipath-relax
  neighbor RR peer-group
  neighbor RR remote-as internal                          ❶
  neighbor RR advertisement-interval 0
  neighbor RR timers 3 10
  neighbor RR timers connect 5
  neighbor swp1 interface peer-group RR
  neighbor swp2 interface peer-group RR
  neighbor swp3 interface peer-group RR
  neighbor swp4 interface peer-group RR
  neighbor swp5 interface peer-group RR
  neighbor swp6 interface peer-group RR
!
  address-family ipv4 unicast
   neighbor RR route-reflector-client                     ❷
   neighbor RR activate
```

```
  maximum-paths ibgp 16                                    ❸
  exit-address-family
!
  address-family l2vpn evpn
   neighbor RR route-reflector-client                      ❷
   neighbor RR activate
  exit-address-family
!

!
! =======================
! Configuration for leaf01
! =======================
!
interface lo
  ip ospf area 0
  ip address 10.0.0.11/32
!
interface swp1
  ip ospf network point-to-point
  ip ospf area 0
  ip address 10.0.0.11/32
!
interface swp2
  ip ospf network point-to-point
  ip ospf area 0
  ip address 10.0.0.11/32
!
vrf evpn-vrf
  vni 104001
!
router ospf
  ospf router-id 10.0.0.11
  passive-interface lo
!
router bgp 65000
  bgp router-id 10.0.0.11
  neighbor RR peer-group
  neighbor RR remote-as internal                           ❶
  neighbor RR advertisement-interval 0
  neighbor RR timers 3 10
  neighbor RR timers connect 5
  neighbor swp1 interface peer-group RR
  neighbor swp2 interface peer-group RR
!
  address-family l2vpn evpn
    neighbor RR activate
    advertise-all-vni
    advertise-svi-ip
  exit-address-family
!
```

```
!
! =========================
! Configuration for exit01
! =========================
!
interface lo
  ip ospf area 0
  ip address 10.0.0.101/32
!
interface swp1
  ip ospf network point-to-point
  ip ospf area 0
  ip address 10.0.0.101/32
!
interface swp2
  ip ospf network point-to-point
  ip ospf area 0
  ip address 10.0.0.101/32
!
interface swp3
  ip ospf network point-to-point
  ip ospf area 0
  ip address 10.0.0.101/32
!
interface swp3
  ip address 169.254.127.1/31
!
interface swp4.2
  ip address 169.254.254.1/31
!
interface swp4.3
  ip address 169.254.254.3/31
!
interface swp4.4
  ip address 169.254.254.5/31
!
interface vrf evpn-vrf
 vni 104001
!
router ospf
  ospf router-id 10.0.0.101
  passive-interface lo

router bgp 65000
 bgp router-id 10.0.0.101
 neighbor swp4.2 interface remote-as internal
 neighbor RR peer-group
 neighbor RR remote-as internal
 neighbor RR advertisement-interval 0
 neighbor RR timers 3 10
 neighbor RR timers connect 5
 neighbor swp1 interface peer-group RR
```

```
  neighbor swp2 interface peer-group RR
  !
  address-family ipv4 unicast
    redistribute ospf                                        ❹
    maximum-paths ibgp 16
  exit-address-family
  address-family l2vpn evpn
   neighbor RR activate
   advertise-all-vni
  exit-address-family
 !
 router bgp 65000 vrf evpn-vrf
  bgp router-id 10.0.0.101
  neighbor swp4.3 interface remote-as external
  !
  address-family ipv4 unicast
   aggregate-address 172.16.1.0/24 summary-only
   aggregate-address 172.16.2.0/24 summary-only
  exit-address-family
  !
  address-family l2vpn evpn
   advertise ipv4 unicast
  exit-address-family
 !
 router bgp 65001 vrf internet-vrf                           ❺
  bgp router-id 10.0.0.101
  neighbor swp4.4 interface remote-as external
  neighbor swp3 interface remote-as external
 !
```

A key point to note is the number of iBGP parameters that need to be tuned from their default values. That said, here are the main differences in the iBGP configuration compared to the eBGP version:

❶ This configuration indicates this is an iBGP peering via remote-as internal.

❷ This configures the spine as an iBGP route reflector. Without this knob, no EVPN routes will be distributed to the leaves.

❸ This is needed to enable ECMP with iBGP. This is only needed for the non-EVPN address family. EVPN doesn't support ECMP, because MAC tables don't support ECMP.

❹ Because all the underlay routes are learned via OSPF, you must enable redistribution of the OSPF routes into iBGP in order for the edge router to see these routes. This in turn allows the leaves and spines in the underlay to access the internet. I've used this line to point out what needs to be done if you want the leaves to communicate with the edge router. However, a more secure configuration prevents access from individual leaves and spines to the external world. You can choose to keep them off the internet either by blocking that subnet from being advertised to the external world at the edge router, or by omitting this redistribution knob in your configuration.

❺ We use a different ASN on the internet-vrf to avoid the problem that was addressed by "Reason for allowas-in 1" on page 379. We discuss this further in the following section.

Because OSPF is used to advertise reachability to the underlay, including VTEPs, we don't advertise them via iBGP again.

The exit leaves also use OSPF to communicate reachability inside the data center for the underlay, and iBGP for the EVPN information. The exit leaves use the same configuration in this section as the edge router and firewall.

allowas-in Versus Separate ASN

Unlike the eBGP configuraiton, the iBGP configuration didn't use `allowas-in 1` to ensure that BGP will accept routes that switch VRFs as they pass through the firewall. To understand why, recall how the AS_PATH loop detection works, as described in "Reason for allowas-in 1" on page 379. Every BGP router receiving a route advertisement will check to ensure that its own ASN isn't already present in the AS_PATH. When using eBGP, the exit leaves have a different ASN than the spines and normal leaves. Therefore, only the exit leaves need to add the `allowas-in 1` knob. But when using iBGP, the spines and leaves have the same ASN as the exit leaves. Therefore, we need to introduce the `allowas-in 1` knob on those nodes as well. This is problematic because we might end up accepting a genuinely looped route. Doing it just at the exit leaves led to a very specific, controlled use of `allowas-in`. With iBGP, it must be configured everywhere, with negative impacts. To avoid this, we adopted a different technique.

FRR (and some other popular routing stacks) support the use of a different ASN for a specific BGP VRF session. Taking advantage of that, we use a different ASN, 65001, on the exit leaves. This enables us to avoid the AS_PATH loop problem. The AS_PATH of the default route on reception by, say, exit01 from the firewall in the evpn-vrf will be {65530, 65001, 65535}. This model changes the configuration only on the exit leaves. Plus it helps preserve a clean AS_PATH, which is useful for troubleshooting.

How about using this option in the eBGP case, avoiding the use of `allowas-in 1` even in that case? You can do that too.

PIM/MSDP Configuration

Let's now look at the configuration when we enable routed multicast underlay to handle the BUM packets. As discussed in "EVPN Bridging with Routed Multicast Underlay" on page 349, we use PIM-SM as the multicast routing protocol with anycast RP. MSDP is the protocol used to synchronize multicast RP routing state between the spines.

Example 17-4. FRR sample configuration for EVPN with PIM/MSDP

```
!
! =========================
! Configuration for spine01
! =========================
!
interface lo
  ip ospf area 0
  ip address 10.0.0.21/32
  ip address 10.0.10.1/32                              ❶
  ip pim                                               ❷
!
interface swp1
  ip ospf network point-to-point
  ip ospf area 0
  ip pim
!
interface swp2
  ip ospf network point-to-point
  ip ospf area 0
  ip pim
!
interface swp3
  ip ospf network point-to-point
  ip ospf area 0
  ip pim
!
interface swp4
  ip ospf network point-to-point
  ip ospf area 0
  ip pim
!
interface swp5
  ip ospf network point-to-point
  ip ospf area 0
  ip pim
!
interface swp6
  ip ospf network point-to-point
  ip ospf area 0
  ip pim
```

```
!
router ospf
  ospf router-id 10.0.0.21
  passive-interface lo
!
router bgp 65000
  bgp router-id 10.0.0.21
  bgp bestpath as-path multipath-relax
  neighbor RR peer-group
  neighbor RR remote-as internal
  neighbor RR advertisement-interval 0
  neighbor RR timers 3 10
  neighbor RR timers connect 5
  neighbor swp1 interface peer-group RR
  neighbor swp2 interface peer-group RR
  neighbor swp3 interface peer-group RR
  neighbor swp4 interface peer-group RR
  neighbor swp5 interface peer-group RR
  neighbor swp6 interface peer-group RR
!
  address-family ipv4 unicast
   neighbor RR route-reflector-client
   neighbor RR activate
   maximum-paths ibgp 16
  exit-address-family
!
  address-family l2vpn evpn
   neighbor RR route-reflector-client
   neighbor RR activate
  exit-address-family
!
ip msdp mesh-group evpn source 10.0.10.21              ❸
ip msdp mesh-group evpn member 10.0.10.22              ❹
ip pim rp 10.0.10.1 238.1.1.0/24                       ❺

!
! ========================
! Configuration for leaf01
! ========================
!
interface lo
  ip ospf area 0
  ip address 10.0.0.11/32
!
interface swp1
  ip ospf network point-to-point
  ip ospf area 0
  ip pim
!
interface swp2
  ip ospf network point-to-point
  ip ospf area 0
  ip pim
```

```
!
interface ipmr-lo                                                   ⑥
  ip pim
!
vrf evpn-vrf
  vni 104001
!
router ospf
  ospf router-id 10.0.0.11
  passive-interface lo
!
router bgp 65000
  bgp router-id 10.0.0.11
  neighbor RR peer-group
  neighbor RR remote-as internal
  neighbor RR advertisement-interval 0
  neighbor RR timers 3 10
  neighbor RR timers connect 5
  neighbor swp1 interface peer-group RR
  neighbor swp2 interface peer-group RR
!
  address-family l2vpn evpn
    neighbor RR activate
    advertise-all-vni
  exit-address-family
!
ip pim rp 10.0.10.1 239.1.1.0/24                                    ⑦
```

Following are some observations on this configuation:

❶ This is the address added as the anycast RP address. Both spine01 and spine02 share the same address.

❷ This advertises that the PIM protocol needs to run on this interface. As described in Chapter 8, this starts sending PIM Hellos on the interface.

❸ This line and the next one identify the members of the MSDP mesh group. As described in Chapter 8, MSDP runs a full-mesh group between all the members; in other words, every member has a connection to every other member in the group. This line tells MSDP that this address is this node.

❹ This line identifies the other members of the MSDP group. In this case, it's only spine02.

❺ This line identifies the PIM-SM RP address for the specified multicast group(s). The multicast group specification can be a subnet too. Thus, 238.1.1.0/24 has 254 possible multicast groups.

❻ `ipmr-lo` is an automatically added device in the Cumulus implementation that identifies a VXLAN tunnel endpoint for multicast routing.

❼ This line identifies the RP for the specified multicast groups.

Exit leaves have a configuration for PIM/MSDP similar to leaf01.

EVPN on the Host

A very small band of network operators are deploying EVPN on the host. The servers themselves (or the hypervisors) are the VTEPs. The rest of the network sees only VXLAN-encapsulated packets. They function as a pure L3 underlay. This mimics the model of network virtualization that cloud service providers use. But cloud service providers might use other tunneling protocols than VXLAN. Using EVPN on the host is an advanced art, and I do not recommend its use unless you're comfortable with installing nondistribution-default kernels, packages, and writing some scripts and programs.

The simplest way to deploy this model is to use iBGP with other centrally located servers as the route reflector servers. The hosts do not peer with the routers in the Clos topology at all. They function as regular dumb hosts. This way, the reduction in network state is quite significant, because the network maintains state only about the underlay.

To ensure that you do not suffer from poor performance due to VXLAN encapsulation, ensure you buy NICs that can provide TCP/UDP offloads on VXLAN-encapsulated packets.

Best Practices

We end this chapter with some best practice recommendations in deploying network virtualization and EVPN in the data center:

- Keep your EVPN configuration as simple as possible. More than any other feature, EVPN has the potential to affect the KISS (keep it simple, stupid) principle of cloud native data center networking. Eschew adding features and complexity pushed by vendors.
- Use a distributed, symmetric routing model, unless you can't.
- One way to keep the configuration simple is to use the single eBGP model first implemented by FRR. This has the fewest moving parts and the simplest of the configurations.
- Avoid routed multicast underlay if you can.

- Consider the use of a different ASN number for peering with the firewall over the internet-vrf instead of allowas-in.

- If you choose to deploy EVPN on the host, ensure that you do not have any BUM packets.

Summary

In this chapter we examined how to configure EVPN in the context of the data center. If there is one takeaway and one alone, it is that the elegance of the cloud native data center has the potential to be submerged in the deluge of complexity that EVPN can drag in. It is up to the network operator to be judicious and minimalistic in the design ethos to ensure that the hounds of complexity and vendor fervor do not slip past the gates.

## CHAPTER 18

Validating Network Configuration

Computers are good at following instructions, but not at reading your mind.
—Donald Knuth

After configuring the network, ensuring that it's working as expected is the next critical step. As discussed in Chapter 10, network automation has unfortunately not progressed much beyond configuration. Old-world tools that rely on Simple Network Management Protocol (SNMP) suffer from critical limitations, especially in the context of the data center. Non-SNMP tools that gather, integrate, and present a unified view of the network are still largely missing, especially in a nonvendor-specific way and certainly not in open source. Although mainstream network operators have made some progress in their journey away from SNMP, the journey has not made much headway, even as much as configuration has.

This chapter deals with providing some ammunition to network operators to automate the validation of their network. It answers questions about how to validate the following:

- Network cabling
- Interface configuration
- Routing configuration
- Network virtualization
- Application connectivity

The lists of questions in this chapter are neither exhaustive or authoritative. Exhaustively listing every question and the ways to obtain the answer is an entire book by itself. Similarly, the way to obtain these answers is not authoritative, because the command syntax and the display can change over time.

Some Notes About the Code

I've relied on JSON outputs from FRR in the Ansible playbooks. Although the JSON outputs vary across the boxes, a similar methodology described in this chapter can be applied for those other boxes, as well. Furthermore, the Ansible playbooks I show you are illustrative and good starting points, not deployment-ready code. All of the playbooks are available in the GitHub repository associated with this book.

Instead of requisitioning a real-world network, I use Vagrant boxes from Cumulus, Ubuntu, and Arista to construct and test networks. Vagrant is a fantastic tool and it is open source. But most traditional network operators do not make their operating systems available via Vagrant. Providing administrative tooling features is a critical part of the cloud native data center ethos.

For FRR, I've relied on an upcoming release (v7.2, release in Oct 2019) to demonstrate some of the commands because of limitations in the current release (v7.1, as of this writing).

FRR's CLI is called *vtysh*. It has a modal interface that network operators should find comfortable; for example:

```
$ sudo vtysh

Hello, this is FRRouting (version 7.2-dev).
Copyright 1996-2005 Kunihiro Ishiguro, et al.

leaf01# conf t
leaf01(config)# router bgp 65010
leaf01(config)# neighbor swp1 interface remote-as external
leaf01(config)# end
leaf01# show ip bgp summary
```

You can also run it via the Bash shell by supplying one or more commands as part of invoking *vtysh* itself. Here's how to execute the same two commands from the previous example, but via Bash:

```
$ sudo vtysh -c "conf" -c "router bgp 65010" \
            -c "neighbor swp1 interface remote-as external"
$ sudo vtysh -c "show ip bgp summary"
```

I use *vtysh* both ways in this chapter. How do you know whether I'm in *vtysh* or the Bash shell? If the command prompt is "$" then it's Bash, and if it's a "<hostname>#", such as "leaf01#", the command is executed inside *vtysh*.

Many of the display outputs exceed 80 characters in column width. To make the displays look readable and fit into the 72 to 75 character limit imposed by the book format, I snip the columns I consider irrelevant to the discussion at hand. I show this by

---

adding "…" in the column display. Further, I snip verbose outputs that span several lines in a similar fashion. In this second case, I show the trimming via "…output snipped for brevity."

Validating the Network State

There are open source tools such as Batfish (*https://www.batfish.org*) that help analyze the configuration to assist in validating the configuration even before it has been deployed. I don't cover Batfish or tools like it in this book, because that would greatly add to the book's length. Instead, I focus on validating the state after deployment. If you use Vagrant to simulate your network, you can achieve a measure of validation before deploying the code in production.

All validation questions are more specific variants of the basic question, "Is my network working as I expect it to be?" For example, a slightly more specific version of this basic question is: "Is my routing protocol working as expected?" An even more specific question is: "Are all my BGP sessions in Established state?" A different strain of specific questions is illustrated by the question: "Is my network cabled properly?" A more specific version of that is: "Is each leaf connected exactly once to all the spines?" Some folks might view these questions in their complementary fashion as assertions ("Assert that each leaf is connected exactly once to all of the spines").

Validation questions can be translated into "how do I" questions. For example, "How do I find the list of established BGP sessions?", "How do I compare my current cabled state with expected cabled state?", and so on. Determining answers to "how" questions help find answers to the more complex "why" questions. After determining how to find answers to your "how" questions, you can string together a bunch of "how" questions to answer a "why" question. The "how" questions are also simpler to understand and approach than the "why" questions, which are much more network and context specific. Thus, we'll look at the "how" questions and their answers before we get to the "why" questions.

Validation is best done by verifying the network starting from the ground up. Isolating a problem close to the source is easier than doing so several layers up. If the network has been mis-cabled, checking for this explicitly and catching the problem at this level is far easier than trying to troubleshoot poor application performance. For this reason, we begin the "how" questions by examining physical cabling.

System Validation

At the most fundamental level, we need to validate that we're running the correct version of the network operating system (or network operating systems) and that the platform has the appropriate CPU, memory, disk, switching silicon, power, fan, and so on. We also need to verify that the various system services are running correctly.

Traditional networking platforms have usually shipped the network operating systems as a single monolithic blob. You can think of them as being akin to a Linux distribution, except that any update, whether it be to SSH, BGP, or a driver, is released as a complete monolithic blob. `show version` therefore encompasses everything you need to know about an OS version. The equivalent on a Linux machine is the command `hostnamectl`. On Ubuntu, the output of this command looks as follows:

```
$ hostnamectl
   Static hostname: server01
         Icon name: computer-vm
           Chassis: vm
        Machine ID: bf712b1790a50163052d66505719d284
           Boot ID: d58dd978139e43eab8ade8bfc9299187
    Virtualization: qemu
  Operating System: Ubuntu 16.04 LTS
            Kernel: Linux 4.4.0-22-generic
      Architecture: x86-64
```

This command doesn't tell you things such as the CPU used and the amount of memory and disk space. For those, you must rely on accessing the useful information such as product name and serial number from */sys/class/dmi/id*. On Cumulus Linux, the outputs from all of these commands is summarized via `net show system`. Most other traditional network operating systems provide similar information via `show system`.

When you automate with Ansible, you get all the useful information via Ansible's *facts*. On Linux machines, Ansible automatically gathers facts, whereas on traditional vendor network operating systems, you need to gather them via a separate command. For example, a playbook for native Linux machines such as Cumulus Linux looks as follows:

```
---
- hosts: routers
  tasks:
    - name: Print the OS/distro version
      debug:
        msg:
          - "{{ ansible_distribution }}"
          - "{{ ansible_distribution_version }}"
```

For Arista's EOS, Cisco's NX-OS, and other traditional network operating systems, a similar playbook looks as follows:

```
- name: "Demonstrate connecting to switches"
  hosts: routers
  vars:
    - ansible_connection: network_cli
    - ansible_network_os: eos
```

```
      - ansible_become: yes
      - ansible_become_method: enable
    gather_facts: no
    tasks:
      - name: Gather facts (eos)
        eos_facts:
        when: ansible_network_os == 'eos'

      - debug:
          msg:
            - "{{ ansible_net_system }}"
            - "{{ ansible_net_version }}"
```

To validate that a router running Cumulus Linux and one running Arista's EOS have the correct version, a playbook might look as follows:

```
---
- hosts: eos
  gather_facts: no
  tasks:
    - name: Gather facts (eos)
      eos_facts:
      when: ansible_network_os == 'eos'

    - name: Verify the version is appropriate
      assert:
        that: ansible_net_version == expected_version

- hosts: vx
  tasks:
    - name: Verify the version is appropriate
      assert:
        that: ansible_distribution_version == expected_version
```

The value of the expected version is put in an appropriate *group_vars* file. For example, all Arista routers can belong to a group called `arista`, and all Cumulus routers can belong to a group called `cumulus`. Now, in a *group_vars* directory created from wherever the playbook is running, create an *arista.yml* and a *cumulus.yml* that contain the appropriate version. In our case, the two files look as follows:

```
$ ls group_vars/
arista.yml  cumulus.yml
$
$ cat group_vars/arista.yml
ansible_connection: network_cli
ansible_network_os: eos
ansible_become: yes
ansible_become_method: enable
expected_version: "4.22.0F"
$
$ cat group_vars/cumulus.yml
```

```
expected_version: "3.7.6"
$
```

Cabling Validation

The main cabling validation question is: "Is my network cabled right?" Here are more-specific versions of this question:

- In a two-tier Clos network, is every leaf connected to every spine exactly once?
- With dual-attached servers, is every server connected to the correct pair of switches?

Three-tier Clos networks have the following additional questions:

- Is each spine hooked up to as many super-spines as there are leaves connected to it?
- Is each spine hooked up only once to a super-spine?

To answer these questions, let's break the problem up into (i) how do you describe the expected cabling behavior, and (ii) how do you determine the current cabling connectivity?

There is no well-accepted model in the network community to describe the expected physical cabling plan. You can use a graph language such as DOT or tools such as Python's NetworkX to describe network connectivity.

Link-Level Discovery Protocol (LLDP) is the basic method for checking whether cabling is correct. LLDP is a standard protocol that is available on every network platform, including Linux servers. In LLDP, peer nodes are called *neighbors*.

I recommend the use of Vincent Bernat's excellent *lldpd* (*https://oreil.ly/NIPSi*) package for Linux servers and Linux-based network operating systems. Packages for easy installation are available for just about every Linux distribution. *lldpd* even runs on macOS and Berkeley Software Distribution (BSD)–based machines.

On Linux servers, you need to configure *lldpd* to advertise interface names instead of interface MAC addresses. The reason for this is probably that the same NIC on a Linux server can change names depending on the order in which nodes were brought up, but the MAC address remains fixed. However, more recent Linux distributions keep the interface name fixed, independent of the order in which the NIC comes up. In any case, you must save your configuration and restart *lldpd* as follows:

```
$ echo "configure lldp portidsubtype ifname" > /etc/lldpd.d/port_info.conf
$ sudo systemctl restart lldpd
```

The most basic LLDP command used with *lldpd* is lldpctl, usually run as sudo lldpctl. Other traditional networking devices provide a similar output via show lldp neighbors. lldpctl's output is neither simple nor columnar, sadly, as shown in Example 18-1.

Example 18-1. Sample lldpctl output for leaf01

```
$ sudo lldpctl
-------------------------------------------------------------------------
LLDP neighbors:
-------------------------------------------------------------------------
Interface:    swp1, via: LLDP, RID: 4, Time: 4 days, 07:55:11          ❶
  Chassis:
    ChassisID:   mac 52:54:00:19:87:4d
    SysName:     server01                                              ❷
    SysDescr:    Ubuntu 16.04 LTS Linux 4.4.0-22-generic #40-Ubuntu...
    MgmtIP:      192.168.121.144
    MgmtIP:      fe80::5054:ff:fe19:874d
    Capability:  Bridge, off                                           ❸
    Capability:  Router, off
    Capability:  Wlan, off
    Capability:  Station, on
  Port:
    PortID:      ifname eth1                                           ❹
    PortDescr:   eth1
    TTL:         120
    PMD autoneg: supported: yes, enabled: yes
      Adv:           10Base-T, HD: yes, FD: yes
      Adv:           100Base-TX, HD: yes, FD: yes
      Adv:           1000Base-T, HD: no, FD: yes
      MAU oper type: 1000BaseTFD - Four-pair Category 5 UTP, full duplex
-------------------------------------------------------------------------
... output snipped for brevity
-------------------------------------------------------------------------
Interface:    swp52, via: LLDP, RID: 1, Time: 4 days, 07:55:23         ❶
  Chassis:
    ChassisID:   mac 52:54:00:07:25:a3
    SysName:     spine02                                               ❷
    SysDescr:    Cumulus Linux version 3.7.6 running on QEMU Standard...
    MgmtIP:      10.0.0.22
    MgmtIP:      fe80::5054:ff:fe07:25a3
    Capability:  Bridge, off                                           ❸
    Capability:  Router, on
  Port:
    PortID:      ifname swp1                                           ❹
    PortDescr:   to Leaf01
    TTL:         120
    PMD autoneg: supported: no, enabled: no
      MAU oper type: 1000BaseTFD - Four-pair Category 5 UTP, full duplex...
  LLDP-MED:
```

```
Device Type:   Network Connectivity Device
Capability:    Capabilities, yes
Capability:    Policy, yes
Capability:    Location, yes
Capability:    MDI/PSE, yes
Capability:    MDI/PD, yes
Capability:    Inventory, yes
Inventory:
  Software Revision: 3.7.6
  Firmware Revision: 1.10.2-1ubuntu1
  Serial Number: Not Specified
  Manufacturer: QEMU
  Model:         Standard PC (i440FX + PIIX, 1996
-------------------------------------------------------------------
```

❶ This is the interface on the local machine that is described by the information that follows it.

❷ This is the name of the peer machine. In the first case, the peering is with the server server01; in the second case, spine02 is the peer.

❸ This is the list of capabilities of the neighbor. For example, server01 is an end station and functions as neither a bridge nor a router. On the other hand, spine02 is a router, not a bridge.

❹ This is the name of the neighbor's interface.

You need to message the output of this command to verify that the physical connection as seen by LLDP matches the cabling description in your configuration. Cumulus Linux comes with a module called the Prescriptive Topology Manager (PTM) that verifies the cabling on any given box. The network operator provides the expected network configuration in the popular graph language, DOT. PTM uses this input along with LLDP's output to validate that the cabling matches that specified by the network operator.

 PTM started as an open source project, but its GitHub repository has not been updated in more than two years. I can assume only that the project is no longer actively updated by the open source community. No other platform that I'm aware of provides an equivalent solution out of the box. But I have seen some GitHub repositories that attempt to duplicate the functionality using Ansible.

Using Ansible to Validate Cabling

Ansible supports *lldpd* natively by providing a module called *lldp* to extract the output in a JSON-friendly manner. First, let me show you a file describing the servers, which I have named *dot.yml*, that we'll read into the playbook (Example 18-2).

Example 18-2. Sample dot.yml file

```
expected_lldp:
  spine01:
        swp1:  leaf01/swp51
        swp2:  leaf02/swp51
... output snipped for brevity
        swp30: exit01/swp51
  spine02:
        swp1:  leaf01/swp52
        swp2:  leaf02/swp52
... output snipped for brevity
        swp30: exit01/swp52
```

The file defines a variable called `expected_lldp` that has multiple keys, one for each spine. Each key has a field called `interfaces` that contains the name of the interface as the key. Each value is the expected LLDP peer machine and interface written out in the format "peer/peer_interface" (for instance, `leaf01/swp51`).

Now we can use the *lldp* module in the playbook shown in Example 18-3 to validate the cabling.

Example 18-3. Playbook showing cabling validation

```
- hosts: spine                                                          ❶
  become: yes
  vars_files:
    - dot.yml                                                           ❷
  tasks:
    - name: Get LLDP                                                    ❸
      lldp:

    - name: Verify Cabling
      assert:                                                          ❹
        that:
          - assertion
        quiet: yes
      vars:
        assertion: >-                                                  ❺
          lldp[item]['chassis']['name'] + '/' + lldp[item]['port']['ifname']
          ==
          expected_lldp[inventory_hostname][item]
      with_items: "{{ expected_lldp[inventory_hostname] }}"            ❻
```

❶ This line determines that the plays that follow are performed only on spines. I used the spines as a way to simplify the specification of the expected lldp peers. As you'll see later in this section, there are other ways to achieve the same goal.

❷ This is the YAML file shown earlier in Example 18-2.

❸ This task retrieves the lldp associated with the spines. On servers and network operating systems running native Linux, the *lldp* module retrieves all of the LLDP information in JSON format.

❹ This is the main task. assert is an Ansible module that tests the veracity of the provided condition. If the condition is true, it succeeds, else it fails. assert offers customizations for related useful activities such as printing the failure message.

❺ For the sake of formatting in this book, I split the single assertion into multiple lines. To do that, you need a variable to hold the multiline string. The assertion tells Ansible to extract from the runtime value of lldp the machine name and interface for the machine on which the play is being executed (identified by the magic variable, inventory_hostname), and then assert that it is equal to the expected output defined in the expected_lldp variable.

❻ Repeat the assertion described in the previous bullet for every interface defined by the expected_lldp variable associated with the machine on which the task is being executed.

You can also put each spine's information in the hostname's file in *host_vars*. Using this method, for example, you get the following:

```
$ ls host_vars/
spine01  spine02

$ cat host_vars/spine01
expected_lldp:
        swp1:  leaf01/swp51
        swp2:  leaf02/swp51
        swp3:  leaf03/swp51
        swp4:  leaf04/swp51
        swp29: exit02/swp51
        swp30: exit01/swp51
```

When done this way, you can access expected_lldp in the playbook directly, without having to use expected_lldp[inventory_hostname]. This does come at the cost of splitting the information into multiple files.

There are multiple ways to formulate *dot.yml* and the validation assertion. For example, if all you want to do is verify that a leaf was connected to all spines once, the spine ports won't interest you. In this case, you can execute the playbook shown in Example 18-4 from the perspective of both the normal leaves and exit leaves.

Example 18-4. Sample playbook verifying cabling without checking interface

```
---
- hosts: leaf:exit
  become: yes
  gather_facts: false
  tasks:
    - name: Get LLDP
      lldp:

    - name: Verify Cabling
      assert:
        that:
          - lldp[item]['chassis']['name'] == expected_lldp[item]
        quiet: yes
      with_items: "{{ expected_lldp }}"
```

This is much simpler than the previous playbook, but it assumes regular cabling; that is, all leaves have the same interface connected to spine01, the same interface connected to spine02, and so on. `expected_lldp` is defined in the file associated with the leaf and exit groups under the *group_vars* directory. That file and directory look as follows:

```
$ ls group_vars/
all  exit  leaf

$ cat group_vars/leaf

# Expected LLDP Peers
expected_lldp:
  swp51: spine01
  swp52: spine02
```

We use the *group_vars* file to keep the code separate from the data. If tomorrow you were to want to run the same validation in a different data center (or you wanted to share it with a friend) where the cabling was such that swp1/swp2 were used instead of swp51/swp52, only the *group_vars* file would change, not the actual validation playbook itself. This helps to keep the playbooks reusable, which is important.

Some of the Ansible modules associated with Arista, Cisco, and Juniper (among others) introduced a way to specify the expected LLDP neighbor node and interface along with the interface configuration. This can be another way for those using those routers to validate the cabling.

Interface Configuration Validation

After you've verified the cabling, next up is ensuring that the interface configuration is valid. The main set of questions associated with ensuring this include the following:

- Is the interface MTU consistent across the network?
- Is the interface VLANs configuration consistent across the two ends of the link?
- On a numbered interface, is the interface addressing from the same subnet across the two ends of the link?
- Is the loopback IP address assigned an address reachable from outside the box?
- Is the interface in the proper VRF?

If you're using dual-attached servers, you're most likely using some form of MLAG, or more recently, EVPN–based multihoming, to connect a server to two different leaves while having the server treat those interfaces like a bond. MLAG is vendor specific and lacks an open source implementation. So I won't be discussing how to answer questions associated with dual-attached servers. However, here are the specific MLAG questions to ask:

- Is the system ID (or domain ID) associated with MLAG the same on both peers?
- Is the peerlink configured correctly? The specifics of this are implementation dependent.
- Is the MLAG-ID associated with the interface to the same server on both MLAG peer switches the same?
- Do the interfaces assigned to the same server share the same attributes (link speed, VLAN set, Access Control Lists [ACLs], etc.)?

On Linux, *iproute2* is the most popular set of tools for examining the runtime state of the interface. You can also use FRR for that purpose. I'll stick with FRR to the extent possible, because most network administrators seem to prefer a single unified tool to perform their tasks. You can obtain the summary of the interfaces across all VRFs via the following:

```
sudo vtysh -c "show interface vrf all brief"
```

You can find the details of a specific interface by using this:

```
sudo vtysh -c "show interface <ifname>"
```

For example, sudo vtysh -c "show int vni13".

Example 18-5 presents the output of show interface vrf all (I show one interface for each type of interface).

Example 18-5. Sample output of `show interface vrf all` *on leaf01*

```
leaf01# show interface vrf all
Interface bond01 is up, line protocol is down          ❶
  Link ups:       0    last: (never)                   ❷
  Link downs:     0    last: (never)
  vrf: default                                         ❸
  index 19 metric 0 mtu 9000 speed 4294967295          ❹
  flags: <UP,BROADCAST,MULTICAST>
  Type: Ethernet
  HWaddr: 44:38:39:00:00:03
  Interface Type bond                                  ❺
  Master interface: bridge                             ❻

... output snipped for brevity

Interface bridge is up, line protocol is up
  Link ups:       0    last: (never)
  Link downs:     0    last: (never)
  vrf: default
  index 21 metric 0 mtu 1500 speed 0
  flags: <UP,BROADCAST,RUNNING,MULTICAST>
  Type: Ethernet
  HWaddr: 44:38:39:00:00:03
  inet6 fe80::4638:39ff:fe00:3/64
  Interface Type Bridge
  Bridge VLAN-aware: yes

... output snipped for brevity

Interface peerlink.4094 is up, line protocol is up
  Link ups:       0    last: (never)
  Link downs:     0    last: (never)
  vrf: default
  index 15 metric 0 mtu 9000 speed 2000
  flags: <UP,BROADCAST,RUNNING,MULTICAST>
  Type: Ethernet
  HWaddr: 44:38:39:00:00:10
  inet 169.254.1.1/30
  inet6 fe80::4638:39ff:fe00:10/64
  Interface Type Vlan
  VLAN Id 4094
  Parent interface: peerlink
Interface swp1 is up, line protocol is up
  Link ups:       0    last: (never)
  Link downs:     0    last: (never)
  vrf: default
  OS Description: to Server01
  index 3 metric 0 mtu 9000 speed 1000
  flags: <UP,BROADCAST,RUNNING,PROMISC,MULTICAST>
  Type: Ethernet
  HWaddr: 44:38:39:00:00:03
```

```
   Interface Type bond_slave
   Master interface: bond01

... output snipped for brevity

Interface swp51 is up, line protocol is up
   Link ups:       0    last: (never)
   Link downs:     0    last: (never)
   vrf: default
   OS Description: to Spine01
   index 11 metric 0 mtu 9216 speed 1000
   flags: <UP,BROADCAST,RUNNING,MULTICAST>
   Type: Ethernet
   HWaddr: 44:38:39:00:00:53
   inet6 fe80::4638:39ff:fe00:53/64
   Interface Type Other
   ND advertised reachable time is 0 milliseconds          ❼
   ND advertised retransmit interval is 0 milliseconds
   ND router advertisements sent: 58 rcvd: 54              ❽
   ND router advertisements are sent every 10 seconds
   ND router advertisements lifetime tracks ra-interval
   ND router advertisement default router preference is medium
   Hosts use stateless autoconfig for addresses.
   Neighbor address(s):
   inet6 fe80::4638:39ff:fe00:54/128                       ❾

... output snipped for brevity

Interface vni13 is up, line protocol is up
   Link ups:       0    last: (never)
   Link downs:     0    last: (never)
   vrf: default
   index 17 metric 0 mtu 9000 speed 0
   flags: <UP,BROADCAST,RUNNING,MULTICAST>
   Type: Ethernet
   HWaddr: 0e:90:8b:ba:ec:54
   Interface Type Vxlan
   VxLAN Id 13 VTEP IP: 10.0.0.112 Access VLAN Id 13
   Master interface: bridge

... output snipped for brevity

Interface vlan13 is up, line protocol is up
   Link ups:       0    last: (never)
   Link downs:     0    last: (never)
   vrf: evpn-vrf
   index 22 metric 0 mtu 1500 speed 0
   flags: <UP,BROADCAST,RUNNING,MULTICAST>
   Type: Ethernet
   HWaddr: 44:38:39:00:00:03
   inet 10.1.3.11/24                                       ❿
   inet6 fe80::4638:39ff:fe00:3/64
```

```
Interface Type Vlan
VLAN Id 13
Parent interface: bridge
```

Here are the main points of interest in this output:

❶   This line names the interface along with listing the administrative status and the operational status.

❷   These two lines show the last times the link came up or went down. Because interfaces come up outside of FRR, never on these lines means that there has been no link status change on this interface after FRR started.

❸   This line specifies the VRF that this interface is part of.

❹   This line lists the ifindex, the MTU, and the speed of the interface.

❺   This line lists the type of interface.

❻   If this interface is a member of another interface, this line lists the name of that container (or master) interface. For example, a member of a bond lists the bond interface here.

❼   This indicates that IPv6 RA is enabled and running on this interface. This is typically the case if that interface is part of a BGP Unnumbered session.

❽   This indicates how many IPv6 RAs have been exchanged on this interface.

❾   If this line is present, you know that the BGP Unnumbered session on that interface can start up.

❿   This line lists the IP address assigned to this interface.

The main difference between this output and what you get from traditional network equipment is the additional information about the interface statistics. On Linux network operating systems, the interface statistics are available via `cat /proc/net/dev`. On Linux endpoints that are not running FRR, the *iproute2* family of commands is your friend. For example, to see details of the interface including addresses, use `ip -d address show`.

Automating Interface Configuration Validation

Just as with cabling in "Using Ansible to Validate Cabling" on page 399, we'll automate the validation of the interface configuration using Ansible. Here, we rely on Ansible's setup module to extract information about the interfaces. Sadly, Ansible

doesn't extract information about VRF or VLANs, so we must rely on other commands to get the information. If the output of the command is not in JSON, it makes
the validation almost impossible, so we ignore those tasks. It's also difficult to validate
without providing a lot more information, including the IP addresses of the interfaces
toward the leaf servers.

With those disclaimers in place, here is a playbook that relies on the same *dot.yml* file
in Example 18-2 to verify interface configuration:

```
- hosts: network
  gather_facts: false                                                ❶
  vars_files:
    - dot.yml
  tasks:
    - name: Verfify non-host local IP address is assigned to loopback
      assert:
        that:
          - ansible_lo.ipv4_secondaries is defined
          - ansible_lo.ipv4_secondaries[0].address|ipaddr('private')

    - name: Verify MTU mismatch
      assert:
        that:
          - ansible_{{item}}.mtu == peer_node.ansible_{{peer_if}}.mtu
      vars:
        - peer_if: "{{ lldp[item]['port']['ifname'] }}"
        - peer_node: "{{ hostvars[lldp[item]['chassis']['name']] }}"
      with_items: "{{ expected_lldp[inventory_hostname].interfaces }}"
      when: inventory_hostname in groups['spine']
```

❶   The reason we have `gather_facts` as false is because this play is part of the PTM
    playbook from the earlier section. Ansible retrieves the system facts for each play
    by default unless instructed not to do so. As we've already obtained the relevant
    information from the first play in the playbook, there is no need for us to retrieve
    it again inside the same playbook.

Routing Configuration Validation

Next up the stack is validating the routing configuration. The answer to the highest-
level questions, "Is my routing configured correctly?" translates to the following specific questions that are independent of the routing protocol used:

- Is my router ID configured correctly? (The loopback IP address is
  recommended.)

- Is the loopback IP address advertised?

- Is my peering with all configured neighbors successful?

- When using numbered interfaces, is the interface address advertised? (The interface address must not be advertised, as we discussed in "Unnumbered Interfaces" on page 98.)
- Is the default route announced by the appropriate router?

A word about the last question. The default route is the one used whenever a router doesn't have a more specific FIB entry to forward the packet. If the default route is not advertised by the correct node, you can blackhole traffic. For example, the default route is how traffic leaves the data center to the external world. Without the correct default route advertisement, connectivity to the external world will be lost. Also, the technique we use to understand who advertises the default route can be used for other routes, as well.

The remaining questions are protocol specific, so we examine these general questions in the context of OSPF and BGP.

Validating an OSPF Configuration

The OSPF-specific questions include the following:

- Are all links configured as point-to-point?
- Do we avoid `redistribute connected` as required in "Configuration with Servers Running OSPF: IPv4" on page 280?
- Are the interfaces in the appropriate areas?

Most of OSPF's configuration can be validated via the following *vtysh* commands:

```
show ip ospf neighbor
show ip ospf interface
```

These commands are useful across all routing suites, including traditional routing suites from Arista and Cisco. Juniper has equivalent commands that display the same information. The default route command is validated using `show ip ospf route`.

I'm assuming the use of OSPF Unnumbered in the following command outputs. We assume the use of OSPF with iBGP for the outputs shown in this section.

`show ip ospf neighbor` shows all sessions where the two sides have passed the initial OSPF Hello exchange and have proceeded beyond the Two-Way Hello state in the session establishment (see "OSPF States" on page 267 for the name and description of OSPF neighbor states). This is the command you use to verify that you have all the successful sessions you need. The output of `show ip ospf neighbor` from the perspective of leaf01 is as follows:

```
vagrant@leaf01:mgmt-vrf:~$ sudo vtysh
```

```
Hello, this is FRRouting (version 7.2-dev).
Copyright 1996-2005 Kunihiro Ishiguro, et al.

leaf01# show ip ospf neighbor

Neighbor ID   Pri State          Dead Time  Address      Interface       ...
10.0.0.21       1 Full/DROther   39.393s    10.0.0.21    swp51:10.0.0.11 ...
10.0.0.22       1 Full/DROther   30.218s    10.0.0.22    swp52:10.0.0.11 ...
```

The output shows the neighbor's router ID in the first column. The `Address` column shows the neighbor's interface IP address. The `Interface` column shows the interface and the IP address of that interface, over which the OSPF peering has occurred. The `State` column must contain the value FRR to indicate that the peering is successful.

However, if the OSPF session is not established, it can be due to one of the following reasons:

- One side has the session configured but the other side does not.
- There's a subnet mismatch, if you're using numbered interfaces.
- There's an MTU mismatch between the two ends of the link.
- There's a mismatch in the OSPF Hello or Dead timer between the two ends of the link.
- There's an OSPF network type mismatch between the two ends of the link.

To see which sessions have not been successful, the helpful command is `show ip ospf interface`. The output is as follows, again from leaf01's perspective:

```
leaf01# show ip ospf interface
lo is up                                                                    ❶
  ifindex 1, MTU 65536 bytes, BW 0 Mbit <UP,LOOPBACK,RUNNING>
  Internet Address 10.0.0.11/32, Area 0.0.0.0                               ❷
  MTU mismatch detection: enabled
  Router ID 10.0.0.11, Network Type LOOPBACK, Cost: 10                      ❸
  Transmit Delay is 1 sec, State Loopback, Priority 1
  No backup designated router on this network
  Multicast group memberships: <None>
  Timer intervals configured, Hello 10s, Dead 40s, Wait 40s, Retransmit 5
    No Hellos (Passive interface)                                           ❹
  Neighbor Count is 0, Adjacent neighbor count is 0                         ❺
  Internet Address 10.0.0.112/32, Area 0.0.0.0                              ❻
  MTU mismatch detection: enabled
  Router ID 10.0.0.11, Network Type LOOPBACK, Cost: 10
  Transmit Delay is 1 sec, State Loopback, Priority 1
  No backup designated router on this network
  Multicast group memberships: <None>
  Timer intervals configured, Hello 10s, Dead 40s, Wait 40s, Retransmit 5
    No Hellos (Passive interface)
  Neighbor Count is 0, Adjacent neighbor count is 0
```

```
swp51 is up                                                                    ❶
  ifindex 11, MTU 9216 bytes, BW 1000 Mbit <UP,BROADCAST,RUNNING,MULTICAST>
  This interface is UNNUMBERED, Area 0.0.0.0                                   ❷
  MTU mismatch detection: enabled
  Router ID 10.0.0.11, Network Type POINTOPOINT, Cost: 100                     ❸
  Transmit Delay is 1 sec, State Point-To-Point, Priority 1
  No backup designated router on this network
  Multicast group memberships: OSPFAllRouters
  Timer intervals configured, Hello 10s, Dead 40s, Wait 40s, Retransmit 5
    Hello due in 2.583s
  Neighbor Count is 1, Adjacent neighbor count is 1                           ❺
... output snipped for brevity
```

This output is more complicated than that of the previous command. Here's the important information that we can extract:

❶ This line lists the name of the interface.

❷ This line lists the interface IP address and the OSPF area associated with the interface. The second interface, swp51, is marked as an unnumbered interface. As described in Chapter 13, in a two-tier Clos with hosts not running OSPF, all of the interfaces should be in area 0. In a three-tier Clos, each pod is in area 1, whereas the interfaces connecting the spine to the super-spine are in area 0. If the hosts run OSPF too, the interfaces facing the servers and the server interfaces are in area 1, and all the other interfaces are in area 0.

❸ This line lists the router ID and the type of interface. This can be used to verify that the router ID is the same as the loopback interface. For the second interface, swp51, this line indicates that via the "Network Type" field the interface is a point-to-point interface from OSPF's perspective.

❹ This line shows that the interface is a passive interface. This means that the interface will not have any OSPF peers.

❺ This line provides the count of active neighbors and successful peerings. For the first interface, lo, which is a passive interface, the count in both cases is 0. For swp51, the count for both is 1, indicating a successful peering. On a point-to-point interface, there can be only a single neighbor. You use this information to determine whether all the nonpassive interfaces have at least a count of 1 on this line, marking a successful peering session.

❻ The loopback interface has two IP addresses: one for the underlay and the other for the VTEP IP address. Each IP address is treated as a different peering session. This is the second IP address associated with the loopback interface. Because we're checking a loopback interface, this is acceptable. Normal peering interfaces have only a single IP address.

Arista's EOS has a nicer output that presents the information in a more readable columnar format.

I find this aspect of OSPF bizarre, and one that hasn't been fixed by any network operating systems or routing suite that I know. It's not difficult to show all the sessions that OSPF is running on and display the state such as "OneWay Hello," "Two-Way Hello," and so on. This makes it painful merely to determine whether OSPF has successfully peered over all the configured sessions. I find this a strong indication of OSPF's poor observability.

If there is an error in the peering, the output of show ip ospf neighbor either might not be present or show the State column as being in a state other than "Full." Here is an example of output indicating an unsuccessful peering session:

```
leaf01# show ip ospf neighbor

Neighbor ID  Pri State          Dead Time Address      Interface
10.0.0.21      1 ExStart/DROther 39.115s 10.0.0.21     swp51:10.0.0.11
10.0.0.22      1 Full/DROther    39.993s 10.0.0.22     swp52:10.0.0.11

leaf01#
```

The state is shown as ExStart instead of Full for the peering session on interface swp51. The output of show ip ospf interface for swp51 is as follows:

```
leaf01# show ip ospf interface swp51
swp51 is up
  ifindex 11, MTU 1500 bytes, BW 1000 Mbit <UP,BROADCAST,RUNNING,MULTICAST>
  This interface is UNNUMBERED, Area 0.0.0.0
  MTU mismatch detection: enabled
  Router ID 10.0.0.11, Network Type POINTOPOINT, Cost: 100
  Transmit Delay is 1 sec, State Point-To-Point, Priority 1
  No backup designated router on this network
  Multicast group memberships: OSPFAllRouters
  Timer intervals configured, Hello 10s, Dead 40s, Wait 40s, Retransmit 5
    Hello due in 1.407s
  Neighbor Count is 1, Adjacent neighbor count is 0
```

The last line in the output indicates that Adjacent neighbor count is 0. Thus, the interface has no connections. To see what the possible error might be, try the following command:

```
sudo journalctl -n -p '1..4' -u frr --since "2 min ago"
```

This shows the last 10 lines with the priority between 1 (critical) and 4 (warning) for the FRR service in the two preceding minutes. For our failed session, the output shows this:

```
$ sudo journalctl -n -p 0..4 -u frr --since '2 min ago'
-- Logs begin at Wed 2019-08-14 05:45:05 UTC, end at ...
```

```
... Neighbor 10.0.0.21 MTU 9216 is larger than [swp51:10.0.0.11]'s MTU 1500
... Neighbor 10.0.0.21 MTU 9216 is larger than [swp51:10.0.0.11]'s MTU 1500
```

This indicates that the error is due to mismatched MTUs on the interface. This should have been caught by the interface-level validation we did in the previous section, which is another example that shows that it is better to catch errors closer to the source than to wait and let them manifest themselves entirely differently in some other place.

Determining the originator of the default route

The output of show ip ospf route uses the topology described in Figure 13-4. I use that topology instead of the usual EVPN topology used in the rest of this chapter because the default route is learned via BGP. The output of the command is as follows:

```
leaf01# show ip ospf route
============ OSPF external routing table ===========        ❶
N E2 0.0.0.0/0            [200/1] tag: 0                     ❷
                          via 10.0.0.21, swp1
                          via 10.0.0.22, swp2
```

❶ The heading indicates that this route is an external route.

❷ This line indicates the default route.

 Unless you're looking at the database of a fully stubby router, the default route is always advertised as an external route because the default route is never the address of any interface. However, on a fully stubby network, the default route is advertised as a "Summary Route."

To find out who advertised this route, you can now issue show ip ospf database as follows:

```
leaf01# show ip ospf database external 0.0.0.0

        OSPF Router with ID (10.0.0.11)

            AS External Link States

    LS age: 1507
    Options: 0x2  : *|-|-|-|-|-|E|-
    LS Flags: 0x6
    LS Type: AS-external-LSA
    Link State ID: 0.0.0.0 (External Network Number)
    Advertising Router: 10.0.0.14                           ❶
    LS Seq Number: 8000000d
    Checksum: 0x2687
```

```
        Length: 36

    Network Mask: /0
            Metric Type: 2 (Larger than any link state path)
            TOS: 0
            Metric: 1
            Forward Address: 0.0.0.0
            External Route Tag: 0
```

❶ This line provides the router ID of the OSPF router that has advertised this route.
In this output, the advertising router has the ID 10.0.0.14. If you used the loopback IP address, you can identify that this is the router leaf04, from Figure 13-3.
We used 0.0.0.0 without the subnet mask because the command doesn't support
looking up a specific prefix, only the linkstate ID of the route. The linkstate ID is
typically (though not always) the route without the subnet mask.

The two preceding examples show how poor observability is with OSPF. It shocks me
how much network operators have put up with for as long as they have, and sadly
continue to do so.

Automating OSPF validation

Validating OSPF configuration is quite straightforward from an Ansible playbook
perspective. It also demonstrates the power of automation, because you can have a
program look across both ends of the interface, unlike a human eyeballing the two
sides. Here's the playbook:

```
---
- hosts: network
  become: yes
  gather_facts: false
  tasks:
    - name: Stuff lldp info into all peers
      lldp:

    - name: Get OSPF interface info
      become: yes
      command: vtysh -c "show ip ospf int json"
      register: ospf_out

    - name: Extract info into JSON object
      set_fact:
        ospf: "{{ ospf_out['stdout']|from_json|json_query('interfaces') }}"

- hosts: leaf:exit
  become: yes
  gather_facts: false
  tasks:
    - name: Extract LLDP info
```

```yaml
    lldp:

- name: Validate all interfaces are present in output
  assert:
    quiet: yes
    that:
      - ospf[item] is defined
  with_items: "{{ expected_ospf_if }}"

  # If interface isn't up, some fields aren't present
- name: Validate all interfaces are up
  assert:
    quiet: yes
    that:
      - ospf[item]['ifUp']
  with_items: "{{ expected_ospf_if }}"

- name: Validate all peering interfaces have 1 valid adjacent neighbor
  assert:
    quiet: yes
    that:
      - ospf[item]['nbrCount'] == ospf[item]['nbrAdjacentCount']
  with_items: "{{ expected_ospf_if }}"
  when: item != 'lo'

- name: Validate all peering interfaces are in P2P mode
  assert:
    quiet: yes
    that:
      - ospf[item]['networkType'] == 'POINTOPOINT'
  with_items: "{{ expected_ospf_if }}"
  when: item != 'lo'

- name: Validate network type is consistent across peers
  assert:
    quiet: yes
    that:
      - ospf[item]['networkType'] == peer_ospf['networkType']
  vars:
    - peer_node: "{{ hostvars[lldp[item]['chassis']['name']] }}"
    - peer_if : "{{ lldp[item]['port']['ifname'] }}"
    - peer_ospf: "{{ peer_node['ospf'][peer_if] }}"
  with_items: "{{ expected_ospf_if }}"
  when: item != 'lo'

- name: Validate timer values are consistent across peers
  assert:
    quiet: yes
    that:
      - ospf[item].timerMsecs == peer_ospf.timerMsecs
      - ospf[item]['timerDeadSecs'] == peer_ospf['timerDeadSecs']
  vars:
```

```
        - peer_node: "{{ hostvars[lldp[item]['chassis']['name']] }}"
        - peer_if : "{{ lldp[item]['port']['ifname'] }}"
        - peer_ospf: "{{ peer_node['ospf'][peer_if] }}"
      with_items: "{{ expected_ospf_if }}"
      when: item != 'lo'
```

The playbook consists of two main plays. The first play retrieves the relevant information for all nodes and stuffs that information into the hostvars dictionary that is maintained by Ansible for all hosts it is processing. The second play verifies the OSPF state, including checking for any mismatches between the two sides. The solution assumes OSPF Unnumbered. The second part also assumes the use of systematic cabling in which all leaves use the same ports to connect to the spines. Doubtless you can write code to handle nonsystematic cabling, but it will require a separate specification for each leaf instead of just one specification across all the leaves. I also used the leaf perspective because there are fewer spines than leaves, which greatly reduces the number of things the user needs to specify. Variables such as peer_node, peer_if, and peer_ospf are used to break down the variable access logic and make the code more readable. It also helps with the formatting in this book.

expected_ospf_if is a variable defined in the *group_vars/leaf* and *group_vars/exit* files. Here's the output of the leaf file:

```
$ cat group_vars/leaf

# Expected LLDP Peers
expected_lldp:
  swp51: spine01
  swp52: spine02

# Expected OSPF interfaces
expected_ospf_if:
  - lo
  - swp51
  - swp52
```

 FRR versions before 7.1 do not contain the correct timer values in the JSON display. If you use older versions, the code in this playbook won't work to validate that the timers are the same on both ends of the peering session.

Validating a BGP Configuration

Because BGP is a multiprotocol routing suite, it raises a few more questions specific to its deployment compared to OSPF. Furthermore, BGP has been adapted to the data center, as we discussed in Chapter 14. As such, here are the BGP-specific routing validation questions:

- Do the spines have the same ASN in a two-tier Clos?

- Do the leaves have their own unique ASN?

- Is as-path multipath-relax configured?

- Are we stripping the private ASN before announcing the routes to the external world?

- Are routes being exchanged for all configured address families?

Here are the two main commands that answer many of these questions:

```
show bgp [vrf <vrf>] <ipv4|ipv6> unicast summary
show bgp bgp [vrf <vrf>] <ipv4|ipv6> unicast neighbor
```

Let's examine the outputs of these commands from the perspective of leaf01 and spine01. There is a single eBGP session for EVPN in the following displays.

We begin with the summary command output (Example 18-6). This is the single command you need in order to determine the state of all your configured peering sessions. I show excerpts of the command's output on two nodes, a leaf and a spine, and will highlight the interesting pieces that help us validate our BGP setup.

Example 18-6. BGP summary for leaf01

```
$ sudo vtysh

Hello, this is FRRouting (version 7.2-dev).
Copyright 1996-2005 Kunihiro Ishiguro, et al.

leaf01# show bgp vrf all summary

Instance default:                                                    ❶

IPv4 Unicast Summary:                                                ❷
BGP router identifier 10.0.0.11, local AS number 65011 vrf-id 0      ❸
BGP table version 13
RIB entries 24, using 4416 bytes of memory
Peers 2, using 41 KiB of memory

Neighbor        ...    AS MsgRcvd MsgSent ...  Up/Down State/PfxRcd
spine01(swp51)  ... 65020     123     115 ... 00:03:38            10 ❹
spine02(swp52)  ... 65020     123     115 ... 00:03:38            10

Total number of neighbors 2                                          ❺

L2VPN EVPN Summary:                                                  ❷
BGP router identifier 10.0.0.11, local AS number 65011 vrf-id 0
BGP table version 0
RIB entries 19, using 3496 bytes of memory
Peers 2, using 41 KiB of memory
```

```
Neighbor       ...     AS MsgRcvd MsgSent ...  Up/Down State/PfxRcd
spine01(swp51) ... 65020   2061    2091  ... 01:40:19         22
spine02(swp52) ... 65020   2121    2111  ... 00:29:15         22

Total number of neighbors 2

Instance evpn-vrf:                                              ❶
% No BGP neighbors found

leaf01#
```

Example 18-7. BGP summary for spine01

```
spine01# show bgp vrf all summary

Instance default:                                              ❶

IPv4 Unicast Summary:                                          ❷
BGP router identifier 10.0.0.21, local AS number 65020 vrf-id 0  ❸
BGP table version 17
RIB entries 22, using 3344 bytes of memory
Peers 6, using 116 KiB of memory
Peer groups 1, using 64 bytes of memory

Neighbor       ...     AS MsgRcvd MsgSent ...  Up/Down State/PfxRcd
leaf01(swp1)   ... 65011    321     330  ... 00:13:57          2 ❹
leaf02(swp2)   ... 65012    330     331  ... 00:13:52          2
leaf03(swp3)   ... 65013    329     330  ... 00:13:52          2
leaf04(swp4)   ... 65014    326     330  ... 00:13:52          2
exit02(swp29)  ... 65042    332     329  ... 00:13:56          4
exit01(swp30)  ... 65041    335     327  ... 00:13:55          5

Total number of neighbors 6                                    ❺

L2VPN EVPN Summary:                                            ❶
BGP router identifier 10.0.0.21, local AS number 65020 vrf-id 0
BGP table version 0
RIB entries 19, using 2888 bytes of memory
Peers 6, using 116 KiB of memory
Peer groups 1, using 64 bytes of memory

Neighbor       ...     AS MsgRcvd MsgSent ...  Up/Down State/PfxRcd
leaf01(swp1)   ... 65011   2153    2124  ... 01:43:30          8
leaf02(swp2)   ... 65012   2169    2126  ... 01:43:25          8
leaf03(swp3)   ... 65013   2171    2125  ... 01:43:25          6
leaf04(swp4)   ... 65014   2168    2125  ... 01:43:25          6
exit02(swp29)  ... 65042   2166    2124  ... 01:43:29          5
exit01(swp30)  ... 65041   2172    2122  ... 01:43:28          5

Total number of neighbors 6                                    ❺
```

❶ Each VRF that BGP knows about is listed in this output. The display marks which VRF is described by the lines that follow. As we see further down, there are no configured neighbors in the evpn-vrf that BGP knows about.

❷ There is a separate listing for every address family that is configured to exchange routes. In this output, we see the output for two address families, IPv4 Unicast and L2VPN EVPN.

❸ This line lists the router ID and the ASN used by this router.

❹ This is a tabular listing of each of the configured BGP sessions for the specified VRF and address family. If the session has been successfully established, it lists the count of valid prefixes received from that peer. If the session has not been successfully established, this column lists the BGP state of the session (Idle, Connect, etc.). FRR supports a BGP capability called "hostname" that supports passing the BGP speaker's hostname to the peer. When used with unnumbered interfaces, this FRR feature renders the display far more interesting than the one you'd get with just about any other routing suite. This significantly improves the observability of the system, because hostnames are far easier to associate with hosts than IP addresses or interface names.

❺ This number allows you to quickly determine whether the number of sessions you expect is the same as the number known in the runtime state. If, for example, you forgot to add a leaf, this count would be off by 1 on the spine.

From these two displays, we can observe that the leaves peer only with spines with the ASN 65020, and that the spine peers with leaves (normal and exit) that each have a different ASN. Thus, BGP's state is kosher as per the configuration we discussed in Chapter 16.

The summaries we have seen do not indicate whether as-path multipath-relax is enabled. This is primarily because the summary display is almost sacrosanct and cannot be expanded, as many tests and text output scrapers rely on the classic format. You can find the information in the JSON output, or via show running-config bgpd, which displays the operational BGP configuration. We use this in the automation section to validate the use of multipath-relax.

The summary displays do not explicitly show the state of the peering session, also for historical reasons. The last column, State/PfxRcd, lists the count of the prefixes received if the peering session has been successfully established. If the peering session was not successful, that last column shows the BGP state of the connection.

The following command can identify whether a peering session has mismatched address families:

```
show bgp [vrf <vrf-name|all>] neighbors
```

Sample output from this command on leaf01 follows, with only the appropriate output shown and with lengthy output columns wrapped:

```
Instance default:
BGP neighbor on swp51: fe80::4638:39ff:fe00:54, remote AS 65020,   ❶
  local AS 65011, external link
Hostname: spine01
  BGP version 4, remote router ID 10.0.0.21, local router ID 10.0.0.11
  BGP state = Established, up for 01:02:19
  Last read 00:00:01, Last write 00:00:01
  Hold time is 9, keepalive interval is 3 seconds
  Neighbor capabilities:
  ... output snipped for brevity
    Address Family IPv4 Unicast: advertised and received        ❷
    Address Family L2VPN EVPN: advertised and received
  ... output snipped for brevity
BGP neighbor on swp52: fe80::4638:39ff:fe00:25, remote AS 65020,   ❶
  local AS 65011, external link
Hostname: spine02
  BGP version 4, remote router ID 10.0.0.22, local router ID 10.0.0.11
  BGP state = Established, up for 01:02:19
  Last read 00:00:01, Last write 00:00:01
  Hold time is 9, keepalive interval is 3 seconds
  Neighbor capabilities:
  ... output snipped for brevity
    Address Family IPv4 Unicast: advertised and received
    Address Family L2VPN EVPN: advertised                       ❸
  ... output snipped for brevity
```

❶ Each neighbor's entry starts with this line and lists the peering address or interface.

❷ This line shows that both sides have advertised that they're willing to process the address family.

❸ This line, which misses the `received` keyword, shows that only one of the sides has advertised that it's willing to process routes with that address family. This should typically be treated as a red flag and investigated.

If a BGP session shows up as not connected but the reason is not a mismatched subnet, this command might indicate the source of the error:

```
sudo journalctl -n -p 0..4 -u frr
```

Determining the originator of the default route

The following command traces the origin of a route in BGP:

```
show bgp [vrf <vrf-name|all>] <address-family> <route>
```

Let's examine how the default route in BGP was populated on leaf01. The output of the command looks as follows:

```
$ sudo vtysh

Hello, this is FRRouting (version 7.2-dev).
Copyright 1996-2005 Kunihiro Ishiguro, et al.

leaf01# show bgp ipv4 unicast 0.0.0.0/0
BGP routing table entry for 0.0.0.0/0
Paths: (2 available, best #2, table default)                            ❶
  Advertised to non peer-group peers:
  spine01(swp51) spine02(swp52)
  65020 65042 65530 65042 25253                                         ❷
    spine02 from spine02(swp52) (10.0.0.22)                             ❸
    (fe80::4638:39ff:fe00:25) (used)
      Origin IGP, valid, external, multipath                           ❹
      Last update: Thu Aug 15 05:41:49 2019                            ❺

  65020 65042 65530 65042 25253
    spine01 from spine01(swp51) (10.0.0.21)
    (fe80::4638:39ff:fe00:54) (used)
      Origin IGP, valid, external, multipath, bestpath-from-AS 65020,  ❻
      best (Older Path)                                                ❼
      Last update: Thu Aug 15 04:30:45 2019
```

❶ This line indicates that leaf01 has received two advertisements for the default route from two peers. Because the leaf is peering with two spines, this makes sense.

❷ This is the ASPATH associated with the route. The ASPATH is listed in the reverse order of the path traversed; that is, starting from the ASN of the last router all the way to the first router that advertised this route. Thus, the router that originated the default route is the one with the ASN 25253. We know that this is the edge router, which is the correct node. Furthermore, this line indicates that the route was propagated via the BGP speakers with the ASNs 65020, 65042, 65530, and 65042. A quick glance at the topology shows that this means the path was propagated as {spine01, exit02, firewall, exit02, internet}. The presence of the firewall is an indication that the original route might have been learned via a different VRF.

❸ This line lists the peer from whom the route was learned. FRR again makes this easy by listing the peer's hostname rather than just the IP address of the peering session.

❹ This line indicates that the route is part of a multipath.

❺ This line indicates when the entry was inserted into BGP's RIB. This is another example of the superb observational property of BGP. OSPF has no equivalent, though this is an implementation issue rather than a protocol concern.

❻ This is the same as point 4, except this is for the other peer from which this route was learned. This line and the next are a single line in the real-life output. It indicates that this is the advertisement accepted as the best path and that this is part of an ECMP.

❼ This line indicates why this path was chosen as the best path and not the previous one. Because this update was received before the previous one, this one was picked as the best path.

In this section, a single command helped identify a lot of useful BGP information that a network operator can use either to validate a route after configuration or to troubleshoot a problem.

Continuing our investigation of how this route got into our BGP RIB, we can examine the presence of this route in the other VRF known to BGP. The whole thing looks more complicated when you examine the same route in the evpn-vrf. Example 18-8 presents the more complex output:

Example 18-8. Sample output of an EVPN imported route

```
leaf01# show bgp vrf evpn-vrf ipv4 unicast 0.0.0.0/0                    ❶
BGP routing table entry for 0.0.0.0/0
Paths: (4 available, best #4, vrf evpn-vrf)
  Not advertised to any peer
  Imported from 10.0.0.41:2:[5]:[0]:[0]:[0.0.0.0], VNI 104001           ❷
  65020 65041 65530 65042 25253
    spine02 from spine02(swp52) (10.0.0.22)
      Origin IGP, valid, external
      Extended Community: RT:65041:104001 ET:8 Rmac:44:38:39:00:00:4b
      Last update: Thu Aug 15 05:41:50 2019

  Imported from 10.0.0.42:2:[5]:[0]:[0]:[0.0.0.0], VNI 104001
  65020 65042 65530 65042 25253
    spine02 from spine02(swp52) (10.0.0.22)
      Origin IGP, valid, external, multipath
      Extended Community: RT:65042:104001 ET:8 Rmac:44:38:39:00:00:0c
      Last update: Thu Aug 15 05:41:49 2019

  Imported from 10.0.0.42:2:[5]:[0]:[0]:[0.0.0.0], VNI 104001
  65020 65042 65530 65042 25253
    spine01 from spine01(swp51) (10.0.0.21)
      Origin IGP, valid, external
      Extended Community: RT:65042:104001 ET:8 Rmac:44:38:39:00:00:0c
      Last update: Thu Aug 15 04:30:47 2019
```

```
Imported from 10.0.0.41:2:[5]:[0]:[0]:[0.0.0.0], VNI 104001
65020 65041 65530 65042 25253
  spine01 from spine01(swp51) (10.0.0.21)
    Origin IGP, valid, external, multipath, ... best (Older Path)
    Extended Community: RT:65041:104001 ET:8 Rmac:44:38:39:00:00:4b
    Last update: Thu Aug 15 04:30:47 2019

leaf01#
```

❶ This command looks for the default route in evpn-vrf. The previous output was
   in the default VRF.

❷ This is a new line and is described in the following paragraph.

Let's unpack the compact information shown near the top of the preceding output:

    `10.0.0.41:2:[5]:[0]:[0]:[0.0.0.0]`

The fields of this format are:

- Router ID of speaker: here, `10.0.0.41`
- Device-specific local encoding of the VNI: here, `2`
- EVPN route type: here, `5` (for RT-5)
- EVPN Ethernet segment: here, `0`
- Prefix length: here, `0`
- IP address: here, `0.0.0.0` (that is, an unnumbered interface)

In short, the line indicates that this route was learned via an RT-5 EVPN route and
that the advertiser was the one with a RD of 10.0.0.41.

Per what we discussed in "Route Distinguisher" on page 342, the format of the RD
consists of the router ID of the speaker followed by a colon and then the device-
specific local encoding of the VNI. Thus, 10.0.0.41 is the router ID of the node that
originated the route. This is router exit01.

If you want to pursue this further, you can look up the original route in EVPN, as
follows:

```
leaf01# show bgp l2vpn evpn route rd 10.0.0.41:2 type prefix
EVPN type-2 prefix: [2]:[EthTag]:[MAClen]:[MAC]
EVPN type-3 prefix: [3]:[EthTag]:[IPlen]:[OrigIP]
EVPN type-5 prefix: [5]:[EthTag]:[IPlen]:[IP]

BGP routing table entry for 10.0.0.41:2:[5]:[0]:[0]:[0.0.0.0]
Paths: (2 available, best #2)
  Advertised to non peer-group peers:
  spine01(swp51) spine02(swp52)
```

```
Route [5]:[0]:[0]:[0.0.0.0] VNI 104001
65020 65041 65530 65042 25253
  spine02 from spine02(swp52) (10.0.0.22)
    Origin IGP, valid, external
    Extended Community: RT:65041:104001 ET:8 Rmac:44:38:39:00:00:4b
    Last update: Thu Aug 15 05:41:49 2019

Route [5]:[0]:[0]:[0.0.0.0] VNI 104001
65020 65041 65530 65042 25253
  spine01 from spine01(swp51) (10.0.0.21)
    Origin IGP, valid, external, bestpath-from-AS 65020,
    best (First path received)
    Extended Community: RT:65041:104001 ET:8 Rmac:44:38:39:00:00:4b
    Last update: Thu Aug 15 04:30:45 2019

... output snipped for brevity

leaf01# show bgp l2vpn evpn route rd 10.0.0.42:2 type prefix
EVPN type-2 prefix: [2]:[EthTag]:[MAClen]:[MAC]
EVPN type-3 prefix: [3]:[EthTag]:[IPlen]:[OrigIP]
EVPN type-5 prefix: [5]:[EthTag]:[IPlen]:[IP]

... output snipped for brevity
```

The output shows that this EVPN route was received from spine01 and spine02. The second path was picked as the best path because it was the first path received. There is no need to support multipath in this route. We're sending the packet encapsulated to 10.0.0.42 because 10.0.0.42 itself is reachable via both spine01 and spine02. You can find this out either from the FIB or from show bgp ipv4 unicast 10.0.0.14 on leaf01. As Example 18-8 shows, we pick both 10.0.0.41 and 10.0.0.42 as the remote VTEPs. You can see this information stored in the router's forwarding table via show ip route,[1] as the following output demonstrates:

```
leaf01# show ip route vrf evpn-vrf 0.0.0.0/0
Routing entry for 0.0.0.0/0
  Known via "bgp", distance 20, metric 0, vrf evpn-vrf, best
  Last update 00:47:08 ago
  * 10.0.0.41, via vlan4001 onlink
  * 10.0.0.42, via vlan4001 onlink

... output snipped for brevity
```

The leading asterisks indicate that these routes are in the FIB.

To track this further and see the VTEP used, follow them via the Linux command, ip neighbor show, like this:

---

1 You can also get the same output via Linux's *iproute2* command, ip ro show vrf evpn-vrf.

```
$ ip neighbor show 10.0.0.41
10.0.0.41 dev vlan4001 lladdr 44:38:39:00:00:4b offload NOARP
$ ip neighbor show 10.0.0.42
10.0.0.42 dev vlan4001 lladdr 44:38:39:00:00:0c offload NOARP
```

You can see that the MAC address used is the one listed as the Rmac in Example 18-8. And to track this MAC address to its encapsulation, for, say, the MAC address of 10.0.0.41, you can enter the following:

```
$ bridge fdb show vlan vlan4001 | grep 44:38:39:00:00:4b
44:38:39:00:00:4b dev vxlan4001 vlan 4001 offload master bridge
44:38:39:00:00:4b dev vxlan4001 dst 10.0.0.41 self offload
$
```

This shows that the MAC address is associated with VTEP 10.0.0.41 via the VXLAN device vxlan4001, which itself has the following attributes:

```
$ sudo vtysh -c 'show int vxlan4001'
Interface vxlan4001 is up, line protocol is up
  Link ups:       2    last: 2019/08/15 04:30:47.04
  Link downs:     9    last: 2019/08/15 04:30:47.03
  vrf: default
  index 20 metric 0 mtu 1500 speed 0
  flags: <UP,BROADCAST,RUNNING,MULTICAST>
  Type: Unknown
  HWaddr: ea:f8:a1:a1:4e:32
  Interface Type Vxlan
  VxLAN Id 104001 VTEP IP: 10.0.0.112 Access VLAN Id 4001
  Master interface: bridge
```

This reveals the VNI and the source VTEP IP address, 10.0.0.112.

Thus, BGP makes it fairly easy to trace the output of a route and verify the information in as much detail as you want, across multiple address families and VRFs.

Stripping the Private ASNs

To verify that the private ASN has been stripped, look first at the neighbor configuration to ensure that it has been configured. To make sure that the advertised routes really have no private ASNs advertised, you can also look at the route as advertised to the peer. To see this, use the following command:

```
show bgp ipv4 unicast neighbors <nbr> advertised-routes
```

The output of this command from the perspective of exit01 looks like that presented in Example 18-9 for routes advertised to the edge router, which is peering on interface swp44.

Example 18-9. Advertised routes output on exit01

```
$ sudo vtysh -c \
 'show bgp vrf internet-vrf ipv4 unicast neighbors swp44 advertised-routes'
BGP table version is 34, local router ID is 10.0.0.41
Status codes: s suppressed, d damped, h history, * valid, > best, = multipath,
              i internal, r RIB-failure, S Stale, R Removed
Origin codes: i - IGP, e - EGP, ? - incomplete

   Network          Next Hop           Metric LocPrf Weight Path
*> 0.0.0.0          ::                                   0 25253 i
*> 10.0.0.11/32     169.254.254.10                       0 ?
... output snipped for brevity
*> 10.0.0.253/32    ::                                   0 25253 i
*> 10.1.3.0/24      169.254.254.10                       0 i
*> 10.2.4.0/24      169.254.254.10                       0 i

Total number of prefixes 14
```

You can see from the right-most `Path` column that the paths have been completely stripped of any private ASN. (In two-byte ASNs, the private ASNs range from 64512-65534.) The only visible ASPATHs are the ones with a nonprivate ASN, 25253. As a comparison, here is the same output, but this time when the `remove-private-AS all` option wasn't enabled for the neighbor swp44:

```
$ sudo vtysh -c \
   'show bgp vrf internet-vrf ipv4 unicast neighbors swp44 advertised-routes'
BGP table version is 34, local router ID is 10.0.0.41
Status codes: s suppressed, d damped, h history, * valid, > best, = multipath,
              i internal, r RIB-failure, S Stale, R Removed
Origin codes: i - IGP, e - EGP, ? - incomplete

   Network          Next Hop        Metric LocPrf ... Path
*> 0.0.0.0          ::                            ... 25253 i
*> 10.0.0.11/32     169.254.254.10                ... 65530 65041 65020 65011 ?
... output snipped for brevity
*> 10.0.0.253/32    ::                            ... 25253 i
*> 10.1.3.0/24      169.254.254.10                ... 65530 65041 i
*> 10.2.4.0/24      169.254.254.10                ... 65530 65041 i

Total number of prefixes 14
```

The following configuration output shows that `remove-private-AS` has been configured:

```
$ sudo vtysh -c 'show ip bgp vrf internet-vrf neighbors swp44'

BGP neighbor on swp44: fe80::4638:39ff:fe00:7...
Hostname: internet
  BGP version 4, remote router ID 10.0.0.253
  BGP state = Established, up for 02:01:56
  Last read 00:00:01, Last write 00:00:01
```

```
  Hold time is 9, keepalive interval is 3 seconds
  Neighbor capabilities:
...output snipped for brevity
 For address family: IPv4 Unicast
  Update group 8, subgroup 8
  Packet Queue length 0
  Private AS numbers (all) removed in updates to this neighbor    ❶
  Community attribute sent to this neighbor(all)
...output snipped for brevity
```

❶ This shows that private ASN stripping has been configured for this neighbor.

Automating BGP validation

We follow the same model as "Automating OSPF validation" on page 412 in validating that the BGP configuration is how we'd like it to be. The playbook consists of three plays and looks as follows:

```
---
- hosts: network                                                  ❶
  become: yes
  tasks:
    - name: Get BGP session state
      command: vtysh -c "show bgp vrf all summary json"
      become: yes
      register: out

    - name: Get JSON output
      set_fact:
        bgp: "{{ out.stdout|from_json }}"

    - name: Verify router-id is the same as the loopback address
      assert:
        that: >-
          bgp|json_query('default.ipv4Unicast.routerId')
          ==
          hostvars[inventory_hostname].ansible_lo.ipv4_secondaries[0].address

    - name: Verify multipath relax is enabled on all nodes
      assert:
        that: bgp|json_query('default.ipv4Unicast.bestPath.multiPathRelax')
      when: inventory_hostname in groups['spine']

- hosts: spine                                                    ❷
  gather_facts: false
  tasks:
    - name: Verify there are as many BGP peers as there are leaves
      assert:
        that: >-
          bgp|json_query('default.ipv4Unicast.peerCount')
          ==
          (groups['leaf']|length + groups['exit']|length)
```

```
    - name: Register just the ipv4 peers
      set_fact:
        bgp_ipv4_peers: "{{ bgp|json_query('default.ipv4Unicast.peers') }}"

    - name: Register just the evpn peers
      set_fact:
        bgp_evpn_peers: "{{ bgp|json_query('default.l2VpnEvpn.peers') }}"

    - name: Verify that all IPv4 Unicast peers are in Established state
      assert:
        that:
          - bgp_ipv4_peers[item].state == "Established"
      with_items: "{{ bgp_ipv4_peers.keys() }}"

    - name: Verify that all EVPN peers are in Established state
      assert:
        that:
          - bgp_evpn_peers[item].state == "Established"
      with_items: "{{ bgp_evpn_peers }}"

- hosts: exit                                                    ❸
  gather_facts: false
  become: yes
  tasks:
    - name: Register just the default VRF IPv4 Unicast peers
      set_fact:
        bgp_default_peers: "{{ bgp['default'].ipv4Unicast.peers }}"

    - name: Register just the EVPN VRF IPv4 Unicast peers
      set_fact:
        bgp_evpnvrf_peers: "{{ bgp['evpn-vrf'].ipv4Unicast.peers }}"

    - name: Register just the internet VRF IPv4 Unicast peers
      set_fact:
        bgp_internet_peers: "{{ bgp['internet-vrf'].ipv4Unicast.peers }}"

    - name: Verify that all default VRF peers are in Established state
      assert:
        that:
          - bgp_default_peers[item].state == "Established"
      with_items: "{{ bgp_default_peers.keys() }}"

    - name: Verify that all Internet VRF peers are in Established state
      assert:
        that:
          - bgp_internet_peers[item].state == "Established"
      with_items: "{{ bgp_internet_peers.keys() }}"

    - name: Verify that all EVPN VRF peers are in Established state
      assert:
        that:
```

```
            - bgp_evpnvrf_peers[item].state == "Established"
        with_items: "{{ bgp_evpnvrf_peers.keys() }}"

    - name: Get edge router's BGP config info
      command: vtysh -c "show ip bgp vrf internet-vrf neighbors swp44 json"
      register: out

    - name: Assert that the remove-private-AS is configured
      assert:
        that: >-
          (out.stdout|from_json).swp44.addressFamilyInfo['IPv4 Unicast']
          ['privateAsNumsAllRemovedInUpdatesToNbr']

    - name: Get advertised routes
      command: >-
        vtysh -c 'show bgp vrf internet-vrf ipv4 unicast neighbors
        swp44 advertised-routes json'
      register: bgp_out

    - name: Get advertised routes as JSON                              ❹
      set_fact:
        all_aspaths: >-
          "{{ bgp_out['stdout']|from_json
          |json_query('advertisedRoutes.*.asPath') }}"

    - name: Assert that there are no private ASNs                      ❺
      assert:
        quiet: yes
        that:
          - item | regex_findall('\\b(6[4-5][0-9]+)') | length == 0
      with_items: "{{ all_aspaths|from_json }}"
```

❶ This play stuffs all of the routers' Ansible states with the outputs of the BGP summary command in JSON format. This also validates that the BGP router ID is the same as the loopback IP address, and verifies that all nodes have multipath-relax configured. The leaves need multipath-relax, too, to allow for multipathing the default route (advertised via exit01/exit02).

❷ This play verifies the peers in the default VRF that is the underlay, for both IPv4 Unicast and EVPN address families.

❸ This play works on the exit leaves. It needs to verify that the BGP sessions in all the VRFs are in Established state. No other leaf has BGP peerings in other VRFs. Exit leaves peer in the default VRF for the underlay, in the internet-vrf with the edge, and in all the VRFs with the firewall. This also verifies that the exit leaves strip out the private ASN from the routes advertised. This section also checks whether remove-private-AS is configured, and whether the private ASNs are actually removed from the output.

❹ This task bears some mention. It takes the output of the command supplied to *vtysh*, converts it to JSON, and uses the `json_query` filter to extract the ASPATHs for all the routes. `all_aspaths` looks like the JSON string shown in Example 18-10 for the output shown in Example 18-9.

❺ This play attempts to find any string that starts with 64 or 65 and has a few following digits. If there are private ASNs, they'll be returned as a list by the `regex_findall` Ansible filter. We can verify that the length of the list returned is always 0; in other words, that there was no match. I'm assuming two-byte ASNs, but a similar regexp can be written for four-byte private ASNs.

Example 18-10. JSON output `all_apaths` *produced by point 4*

```
[
        "",
        "",
        "",
        "",
        "",
        "",
        "25253",
        "",
        "25253",
        "",
        "",
        "",
        "",
        "",
        ""
]
```

Validating Network Virtualization

In addition to checking the underlay routing configuration, as discussed in the previous section, validating the configuration of the network virtualization control plane involves seeking answers to the following questions:

- Is information about all my virtual networks advertised? This includes MAC addresses for EVPN, IP address if ARP suppression is enabled, and any routes that are announced.

- Is an appropriate L3 VNI configured and mapped to the correct VRF in case of symmetric EVPN routing?

- If centralized routing is used, are the default route and associated MAC address advertisement configured?

- Is my VTEP IP advertised?
- Is the handling of BUM traffic configured consistently on all nodes?
- Is every VTEP having an active VNI known to every other VTEP with that same active VNI?

FRR simplifies EVPN configuration considerably compared to most other routing suites. As a consequence, you need far fewer checks, particularly to validate the configuration of the RD, export RT, and import RT. If a routing suite supports `rd auto`, `route-target import auto`, and `route-target export auto`, use them to get the same behavior as FRR's default behavior. Furthermore, these other routing suites require additional configuration for EVPN neighbors, such as `send-community` and `send extended-community`. You don't need to worry about these with FRR. FRR does the right thing by default for the data center configuration.

The main FRR command to validate the EVPN configuration is `show bgp l2vpn evpn vni`. The output of this command on leaf01 is as follows:

```
$ sudo vtysh

Hello, this is FRRouting (version 7.2-dev).
Copyright 1996-2005 Kunihiro Ishiguro, et al.

leaf01# show bgp l2vpn evpn vni
Advertise Gateway Macip: Disabled                              ❶
Advertise SVI Macip: Disabled                                  ❷
Advertise All VNI flag: Enabled                                ❸
BUM flooding: Head-end replication                             ❹
Number of L2 VNIs: 2                                           ❺
Number of L3 VNIs: 1                                           ❻
Flags: * - Kernel
  VNI     Type RD              Import RT       Export RT       Tenant VRF
* 24      L2   10.0.0.11:3     65011:24        65011:24        evpn-vrf     ❼
* 13      L2   10.0.0.11:2     65011:13        65011:13        evpn-vrf
* 104001  L3   10.2.4.11:4     65011:104001    65011:104001    evpn-vrf
```

❶ This indicates whether this node is configured as a centralized routing gateway for EVPN. If so, this field will show `Enabled`.

❷ This indicates whether the node is advertising the gateway IP address configured on the VNIs on this router.

❸ This indicates whether the node is advertising information about all the locally configured VNIs.

❹ This indicates the model for handling BUM traffic. In this example, it is "Head-end replication," also called "Ingress replication."

⑤ This indicates the number of Layer 2 virtual networks that are advertised.

⑥ This indicates the number of Layer 3 virtual networks that are advertised. If you're using only EVPN bridging, this will have a count of 0. Otherwise, it should show the correct number of VRFs used for EVPN.

⑦ This indicates specific information about each VNI. The asterisk at the start of each line indicates that this VNI is also known to the kernel. Lines that do not have an asterisk as the first character are not present in the data plane and so are not advertised.

To map the L3 VNI to a specific local VRF instance, specify the VNI number in the previous command, and you'll get details for that VNI. For example, on leaf01 the output looks like this:

```
leaf01# show bgp l2vpn evpn vni 104001
VNI: 104001 (known to the kernel)
  Type: L3
  Tenant VRF: evpn-vrf                      ❶
  RD: 10.2.4.11:4
  Originator IP: 10.0.0.112                  ❷
  Advertise-gw-macip : n/a
  Import Route Target:
    65011:104001
  Export Route Target:
    65011:104001
leaf01#
```

❶ This line indicates the local VRF instance that represents this VNI.

❷ This is the VTEP IP address used with this VNI. All VNIs have the same VTEP IP address.

To know whether your VTEP IP is advertised, identify the VTEP IP address such as in the earlier output, and look up the related information in BGP's RIB. Remember, the VTEP IP is advertised via the default VRF, which is where the underlay resides. The output for leaf01's VTEP IP address, which the previous example showed to be 10.0.0, looks as follows:

```
leaf01# show bgp ipv4 unicast 10.0.0.112
BGP routing table entry for 10.0.0.112/32
Paths: (1 available, best #1, table default)
  Advertised to non peer-group peers:
  spine01(swp51) spine02(swp52)                             ❶
  Local                                                     ❷
    leaf01 from 0.0.0.0 (10.0.0.11)
      Origin incomplete, metric 0, weight 32768, valid, sourced,
      bestpath-from-AS Local, best (First path received)
      Last update: Thu Aug 15 04:30:52 2019
```

❶ You can see that this has been advertised to both its peers in the underlay, the two spines. As mentioned earlier, displaying the hostnames to which this has been advertised helps in immediately eyeballing a problem.

❷ This line indicates that this is a connected route. If this is not a local route, we have a problem, because some other node is advertising our VTEP IP address, and our local configuration of the VTEP IP address has failed.

To track whether every VTEP with an active VNI knows about all other VTEPs with that same active VNI requires looking across multiple devices. But even if a user must look at only a handful of VNIs this way across more than a handful of boxes, the task quickly becomes monotonous, laborious, and therefore error prone. Some tool or script that gathers all of this information and munges it together to produce the appropriate output would be phenomenally helpful. Alas, none exists except for a handful of vendor-specific tools such as Cumulus' NetQ or Arista's CloudVision. But if someone were to attempt to write such a tool, the command that would be useful on every device to summarize the EVPN info is show evpn vni, which produces an output that looks as follows:

```
leaf01# show evpn vni
VNI          Type VxLAN IF          # MACs  # ARPs  # Remote VTEPs Tenant VRF
24           L2   vni24             8       8       1              evpn-vrf
13           L2   vni13             8       8       1              evpn-vrf
104001       L3   vxlan4001         3       3       n/a            evpn-vrf
leaf01#
```

This command also produces output in JSON format, which is much more consumable in a tool. To get even more useful information per VNI, use show evpn vni detail. This provides information such as which L2 VNIs use which L3 VNI for routing, the local VTEP IP address, and so on. An even more simplified summary is available via show evpn, which produces output like the following:

```
leaf01# show evpn
L2 VNIs: 2
L3 VNIs: 1
Advertise gateway mac-ip: No
Advertise svi mac-ip: No
Duplicate address detection: Enable
  Detection max-moves 5, time 180
```

Automating EVPN validation

This section shows another playbook demonstrating the validation of the EVPN configuration. This playbook is a little trickier than the previous ones, and some of the code bears additional explanation. This playbook consists of three plays. The first one, similar to the previous playbooks, consists of gathering the data and getting it ready for actual work performed in the next two plays:

```
---
- hosts: leaf:exit                                                          ❶
  gather_facts: false
  become: yes
  tasks:
    - name: Retrieve the VNI info from all nodes
      command: vtysh -c 'show evpn vni json'
      register: out

    - name: Pull out the information into JSON
      set_fact:
        vni: "{{ out.stdout|from_json }}"

    - name: Retrieve EVPN info from all nodes
      command: vtysh -c 'show bgp l2vpn evpn vni json'
      register: out

    - name: Pull out the information into JSON
      set_fact:
        evpn_vni: "{{ out.stdout|from_json }}"

    - name: Extract the tunnel IP
      set_fact:
        vtep_ip: "{{ evpn_vni[(vni|list)[0]].originatorIp }}"

- hosts: leaf:exit                                                          ❷
  gather_facts: false
  become: yes
  tasks:
    - name: Verify VNIs are advertised
      assert:
        that:
          - evpn_vni.advertiseAllVnis == "Enabled"

    - name: Retrieve the route for VTEP IP                                  ❸
      command: 'vtysh -c \"'show ip route ' + cmdarg + '\"' }}"
      register: route_out
      vars:
        - cmdarg: "{{ hostvars[item].vtep_ip + '/32 longer-prefixes' }}"
      loop: "{{ groups.leaf + groups.exit }}"

    - name: Verify that all VTEP IPs are reachable                          ❹
      assert:
        quiet: yes
        that:
          - item.stdout != ""
      loop: "{{ route_out.results }}"

- hosts: leaf01                                                             ❺
  gather_facts: false
  tasks:
    - name: Verify that {VNI, VTEP} pair is consistent across network       ❻
```

```
          assert:
            that: >-
              vni[item.0].numRemoteVteps
              ==
              hostvars[item.1].vni[item.0].numRemoteVteps
          loop: "{{ vni | product(groups.leaf + groups.exit) | list }}"
          when: hostvars[item.1].vni[item.0] is defined

        - name: Verify BUM Handling is consistent                    ❼
          assert:
            that: >-
              evpn_vni.flooding == hostvars[item].evpn_vni.flooding
          loop: "{{ groups.leaf + groups.exit }}"
```

❶ This is the first play, which gathers and prepares data. Data is gathered from the two commands that we discussed earlier: show evpn vni json and show bgp l2vpn evpn vni json.

❷ This is the second play. It is executed on every leaf and exit node defined.

❸ Having retrieved and stored the VTEP IP address of every VTEP in the first play, we check whether the route is known to the router on which Ansible is currently executing. We use FRR to extract the route information because Linux's ip route show doesn't show a connected route. We use a precise match of the specified prefix (via the longer-prefixes option) rather than some summarized prefix for the VTEPs, such as the default route. I use the cmdarg variable just for formatting in the book. The command given to Ansible is vtysh -c "show ip route <vtep_ip>/32 longer-prefixes", where <vtep_ip> is dynamically constructed in a loop in that task. To assemble the command with the new <vtep_ip> each time, we have to concatenate multiple strings.[2]

❹ This verifies that none of the ip route entries retrieved in the previous step was an empty string. If the route was unknown to this box, the output would be the empty string, in which case Ansible reports the error.

❺ In this third play, we verify that a given VNI is known across all the VTEPs that have declared as having that VNI. For example, in our EVPN topology, the exit leaves do not have any information about the tenant VNIs, 13 and 24. But all the leaves—normal and exit—support the L3 VNI needed for symmetric routing support. Because the data has all been gathered in the first play, we need to validate the information only in the context of a single leaf.

---

2 There's a slight chance that the route exists in FRR's RIB but not the FIB, and we need to check that the route is in the FIB, too, but I'm ignoring that for now.

⑥ What we validate is that for a given VNI, all VTEPs having that VNI define the same number of remote VTEPs. This is a slightly clever trick to get past the more complicated code to verify that for each VNI on every VTEP, the other VTEP IPs are all present.

⑦ Finally, we validate that the Broadcast, Unknown unicast, and Multicast (BUM) handling is consistent across all VTEPs.

Application's Network Validation

In the data center, what's important to the application is proper connectivity to the appropriate services and nodes. Facebook has published papers (*https://oreil.ly/aymgW*) and code stating how they used their own pinger and *traceroute* to detect packet latency and loss between servers as a measure of how well their network was working, and used the output to pinpoint when problems occurred. Microsoft has done the same (*https://oreil.ly/7m1qL*).

Typically, trying to ping from a server in one rack to one or two servers in every other rack is sufficient. When you run *ping*, ensure that you test the path MTU, as well. This is especially true in the presence of VXLAN. *ping* also supports the following options to test the path MTU:

```
ping -s <MTU> -M do <ip_destination>
```

In our example, this command is as follows:

```
ping -s 9000 -M do 10.0.0.253
```

However, this command doesn't work as expected in the Vagrant and libvirt simulation, so I don't show the output.

Instead, here is an example of a *traceroute* with the appropriate flags for testing Path MTU. This is a *traceroute* run from server01 to the loopback IP address of the edge router, 10.0.0.253.

```
$ traceroute -n --mtu 10.0.0.253
traceroute to 10.0.0.253 (10.0.0.253), 30 hops max, 65000 byte packets
 1  10.1.3.12  0.835 ms F=9000  0.550 ms  0.487 ms              ❶
 2  10.0.0.42  2.093 ms F=1500 10.0.0.41  2.130 ms  1.661 ms    ❷
 3  10.0.0.100  2.018 ms  1.959 ms  2.071 ms
 4  10.0.0.41  2.359 ms  1.992 ms  2.134 ms
 5  10.0.0.253  2.677 ms  2.529 ms  2.478 ms

$ ip ro show vrf evpn-vrf 10.0.0.253
10.0.0.253  proto bgp  metric 20
        nexthop via 10.0.0.41  dev vlan4001 weight 1 onlink
        nexthop via 10.0.0.42  dev vlan4001 weight 1 onlink
$
```

❶ This line indicates that *traceroute* tries to start with an MTU of 9,000 bytes, which is the MTU of its local outgoing interface

❷ This line shows two things. First, the MTU is beaten down to 1,500 bytes by the two routers, 10.0.0.41 and 10.0.0.42. This also indicates that the packet is being multipathed between 10.0.0.41 and 10.0.0.42 as the exit VTEPs. How do we know this? The first hop shown is the default gateway of the server, which is the anycast IP address 10.1.3.1; the actual gateway servicing the request uses its own unique IP address in the responses, in this case 10.1.3.12. Because the server is dual-attached to leaf01 and leaf02 via a bonded interface, the kernel picks the link to leaf02 (10.1.3.12) as the path to use. The server interfaces are mapped to evpn-vrf, and a lookup of the FIB shows that 10.0.0.253 is reachable via 10.0.0.41 and . 42 via the vlan4001 interface. From the route tracing we did in "Determining the originator of the default route" on page 418, we know that these two paths lead to the exit leaves' VTEPs.

Facebook's tools for pinger have not been updated in four years and the project has been archived. Long before these tools, the well-regarded Center for Applied Internet Data Analysis (CAIDA) produced a tool called *scamper* (*https://oreil.ly/zNXKF*) that is useful for measuring and reporting latency and loss in a manner similar to the tools described by Facebook and Microsoft. *scamper* is even available as a readily down-loadable package on Ubuntu and other popular Linux distributions. *scamper* supports testing multiple IP addresses and generating a periodic report. I recommend the use of scamper for application measurement of loss and latency.

scamper presents the multipath information much more succinctly, as shown in the following output, although it can't test the path MTU information in this mode:

```
$ scamper -I 'tracelb  10.2.4.104'
tracelb from 10.1.3.101 to 10.2.4.104, 2 nodes, 1 links, 13 probes, 95%
10.1.3.12 -> (10.1.3.13, 10.1.3.14) -> 10.2.4.104
```

To test all this in a virtualized environment, the router needs to support path selection based on TCP/UDP ports in case of multipath. Linux only recently added support for this. Until then, Linux load balanced packets across multiple paths to a destination only based on source and destination IP address. This meant that tools such as scamper and *traceroute* cannot identify the multiple paths in a simulation environment unless the right kernel versions are used. For example, Cumulus Linux version 3.7 and later support this option, but Arista's EOS simulation does not. However, even Cumulus Linux doesn't support it by default. Ubuntu 18.04 and later versions support this option.

To enable this option, you must run the following command:

```
sudo sysctl -w net.ipv4.fib_multipath_hash_policy=1
```

If you're using IPv6, repeat the command for IPv6, too:

```
sudo sysctl -w net.ipv6.fib_multipath_hash_policy=1
```

Data-Plane Validation

Validating application connectivity is a proxy for data-plane validation. Nevertheless, it is useful to know a set of commands to query the data-plane state on a device. The main things to look at from a data-plane perspective are forwarding tables and tunnel tables.

This section offers a brief listing of useful commands to validate the data plane. Two versions of the commands are provided, if available: Linux's native command and FRR's command. The benefit of FRR's command is that the output and the command syntax might be more familiar to network administrators accustomed to working with traditional networking suites. The Linux command version will be more familiar to those who have a Linux background. I show both versions of the command, with the Linux version always shown first.

MAC table entries

These commands display the MAC table entries on a node:

```
bridge fdb show [vlan <vlan>]
show evpn mac vni <VNI|all> [detail]
```

Neither command can look up a specific MAC address. To see the MAC table entries populated by a specific VTEP alone, issue the following:

```
show evpn mac vtep vni <VNI|all> <VTEP-IP-Address>
```

For example, in our topology you can run this:

```
show evpn mac vni all vtep 10.0.0.134
```

Routing table

These commands display the routing table of the specified VRF:

```
ip route show [vrf <vrf-name>]
show ip route
```

The Linux command to see the routing table of all VRFs is as follows:

```
ip route show table all
```

ARP or ND cache

These commands display the Address Resolution Protocol/Neighbor Discovery (ARP/ND) cache on the node:

```
ip neighbor show
show evpn arp-cache [vni <VNI|all>] [detail]
```

Summary

This chapter was dedicated to validating the network configured in the previous chapters. Specifically, the chapter highlighted specific questions that can be asked of cabling, interface, routing, network virtualization, and the application-level network to verify that the configuration has built a network that performs as expected. Besides looking at individual box-specific commands to answers the questions posed, I provided model playbooks that automated the derivation of the answers.

## CHAPTER 19

Coda

In computers, every "new explosion" was set off by a software product that allowed users to program differently.

—Alan Kay

I leave you with a poem that its author, who also happens to be the editor of this book, Andy Oram, wrote about networks. In its ending, I hear the beating heart of network operators as they deploy a new network, or make a change to one that's working. I hope the concepts and practices explained in this book, in some way, can help you to build robust, predictable networks.

Neural net

For Dinesh G. Dutt

I'm thinking

it's time to configure a new protocol   of notifications from an unaccounted future

for a brain   partitioned — non-consistent

that repeatedly

drops packets as it   lacks a fully connected network

traces a path away from enlightment   is pervasively exposed to

well-intended candy wrappers   people who say pronouns can lie   crackpots on Byzantine platforms

decked out with extraneous existences   flagrantly exposed to malignant scrutiny   slashing significance from protocols
stock vacation images   undeterred by ancient understandings   kept alive by opaque handshakes
every brusque weekly commonplace   furiously hidden from tabulation   heaving highly compressed projectiles

They tunnel funny payloads
within fragments incompletely formed

If I must

massage the message I retransmit   be liberal in what I accept

placing backpressure   at moments of extreme disconnect
on too promiscuous nodes   not in harmony with today's traffic

can the network survive   can the network survive can the network survive can the network survive can the network survive

Andy Oram,
August 29, 2019

Glossary

This book makes use of many acronyms and abbreviations that you can find expanded here:

ABR
Area Border Router

access-agg
access-aggregation-core

ACI
Application-Centric Infrastructure

ACLs
Access Control Lists

AFI
Address Family Indicator

AI
artificial intelligence

API
Application Programming Interface

ARP
Address Resolution Protocol

AS
Autonomous System

ASBR
Autonomous System Border Routers

ASIC
Application-Specific Integrated Circuit

ASN
Autonomous System Number

ASN.1
Abstract Syntax Notation One

AWS
Amazon Web Services

BFD
Bidirectional Forwarding Detection

BGP
Border Gateway Protocol

Bidir PIM
Bidirectional Protocol-Independent Multicast

BSD
Berkeley Software Distribution

BUM
Broadcast, Unknown unicast, and Multicast

CLI
command-line interface

CNCF
Cloud Native Computing Foundation

CNI
Container Network Interface

CNM
Container Network Model

DHCP
Dynamic Host Configuration Protocol

DIY
do it yourself

DPDK
Data Path Development Kit

DR
designated router

eBGP
external Border Gateway Protocol

ECMP
Equal-Cost Multipath

ECS
Elastic Compute Service

EGP
Exterior Gateway Protocol

EIGRP
Enhanced Interior Gateway Routing Protocol

ELK
Elastic, Logstash, and Kibana

EOS
Extensible Operating System

EVPN
Ethernet Virtual Private Network

FDDI
Fiber Distributed Data Interface

FHR
first-hop router

FHRP
First Hop Routing Protocol

FIB
Forwarding Information Base

FoRCES
Forwarding and Control Element Separation

FRR
Free Range Routing

FUD
Fear, Uncertainty, Doubt

GARP
gratuitous Address Resolution Protocol

GPL
General Public License

GPUs
Graphical Processing Units

GRE
Generic Routing Encapsulation

GUI
graphical user interface

HAL
Hardware Abstraction Layer

HSRP
Hot Standby Routing Protocol

iBGP
internal Border Gateway Protocol

ICMP
Internet Control Message Protocol

IEEE
Institute of Electrical Engineers

IETF
Internet Engineering Task Force

ifMIB
interface Management Information Base

IGMP
Internet Group Membership Protocol

IGP
Interior Gateway Protocol

IPAM
IP Address Management

IPC
Interprocess Communication

IPTV
Internet Protocol Television

IPVS
IP Virtual Server

IS-IS
Intermediate System to Intermediate System

ISL
inter-switch link

ISSU
In-Service Software Upgrade

L1
Layer 1

L2
Layer 2

L3
Layer 3

L4
Layer 4

LACP
Link Aggregation Control Protocol

LAN
local area network

LHR
last-hop router

LISP
Locator Identity Separation Protocol

LLA
link-local address

LLDP
Link Level Discovery Protocol

LPM
longest prefix match

LSA
Link-State Advertisement

MIB
Management Information Base

MLAG
Multichassis Link Aggregation

MOSPF
Multicast Open Shortest Path First

MPLS
Multiprotocol Label Switching

MSDP
Multicast Source Discovery Protocol

MSTP
Multi-Instance Spanning Tree Protocol

MTU
maximum transmission unit

NAT
Network Address Translation

NDP
Neighbor Discovery Protocol

NETCONF
Network Configuration Protocol

NICs
Network Interface Cards

NLRI
Network Layer Reachability Information

NMS
Network Management System

NOS
network operating system

NSSA
not-so-stubby area

NTP
Network Time Protocol

NVE
Network Virtualization Edge

NVGRE
Network Virtualization over Generic Routing Encapsulation

NVO3
Network Virtualization Overlay over L3

OCP
Open Compute Project

ODMs
original design manufacturers

OID
Object ID

ONF
Open Network Foundation

ONIE
Open Network Installer Environment

OS
operating system

OSI
Open Systems Interconnection

OSPF
Open Shortest Path First

OTV
Overlay Transport Virtualization

OUI
Organizationally Unique Identifier

OVS
Open Virtual Switch

PCIe
Peripheral Component Interconnect express

PC
personal computer

PIM
Protocol-Independent Multicast

PIM-DM
PIM Dense Mode

PIM-SM
PIM Sparse Mode

PIM-SSM
PIM Source-Specific Multicast

PMSI
Provider Multicast Service Interface

PoC
proof-of-concept

PTM
Prescriptive Topology Manager

PVST
Per-VLAN spanning tree

PXE
Pre-boot eXecution Environment

RA
router advertisement

RD
Route Distinguisher

RIOT
Routing In and Out of Tunnels

RIP
Routing Information Protocol

RP
rendezvous point

RPF
Reverse Path Forwarding

RR
Route Reflector

RPT
rendezvous point tree

RT
Route Target

SAFI
Subsequent Address Family Indicator

SAI
Switch Abstraction Interface

SDN
software-defined networking

SD-WAN
software-defined wide area network

SNMP
Simple Network Management Protocol

SONET
Synchronous Optical Network

SPB
Shortest Path Bridging

SPF
shortest path first

SPT
Shortest Path Tree

SSH
Secure Shell

STP
Spanning Tree Protocol

SVI
Switched VLAN Interface

TCP
Transmission Control Protocol

TFTP
Trivial File Transfer Protocol

TLV
Type, Length, and Value

ToR
top of rack

TRILL
Transparent Interconnection of Lots of Links

TTL
time-to-live

UCMP
Unequal-Cost Multipath

UDLD
Unidirectional Link Detection

UDP
User Datagram Protocol

UI
user interface

USE
Utilization, Saturation, and Errors

veth
Virtual Ethernet

VLAN
virtual local area network

VM
virtual machine

VNI
VXLAN Network Identifier

VPC
Virtual Private Cloud

VPLS
Virtual Private LAN Service

VPN
virtual private network

VRF
Virtual Routing and Forwarding

VRRP
Virtual Router Redundancy Protocol

VTEP
VXLAN Tunnel Endpoint

VTP
VLAN Trunking Protocol

VXLAN
Virtual eXtensible Local Area Network

WAN
wide area network

YAML
YAML Ain't Markup Language

YANG
Yet Another Next Generation

Index

about, 288-294
adapting, 295-300
advertisement interval timer, 300
ASN numbering scheme, 296
attributes/communities/extended communities with, 291
automating validation of, 425
autonomous system number, 290
best practices, 333
best-path computation, 292
BUM handling choice with, 345
capabilities, 291
communities, 291, 353
configuration concepts with, 301-303
connect timer, 300
count-to-infinity, 297
eBGP versus iBGP, 295
eliminating interface IP addresses, 316-325
fixing convergence time, 299
FRR, 320-322, 344
GRACEFUL_SHUTDOWN, 332
hold timers, 300
interoperability, 323
IPv4, 303-307
IPv6, 318, 318, 325
keepalive time, 300
link bandwidth extended community and, 34
Max-MED, 332
multipath selection, 298
neighbor command, 307
neighbor listen command, 331
network configuration complexity and, 202
OSPF versus, 258
path hunting, 297
peering, 289, 307, 328-331
private ASNs, 296
protocol overview, 288
providing defaults, 314
RFC 5549, 319-322
route distinguisher, 342
route maps, 310-314
route target, 343
routing configuration, 101
routing configuration validation, 414-423
routing policy with, 308-314
state machine, 290
summarizing routes, 377
support for multiple protocols with, 293

supporting virtual network routes, 341-346
unnumbered interfaces, 99
upgrades, 331
VRFs and, 326-328
border leaf, 185, 187
box-by-box approach to observability, 237
bridging, 6-12
    access-aggregation-core, 6-12
    broadcast storms and, 9
    Clos topologies, 22
    EVPN, 346-354
        (see also EVPN bridging)
    flooding and, 10
    hardware packet switching and, 6
    lack of configuration and, 8
    mitigating failure, 12
    proprietary enterprise network stacks, 7
    PVST (per-VLAN spanning tree), 11
    redundancy, 11
    scalable, 9-12
    self-learning transparent, 8
    switch versus, 7
    terminology, 7
    VXLAN, 131-140
brite boxes, 49
broadcast storms, 15
    access-aggregation-core and, 9
    STP and, 9
Broadcom, 48
bugs, fixing, 55
BUM handling choice, 345
Busybox, 47

C

cabling
    Clos topology and, 33
    validation, 396-401
Calico, 106
Catalyst 5000, 3
Catalyst 6500, 3
centralized control model, 129
Cgroups (control groups), 142
chassis
    Clos topology, 36
    defined, 36
    spine switch, 35
Cisco NX-OS, 71
CLAG, 37, 370
CLI (command-line interface), 72, 203

flow tables, 55
flow, definition, 23, 121
Forwarding and Control Element Separation
(FoRCES), 58
Forwarding Information Base (FIB), 87-90
Free Range Routing (FRR)
ASN use with, 385
container networking with, 148
defining defaults, 315
EVPN simplified with, 429
RD and RT with, 344
RFC 5549 and, 320-322, 325
unnumbered interfaces supported by, 222

G

GPUs (Graphical Processing Units), 26
Graphical Processing Units (GPUs), 26
Gregg, Brendan, 241
group_vars, 219

H

hairpinning, 153
hardware
disaggregation, 40
network disaggregation, 48-50
network virtualization, 126
Hardware Abstraction Layer (HAL), 69
hardware packet switching, 6
hardware switch, 7
head end replication, 135, 162
Hello Interval, 266
host attach models, 36
host-switch interconnect model, 355
hostnamectl command, 394
host_vars, 219
Hot Standby Routing Protocol (HSRP), 12
hybrid cloud connectivity, 190-193
hybrid model, 64
hypervisor, 112

I

iBGP (see internal BGP)
IBM, 46
IETF (Internet Engineering Task Force), 50
ifupdown2, 369
IGMP (Internet Group Membership Protocol),
165
IGMPv3, 166

import RT, 343
In-Service Software Upgrade (ISSU), 12, 14,
252
incremental shortest path first algorithm, 97
ingress replication, 162, 347-349
inline network virtualization, 117
Intel, 41
Intel x86/ARM processors, 62
interconnect link speeds, 25
interface configuration validation, 402-406
interface IP addresses, eliminating, 316-325
interfaces, unnumbered (see unnumbered
interfaces)
Intermediate System to Intermediate System
(IS-IS), 34, 95, 98, 168
internal BGP (iBGP), 385, 389
characteristics, 338-340
eBGP versus, 295
overlay, 380-389
Internet Engineering Task Force (IETF), 50
Internet Group Membership Protocol (IGMP),
165
interprocess communication (IPC), 144
inventory, Ansible, 210
IP address prefix, 83
IP addresses, network automation, 201
ip route show, 89
ipmr-lo, 389
IPv4, 268-277, 280-285, 303-307
mask length, 83
IPv6, 277, 325
link-local address, 318
mask length, 83
router advertisement, 318
support, 261
IS-IS (Intermediate System to Intermediate System), 34, 95, 98, 168
ISSU (In-Service Software Upgrade), 12, 14,
252

J

JSON, 392
Juniper, 42, 229
Junos OS, 229
just-in-time monitoring, 242

K

Kubernetes, 141, 159, 262

reasons for, 258
requirements, 262
route types, 263-266
security and safeguards, 106
summarizing routes in, 284
support for IPv6, 261
support for VRFs, 262
timers with, 266
underlay, 380-389
unnumbered interfaces, 99
upgrades, 284
overlay network virtualization, 117
overlay networks, 138, 154-156
oversubscription, 24
OVS (Open Virtual Switch), 60
OVSDB, 60

P

packet load balancing, 121
packet networks, 112
packet, defined, 7
packet-switching silicon, 42, 43, 48
PCs (personal computers), 41, 46
peer group, 307
peering, BGP and, 289, 328-331
per-VLAN spanning tree (PVST), 11
peripheral input/output bus, 63
Perlman, Radia, 9, 17
personal computers (PCs), 41, 46
PID namespace, 144
PIM (Protocol-Independent Multicast), 166, 345
PIM Dense Mode (PIM-DM), 166
PIM Source-Specific Multicast (PIM-SSM), 135, 167
PIM Sparse Mode (PIM-SM), 168-182
    building multicast distribution tree, 168-179
    data center use, 180-182
    rendezvous point, 168
    unnumbered OSPF, 182
    use case, 166
PIM-DM (PIM Dense Mode), 166
PIM-SM (see PIM Sparse Mode)
PIM-SSM (PIM Source-Specific Multicast), 135, 167
PIM/MSDP configuration, 386-389
Ping, 145
playbooks for Ansible, 212-215, 217

PMSI (Provider Multicast Service Interface), 345
pod model
    applications choosing, 31
    build out, 32
Pre-boot eXecution Environment (PXE), 46
private ASNs, 296, 423-428
programmability of network device, 54
programming switching silicon, 66-70
    switch abstraction interface, 69
    switchdev, 69
propagation delay
    in distance and link-state vector protocols, 97
    in routing protocols, 97
proprietary enterprise network stacks, 7
protocol-based control model, 129
Protocol-Independent Multicast (PIM), 166, 345
Provider Multicast Service Interface (PMSI), 345
PVST (per-VLAN spanning tree), 11
PXE (Pre-boot eXecution Environment), 46
Python, 198

R

RA (router advertisement), 318
rack space limitations, 26
RD (route distinguisher), BGP, 342
Red Hat, 205
redistribute command, 306
redistribute connected, 312
redistributing routes, 264
rendezvous point (RP), 168, 386
Retransmit Interval, 266
RFC 5549, 319-322
    FRR and, 320-322
    packet forwarding with, 320
RIB (Routing Information Base), 87-90
rollback, network automation, 228
route distinguisher (RD), BGP, 342
route filtering, 106
route maps, 310-314
    classifiers, 310
    writing secure, 312
Route Reflectors (RR), 338
route summarization, 105
route target (RT), BGP, 343
routed multicast underlay, 349-353

About the Author

Dinesh G. Dutt has been in the networking industry for the past 20 years, most of it at Cisco Systems. His most recent job was as the chief scientist at Cumulus Networks. Before that, he was a Fellow at Cisco Systems. He has been involved in enterprise and data center networking technologies, including the design of many of the Application-Specific Integrated Circuits (ASICs) that powered Cisco's megaswitches such as Cat6K and the Nexus family of switches. He also has experience in storage networking from his days at Andiamo Systems and in the design of Fibre Channel over Ethernet (FCoE). He is a coauthor of TRILL and VXLAN and has filed more than 40 patents.

Colophon

The bird on the cover of *Cloud Native Data Center Networking* is a great shearwater (*Ardenna gravis*). Great shearwaters live in the open waters and islands of the Atlantic coast of North and South America. These common seabirds have a limited breeding range because they prefer cold-water environments.

Great shearwater gulls can be about 18–20 inches from head to tail and 43–45 inches across the wingspan. In flight, their wings bow and enable them to glide for long periods, which gives their flight a stiff appearance. From below, great shearwaters look mostly white with just one brown patch under the belly. From above, they are dark with white only in a ring at the neck and a "horseshoe" at the tail.

With dark and slightly hooked bills, great shearwaters dive for fish and squid. They are quick birds and might feed among dolphins and whales near the surface.

Many of the animals on O'Reilly covers are endangered; all of them are important to the world.

The cover illustration is by Karen Montgomery, based on a black and white engraving from *British Birds*. The cover fonts are Gilroy Semibold and Guardian Sans. The text font is Adobe Minion Pro; the heading font is Adobe Myriad Condensed; and the code font is Dalton Maag's Ubuntu Mono.

O'REILLY®

There's much more where this came from.

Experience books, videos, live online training courses, and more from O'Reilly and our 200+ partners—all in one place.

Learn more at oreilly.com/online-learning